# Sacred Space in Early Modern Europe

The medieval landscape was marked by many sacred sites – churches and chapels, pilgrimage sites, holy wells – places where the spiritual and temporal worlds coincided. Although Max Weber argued that the Reformation brought about the 'disenchantment of the world', this volume explores the many dimensions of sacred space during and after the religious upheavals of the early modern period. The chapters examine the subject not only through a variety of contexts across Europe from Scotland to Moldavia, but also across the religious spectrum of the Catholic, Orthodox, Lutheran and Calvinist Churches. Based on original research, these essays provide new insights into the definition and understanding of sanctity in the post-Reformation era and make an important contribution to the study of sacred space.

WILL COSTER is Senior Lecturer and Head of History at De Montfort University, Bedford. His previous publications include *Family and Kinship in England* (2001) and *Baptism and Spiritual Kinship in Early Modern England* (2002).

ANDREW SPICER is Senior Lecturer in Early Modern European History at Oxford Brookes University. He is author of *The French-Speaking Reformed Community and their Church in Southampton, 1567– c. 1620* (1997) and the co-editor of *Society and Culture in the Huguenot World, 1559–1685* (2002).

# Sacred Space in Early Modern Europe

Edited by

Will Coster and Andrew Spicer

CAMBRIDGE
UNIVERSITY PRESS

CAMBRIDGE UNIVERSITY PRESS
Cambridge, New York, Melbourne, Madrid, Cape Town, Singapore, São Paulo

Cambridge University Press
The Edinburgh Building, Cambridge CB2 2RU, UK

Published in the United States of America by Cambridge University Press, New York

www.cambridge.org
Information on this title: www.cambridge.org/9780521824873

First published 2005

Printed in the United Kingdom at the University Press, Cambridge

*A catalogue record for this book is available from the British Library*

*Library of Congress Cataloguing in Publication data*
Sacred space in early modern Europe / edited by Will Coster and Andrew Spicer.
   p.   cm.
Includes bibliographical references and index.
ISBN 0 521 82487 7 (hardback)
1. Sacred space – Europe – History.   I. Coster, Will, 1963–   II. Spicer, Andrew.
BV896.E85S23   2005
63′.0424′0903 – dc22   2004054036

ISBN-13 978-0-521-82487-3 hardback
ISBN-10 0-521-82487-7 hardback

# Contents

*List of illustrations*                                     *page* vii
*List of figures*                                                    ix
*Notes on contributors*                                              x
*List of abbreviations*                                           xiii

1  Introduction: the dimensions of sacred space in
   Reformation Europe                                                 1
   WILL COSTER AND ANDREW SPICER

2  Sacred church and worldly tavern: reassessing an early
   modern divide                                                     17
   BEAT KÜMIN

3  Sacred image and sacred space in Lutheran Germany             39
   BRIDGET HEAL

4  Places of sanctification: the liturgical sacrality of
   Genevan Reformed churches, 1535–1566                            60
   CHRISTIAN GROSSE

5  'What kinde of house a kirk is': conventicles,
   consecrations and the concept of sacred space in
   post-Reformation Scotland                                        81
   ANDREW SPICER

6  Psalms, groans and dogwhippers: the soundscape of
   worship in the English parish church, 1547–1642               104
   JOHN CRAIG

7  A microcosm of community: burial, space and society
   in Chester, 1598 to 1633                                        124
   WILL COSTER

8   *Apud ecclesia*: church burial and the development of
    funerary rooms in Moldavia                                    144
    MARIA CRĂCIUN

9   Reading Rome as a sacred landscape, *c.* 1586–1635            167
    SIMON DITCHFIELD

10  Gardening for God: Carmelite deserts
    and the sacralisation of natural space
    in Counter-Reformation Spain                                  193
    TREVOR JOHNSON

11  Holywell: contesting sacred space in
    post-Reformation Wales                                        211
    ALEXANDRA WALSHAM

12  The sacred space of Julien Maunoir: the
    re-Christianising of the landscape in
    seventeenth-century Brittany                                  237
    ELIZABETH TINGLE

13  Sacralising space: reclaiming civic culture in
    early modern France                                           259
    AMANDA EURICH

14  Breaking images and building bridges: the making of
    sacred space in early modern Bohemia                          282
    HOWARD LOUTHAN

15  Mapping the boundaries of confession: space and
    urban religious life in the diocese of Augsburg,
    1648–1750                                                     302
    DUANE J. CORPIS

    *Index*                                                       326

# Illustrations

2.1 The 'Old Innkeeper' (*Alte Wirt*) at Obermenzing in
Bavaria. (Photograph by Michelle Kümin.)                    *page* 21

2.2 The Schangnau valley in the Bernese Emmental, from
a border atlas of the Republic of Bern compiled by Samuel
Bodmer in 1705–10. (Reproduced by kind permission of
the State Archives of Bern.)                                         22

2.3 (a) The villages of Neuenegg and Sensebrücke.
(Reproduced by kind permission of the State Archives
of Bern.)                                                                   29

2.3 (b) Map of the border area between Bern and Fribourg.
(Reproduced by kind permission of the State Archives
of Bern.)                                                                   30

2.4 Prospect of the Holy Mountain at Andechs near Munich
from the Bavarian topography published by Matthäus
Merian in the mid-seventeenth century. (Reproduced by
kind permission of Bärenreiter Verlag, Kassel.)             35

3.1 Johann Ulrich Krauss (after Johann Andreas Graff), *Interior
of the Frauenkirche*, engraving 1696, Germanisches
Nationalmuseum, Nuremberg.
© Germanisches Nationalmuseum, Nuremberg.               40

3.2 Johann Ulrich Krauss (after Johann Andreas Graff), *Interior
of the Lorenzkirche*, engraving 1685, Germanisches
Nationalmuseum, Nuremberg.
© Germanisches Nationalmuseum, Nuremberg.               49

3.3 Peter Vischer the Elder and sons, *The Tomb of St Sebald*,
1508–19, Sebalduskirche, Nuremberg. (Reproduced
courtesy of the Conway Library, Courtauld Institute
for Art.)                                                                   52

5.1 South Queensferry, Old Parish Church. (Crown
Copyright: Royal Commission on the Ancient and
Historical Monuments of Scotland.)                            101

8.1 Votive image at Dobrovăţ.                                    156

8.2 Votive image at Suceviţa.                                              157
8.3 Vir Dolorum at Probota.                                                165
9.1 (a) *Roma sotteranea.*                                                 181
9.1 (b) *Roma sotteranea.* Plan of the catacombs of Pontiano on
    the via Portense.                                                      182
9.2 (a) *Roma sotteranea.* Second chamber of the catacombs of
    St Priscilla and other martyrs on the via Salaria nuova.              185
9.2 (b) *Roma sotteranea.* Different Christian symbols in the
    catacombs (detail).                                                    186
9.3 (a) *Roma sotteranea.* Some examples of Christian
    sepulchres.                                                            187
9.3 (b) *Roma sotteranea.* Glass and pottery vases containing
    the blood and ashes of holy martyrs found in the
    catacombs of Calixtus.                                                 188
11.1 Exterior of the chapel over St Winefride's Well. (Crown
    copyright: Royal Commission on the Ancient and
    Historical Monuments of Wales.)                                        214
11.2 Bathing pool of St Winefride's Well. (Crown copyright:
    Royal Commission on the Ancient and Historical
    Monuments of Wales.)                                                   215
11.3 Interior of the chapel over St Winefride's Well. (Crown
    copyright: Royal Commission on the Ancient and
    Historical Monuments of Wales.)                                        216
11.4 Robert, abbot of Shrewsbury, *The Admirable Life of Saint
    Wenefride Virgin, Martyr, Abbesse,* trans. J[ohn] F[alconer]
    ([St Omer], 1635), title-page and frontispiece.
    (Reproduced by permission of the Abbess of Syon Abbey,
    Brent Eleigh, Devon, and the University of Exeter
    Library. Shelfmark Syon Abbey 1635/ROB.)                               224
11.5 The martyrdom of St Winefride, in Giovanni Battista de
    Cavalleriis, *Ecclesiae Anglicanae Trophaea* (Rome [1584]).
    (Reproduced by permission of the British Library.
    Shelfmark 551.e.35.)                                                   226
12.1 Fountain of St Philibert, commune of Trégunc, Finistère,
    France.                                                                253
12.2 Menhir at Men-Marz, commune of Brigognan, Finistère,
    France.                                                                255
14.1 Photograph of Caspar Bechteler's carving of the
    iconoclasts in St Vitus' Cathedral, Prague.                            289
14.2 Ferdinand Brokoff, St Elizabeth, St Margaret and
    St Barbara, Charles Bridge, Prague.                                    295
14.3 Matthias Braun, St Luitgard, Charles Bridge, Prague.                  297
14.4 Luther, Charles Bridge, Prague.                                       300

# Figures

7.1 Map of the parish of Holy Trinity, Chester. *page* 125
7.2 Plan of the church of Holy Trinity, Chester. 128
7.3 Graph of the ratio between church and churchyard burials
at Holy Trinity, Chester, 1598–1633. 140
8.1 Plan of the church at Neamţ after Grigore Ionescu.
(Drawn by Pavel Bugnar.) 145
8.2 Plan of the church at Rădăuţi, after Grigore Ionescu.
(Drawn by Pavel Bugnar.) 148
8.3 Plan of the church at Bistriţa after Ioan Bălan; plan of the
church at Probota after Vasile Drăguţ. (Drawn by Pavel
Bugnar.) 149
13.1 Map of Orange, *c.* 1650. 265

# Notes on contributors

DUANE J. CORPIS is Assistant Professor at Georgia State University in Atlanta, Georgia, where he teaches early modern European and World History. He is currently revising a book manuscript entitled *Crossing the Boundaries of Belief: The Geography of Religious Conversion in Southern Germany, 1648–1800*. He is also a regular contributor and member of the editorial board of *Radical History Review*.

WILL COSTER is Senior Lecturer in History at De Montfort University, Bedford. He has published numerous articles and chapters on early modern social and religious history and is the author of *Baptism and Spiritual Kinship in Early Modern England* (2002).

MARIA CRĂCIUN is Senior Lecturer in the Department of Medieval and Early Modern History Babeş-Bolyai University of Cluj, Romania. As well as a number of articles on the the religious life of Moldavia and Transylvania in the early modern period, she is the author of *Protestantism şi Ortodoxie în Moldova secolului al XVI-lea* (1996), and co-edited *Ethnicity and Religion in Central and Eastern Europe* (1995), *Church and Society in Eastern Europe* (1998), *Confessional Identity in East-Central Europe* (2002).

JOHN CRAIG is Associate Professor of History at Simon Fraser University in British Columbia, Canada. He is the author of *Reformation, Politics and Polemics: The Growth of Protestantism in East Anglian Market Towns, 1500–1610* (2001) and one of the editors of *Conferences and Combination Lectures in the Elizabethan Church, 1582–1590* (2003). He is currently writing *The Politics of Reading in the English Parish, 1536–1642*.

SIMON DITCHFIELD is Senior Lecturer in History at the University of York. He has published widely on Roman Catholic uses of the past in early modern Italy. His monograph study, *Liturgy, Sanctity and History in Tridentine Italy*, was published in paperback by Cambridge University Press in 2002.

AMANDA EURICH is Professor of History at Western Washington University, Bellingham, Washington. She is the author of *The Economics of Power: The Private Fortunes of the House of Foix-Navarre-Albret During the Religious Wars* (1994) and has written a number of articles on confessional identity and community in early modern France. She is currently engaged in writing a book on the politics and practice of religious toleration and violence in southern France during the seventeenth century.

CHRISTIAN GROSSE lectures in the Département d'histoire générale at the Université de Genève. He has published *L'excommunication de Philibert Berthelier. Histoire d'un conflit d'identité aux premiers temps de la Réforme genevoise (1547–1555)* (Geneva, 1995) and he completed his dissertation on 'Les rituels de la cène. Une anthropologie historique du culte eucharistique réformé à Genève (XVIᵉ–XVIIᵉ siècles)' at the University of Geneva in 2001.

BRIDGET HEAL is Lecturer in Early Modern History at the University of St Andrews. She is currently working on a book on Marian imagery and devotion in early modern Germany.

TREVOR JOHNSON is Senior Lecturer in History at the University of the West of England, Bristol and the editor (with Bob Scribner) of *Popular Religion in Germany and Central Europe, 1400–1800* (1996).

BEAT KÜMIN is Senior Lecturer in Early Modern European History at the University of Warwick. His research interests focus on social centres in pre-modern towns and villages, particularly in England and German-speaking Europe. After a comparative study of English parishes in the age of the Reformation (which appeared as *The Shaping of a Community* (1996)), he is now completing a social and cultural history of public houses in Bern and Bavaria. Recent publications include the (co-)edited collections *The World of the Tavern: Public Houses in Early Modern Europe* (2002) and *Landgemeinde und Kirche im Zeitalter der Konfessionen* (2004).

HOWARD LOUTHAN is Associate Professor of History at the University of Florida. He is the author of the *Quest for Compromise* (1997). He is nearing completion on a project that examines the creation of a Catholic identity in the Bohemian kingdom during the seventeenth and eighteenth centuries.

ANDREW SPICER is Senior Lecturer in Early Modern European History at Oxford Brookes University. He has written on immigrant communities, Reformed death and burial, and the impact of the Reformation on church architecture. His publications include *The French-speaking Reformed Community and their Church in Southampton, 1567– c. 1620* (1997) and he is the co-editor of *Society and Culture in the Huguenot World, 1559–1685* (2002), and *Defining the Holy: Sacred Space in Medieval and Early Modern Europe* (forthcoming). He is currently completing a monograph entitled, *The Reformed Church: Architecture and Society*.

ELIZABETH TINGLE is Senior Lecturer in History at University College, Northampton. She has published on the social, economic and cultural history of Brittany and the Saintonge region of France. Her current research interests are the French Wars of Religion and the Catholic Reform movement in the west of France, particularly in Brittany. She is currently preparing a monograph entitled *Authority and Society in Nantes during the French Wars of Religion 1558–1598*.

ALEXANDRA WALSHAM is Professor of History at the University of Exeter. As well as many essays and articles, she has written *Church Papists: Catholicism, Conformity and Confessional Polemic in Early Modern England* (1993) and *Providence in Early Modern England* (1999), and co-edited with Julia Crick *The Uses of Script and Print 1300–1700* (2004). She is currently completing a survey of *Tolerance and Intolerance in England 1500–1700* and carrying out research for a monograph on *Holy Wells and Healing Springs in Early Modern Britain*.

# Abbreviations

BL  British Library
*JEH*  *Journal of Ecclesiastical History*
*P&P*  *Past & Present*
PRO  Public Record Office
SCH  Studies in Church History
*SCJ*  *Sixteenth Century Journal*

# 1    Introduction: the dimensions of sacred space in Reformation Europe

## Will Coster and Andrew Spicer

Perhaps the most significant aspect of sacred space in Reformation studies over the last forty years has been its absence. This lacuna is striking because, since Mircea Eliade coined the phrase there has been a huge body of work on this subject generated by anthropologists, sociologists, geographers, students of architecture, archaeologists and even by historians of other eras, stretching from ancient Greece to modern America.[1] Despite pioneering work by Natalie Zemon Davis on sixteenth-century Lyon, this picture has only recently begun to change.[2] Sacred space is fast becoming one of the major areas of study in late medieval and early modern religion.[3] To date, however, there has been no serious and sustained attempt to investigate this important facet of the period in the variety of contexts that prevailed across the continent of Europe.

---

[1] M. Eliade, *The Sacred and the Profane: The Nature of Religion* (New York, 1959). On the ancient world see S. E. Alcock and R. Osborne (eds.), *Placing the Gods, Sanctuaries and Sacred Space in Ancient Greece* (Oxford, 1998); B. Z. Kedar and R. J. Z. Werblowsky (eds.), *Sacred Space: Shrine, City, Land: Proceedings of the International Conference in Memory of Joshua Prawer* (Basingstoke, 1998); S. D. Kumin, *God's Place in the World: Sacred Space and Sacred Place in Judaism* (London, 1998); D. Frankfurter (ed.), *Pilgrimage and Holy Space in Late Antique Egypt* (Leiden, 1998). On America see, D. Chidester and E. T. Lithenthal (eds.), *American Sacred Space* (Bloomington, Ind., 1995); E. T. Lithenthal, *Sacred Ground: Americans and Their Battlefields* (Urbana, Ill., 1993); D. C. Sloane, *The Last Great Necessity: Cemeteries in American History* (Baltimore, Mass., 1991); P. W. Williams, *Houses of God: Region, Religion, and Architecture in the United States* (Urbana, Ill., 1997). In the aftermath of '9/11' the concept of sacred space has been frequently applied to 'Ground Zero'. See the useful review by P. W. Williams, 'Sacred space in North America', *Journal of the American Academy of Religion* 70 (2002), 593–609.

[2] N. Z. Davis, 'The sacred and the body social in sixteenth-century Lyon', *P&P* 90 (1981), 40–70.

[3] For examples of recent work, see, J. M. Minty, '*Judengasse* to Christian Quarter: the phenomenon of the converted synagogue in the late medieval and early modern Holy Roman Empire', in R. W. Scribner and T. Johnson (eds.), *Popular Religion in Germany and Central Europe, 1400–1800* (Basingstoke, 1996), pp. 58–86; P. Roberts, 'Contesting sacred space: burial disputes in sixteenth-century France', in B. Gordon and P. Marshall (eds.), *The Place of the Dead: Death and Remembrance in Late Medieval and Early Modern Europe* (Cambridge, 2000), pp. 131–48; T. M. Lucas, *Landmarking, City, Church and Jesuit Urban Strategy* (Chicago, 1997); R. McCoy, *Alternations of State, Sacred Kingship in the English Reformation* (New York, 2002), ch. 2.

The aim of this volume is to explore the many dimensions of sacred space in the context of one of the most significant events of this period of European history, the Reformation, in locations ranging from Britain to Moldavia, in a variety of cultural and religious contexts. The areas investigated cross not only the continent, but also the confessional divide, between the Catholicism that continued to dominate in the centre and the south (as well as the Orthodox faith to the east), and the Lutheranism and Calvinism that gained a foothold in the north, west and parts of eastern Europe. Each chapter provides a detailed investigation of an aspect of the general theme in a national or local context based on original research. The collection does not attempt to be a comprehensive study of this phenomenon, but enables the reader to draw his or her own comparisons across Europe and the period under study in a critical age that has undergone a revolution in perception in recent years.

It is no longer possible to argue that the Protestant Reformation and the Catholic Counter-Reformation were inevitable or even welcome events with roots deep in the failings and unpopularity of the medieval Church. Instead 'revisionism' has made it necessary to appreciate the ubiquity, functionality and popularity of late medieval Catholicism.[4] Such an appreciation raises issues about the ability of reformers to impose or facilitate a transformation of religious life. This has turned the interest of historians away from the purely theological and administrative structures of rival churches, towards the impact of what is usually referred to as 'popular religion'.[5] This shift has coincided with the rise of a form of cultural history with very similar aims, which has virtually subsumed the economic and social history that once dominated in academic circles.[6]

Such a form of investigation cannot be embarked upon in the same way as religious history was once undertaken. It demands different sources, such as wills, churchwardens' accounts, parish registers, court records,

---

[4] C. Haigh, *Reformation and Resistance in Tudor Lancashire* (Cambridge, 1975) and G. Strauss, 'Success and failure in the German Reformation', *P&P* 67 (1975), 30–65, are important points of departure.

[5] On popular religion in general see B. Reay, 'Popular religion', in B. Reay (ed.), *Popular Culture in Seventeenth-Century England* (London, 1985), pp. 91–128; Scribner and Johnson (eds.), *Popular Religion*, particularly the introduction by Scribner, pp. 1–15; K. von Greyerz, *Religion and Society in Early Modern Europe 1500–1800* (London, 1984); R. W. Scribner, *Popular Culture and Popular Movements in Reformation Germany* (London, 1987).

[6] P. Burke, *Popular Culture in Early Modern Europe* (London, 1978); R. Muchembled, *Popular and Elite Culture in Early Modern France 1400–1750* (1978, Baton Rouge, La., 1985); B. Reay, *Popular Cultures in England 1550–1750* (London, 1998); S. L. Kaplan, *Understanding Popular Culture Between the Middle Ages and the Nineteenth Century* (Berlin, 1984); T. Harris (ed.), *Popular Culture in England 1500–1850* (London, 1995), especially ch. 1 by the editor, 'Problematising popular culture'; R. W. Scribner, 'Is a history of popular culture possible', *History of European Ideas* 10 (1987) 175–91.

as well as the visual and structural evidence provided by archaeology, art and architecture; it gives us the opportunity to understand the reception and impact of religion on the people, many aspects of which are reflected in the chapters present in this volume. But one of the strengths of the work in this collection is that the contributors are able to bring to bear an understanding of more traditional sources, including liturgical, theological and spiritual works, albeit with a new intellectual focus.

There has also been a shift towards seeing a plurality of Reformations, including those that can be described as magisterial, radical and Catholic, which has led to increasing scholarly fragmentation and an appreciation of the diverse nature of experiences of religious change.[7] Moreover, where the Reformation was once seen as a single and abrupt watershed, historians now routinely talk of a 'long sixteenth century', whereby religious change stretches back to include earlier movements for reform. Other scholars have adopted a 'long reformation' that includes the seventeenth and even the eighteenth centuries.[8]

If post-revisionism can be defined as an attempt to investigate the ways in which the slow, hesitant and difficult process of religious change was undertaken on a broad canvas, it is hardly surprising that its proponents have begun to focus on understanding the concept of space within early modern religion. The ways in which space was created, and re-created, are an obvious means of investigating how change was achieved, or, just as importantly, how limited was its extent. Space is also much more than a physical issue; what is of chief concern to most of the historians currently working in this field is not the purely architectural utilisation of space, but what that can tell us about the *mentalité* of the people of Reformation Europe: how it reflected and reinforced their understanding of sanctity, divinity and themselves. Thus sacred space can be seen as situated at the crossroads of the major trends in the study of the Reformation, as a meeting place between popular religion and the attempt to reorder that religion. What is more, the collapse of the major intellectual structures that have dominated thinking about the Reformation, has also led to the study of sacred space beyond the initial period of change.

Late medieval Europe has long been seen as a landscape filled and defined by points of access to the holy: in the striking terminology of Henri Lefebvre, arguably the pre-eminent philosopher of space, it was a

---

[7] C. Haigh, *English Reformations, Religion, Politics and Society under the Tudors* (Oxford, 1993); C. Lindberg, *The European Reformations* (Oxford, 1996); J. D. Tracy, *Europe's Reformations* (Lanham, Md, 1999).

[8] N. Tyacke (ed.), *England's Long Reformation 1500–1800. The Neale Colloquium in British History* (Cambridge, 1998); see also Lindberg, *European Reformations*, p. 13 on the 'long sixteenth century'.

land 'haunted by the Church'.[9] These included parish churches, chapels and cathedrals; abbeys, priories and nunneries; shrines, wells, springs and crosses; not to mention the caves and chambers of hermits and anchorites, the routes of pilgrimage, the sites of the dead and of martyrdom. Indeed, there were so many forms of sacred space in pre-Reformation Europe that it is impossible to compile a comprehensive list. It is not unreasonable to characterise late medieval Catholicism as a religion dependent on a highly complex landscape of the sacred.

It would, however, be misleading to depict the use of space across Catholic Europe as uniform. In a series of studies, Lionel Rothkrug, drawing a contrast with France, has pointed to the greater significance of holy sites over holy objects in late medieval Germany. Noting the different densities of such sites in the northern and southern empire, he even goes so far as to argue that there was a correlation between the success of the Reformation in those areas with few sacred sites and its failure in those regions with many.[10] Some historians have taken exception to these conclusions, but they do, at the least, raise the possibility that there was a relationship between sacred space and the achievement of religious change. Such a relationship could be complex, as a religion that is closely tied to a map of the sacred may permeate the popular consciousness, but it is also highly vulnerable if that map is redrawn.[11]

It is just such a reconfiguration that is associated with the Reformation. Reformers attacked the distinctiveness and efficacy of many sacred rites, assailed holy objects, broke down the barriers between the consecrated individual and the multitude, but they also launched an offensive on the sanctity of space. Luther denounced the dedication of churches as the first among 'the Pope's bag of impostures' and Calvin even more explicitly saw churches as not having any 'secret sanctity', but as convenient temples to house congregations.[12] This, linked to attacks on monasticism, purgatory

---

[9] H. Lefebvre, *The Production of Space*, trans. D. Nicholson-Smith (1974, Oxford, 1991), p. 254.

[10] L. Rothkrug, 'Popular religion and holy shrines', in J. Obelkerich (ed.), *Religion and the People* (Chapel Hill, 1979), pp. 20–86; L. Rothkrug, 'Religious practice and collective perceptions, hidden homologies in the Renaissance and Reformation', *Historical Reflections* 7 (1980); L. Rothkrug, 'Holy shrines, religious dissonance and Satan in the origins of the German Reformation', *Historical Reflections* 14 (1987), 143–286; L. Rothkrug, 'German holiness and Western sanctity in medieval and modern history', *Historical Reflections* 15 (1988), 161–249.

[11] A. Walsham, 'The reformation of the landscape: religion, memory and legend in early modern Britain', paper delivered at the Reformation Studies Colloquium at Easter 2004. Forthcoming publication of this research is planned.

[12] F. Bente and W. H. T. Dau (eds.), *Triglot Concordia: The Symbolical Books of the Evangelical Lutheran Church* (St Louis, 1921), pp. 453–529; F. L. Battles (ed.), *John Calvin, Institutes*

and the cult of the saints, meant that shrines, relics and pilgrimage were destroyed; monasteries and chantries were dissolved; rood screens ripped down; altars stripped and moved; most strikingly iconoclasm 'purified' the internal landscape of churches and turned them from repositories of supernatural power to mere meeting houses.[13]

Thus the Reformation has traditionally been perceived as a process by which the sanctity of space, along with the other elements of the 'magic of religion' was destroyed: that it promoted, in Max Weber's famous phrase a 'disenchantment of the world'.[14] In recent years Weber's thesis has been seriously undermined and there has been a growing awareness that Protestantism in its many forms could not entirely dispense with all elements of Catholic practice.[15] Just as some of the sacraments were retained, so fonts, altars or communion tables, even churches themselves, could not be completely divorced from intimations of sanctity. As Bob Scribner put it, 'Protestantism was as caught up as Catholicism in the same dilemmas about the instrumental application of sacred power to secular life because it was positioned in the same forcefield of sacrality.'[16] As the current research of Alex Walsham demonstrates, holy wells and other features in the landscape could remain centres of recusant worship in an overwhelmingly Protestant state, suggesting that the Reformation led not to the eradication of older patterns of sanctity in space, but to a modification of those views.[17]

---

of the Christian Religion, 1536 Edition (Grand Rapids, Mi., 1986), p. 73. For more detail of the Lutheran and Calvinist positions on the sanctity of churches see the contributions to this volume by Bridget Heal, Christian Grosse and Andrew Spicer.

[13] C. M. N. Eire, War Against the Idols: The Reformation of Worship from Erasmus to Calvin (Cambridge, 1986); E. Duffy, Stripping of the Altars: Traditional Religion in England 1400–1580 (New Haven and London, 1992) and M. Aston, England's Iconoclasts, I: Laws Against Images (Oxford, 1988). For comments on icons and their context see L. P. Wandel, Voracious Idols and Violent Hands, Iconoclasm in Reformation Zurich, Strasbourg, and Basel (Cambridge, 1995), pp. 44, 133–47; N. Z. Davis, 'The rites of violence' in her Society and Culture in Early Modern France (Oxford, 1987), pp. 152–87; K. Thomas, Religion and the Decline of Magic: Studies in the Popular Religion of Sixteenth and Seventeenth Century England (London, 1970), p. 35.

[14] M. Weber, The Protestant Ethic and the Spirit of Capitalism, trans. T. Parsons (1930, London, 1985), p. 105. For Weber, Calvinism was the major step in this process. See also Thomas, Religion and the Decline of Magic, pp. 58–89.

[15] R. A. Mentzer, 'The persistence of "superstition and idolatry" among rural French Calvinists', Church History 65 (1996), 220–33; see also W. G. Naphy and H. Parish (eds.), Religion and Superstition in Reformation Europe (Manchester, 2003).

[16] R. W. Scribner, 'The Reformation, popular magic and the disenchantment of the World', Journal of Interdisciplinary History 23 (1993), 475–94; R. W. Scribner, 'The impact of the Reformation on daily life', in Mensch und Mittelalter und in der frühen Neuzeit. Leiben, Altag, Kultur (Vienna, 1990).

[17] Walsham, 'The reformation of the landscape'; see also her chapter in this volume.

Some Protestants consciously retained the existing landscape of the holy. In Lutheran cities such as Nuremberg and Lübeck, the sacred topography of Catholicism was assimilated into Protestantism. Moreover, those religious communities that were forced to create new spaces for worship and ritual had to find precedents and develop their own concepts of how space should be organised and apportioned, even in the heart of the Calvinist movement, the 'new Jerusalem' of Geneva, what took place was not a process of desacralisation, but rather a rearrangement of space according to a new conception of the sacred. Beyond Geneva, there was an apparent contradiction in the Reformed Church's practice of combating the 'superstitious customs' that reflected a continued belief in the sanctity of the church, while also attempting to protect the building from profanation.[18]

On the other side of the religious divide the Council of Trent placed an emphasis on the repair of ruined churches and shrines and on order and reverence within church services, but the Catholic Church could not hope simply to maintain its map of the sacred intact.[19] The resurgence of ecclesiastical patronage, the construction and refurbishment of the churches of Rome, in the late sixteenth and seventeenth centuries, culminating in the completion of St Peter's Basilica, made an emphatic and symbolic statement of the importance and sanctity of the Eternal City. The exuberance of the Baroque was part of a wider readjustment to the changed religious landscape. At the centre of the Catholic world, a number of writers redrew and redefined the sacred space of Rome for visitors and devout inhabitants, linking the present with their sacred past.[20] Beyond Rome, the fact that many areas of Europe were converted to Protestantism inevitably meant a wider realignment of the geography of holiness, and the war against heresy also created new centres of sanctity and the need to resanctify territory and sites restored to Catholic control.[21] In the reconquered kingdom of seventeenth-century Bohemia, this necessitated the creation of new religious identities in the resanctification of 'heretical' space. But as the research of Elizabeth Tingle and Alexandra Walsham shows us, the Counter-Reformation was linked to the reordering of the physical world and a revisiting and reintegration of the pre-Christian landscape into a system of sacred spatial organisation. It reminds us that sacred space was transformed by the rise of new and the renewal of old religious

[18] See the chapters by Bridget Heal, Christian Grosse and Andrew Spicer below.
[19] J. Waterworth (ed.), *The Canons and Decrees of the Sacred and Oecumenical Council of Trent* (London, 1848), pp. 150–1, 161, 265–6.
[20] See Simon Ditchfield's chapter in this volume.
[21] T. M. Buttner, 'The significance of the Reformation for the re-orientation of geography of religion in Germany', *History of Science* 17 (1979), 151–69.

movements within the Catholic Church, but had also been appropriated by the Church in the past from other religions.[22] Thus one of the by-products of the Counter-Reformation was a reassessment and a reassertion of the place of the holy on earth.

In the light of these findings it is necessary to re-evaluate our traditional view of the Reformation and Counter-Reformation as, respectively, movements for the destruction and preservation of sacred space. Instead we need to consider both as creative and adaptive forces, retaining functional elements of the existing system and developing new organisations of the holy. Across Europe and the religious divide, the removal of traditional social events such as dances, courts, communal meetings and ales from churches can be seen as a part of a process of the re-sacralisation of the church.[23] It seems then this period saw a 're-formation' of sacred space, in more than one sense.

If sacred space was not simply swept away by the Reformation then we need to consider how it survived and its nature in what was inevitably a much more complex and contradictory picture of religious experience than the one that historians have traditionally drawn. These may be defined as the problems of contestation, liminality, subdivision, polarity, dimension and meaning.

The simple division of topography into sacred and profane spheres assumes a set of shared values and beliefs, but that consensus could be absent. Even within the orthodox Catholic Church of the pre-Reformation era there were many instances where the sanctity of different sites was a subject of negotiation or dispute, and there existed groups within medieval society, most obviously the Jews, with clearly distinct views of the sanctity of space.[24] This problem was all the more acute after the Reformation in those places where the high tide of reform had left pools of alternative belief. Recent work by Lisa McClain and Frances Dolan has drawn attention to the implications of this problem among the English Catholic minority in the late sixteenth and early seventeenth

---

[22] See chapters by Howard Louthan, Elizabeth Tingle and Alexandra Walsham below; A. G. Remensnyder, 'The colonization of sacred architecture: the Virgin Mary, mosques and temples in medieval Spain and early sixteenth-century Mexico', in S. Farmer and B. H. Rosenwein (eds.), *Monks and Nuns, Saints and Outcasts. Religion in Medieval Society* (Ithaca, 2000), pp. 189–219.

[23] C. J. Sommerville, *The Secularization of Early Modern England, From Religious Culture to Religious Faith* (Oxford, 1992), p. 30, observes that, 'Reformation changes in the use of space within churches might well strike us as a sacralization of these buildings, rather than a secularization.'

[24] C. Zika, 'Hosts, processions and pilgrimage: controlling the sacred in fifteenth-century Germany', *P&P* 181 (1988), 25–64; K. R. Stow, 'Holy body, holy society: medieval structural conceptions', in Kedar and Werblowsky (eds.), *Sacred Space: Shrine, City, Land*, pp. 151–71.

centuries, while in contrast Penny Roberts has illustrated the difficulties faced by the Huguenots in France.[25] Norman Jones has seen these circumstances as creating areas of 'neutral space'.[26] In an urban context, confessional divides within communities necessitated the careful articulation of space to maintain separate and distinct places. But this negotiated sacred topography presented a number of battlegrounds for confessional conflict and contestation, especially when the balance between the religious faiths was altered.[27]

To understand these borders we have to approach the much-discussed concept of liminality. This was originally identified by Arnold van Gennep to highlight the boundaries surrounding ritual states, movement between which is facilitated by rites of passage.[28] In liminality the bridges between states, in this case between zones of sanctity and profanity, act as places of possibility and danger. Some historians have been unconvinced by the rigidity of these boundaries and have concluded that the contrast was not between sacred and profane worlds, rather in the words of R. W. Scribner, 'the sacred is . . . experienced from *within the profane*'.[29] Furthermore if we consider this from another perspective, 'one of the defining characteristics of baroque style is this fusion of sacred and profane imagery'.[30] Therefore we need not consider sacred and profane space as distinct and totally opposed zones.

It has long been noted that in the early Church the location of the tombs of saints, usually outside of an urban centre, often led to the establishment of ecclesiastical buildings on or near such sites, acquiring sanctity by association, like pieces of iron undergoing polarisation by a magnet.[31]

---

[25] L. McClain, 'Without church, cathedral or shrine: the search for religious space among Catholics in England, 1550–1625', *SCJ* 33 (2002), 381–99; F. E. Dolan, 'Gender and the "lost" spaces of Catholicism', *Journal of Interdisciplinary History* 32 (2002), 641–60; P. Roberts, 'The most crucial battle of the wars of religion? The conflict over sites for reformed worship in sixteenth-century France', *Archiv für Reformationsgeschichte* 89 (1998), 247–66.

[26] N. Jones, *The English Reformation: Religion and Cultural Adaptation* (Oxford, 2002), pp. 33–4.

[27] See the chapters by Duane Corpis and Amanda Eurich below; G. (Ineke) Justiz, 'Reforming space, reordering reality: Naumberg's Herren Gasse in the 1540s', *SCJ* 33 (2002), 625–48.

[28] A. van Gennep, *The Rites of Passage*, trans. M. B. Vizdeom and G. L. Caffee (Chicago, 1960); V. Turner and E. Turner, *Image and Pilgrimage in Christian Culture* (New York, 1978); Kumin, *God's Place in the World*, pp. 30–8.

[29] R. W. Scribner, 'Cosmic order and daily life: sacred and secular in pre-industrial German society', in his *Popular Culture and Popular Movements in Reformation Germany* (London, 1987), p. 2.

[30] B. L. Brown, 'Between the sacred and profane', in L. Brown (ed.), *The Genius of Rome, 1592–1623* (London, 2001), pp. 276–303; quotation at p. 281.

[31] P. Brown, *The Cult of the Saints: Its Rise and Function in Latin Christianity* (Chicago, 1981).

Routes to these sites of pilgrimage, particularly like those to the most famous shrines could themselves become veins of sacred force, and the chapels or shrines erected along them began to acquire their own status as holy ground.[32] As Edward Muir has argued in relation to Italian cities, the distinction between the sacred church and the profane world around it was blurred by holy images 'extending the sacrality of the church outward'.[33] Ecclesiastical buildings themselves demonstrate a complex language of space, an interaction between ideals of the utilisation of existing topography and the continuing development of a long tradition of the architectural mapping of sanctity that can be seen most obviously in the great cathedrals and monasteries.[34] Moreover, as Barbara Rosenwein has demonstrated in a wide-ranging study, ideas of immunity and sanctity created by space have long been a subject of negotiation between the church and the state.[35] Thus the division or relationship between profane and sacred space was constantly in flux; sacred objects and sacred places tended to become surrounded by other zones of sanctity that could be different in their character and intensity.[36]

The results of these factors were gradations of holiness within sacred sites: for example, the church within the churchyard, the chapel within the church, the altar within the chapel. In late medieval Catholicism Christians crossed boundaries of holiness between different zones, or had their representative, the priest, cross these boundaries on their behalf, moving closer to the holy. In this way, sacred space defined religious experience, but it also reflected social experience. As a number of historians have noted, these concerns meant that sacred space was often sub-divided in ways that reflected and reinforced the nature of the social order. Seating in churches, which had begun to be employed in the late medieval period, was sometimes used to separate men from women, the young from the old, but most frequently it reflected the hierarchical social structure of early modern society.[37] The greater status of some points in

---

[32] Turner and Turner, *Image and Pilgrimage*; R. A. Fletcher, *Saint James' Catapult: The Life and Times of Diego Gelmirez of Santiago de Compostela* (Oxford, 1986).

[33] E. Muir, *Civic Ritual in Renaissance Venice* (Princeton, 1981).

[34] M. Cassidy-Welch. *Monastic Spaces and Their Meanings: Thirteenth-Century English Cistercian Monasteries*, Medieval Church Studies 1 (Turnhout, Belgium, 2001); R. Gilchrist. *Gender and Material Culture: The Archaeology of Religious Women* (London, 1994) and see also her *Contemplation and Action: The Other Monasticism* (Leicester, 1995) for a consideration of less prominent sites.

[35] B. H. Rosenwein, *Negotiating Space: Power, Restraint and Privileges of Immunity in Early Medieval Europe* (Ithaca, 1999).

[36] F. De Polignac, *Cults, Territory and the Origins of the Greek City State*, trans. J. Lloyd (Chicago, 1995).

[37] M. Aston, 'Segregation in church', in D. Webb (ed.), *Women in the Church*, SCH 27 (Oxford, 1990), pp. 237–94; C. Marsh, '"Common Prayer" in England 1560–1640: the

the church was thus echoed in seating patterns, but space could also be sub-divided by other factors.

The issue of gender in sacred space has received some attention in recent years, while gendered space has become a major area of investigation in both late medieval and early modern social history.[38] Although we have important work on female monasticism, there has been very little exploration of the ways in which these two factors met to create lay versions of gendered sacred space, for example in terms of shrines, or the organisation of churches.[39] Perhaps for the epitome of gendered sacred space we have to look to the growth of 'twin' religious houses with communities of both monks and nuns. A number of the chapters in this volume indicate the ways in which gender not only provided sub-divisions, but also led to single-gendered spaces.[40]

The character of sacred space not only reflected relations between parishioners, but the church and churchyard, serving as the places of burial and ritual, have been seen as structuring the relationships between the 'age groups' of the living and of the dead.[41] It has become a commonplace of Reformation historiography that Protestantism, by abolishing Purgatory and the cult of the saints, severed these relationships.[42] This view has recently been challenged, by pointing to continuing concerns among Protestants regarding their deceased relatives and ancestors.[43] Not

---

view from the pew', *P&P* 171 (2001), 66–94; C. Marsh, 'Sacred space in England, 1560–1640: the view from the pew', *JEH* 53 (2002), 286–311; A. Spicer, '"Accommodating of Thame Selfis to Heir the Word": preaching, pews and Reformed worship in Scotland, 1560–1638', *History* 88 (2003), 405–22.

[38] For examples of gendered sacred space for other periods see: D. Spain, *Gendered Spaces* (Chapel Hill, NC, 1992); S. Ardener, *Women and Space: Ground Rules and Social Maps* (Berg, 1993); L. Mcdowell and J. P. Sharp (eds.), *Space, Gender, Knowledge, Feminist Readings* (Oxford, 1997); A. I. Kahera, *Deconstructing the American Mosque: Space, Gender and Aesthetics* (Austin, 2002). For women's space in society see B. A. Hanawalt, 'At the margins of women's space in medieval Europe', in her *'Of Good and Ill Repute': Gender and Social Control in Medieval England* (Oxford, 1998); A. J. Chutte, T. Kuchn and S. S. Menchi (eds.), *Time, Space and Women's Lives in Early Modern Europe* (Kirkville, Mo., 2001); B. Capp, *When Gossips Meet Women, Family, and Neighbourhood in Early Modern England* (Oxford, 2003).

[39] Gilchrist, *Gender and Material Culture*; U. Strasser, 'Bones of contention: cloistered nuns, decorated relics, and the contest over women's place in the public sphere of Counter-Reformation Munich', *Archiv für Reformationsgeschichte* 90 (1999), 254–88.

[40] For sub-division by gender see the chapter by Will Coster and for male space see that by Trevor Johnson below.

[41] N. Z. Davis, 'Some tasks and themes in the study of popular religion', in C. Trinkaus and H. A. Oberman (eds.), *The Pursuit of Holiness in Late Medieval and Renaissance Religion* (Leiden, 1974), pp. 327–8.

[42] *Ibid.*, p. 330; Duffy, *Stripping of the Altars*, pp. 474–5; S. C. Karant-Nunn, *The Reformation of Ritual: an Interpretation of Early Modern Germany* (London, 1997), p. 178; Cressy, *Birth, Marriage and Death*, p. 396.

[43] P. Marshall, *Beliefs and the Dead in Reformation England* (Oxford, 2002), pp. 188–231.

only did the utilisation of the church and churchyard in late sixteenth- and early seventeenth-century England point to the continued concerns and proximity of the living worshippers and the deceased, but it also served as a focus of communality, reflecting both the mutuality and inequalities between the living. The circles of holiness that radiated out from the altars and shrines within a medieval church and churchyard still determined the expression of these factors. Even further afield in the Orthodox world, changes in funerary practice could reinforce and expand political relationships between the rulers and the divine and therefore between the elite and the people.[44]

The concept of sacred space is ultimately founded in Emile Durkheim's observation of the division into sacred and profane spheres in all religions. Yet it is already clear that such a bi-polar model of religious behaviour oversimplifies a complex picture. It is not difficult to find aspects of the organisation of space that appear multi-polar, or where other bi-polarities cut across religious boundaries.

The most obvious area where simple bi-polarity cannot describe a complex pattern is in attitudes to nature. While there is an obvious corollary between the natural and the profane, commentators have long been aware that wilderness and natural landscape can provide one key focus for the sanctity of space.[45] There is a complex triangular relationship between the sacred, profane and natural. The Spanish Carmelite deserts in the Counter-Reformation and the baroque illustrate the processes behind the sacralisation of natural space and religious attitudes towards the natural world that allowed the evocation and representation of a specific spirituality.[46] What is natural is not necessarily profane and, in a divine creation, can be seen as mirroring or even being part of a celestial plan.

Space must also be understood in the context of dichotomies between the rural and the urban and a number of the chapters in this collection reflect the different natures of urban and rural space.[47] For England these were highlighted by Raymond Williams in his work on the *Country and*

---

[44] See the chapters by Will Coster and Maria Crăciun below; H. Colvin, *Architecture and the After-Life* (New Haven, 1991), esp. pp. 253–82, 295–326; V. Harding, *The Dead and the Living in Paris and London, 1500–1670* (Cambridge, 2002), chs. 5, 6; A. Spicer, '"Defyle not Christ's kirke with your carrion": burial and the development of burial aisles in post-Reformation Scotland', in Gordon and Marshall (eds.), *The Place of the Dead*, pp. 149–69.

[45] L. H. Graber, *Wilderness as Sacred Space* (Washington, 1976).

[46] See the chapter by Trevor Johnson below; Walsham, 'The Reformation of the Landscape'.

[47] Those by Duane Corpis, Will Coster, Simon Ditchfield, Amanda Eurich and Christian Grosse reflecting urban space and those by Trevor Johnson and Elizabeth Tingle focusing specifically on rural contexts.

*the City* and recent re-evaluations of this opposition have emphasised the emergence of civic culture in the separation of these spheres.[48] Despite the overwhelmingly rural nature of pre-industrial society, towns have long held a place of particular significance in the study of medieval society and as the vessels in which the Reformation first fermented. The divide between urban and rural topography provided very different contexts for the organisation of sacred space and these can be seen in the contrasting utilisations of similar institutions, such as monasticism and in divergent ecclesiastical structures. In this sense the urban/rural divide could cut across the boundaries of sanctity. By the same token sacred space could bridge this divide, for example where parochial units crossed civic frontiers, encompassing both rural and urban settlements, as they did in many late medieval and early modern towns.

Urban historians have been particularly interested in the division between private and public space, which can be expressed in terms of both ownership and function.[49] Sacred space could be both private and public; the former can be seen in the family chapel and mausoleum, the latter in the graveyard or public shrine. David Postles has inverted the usual model of the church as sacred space utilised for secular purposes, by pointing to the utilisation of the market place for religious purposes.[50] It would be wrong to depict the Reformation and Counter-Reformation as processes for the privatisation of sacred space. The dissolution of monasteries might have resulted in the redistribution of lands into private hands, but the ruins of the great abbeys and priories had, as Margaret Aston has observed, a common melancholic aspect.[51] There is a tension inherent in all religions between the ownership of sacred space by the individual, the institution or the community and of the division into the visible and the unseen. These tensions and complexities became all the more acute

---

[48] R. Williams, *The Country and the City* (Oxford, 1973) and G. MacLean, D. Landry and J. P. Ward (eds.), *The Country and the City Revisited: England and the Politics of Culture 1550–1850* (Cambridge, 1999).

[49] V. Harding, 'Real estate: space, property and propriety in urban England', *Journal of Interdisciplinary History* 32 (2002), 549–71; M. Boon, 'Urban space and political conflict in late Medieval Flanders', *Journal of Interdisciplinary History* 32 (2002), 621–40; M. Camille, 'Signs of the city: place, power, and public fantasy in medieval Paris', in B. A. Hanawalt and M. Kobialka (eds.), *Medieval Practices of Space* (Minneapolis, 2000), pp. 1–36; C. Burroughs, 'Spaces of arbitration and the organisation of space in late medieval Italian cities', in Hanawalt and Kobialka (eds.), *Medieval Practices*, pp. 64–100; D. Barthélemy and P. Contamine, 'The use of private space', in G. Duby (ed.), *A History of Private Life*, II: *Revelations of the Medieval World* (Harvard, 1988), pp. 395–505.

[50] D. Postles, 'The market place as space in early modern England', *Social History* 29 (2004), 41–58.

[51] M. Aston, 'English ruins and English history: the dissolution and the sense of the past', in her *Lollards and Reformers: Images and Literacy in Late Medieval Religion* (London, 1984).

at the Reformation where the ownership of space and the public nature of worship became flashpoints for conflict, both theological and physical. They also became mechanisms for an emerging grudging toleration as in many places the private chapel and the home became divorced from the strictures of uniform worship and action.[52] But within the wider community the relationship between the early modern church and the public space of the tavern challenges the simple dichotomy of sacred and profane from a different perspective and points to a more complex set of spatial interactions within early modern communities.[53]

Thus, if nature can be said to complicate the divide between sacred and profane spheres by adding a third overlapping set, in modern mathematical terms, we might see the urban/rural divide as presenting us with a second axis on a graph. If we add the complication of public and private space, we have infinite room for variation in the topography of holiness.

As if this did not provide us with sufficient complexity we must also look beyond the obvious three dimensional configuration of sacred space. If the ancestry of the concept can be found in the work of Durkheim it is worthwhile considering that he also identified time as a key characteristic of the sacred/profane dichotomy.[54] We can see time as providing us with a fourth dimension to sacred space. The sanctity of space was not immutable; it could vary between different points in the liturgical calendar, the week or even the day. For example, the sanctity of the shrine was enhanced on the day of commemoration for a saint, or, for some Protestants a church became more intensely a locus of the sacred on the Sabbath.[55] Therefore, we cannot see sacred space as immutable and fixed, but as interacting with a complex range of factors.

[52] A point made with some force in B. J. Kaplan, 'Fictions of privacy: house chapels and the spatial accommodation of religious dissent in early modern Europe', *American Historical Review* 107 (2002), 1031–64.

[53] See Beat Kümin's chapter below.

[54] E. Durkheim, *The Elementary Forms of Religious Life*, ed. M. S. Cladis, trans. C. Cosman (1912, repr. Oxford, 2001). The impact of the Reformation on concepts of time has received more serious investigation than space. See particularly E. Muir, *Ritual in Early Modern Europe* (Cambridge, 1997), pp. 55–80; C. Phythian-Adams, 'Ceremony and the citizen: the communal year at Coventry 1450–1500', in P. Clark and P. Slack (eds.), *Crisis and Order in English Towns, 1500–1700, Essays in Urban History* (Toronto, 1972), pp. 57–85; J. Le Goff, 'Merchant's time and church's time in the Middle Ages', in his *Time, Work and Culture in the Middle Ages*, trans. A. Goldhammer (Chicago, 1980), pp. 29–42; D. Cressy, *Bonfires and Bells: National Memory and the Protestant Calendar in Elizabethan and Stuart England* (Berkeley and Los Angeles, 1989).

[55] B. Nilson, *Cathedral Shrines of Medieval England* (Rochester, NY, 1998); J. Sumption, *Pilgrimage: An Image of Mediaeval Religion* (Totowa, NJ, 1975); C. Hahn, 'Seeing is believing: the construction of sanctity in early medieval saints' shrines', *Speculum* 72 (1997); J. T. Schulenburg, 'Gender, celibacy, and proscriptions of sacred space: symbol and practice', in M. Frassetto (ed.), *Medieval Purity and Piety: Essays on Medieval Clerical Celibacy and Religious Reform* (New York, 1998), pp. 353–76; P. Collinson,

To add to this already multifaceted picture, space must be understood in more than simply visual or physical dimensions. It is necessary to think in terms of the soundscape of sacred space if we are to comprehend fully the nature of religious experience in this period. In biconfessional cities or countries with recognised religious minorities, the faiths competed audibly with the chiming of bells for services, or challenged the rival faiths through singing.[56] We can pursue this theme further and consider the other senses, including the smells and tangibility or intangibility of holy places, which must have had a profound impact on the emotional reception of religion. How different was the air of the late medieval parish church, filled with incense and the smoke of burning candles, from that of the whitewashed halls of post-Reformation meeting houses? How significant were the contrasts between standing in the spaces of a great cathedral church to witness mass, with sitting in the boxed pews of later seventeenth-century chapels with prayer book, Bible or hymnal tangibly in hand? Out of such sensory encounters are religious experiences fashioned. As proposed by Rudolph Otto, the encounter with sacred power produced a 'numinous' experience, affecting the human consciousness with the 'creature-feeling', that is, an awareness of one's own fragile mortal nature and *mysterium tremendum*, a sense of the majesty of the divine.[57] We cannot fully understand the sanctity of space without appreciating these emotional and psychological aspects.

Space can also be extended and modified by representation, in both artistic and literary forms. In recent scholarship this process of mapping space in drama, literature, cartography and politics has been very much to the fore.[58] The great works of baroque art might have been confined to the private chapels of the wealthy and a few great cathedrals, but even modest medieval parish churches contained a multiplicity of artistic representations, most obviously the doom paintings that

'The beginnings of English Sabbatarianism', in C. W. Dugmore and C. Dugan (eds.), *SCH* 1 (Oxford, 1964), pp. 207–21; K. Parker, *The English Sabbath, a Study of Doctrine and Discipline from the Reformation to the Civil War* (Cambridge, 1988).

[56] See John Craig's chapter below; P. Benedict, 'Un roi, une loi, deux fois: parameters for the history of Catholic-Reformed co-existence in France, 1555–1685', in O. P. Grell and B. Scribner (eds.), *Tolerance and Intolerance in the European Reformation* (Cambridge, 1996), p. 82; S. Deyon, 'La destruction des temples', in R. Zuber and L. Theis (eds.), *La révocation de l'edit de Nantes et le protestantisme français en 1685* (Paris, 1986), pp. 252–4.

[57] R. Otto, *The Idea of the Holy: An Enquiry Into the Idea of the Divine and Its Relation to the Rational* (London, 1925), pp. 6–41.

[58] A. Gordon and B. Klein (eds.), *Literature, Mapping and the Politics of Space in Early Modern Britain* (Cambridge, 2001); B. Klein, *Maps and the Writing of Space in Early Modern England and Ireland* (Basingstoke, 2001); G. Bachelard, *The Poetics of Space*, trans. M. Jolas (New York, 1993); U. Chaudhuri, *Staging Space: the Geography of Modern Drama* (Michigan, 1995).

enlarged the interior of the church to include a celestial landscape. Similarly, literary expansion can be seen in devotional works that underlined the significance of topography, and also in items such as liturgical writings, that brought divinity within sacred space. In the age of cyberspace we should need no reminding that space can exist beyond the physical world.

Finally, we have to consider the meaning of sacred space. Even if we take into account the many facets of this phenomenon there is a danger of interpreting it according to a one-dimensional formula: to assume that it had one meaning. Some historians have concluded that this phenomenon is closely connected to the utilisation and demonstration of power, but an examination of sacred space indicates that Michel Foucault's emphasis on the power of the state expressed in the organisation of space from the eighteenth century, disregards the degree to which different forms of power could be expressed and re-enforced.[59] Going further from a model of space as the medium of power, more recent, postmodern interpretations treat sacred locations as 'ritual space for the expression of a diversity of perceptions and meanings' which individuals themselves bring to the site of sanctity.[60] One of the many problems historians have with such views is that they disregard the ways in which culture or religion can provide a shared framework for such interpretations. However, these possibilities do raise an important point about the analysis of space. As Lefebvre noted, it would be erroneous to reduce space to the status of a *message*, and thereby its use to merely a *reading*. There is a complex interrelationship between space, which has often been inherited, modified and reinterpreted, and the 'messages' that it can provide.[61] Neither traditionalists nor reformers were necessarily clear about the significance of all aspects of the sanctity of space. Even the famous (or infamous) iconoclast William Dowsing, who worked his way through Civil-War East Anglia removing the remnants of idolatry, left items such as fonts and heraldic stained glass intact.[62]

Moreover, although Weber's thesis of disenchantment has been overturned, something significant still occurred to space in the Reformation. We should not assume that all space connected with religion is sacred. In the language formulated by Harold Turner, there is a distinction between sacred space as *domus dei*, where it contained the presence of God, and sacred space as *domus ecclesiae*, which acted as a vessel to contain worship

[59] M. Foucault, 'Space, knowledge and power', in *The Foucault Reader*, ed., P. Rainbow (London, 1984), pp. 239–56.
[60] J. Eade and M. Sallnow (eds.), *Contesting the Sacred* (London, 1991), pp. 9–10.
[61] Lefebvre, *The Production of Space*, pp. 7, 36–8.
[62] Aston, *England's Iconoclasts*, pp. 82–3.

or service and we need to be aware of such contrasts, when considering space before and after the Reformation.[63]

This period also gave rise to a new view of cosmology, of space in its greatest sense, which, by rejecting Aristotelian and Ptolemaic views of the universe, for some, removed the immediate presence of both heaven and hell, no longer above the sky and directly below the ground.[64] This in turn produced different views of the possibility of experiencing the holy on a more isolated 'island' earth and helped to make such encounters more metaphysical than physical. It has long been argued that both the Reformation and Counter-Reformation were processes that led to the internalisation and individualisation of religion. To the extent that this is true, the transformation of sacred space meant that its function was no longer to act, as Raymond Christinger put it, as 'spatial gates' between the earthly 'known realm' and the sacred 'unknown realm'.[65] Instead it allowed individuals to find a deeper level of spirituality by reminding them of the elements of the divine. The degree to which such changes penetrated the popular religious consciousness, and the point at which a reflection of holiness took on associations of sanctity, remain important areas of investigation to be revisited throughout this collection.

As a result of these complexities, the analysis of sacred space can be seen to lie within the remit of dominant 'post-revisionist' scholarship, but it also represents an opportunity to move beyond current thinking about the Reformation. The next stage in this process is unlikely to be a return to fatalistic and optimistic views of traditional religion and its reform, but the thematic cohesion of the chapters in this volume perhaps present an opportunity to restore some order and unity to the fragmented studies that have come to dominate recent thinking. It is perhaps time to reiterate that the Reformation was something distinct and significant, suggesting perhaps a return to a capitalised and singular Reformation. The acknowledgement of the continued existence and reproduction of sacred space during and after this process, between Catholics and Protestants, across and beyond the continent of Europe and the entire length of an expanded chronology, suggests that it is one means of developing a new agenda in the study of the Reformation and an important contribution to our understanding of religious experience and change in this vital period.

[63] H. Turner, *From Temple to Meeting House: The Phenomenology and Theology of Places of Worship* (The Hague, 1979).

[64] Lefebvre, *The Production of Space*, p. 45.

[65] R. Christinger, 'Notions préliminaires d'une géographie mythique', *Le Globe* 105 (1965), 119–59.

## 2    Sacred church and worldly tavern: reassessing an early modern divide

*Beat Kümin*

Ever since Emile Durkheim identified the distinction between the sacred and the profane as a characteristic of all religions, sociologists, anthropologists and historians have examined the manifold manifestations of this polarity and the 'liminal' areas in between.[1] Recent research on the European Confessional Age suggests that the late sixteenth and seventeenth centuries witnessed renewed and particularly strenuous efforts to demarcate the two spheres. Calvinism is usually credited with the fiercest campaigns against profanations of spiritual matters, as exemplified by 'Puritan' sabbatarianism and the pressure for greater moral discipline in post-Reformation England.[2] And yet, Catholic confessionalisation involved comparable efforts to disentangle the sacred and the profane, as recently shown for the prince-bishopric of Münster in Germany.[3]

Church–tavern relations provide an ideal opportunity for a closer examination of this process. As multifunctional institutions, public houses ranked among the most prominent social centres in European towns and villages. Apart from food and drink, they offered spatial settings for an infinite range of socio-economic, political and cultural activities.[4] Current scholarly opinion portrays church–tavern relations as inherently delicate and increasingly polarised over the course of the early modern period. In an influential study, Peter Clark observed a gradual shift in the relative importance of the two institutions for the population at large. In the wake

---

[1] 'The division of the world into two domains, the one containing all that is sacred, the other all that is profane, is the distinctive trait of religious thought.' E. Durkheim, *The Elementary Forms of the Religious Life: A Study in Religious Sociology*, trans. J. W. Swain (London, 1915, repr. 1971), p. 37. For a survey of relevant scholarship see the introduction to this volume.

[2] R. Hutton, *The Rise and Fall of Merry England: The Ritual Year 1400–1700* (Oxford, 1994), esp. chs. 4–6; see also the contribution by John Craig in this volume.

[3] A. Holzem, *Religion und Lebensformen: Katholische Konfessionalisierung im Sendgericht des Fürstbistums Münster* (Paderborn, 2000); cf. the chapter by Elizabeth Tingle in this volume.

[4] For the medieval origins see H. C. Peyer, *Von der Gastfreundschaft zum Gasthaus: Studien zur Gastlichkeit im Mittelalter* (Hanover, 1987). A survey of recent approaches appears in B. Kümin and B. A. Tlusty (eds.), *The World of the Tavern: Public Houses in Early Modern Europe* (Aldershot, 2002).

of post-Reformation campaigns of re-sacralisation (or, more precisely, sustained endeavours to 'de-profanise' religious buildings), public houses gradually replaced parish churches as the main social centres. If popular ceremonies and customs such as church ales were no longer acceptable within ecclesiastical precincts, people turned to alehouses instead.[5] A similar development has been identified elsewhere, often with sinister implications. For the sociologist Gabriel le Bras, the early modern French publican acted as the 'anti-curé' of his village, competing for the same audience, offering similar opening hours and succeeding in the establishment of a 'contre-Église'.[6] Political scientists like James C. Scott, furthermore, associate taverns more generally with the subculture of the oppressed, where an anti-establishment 'hidden transcript' could be articulated.[7] In short, reinforced demarcations between the sacred and the profane in early modern communities found spatial expression in the institutional dichotomy of parish churches (as religious sites) and public houses (as secular, if not immoral, criminal and subversive centres).

Such an interpretation can point to a substantial body of evidence from the period. As early as the fourteenth century, a French author was in no doubt about the nature of a public house: 'the devil's school is there, where his little disciples study, and also the chapel, where he is worshipped'.[8] A few hundred years later, Hippolytus Guarinonius, a medical doctor from seventeenth-century Tyrol, similarly defined the public house as a site 'where one serves the devil and forgets about God'.[9] Moral literature, however, may not be the most reliable guide by which to judge the early modern public house.

This chapter aims to reassess the relationship in more nuanced terms. While acknowledging the disorderly potential of public houses and numerous incidents of conflict, churches and taverns will be portrayed as closely connected and mutually dependent focal points of local cultural life. Examining a range of sources from a long-term perspective, it is argued that the 'polarisation thesis' fails to reflect the complexity of church–tavern interactions in early modern towns and villages. The case

---

[5] P. Clark, *The English Alehouse: A Social History 1200–1830* (London, 1983), esp. pp. 27, 152.

[6] Cited in G. Maistre, 'La lutte du clergé contre les cabarets du XVIIe au XIXe siècle', in *Vie religieuse en Savoie* (Annecy, 1988), pp. 307–18, esp. 309. See also the wider European comparison in A. L. Martin, *Alcohol, Sex and Gender in Late Medieval and Early Modern Europe* (Basingstoke, 2001), pp. 60–1.

[7] J. C. Scott, *Domination and the Arts of Resistance: Hidden Transcripts* (New Haven, 1990), esp. ch. 5.

[8] 'L'escole au déable y est où ses petits desciples estudient, et la chapèle où on fait son service', *Le mireour du monde*, ed. F. Chavannes (Lausanne, 1845), p. 170.

[9] *Die Grewel der Verwüstung menschlichen Geschlechts* (Ingolstadt, 1610; facsimile edn, Bozen, 1993), p. 828.

is substantiated primarily for the Zwinglian Swiss city republic of Bern and the Catholic princedom of Bavaria in the Holy Roman Empire, with glimpses into other European areas as well.[10] The juxtaposition of evidence from heterogeneous case studies is not meant to deny significant contextual differences (which cannot be elaborated here), but highlights the existence of a comparable structural framework in local communities right across the continent. The argument unfolds in four sections: first, a brief examination of the spatial relationship in the narrower sense of the term, that is the geographical and topographical setting; second and third, sketches of contrasting forms of interaction between 'sacred church' and 'worldly tavern'; and finally, a reassessment of the relationship from a wider conceptual perspective.

## I

A 'proper' town or village needed both a church and a public house.[11] From the later Middle Ages local communities all across the continent lobbied to improve their religious and socio-economic infrastructure. Villages without easy access to sacramental provision petitioned bishops and even popes for the grant of at least a chapel of ease, while those lacking appropriate hostelries approached manorial lords or territorial authorities for permission to open an alehouse, tavern or – ideally – a fully privileged inn.[12] Yet the topography of provision remained heterogeneous. The parochial network in realms like England looks very uneven: while London and southeastern counties boasted a disproportionate number of parishes, northern regions numbered extremely few.[13] The same is true for the distribution of public houses. Busy commercial centres or pilgrimage sites in central Europe easily reached a ratio of one establishment for fewer than one hundred inhabitants, while provision

[10] The chapter draws on a wider research project on German-speaking Central Europe forthcoming as *The Social Construction of Early Modern Public Houses*.

[11] 'A Bavarian village without a "proper" public house is not a "proper" Bavarian village.' T. Drexler (ed.), *Kellnerin, a Maß! Das Wirtshaus – die weltliche Mitte des Dorfes* (Fürstenfeldbruck, 1997), p. 6.

[12] Examples of ecclesiastical petitions from England are given in B. Kümin, *The Shaping of a Community: The Rise and Reformation of the English Parish c. 1400–1560* (Aldershot, 1996), pp. 167–79; evidence for village petitions for the creation or preservation of public houses from the German principality of Lippe is shown in Roland Linde, 'Ländliche Krüge. Wirtshauskultur in der Grafschaft Lippe im 18. Jahrhundert', in S. Baumeier and J. Carstensen (eds.), *Beiträge zur Volkskunde und Hausforschung* (Detmold, 1995), pp. 7–50, esp. 47.

[13] A structural analysis of the network appears in P. Hughes, *The Reformation in England* (London, 1950), I, p. 35. Cf. B. Kümin, 'The English parish in a European perspective', in K. French, G. Gibbs and B. Kümin (eds.), *The Parish in English Life 1400–1600* (Manchester, 1997), pp. 15–32.

on the northern and southern periphery of the continent remained minimal.

Kevelaer on the Lower Rhine, a pilgrimage centre to the present day, counted no fewer than seventy-six public houses in 1770, at a time when it had a mere 1,500 inhabitants (a ratio of 1:20).[14] Travelling through the Pennine region in northern England, however, Fynes Moryson remarked around 1600: 'I did neuer see nor heare that they haue any publike Innes with signes hanging out, but the better sort of Citizen . . . will entertaine passengers vpon acquaintance or entreaty'. Here, the ancient tradition of private hospitality predominated.[15] There were thus all sorts of spatial combinations in early modern Europe: places (like most major cities) with an inextricable, densely interwoven patchwork of sacred and profane social sites; places (as on the continent's periphery) punctuated by the holy grounds of chapels or parish churches, but hardly any hostelries; places (for example those on mountain pass routes) with only an isolated public house; and hamlets with no ecclesiastical or gastronomic provision at all. A first conclusion, therefore, is that the physical setting for church–tavern relations varied dramatically from one place to the other.

A similar impression emerges when we zoom in on the local topography. An 'ideal type' central European settlement is often visualised as nestling around a parish church, with the local inn in the immediate vicinity. This is indeed a common pattern, as illustrated in plate 2.1. From the window of the 'church lounge' on one side of the 'old innkeeper' at Obermenzing near Munich, the church building is all that can be seen. In such a setting, churchgoers must have been acutely aware of what went on in the public house, and vice versa. On the other hand, even more public houses were situated at quite some distance from the local church. The principal precondition for a successful hostelry was a good location, and the best location of all was a busy thoroughfare. Countless public houses stood on main roads or highway junctions, alongside canals or near bridges, sometimes outside the settlement proper, and thus way out of sight of the local vicar.[16] Urban hostelries, particularly numerous and heavily differentiated, targeted specific customer segments. Important guests liked to stay in the top establishments situated around the market

---

[14] P. Hersche, 'Die Lustreise der kleinen Leute – zur geselligen Funktion der barocken Wallfahrt', in W. Adam (ed.), *Geselligkeit und Gesellschaft im Barockzeitalter* (Wiesbaden, 1997), pp. 321–32, esp. 326.

[15] *An Itinerary* (London, 1617; facsimile edn, Amsterdam, 1971), part 3, p. 156.

[16] Almost all public houses in the English Chilterns were situated along the London highways or along waterways: M. Frearson, 'Communications and the continuity of dissent in the Chiltern Hundreds during the sixteenth and seventeenth centuries', in M. Spufford (ed.), *The World of Rural Dissenters 1520–1725* (Cambridge, 1995), pp. 273–87, esp. map 6.

Plate 2.1 The 'Old Innkeeper' (*Alte Wirt*) at Obermenzing in Bavaria, now a suburb of Munich. Located immediately adjacent to the churchyard of the parish of St George, the building dates from 1589–90.

square, carriers preferred inns with spacious yards just outside the city gates, while tradesmen and artisans sealed business deals in the taverns nearest to their residences.[17] Given the choice between proximity to a church or a commercial site, most publicans would not have hesitated to opt for the latter. One example is the tavern of the valley of Schangnau (Bernese Emmental), where the right to hold a hostelry seems to have been associated with the site of a rural fair, rather than the settlement around the local church (plate 2.2).[18]

In cases where the two institutions merged, however, spatial distinction no longer applied. On the one hand, some ecclesiastical buildings acted as public houses. In Bavaria, for instance, church-managed alcohol retailing has always been a characteristic of the catering trade. The former Benedictine monastery of Weihenstephan near Freising, which dates its brewing tradition back to 1040, is among the many contenders for the coveted

---

[17] Cf. the topography of Augsburg public houses sketched in B. A. Tlusty, *Bacchus and Civic Order: The Culture of Drink in Early Modern Germany* (Charlottesville, 2001), pp. 22–34.

[18] For details of the complex legal situation see F. Häusler, *Die alten Dorfmärkte des Emmentals* (Langnau, 1986), pp. 82–3.

Plate 2.2  The Schangnau valley in the Bernese Emmental, from a border atlas of the Republic of Bern compiled by Samuel Bodmer in 1705–
1710. The village centre with the church appears in the middle of the
picture, the public house (*Wirtzhus*) in the hamlet Wald at some distance
in the top left-hand corner. (StA BE, Atlanten Nr. 1–4, vol. II, fol. 223.)

attribute of 'oldest brewery in the world'.[19] Beer was sold in, below or
immediately adjacent to 'sacred' buildings, as in countless other localities with monastic foundations, for example in the brew house of the
abbey of Seemanshausen. By the sixteenth century, some members of
the secular Bavarian clergy used their rectories for the same purpose.[20] In
Bern, meanwhile, parsons obtained their income partly in kind. Depend-
ing on the setting wine could make up a substantial part of tithe and
rent revenues. Reluctant or unable to consume this bounty privately,

---

[19] The company's website, a classic example of the instrumentalisation of history for commercial purposes, locates the first reference to hops in AD 768. In 1040, 'Abbot Arnold
succeeded in obtaining from the City of Freising a licence to brew and sell beer. That
hour marked the birth of the Weihenstephan Monastery Brewery': http://www.brauerei-
weihenstephan.de (consulted 12 February 2003).

[20] Munich, Bayerisches Hauptstaatsarchiv (hereafter: Bay HStA), StV 1853, fol. 124r
(Seemanshausen); H. T. Gräf and R. Pröve, *Wege ins Ungewisse: Reisen in der frühen
Neuzeit 1500–1800* (Frankfurt, 1997), p. 161 (rectories).

Zwinglian ministers ran church taverns throughout the early modern period, normally from their official residences. Examples include the villages of Jegenstorf and Ursenbach (1497), Neuenegg (1512), Münsingen (1688), Corcelles, Krauchthal and Morrens (1786).[21] Over the tax year 1687–88, for instance, the parson of Münsingen accounted for total sales of over 8,000 litres of wine. The annual proceeds from this minister's tavern amounted to no less than 2,500 artisan day wages.[22] One would love to know how clerical publicans squared economic interests with moralising sermons delivered from the pulpit; and equally, whether patrons felt any different when they drank at the rectory rather than in the nearby public house. During the Enlightenment, anticlerical critics duly capitalised on apparent church hypocrisy. With explicit reference to the diocese of Freising in Bavaria, Johann Pezzl accused monasteries of being 'keen to stage processions, and even keener to brew beer, in order to refresh . . . throats dried up from praying'.[23] It is certainly hard to avoid the impression that clerical public houses flew in the face of official endeavours to separate sacred and profane places.

On the other hand, some public houses acquired 'sacral' attributes of their own. In 1484, the abbot of St Alban's granted a licence for the celebration of divine service in the chapel of the town's George Inn, underlining that there were no boundaries to the multifunctionality of public houses.[24] A few decades later in northern Germany, the inn (*Krug*) of Nortorf (in present-day Schleswig Holstein) temporarily stepped in as the local religious site after the parish church had burnt down in 1528.[25] During the turbulent times of the early 1640s and in somewhat less orthodox fashion, cobbler Samuel How preached a sermon at the Nag's Head Tavern near Coleman Street, London, to 'aboue a hundred people'.[26] Towards the end of our period, Augsburg's premier inn The

---

[21] B. Haller (ed.), *Bern in seinen Rathsmanualen 1465–1565* (3 parts, Bern, 1900–2), part 3, pp. 114–17 (Jegenstorf, Neuenegg, Ursenbach); State Archives of Bern (hereafter: StA BE), B VIII 499, 15/8/1688 (Münsingen); and B V 148, *passim* (other examples).

[22] StA BE, B VIII 499, 15/8/1688.

[23] *Reise durch den Baierischen Kreis* (Munich, 1973; reprint of the Salzburg edn, 1784), p. 65 (monasteries, 'die fleißig Prozessionen halten, und noch fleißiger Bier sieden, um die durch Beten ausgetrockneten Freysinger zu laben').

[24] H. T. Riley (ed.), *Registra quorundam abbatum monasterii S. Albani*, Rolls Series 2 (London, 1872), pp. 269–70; cf. the undated licence granted to Thurstan Smyth of Oundle for travelling priests to say mass in 'le Tabard', with others in attendance, provided there is no prejudice to the cure of Oundle, during the bishop's pleasure. Lincolnshire Archives Office, FOR 2, fol. 9v. I am grateful to Robert Swanson for these references.

[25] The document states: 'Szo leten ße missen hollden in dem kroge': H. H. Hennings (ed.), *Kloster Itzehoe 1256–1564* (Neumünster, 1993), p. 228. I am grateful to Enno Bünz for this reference.

[26] *The Vindication of the Cobler* (1640) (Short Title Catalogue, 2nd edn, 13855.4).

Three Moors offered its patrons the convenience of a private chapel.[27] Systematic searches in local archives would doubtless produce many more instances of religious activities conducted in public houses.

To conclude this first section, while spatial distance by no means determined the nature of church–tavern relations – secluded public houses were sometimes ignored and sometimes demonised[28] – 'ungodly' behaviour may have appeared particularly startling at inns situated right next to a church. All the more so if it occurred during divine service, suggesting that the variable 'time' had a bearing on the perception of spatial dichotomies. Equally plausible seems the assumption that different sets of patrons had different thresholds with regard to what exactly was deemed unacceptable behaviour, pointing to the variable 'audience' in the construction and interpretation of social space.[29] There were, in short, countless specific settings for church–tavern relations, including spatial fusions, as well as a number of important other variables, and it would be surprising if all of these combinations produced exactly the same (antagonistic) pattern. In addition, there were further secular sites with a potential to upset the early modern Church. At times, what went on in the streets, woods and camping closes, bathing and bawdy houses may have looked rather more threatening than the sociability at an ordinary public house.[30] One recent observer, in fact, interprets taverns as 'a means of defining and enforcing order' in local communities. As providers of 'public' services to overwhelmingly respectable people, they proved indispensable for the smooth running of early modern society.[31]

## II

Moving to the vast spectrum of church–tavern interactions, it is impossible to ignore some serious tensions. Folkloric tradition explicitly associates public houses with ungodly activities and the disruption of religious life. According to a colourful story recounted to this day, the terrible

---

[27] P. W. Gercken, *Reisen durch Schwaben, Baiern, angränzende Schweiz* (4 parts, 1783), part 1, p. 217.

[28] The moral dangers and criminal associations of isolated public houses inspired an entire early modern literary genre, represented by sensational tracts such as *Fortunatus* (1509) or *The Bloody Innkeeper, or Sad and Barbarous News from Gloucestershire* (1675). Further examples and commentary are given in Friedrich Rauers, *Kulturgeschichte der Gaststätte* (Berlin, 1941), pp. 807–43.

[29] Recent sociological work emphasises human agency in the constitution of space, see M. Löw, *Raumsoziologie* (Frankfurt am Main, 2001), p. 228.

[30] R. Jütte, *Poverty and Deviance in Early Modern Europe* (Cambridge, 1994), esp. ch. 8; D. Dymond, 'A lost social institution: the camping close', *Rural History* 1 (1990), 165–92.

[31] Tlusty, *Bacchus*, p. 212.

thunderstorm which destroyed the parish church of Widdecombe in the Moor (Devon) on 21 October 1638 was the work of the devil, who had been spotted drinking earlier the same day at the Tavistock Inn in the hamlet of Poundsgate, a mere three miles away.[32]

As for clerical discourse, medieval preachers had long warned of the dangers of tippling for the health of people's souls.[33] Reformers of all confessions elaborated on this theme. None of the mainstream religious leaders in the early modern period banned the drinking of alcohol outright, but most emphasised the need for moderation.[34] In a sermon delivered at Wittenberg on 18 May 1539, Martin Luther clarified his position:

Germany is a land of hogs and a filthy people which debauches its body and its life. If you were going to paint it, you would have to paint a pig . . . We would not forbid this; it is possible to tolerate a little elevation, when a man takes a drink or two too much after working hard and when he is feeling low. This must be called a frolic. But to sit day and night, pouring it in and pouring it out again, is piggish . . . It is now becoming a custom even in evangelical cities to establish taprooms; a donkey goes in, pays a penny, and drinks the whole day long; and the government does nothing about it . . . Just because the magistrates and princes do not denounce and punish these vices, we shall not fail to perform our office . . . If we are aware of what is going on, we know that such persons should be excluded from all the sacraments and will make it public, just as we would in the case of a murderer . . . Peter states the reason why it is necessary for us to be sober. Why? In order to be able to pray . . . God does not forbid you to drink, as do the Turks; he permits you to drink wine and beer; he does not make a law of it. But do not make a pig of yourself; remain a human being.[35]

Something thus had to be done about excessive drinking and authorities associated with all major confessions took appropriate action. While late medieval tavern laws in Augsburg had focused on matters like prices, quality of drink and licensing, the moral fervour surrounding the Lutheran Reformation prompted city fathers to brandish drunkenness as an offence in its own right, even a *sin* threatening the entire community. At the same time, alcohol became the subject of a lively published debate denouncing traditions like *Zutrinken* (pledging health), which was closely linked with economic and moral decline.[36]

[32] C. Barber, *Widdecombe in the Moor* (Exeter, 1996), pp. 10–11.

[33] J. A. Galloway, 'Driven by Drink? Ale consumption and the agrarian economy of the London region c. 1300–1400', in M. Carlin and J. T. Rosenthal (eds.), *Food and Eating in Medieval Europe* (London, 1998), pp. 87–100, esp. 95.

[34] F. Blanke, 'Reformation und Alkoholismus', *Zwingliana* 9 (1953), 75–89.

[35] 'Sermon on soberness and moderation against gluttony and drunkenness, I Pet. 4: 7–11, May 18, 1539', in J. W. Doberstein (ed.), *Luther's Works, vol. 51: Sermons I* (Philadelphia, 1959), pp. 291–9, esp. 292–3.

[36] Tlusty, *Bacchus*, p. 80 and ch. 3.

Reformed territories typically pursued the strictest policies. In Elizabethan England, central legislators, county magistrates and godly reformers embarked on a concerted campaign against alehouses, which they equated with irreligious and disorderly behaviour.[37] Zwinglian consistories in Zurich and Bern denounced drunkenness, restricted tavern hours and charged publicans to report all blasphemers and moral offenders. Prompted by the synod, the council of Zurich reduced the number of hostelries in 1530. Even more dramatic action was taken in Geneva: on 29 April 1546 all public houses were closed and replaced with 'Bible clubs', where meals started with a prayer, where the Scriptures were openly displayed and where only psalms and spiritual songs were to be tolerated as musical entertainments. After a mere three months, however, this extremist measure had to be withdrawn and public houses reopened.[38]

Catholic authorities, too, promoted godlier lifestyles, even though a larger number of public holidays and an emphasis on ceremonial splendour set certain limits. In 1604, Duke Maximilian of Bavaria issued a mandate confirming previous decrees against the 'awful/unchristian' vice of blasphemy. Given that this serious offence, which incurred 'terrifying divine wrath' as well as punishments like wars and diseases, was 'most commonly committed in guest- and public houses', specially appointed commissioners were to keep watchful eyes on them.[39] The seventeenth-century French theologian César de Bus complained that 'towns and villages are full of profaners of the holy Sunday: for, how many labourers, vintners, artisans and other people spend all they earned by the sweat of their brows during the week on eating and drinking in the public house on Sundays?'[40] From about the same time, when Catholic reform efforts started to take root, ecclesiastical courts in the prince-bishopric of Münster clamped down on tavern-going during divine service and increasingly portrayed 'the public house as a den of vice, even blasphemy and unchristian anti-religion'.[41] A comparative examination, however, suggests that Catholic flocks still enjoyed a greater range of legitimate tavern-activities than those in reformed areas. Public dancing, for instance, was banned outright in Zwinglian Bern, but merely regulated in Catholic Bavaria.

---

[37] P. Clark, 'The alehouse and alternative society', in D. Pennington and K. Thomas (eds.), *Puritans and Revolutionaries* (Oxford, 1978), pp. 47–72; K. Wrightson, 'Alehouses, order and reformation in rural England 1590–1660', in S. and E. Yeo (eds.), *Popular Culture and Class Conflict 1590–1914* (Brighton, 1981), pp. 1–27.

[38] Blanke, 'Alkoholismus', 84–86.

[39] Bay HStA, Mandatensammlung, 2 December 1604.

[40] Cited in R. Beck, *Histoire du dimanche. De 1700 à nos jours* (Paris, 1997), pp. 79–80.

[41] 'Das Wirtshaus wurde zunehmend zu einem Ort des Lasters, ja der Lästerung Gottes und der unchristlichen Gegenreligion stilisiert', Holzem, *Religion*, p. 399.

As with most other objectives of the European-wide campaign for greater 'social discipline', success on the ground remained patchy.[42] Geneva had to reopen public houses; Bavarian blasphemy mandates required frequent reissuing; and the number of English alehouses continued to grow.[43] Even the most radical Reformed groups, whose written confessions stigmatised drinking,[44] found it difficult to avoid public houses altogether. As Marion Kobelt-Groch has shown, Anabaptists appreciated their services for practical purposes when travelling, for meetings with sympathisers and even for religious discussions, missionary campaigns and as 'safe houses' for established local groups.[45]

Church–tavern relations crystallised in the characters of pastors and publicans. Again, evidence for friction is plentiful. Two examples may illustrate 'classic' confrontations: the first features Johann Jacob Hürsch, Zwinglian minister in the village of Neuenegg near Bern in the mid-seventeenth century, who ran an energetic campaign to improve the moral standards of his flock. One of the prime targets of his efforts was the Bear, the local inn located a few minutes' walk away from the rectory. One Sunday in 1659, he bravely preached a sermon against 'those people who prefer to be in the house of gluttony rather than that of the Lord', but – upon leaving the church – Bentz Juncker, the heavily inebriated son of the innkeeper, embarked on a tirade of insults. Hürsch immediately summoned him before the consistory, where the young man was censured by Bern's local government official: 'How dare he get drunk the very day the minister warned against gluttony?' Proceedings dragged on, so that the consistory adjourned to the Bear! Eventually, the offender admitted his guilt and apologised to the minister.[46] The second example comes from Bayerbach (Bavaria), where vicar Paul Prucker clashed with innkeeper Joseph Mayrhofer over a dance event held on Easter Tuesday

---

[42] H. R. Schmidt, *Dorf und Religion. Reformierte Sittenzucht in Berner Landgemeinden der frühen Neuzeit* (Stuttgart, 1995), p. 375.

[43] The most recent estimate puts the number of English drinking outlets in the late sixteenth century somewhere between 20,000 and 24,000 premises, but at over 47,000 in 1695, J. Chartres, 'The eighteenth-century English inn: a transient "golden age"?', in Kümin and Tlusty (eds.), *World of the Tavern*, pp. 205–26, esp. 207.

[44] No. 4 of the Schleitheim Articles of 1527 emphasises that the faithful shall 'dissociate' themselves 'from all evil, which the devil has planted in the world', including, explicitly, 'wine houses': http://www.anabaptists.org/history/schleith.html (consulted 12 December 2003).

[45] M. Kobelt-Groch, 'Unter Zechern, Spielern und Häschern: Täufer im Wirtshaus', in N. Fischer and M. Kobelt-Groch (eds.), *Aussenseiter zwischen Mittelalter und Neuzeit* (Leiden, 1997), pp. 111–26; cf. R. W. Scribner, 'Oral culture and the diffusion of Reformation ideas', in his *Popular Culture and Popular Movements in Reformation Germany* (London, 1987), pp. 49–69, esp. 57.

[46] Neuenegg, Gemeindearchiv: Chorgerichts-Manual 1.1, 9/1/1659 ('die jenigen menschen, welche lieber im Fräß vnd Sauff hauß sind v. blieben wöllen, als ins Herren Hauß').

in 1756. According to the latter's court deposition, Prucker had entered the inn, banged his stick on a table and asked the revellers to leave the premises at once. Furthermore, he warned the musicians that he would ban them from playing. Confronted by Mayrhofer, who argued that such actions were the prerogative of secular lords, the priest exclaimed 'You ruffian!' and threatened to hit him. Moreover, vicar Prucker regularly sold wheat beer to the public himself, to the great detriment of the innkeeper's turnover. To add insult to injury, Prucker publicly branded Mayrhofer a disobedient and negligent parishioner from the pulpit, all of which the publican dismissed as a smear campaign. Defending his own behaviour in court, the priest charged the publican with ignoring many warnings and verbally abusing the clergy. The landlady, furthermore, allegedly provoked Prucker's anger by saying that similar 'dances were staged . . . elsewhere, that they were not Lutherans and that they still hoped to go to heaven etc.'. In the end, the Bavarian official admonished Prucker not to act independently, but to alert the appropriate state authorities to any future misdemeanours.[47]

Churchmen, of course, also had bones to pick with the patrons of public houses. Returning to Neuenegg, the ministers' mission was complicated by an unusually delicate spatial setting. Not only was the Bear, the principal focus of neighbourly conviviality, situated within a small distance of church and rectory, but much more seriously, it was only a short walk away from the river Sense. This waterway marked the border between Zwinglian Bern and Catholic Fribourg, two allied members of the biconfessional Swiss Confederation (see plate 2.3(a)). Catholic sociability across the river included kermis and many official holy days, most of which were celebrated with manifold revels. Games, dances and other entertainments staged by the Custom House at Sensebrücke, which doubled up as an inn, proved irresistible temptations to the people of Neuenegg. During popular feasts, dozens of them crossed the bridge, no doubt fully aware of the fuming disapproval of the Reformed minister who must have looked on (his house and church were a few hundred yards to the right of the Bear, on a small elevation just outside the plan on plate 2.3(a); cf. plate 2.3(b)). The consistory manuals kept by clergyman Hürsch and his successors abound with examples of husbands and wives as well as girls and boys summoned and fined for 'dancing at the Custom House'. No fewer than forty-five women stood accused of this offence

---

[47] W. Hartinger, 'Tanz am Osterdienstag, Bayerbach im Rottal', *Storchenturm* 46–7 (1989), 114–24, esp. 117 ('Die Wirthin hingegen versezte, man mache . . . anderwo auch auf, sye seyen ja auch keine lutherische, hoffen ja auch in Himmel zu khommen und dergleichen').

Plate 2.3(a) The villages of Neuenegg (in Zwinglian Bern; bottom right of the picture) and Sensebrücke (in Catholic Fribourg; top right), located on the border between the two Swiss Cantons marked by the river Sense. The large house nearest the bottom of the picture is the Bear inn, the building with the turrets at the top is the Custom House, a customs-cum-public house immediately adjacent to the Catholic chapel of St Beatus, which is just visible on its left hand side. On the Fribourg-side of the bridge, a cross alerts travellers to the fact that they enter Catholic territory. (From the border atlas by Samuel Bodmer 1705–10: StA BE, Atlanten Nr. 1–4, vol. III, fol. 7.)

during kermis in 1752.[48] To aggravate the situation, the main highway between the capitals of Fribourg and Bern led over the bridge and thus right through Neuenegg and Sensebrücke, bringing locals into constant contact with travellers of many different religious persuasions. Here, then, we find a multi-dimensional combination of spatial dichotomies between the sacred and the profane, not only between church and public house, but the respective pairings in rival confessional contexts.

---

[48] Details in B. Kümin, 'Public houses and their patrons in early modern Europe', in Kümin and Tlusty (eds.), *The World of the Tavern*, pp. 44–62, esp. 57.

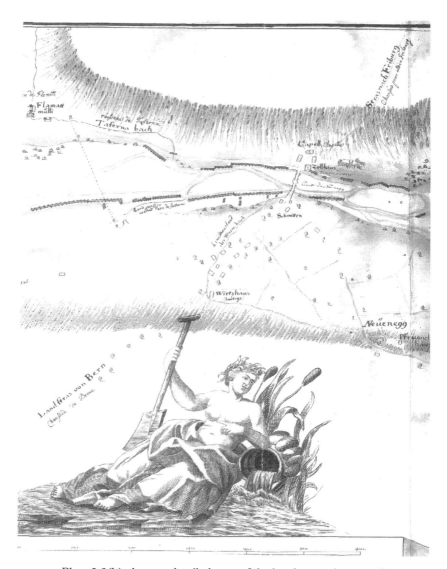

Plate 2.3(b)  A more detailed map of the border area between Bern and
Fribourg, showing the complex spatial relationship between 'sacred' and
'profane' sites. On the Neuenegg side: the Bear inn (*Wirtshaus*; centre)
and the Reformed parish church with rectory (marked *Neüenegg* and
*Pfruendhaus*; centre right); on the Sensebrücke side across the bridge:
the customs-cum-public house (*Zollhaus*; top centre) adjacent to the
Catholic chapel of St Beatus (*Capell*). *Stras nach Friburg* (top right) and
*Landstras von Bern* (bottom left) designate the busy highway between
the capital cities of Bern and Fribourg. (From a plan drawn by J. A.
Riediger in 1725: StA BE, AA v, Nr. 1.)

Most church court records provide comparable anecdotes of inappropriate and ungodly tavern behaviour. Even the most cursory browsing will yield examples of blasphemy, vomiting, fighting and sexual offences associated with public houses.[49] However, this has to be judged in light of the fact that the local inn, tavern or alehouse was the main secular centre and thus inevitably a prominent stage for interpersonal relations, whether 'good' or 'bad'. Some cases, furthermore, are not so easy to interpret. In the Emmental region of the Bernese state, the consistory of Lauperswil summoned Christen Dällenbach in February 1631, as he 'had carried the table of our Lord Jesus Christ into the [Lion] inn, on which a wedding party then ate and drank'.[50] Was this a harmless insensitivity carried out by a sociable parishioner, a deliberate act of desecration by a crypto-Anabaptist (there were many of them in the Emmental) or even a symbol of communal assertiveness, demonstrating that church goods belonged to the people? Over a century later, in 1764, butcher Heinrich Märki appeared before the consistory of Birr (Bernese Aargau), as he had allegedly raised a toast to the churchwarden with the parochial chalice. Again, many possible readings present themselves. Surely Märki knew that he would offend the vicar by abusing a sacred object. But where exactly did he do it: in the choir, in the nave or even on 'profane' ground, for example when buying new silverware for the parish? Did it matter that the offence happened at Easter, that is, might it have gone unnoticed on a normal weekday? Was the real issue that he simultaneously criticised both the minister and Bern's secular authority?[51]

In Bavaria, quasi-sacrilegious acts were also reported. Two peasants got into trouble at Altötting in 1594, after speculating over a beer that the Jesuits had been sent by the devil. Publican Hans Härtl of Maisach was fined £1 for causing 'scandal' on a Sunday in 1582: just when he saw parishioners passing his inn on their way to church, he opened the windows to advertise games as a rival attraction. Furthermore, in an intriguing parallel to the spatial situation at Neuenegg (albeit in a different confessional setting), inhabitants of eighteenth-century Landshut avoided (fasting) restrictions at home by crossing the bridge into the

---

[49] See e.g. the cases of godparents and fathers who were too drunk to attend baptismal ceremonies reported by the Kulmbach visitor in 1586: C. S. Dixon, *The Reformation and Rural Society: The Parishes of Brandenburg-Ansbach-Kulmbach 1528–1603* (Cambridge, 2002), p. 109.

[50] H. Minder (transcriber), *Die Chorgerichtsmanuale der Kirchhöri von Lauperswil von 1594–1798: Part II* (Lauperswil, 1997), vol. I, fol. 230 ('von wegen das er den Tisch unseres Herren Jesu Christi in das Wirtzhuss tragen, daruff man an einem Hochzyt gessen und getrunken').

[51] F. Müller, 'Bären Birr', in *Brugger Neujahrsblätter* (1988), 129–44, esp. 132.

territory of Regensburg, in order to quench their thirst and fill their stomachs on one of the biconfessional city's local holy days.[52]

## III

So far, church–tavern relations look problematic indeed, but it is time to balance the account. Interactions appear in a different light when we consider two aspects in greater detail. First, practical advantages of public houses for the Church; and second, evidence for various forms of cultural exchange.

Starting with practical advantages, numerous public houses were run from holdings or tenements owned by the Church and thus sources of ecclesiastical revenues. Examples from Bern include the inn-cum-village-hall at Twann, which paid rent to the local churchwarden in support of church and school funds, while the Bavarian public house of Unterdolling belonged to the parish church of Sollern.[53] In cities like pre-Reformation Erfurt, ecclesiastical taverns capitalised on the Church's tax exemptions to sell drinks more cheaply, something which clearly endeared them to the local population.[54] Furthermore, the right to allocate public houses afforded clergymen a powerful instrument of patronage. Confronted with a strong Protestant movement in the Swiss valley of Toggenburg, the early modern Prince-Abbots of Saint Gall deliberately fostered reliable Catholics as publicans, in order to encourage the 'right' sort of sociability and to deprive the Reformed confession of key communication facilities.[55]

Inns also provided indispensable service like food, drink and accommodation for countless members of the Church. In spite of official prohibitions, clergymen found it impossible to avoid public houses altogether, for instance when travelling, attending synods, conducting visitations or holding ecclesiastical courts in distant towns and villages. At Neuenegg, members of the consistory were repeatedly treated to a dinner at the Bear,

---

[52] Examples taken from H. Rankl, *Landvolk und frühmoderner Staat in Bayern 1400–1800* (Munich, 1999), p. 530; J. Focht, '"Gespann, mach auf!" Historische Beispiele der Gebrauchsmusik im ländlichen Wirtshaus', in Drexler (ed.), *Kellnerin*, pp. 49–81, esp. 65; Johann Pezzl, *Reise durch den Baierschen Kreis* (2nd edn, 1784; facsimile, Munich, 1973), pp. 51–2.

[53] StA BE, B V 147, p. 308; Bay HStA, GR 878/186, p. 96. The Crown and Bull inns at Burford (Oxfordshire) equally belonged to the church: R. Moody, *The Inns of Burford* (Burford, 1996), part 1, pp. 7, 20.

[54] R. W. Scribner, 'Anticlericalism and the cities', in his *Religion and Culture in Germany 1400–1800*, ed. L. Roper (Leiden, Boston and Cologne, 2001), pp. 149–71, esp. 154.

[55] F. Brändle, 'Public houses, clientelism and faith: strategies of power in early modern Toggenburg', in Kümin and Tlusty (eds.), *World of the Tavern*, pp. 83–92, esp. 89.

with expenses shared equally among the parties contesting a case.[56] Other ecclesiastical dignitaries seem to have frequented wine and beer houses off-duty or even at rather inappropriate times. When the parishioners of Great Abington (Cambridgeshire) congregated for a service one day in 1585, they made a startling discovery: 'we were all at the churche and our minister was at the Alehouse'![57] Clergymen of all confessions feature in similar episodes. Veith Neumair, Catholic parson of Bruck in Bavaria, behaved 'in a drunken and very loud fashion' when visiting the public house of Tuntenhausen in 1566, even 'chanting out of the window', for which he was fined four pounds.[58] Complaining about two evangelical ministers in 1527, two Anabaptists from Benfeld (Alsace) reported that they had 'preached the Gospel according to Scripture in the morning, but then led the excessive behaviour at the inn after noon, with their women also attending the dancing'.[59]

Some of these offenders, however, may have recognised the 'pastoral' potential of public houses. Clergymen often felt the expectation and/or desirability of participating in local sociability, which afforded the twin benefits of staying in touch with one's flock and keeping an eye on behaviour. Clergymen who preached the incompatibility of pious devotion and popular pastimes could find themselves marginalised and victimised, as evident from a complaint by the parson of Gaukönigshofen (Diocese of Würzburg, Germany) in 1530: 'if I gambled, drank, feasted and did other disorderly things with [my parishioners, then] I would be a good clergyman', but since he refused to do so, his insistence on godly behaviour sparked tensions and conflict in the community.[60] Echoing Martin Luther's endorsement of moderate alcohol consumption, one Zwinglian clergyman argued that extreme prohibitions were counterproductive. For the minister of Ferenbalm (Bern) in 1764, it was evident

[56] Neuenegg, Gemeindearchiv: Chorgerichts-Manuale, 29/3/1663, 6/7/1665, 9/3/1671; C. Marsh, *Popular Religion in Sixteenth-Century England* (New York, 1998), p. 108 (ecclesiastical visitors administering justice at English inns). Travelling through Bavaria on 2 May 1782, Pope Pius VI briefly rested at the inn of Schwabhausen (as commemorated by a plaque on the building).

[57] Marsh, *Popular Religion*, p. 46.

[58] Focht, 'Gebrauchsmusik', p. 62 ('in bezechter weis vnd im Würtshauss gar polderisch gehalten vnd zum Venster aus geiuchizt').

[59] Kobelt-Groch, 'Täufer', p. 116 ('am morgen das evangelium nach dem text geprediget, nach mittag aber die ersten in vppigem weßen im würtzhuß . . . gewesen, jre weiber auch bey den täntzen vmbhergeloffen').

[60] E. Bünz, '"Die Kirche im Dorf lassen . . .": Formen der Kommunikation im spätmittelalterlichen Niederkirchenwesen', in W. Rösener (ed.), *Kommunikation in der ländlichen Gesellschaft vom Mittelalter bis zur Moderne* (Göttingen, 2000), pp. 77–167, esp. 155. A similar case is mentioned in R. W. Scribner, 'Pastoral care and the Reformation in Germany', in his *Religion and Culture*, pp. 172–94, esp. 180.

that hard-working men needed 'restoration from time to time' and that drinking wine at a tavern could have advantageous psychological effects.[61]

Furthermore, in many large parishes, there was simply no way to conduct regular worship without adequate catering facilities nearby. When a new church was built in Eggiwil in the Bernese Emmental in the 1630s, the government bailiff acknowledged that 'a tavern was needed due to the multitude of people'. A little later, the publican obtained permission to serve hot meals as well, explicitly because 'the parishioners flock to this church from distant valleys, and older or weaker people would no longer be able to do so without the availability of some food and drink'. The local official – perhaps a little optimistically – anticipated no particular problems, as 'the tavern is located . . . near the parsonage, so that no scandalous activities can be carried out there'.[62] Indeed, for most parishioners, a visit to the public house did not amount to a profanation of the sabbath; for them, church and tavern belonged together as the two sides of the same coin. In 1696, the parish of Arnage in France petitioned the bishop of Mans for a 'reasonable' mass time, which allowed them to visit the *cabaret* thereafter. The proximity of communal sociability to religious services and buildings gave it 'a certain sacrality' of its own.[63] In return, there are repeated examples of 'worldly' publicans providing the local clergy with wine for communion, for example at Worb (Bern) and Obermenzing (Bavaria).[64]

A cornerstone of post-Tridentine Catholicism, to add a final 'practical' example, equally depended on the facilities of public houses. Mass pilgrimages to distant holy sites were unthinkable without an adequate network of inns, taverns and alehouses along the way and, crucially, in the immediate vicinity of the holy site. According to Peter Hersche, early modern pilgrimages can be interpreted as 'pleasure trips for humble people', during which spiritual and secular activities intermingled in a complex pattern, with the visit to the tavern the profane equivalent of participation in processions and other religious observances.[65] Visual expression of this relationship can be found in a seventeenth-century depiction of the Holy Mountain of Andechs near the Bavarian capital, which remains both a prominent pilgrimage site and home of a notable brewery to the present day (plate 2.4).

---

[61] StA BE, B III 207, no. 45, p. 7.
[62] StA BE, B V 143, p. 19.      [63] Beck, *Dimanche*, pp. 79–80.
[64] Worb, Kirchgemeindearchiv, vol. 146: Seckelmeisterrechnungen ('3 crowns and 5 *batzen* paid to the innkeeper of the Lion for communion wine in the accounting period 1733–36'); Adolf Thurner, 'Der "alte Wirt" in Obermenzing', *Amperland* 22 (1986), 268–71, esp. 269 (according to manorial records of 1684, innkeeper Steyrer had to provide mass wine free of charge, probably in lieu of a customary monetary payment).
[65] Hersche, 'Lustreise', p. 326.

Plate 2.4 Prospect of the Holy Mountain at Andechs near Munich from the Bavarian topography published by Matthäus Merian in the mid-seventeenth century. A series of processions make their way to the church, passing the *Klostergasthof* (the monastic inn identified by a sign protruding from the top of the building) half-way up the mountain on their left. (From Martin Zeiller, *Topographia Bavariae* (2nd edn, Frankfurt, 1657; facsimile edn, Kassel, 1962), pp. 114–15.)

Proceeding to the field of cultural exchange, religious inn names like Angel or Cross Keys (emblem of the Apostle Peter) provide a first indication. More significantly, there were numerous ways in which church and tavern intersected in communal festive life. Religious feasts are a case in point, exemplified by the *Kirchweih* woodcuts of the Beham brothers dating from the early Reformation period. During kermis, that is, the celebrations marking a church's dedication day, ecclesiastical observances led smoothly on to village fairs staged near inns or taverns (as observed at Sensebrücke above). A recent reassessment of the prominence of heavy drinking, gaming, dancing and other controversial delights in these festival prints concludes that the artists were not just promulgating moralising messages or engaging in anti-peasant ridicule, but documented tensions within a society 'at the same time undergoing reevaluation and attempts at reform', in which traditional tavern sociability was 'still alive, thriving and extremely popular'.[66] Rites of passage associated with the life cycle often entailed a similarly seamless sequence of church- and tavern-attendance. The wine house in the French-speaking Swiss village of Mézières for example owed its seventeenth-century licence explicitly to the 'requirements of weddings and baptisms', while many Bavarian manors granted their innkeepers a legal monopoly on the staging of family and kinship banquets.[67]

Most importantly, there is a flood of evidence for the spread and discussion of religious ideas in or through public houses. This has long been noted as a key factor in the rapid dissemination of Lutheran doctrine in Reformation Germany. Literary and legal sources speak of peasants hotly debating the Gospel over a drink and reveal numerous ways in which new views were promulgated. In Brandenburg in 1524, for example, 'a number of wandering apprentices sang Lutheran songs to travellers in the inns'.[68] In August of the same year, a radical clergyman caused great commotion in the Imperial Free City of Memmingen. Disguised as a peasant, he pronounced that priests 'have long kept us from the truth' in Felix Mayer's tavern and, later the same day in another public house, he caused a theology student to curse all evangelicals: 'God may strike Luther and his followers with the plague.'[69] Throughout the late-medieval and early modern period, judging from a survey of relevant scholarship, religious minorities used 'known' public houses as logistical bases for the distribution of their ideas and tracts.[70]

Surprising as it may seem, religious culture clearly permeated tavern walls. By the eighteenth century, travellers were intrigued to hear Swiss peasants singing psalms and other religious songs in the public house.[71] Whether this was out of genuine piety, the lack of an alternative musical repertory or for deliberate provocation, is difficult to tell, but some form of cultural transmission had clearly occurred. Even publicans, often viewed as the 'anti-curés' of local communities, opened their hearts and doors to spiritual messages. There were religious ballads with acceptable Protestant imagery on the walls of many early modern English alehouses

[66] A. Stewart, 'Taverns in Nuremberg prints at the time of the German Reformation', in: Kümin and Tlusty (eds.), *World of the Tavern*, pp. 95–115, esp. 100–1 (Sebald Beham's *Large Kermis* of 1535) and 115 (quotation).

[67] StA BE, B V 144, p. 72 (Mézières); Bay HStA GR 878/186, pp. 469, 523 (manor of Oberzell and county of Ismaning).

[68] Scribner, 'Oral culture', pp. 57–8 and 60.

[69] P. Blickle, 'Memmingen – A centre of the Reformation', in his *From the Communal Reformation to the Revolution of the Common Man* (Leiden, 1998), pp. 16–79, esp. 16.

[70] Marsh, *Popular Religion*, p. 169 (English Lollards); Kobelt-Groch, 'Täufer', *passim* (Anabaptists); Frearson, 'Communications', pp. 273–87, esp. 276, 286 (Quakers).

[71] C. Meiners, *Briefe über die Schweiz* (2nd edn, Berlin, 1788), part 1, p. 315; J. G. Heinzmann, *Beschreibung der Stadt und Republik Bern* (Bern, 1794), part 1, p. 63.

and pious innkeepers like John Ormesbye of Norwich provided John Foxe's *Book of Martyrs* and other religious classics for perusal on their premises.[72]

## IV

In conclusion, a survey of church–tavern interactions highlights the complex relationship between the sacred and the profane in early modern Europe. Holy and worldly things could not be neatly separated and 'space' was no static or absolute entity.[73] While all mainstream confessions strove to purify or 'de-profanise' religious buildings and precincts, fearing above all the corrosive influence of drink, such campaigns met with at best partial success. Pious crusaders against public houses failed to grasp that church and tavern were inextricably intertwined in communal life. Simple notions of polarity and conflict overlook the vastly heterogeneous spatial settings and the importance of variables like timing, situation and audience. While tensions undoubtedly existed, there were also mutual benefits and cultural exchanges. Church–tavern relations could be 'complementary' and 'symbiotic' just as well as 'antagonistic'. As prominent social centres, churches and public houses constantly defined and re-defined their respective roles, both individually, and with regard to each other; both in response to internal and external pressures.

Seen in their wider context, furthermore, church and tavern represented merely two focal points of a larger entity, that is, 'holistic' communal experience. Geometrically speaking, interactions between churches and taverns formed but one side of a triangular network of relationships characterising local communities throughout premodern Europe. At each end-point of this triangle was an institutionalised social centre, which specialised in one key communal concern: *politics* in the case of the town or village hall, *religion* in the case of the church, and *socio-cultural relations* in the case of the tavern. In everyday life, of course, these three spheres could not be neatly demarcated and frictions were hard to avoid.[74] Yet,

---

[72] T. Watt, *Cheap Print and Popular Piety 1550–1640* (Cambridge, 1991), pp. 194–6, 331–2 (ballads). In 1603, John Ormesbye, innkeeper of Norwich, listed 'a boocke of martirs and a deske' (worth 20s.), 'a bible and a deske' (10s.) and 'a Frame and the X commandments written' (2s. 6d.) in his inventory for the George Inn: Norfolk Record Office, Inv. 19/145B. (I am grateful to John Craig for this reference.)

[73] For comparable conclusions cf. J. Eade and M. J. Sallnow (eds.), *Contesting the Sacred: the Anthropology of Pilgrimage* (Urbana, 2000), esp. 'Introduction'; Löw, *Raumsoziologie*.

[74] This line of thought is elaborated in: B. Kümin, 'Rathaus, Wirtshaus, Gotteshaus. Von der Zwei- zur Dreidimensionalität in der frühneuzeitlichen Gemeindeforschung', in F. Šmahel (ed.), *Geist, Gesellschaft, Kirche im 13.–16. Jh.* (Prague, 1999), pp. 249–62.

however hard anybody tried, townspeople and villagers would and could not accept the marginalisation or even elimination of any one of these indispensable establishments.

Powered by the spiritual energy and moral fervour of the Reformation, the role of the Confessional Age may have been that of a 'catharsis', when Churches went out on a limb to maximize their influence over people's bodies and minds, but saw their ultimate ambitions thwarted. As a result, churches and public houses retained their prominence in communal sociability well into modern times.

# 3 Sacred image and sacred space in Lutheran Germany

*Bridget Heal*

In 1845 George Gilbert Scott, the most famous architect of England's Gothic revival, praised the appearance of Germany's Lutheran churches, writing that 'while . . . one party in our own church is searching, with but little success, for ancient stone altars; and another is much more successfully seeking for judgments against new ones, the Lutherans quietly and universally retain and use their ancient stone high altars, and even minor altars which are not used are still preserved'. He admired in particular the 'triptychs, gorgeously decorated with paintings and imagery, which retain their places not only over the high altars but in many instances even over the small and disused altars'. In addition, 'the magnificent tabernacle, a feature almost unknown in England, still stands by the side of the altar . . . The rood-lofts often remain decorated with splendid sculpture or with panels filled by most beautiful paintings of saints, or other Catholic subjects. Above, very frequently, hangs the rood itself, never having been removed.'[1]

This eloquent evocation of the appearance of Germany's churches prior to the widespread destruction of the Second World War testifies to what has recently been described as the 'preserving power' of Lutheranism.[2] Official Lutheran teaching on sacred images and sacred spaces differed markedly from that of the Catholic Church: consecration rituals were no longer used to sanctify church buildings, altars and liturgical objects, setting them aside from the profane world; altars and chancels, traditionally the most sacred parts of the church, were henceforth to be regarded as no more than convenient places for the distribution of communion; and believers were no longer encouraged to seek God's assistance and the beneficent intercession of saints at sites made holy by the presence of relics and miraculous images. Yet the appearance of Lutheran churches – the

---

[1] G. G. Scott, *Personal and Professional Recollections* (London, 1879), pp. 138–9.
[2] J. M. Fritz (ed.), *Die bewahrende Kraft des Luthertums: Mittelalterliche Kunstwerke in evangelischen Kirchen* (Regensburg, 1997).

Prospectiva Ædis ad Divum B. MARIÆ Virginis NORIBERGÆ. Prospect der MARIÆ-Kirche, zu unser Lieben Frauen genannt in NÜRNBERG.

Plate 3.1 Johann Ulrich Krauss (after Johann Andreas Graff), *Interior of the Frauenkirche*, engraving 1696. © Germanisches Nationalmuseum, Nuremberg.

ways in which they were marked out as sacred spaces using altars and images – changed remarkably little. As plate 3.1, a late-seventeenth-century engraving of the Frauenkirche in Nuremberg, demonstrates, the sacred topography of a Lutheran city was, at least at first glance, often barely distinguishable from that of a late-medieval city.[3]

This visual continuity seems odd in the light of what we know about Reformation attempts to destroy or desecrate holy places. Reformers sometimes went to considerable lengths to demonstrate that spaces and images were not divinely empowered. While adherents of Reformed Protestantism or the Radical Reformation were, of course, responsible for the most extreme attacks, even in Lutheran areas iconoclasm could sometimes be a major force. Sergiusz Michalski points, for example, to the extensive iconoclasm of 1524–6 and 1529 on the Baltic coast, which

[3] The original occasion for the production of this engraving is not known, but during the eighteenth century it was used alongside equivalent engravings of Nuremberg's other churches to illustrate a manuscript describing the city. Stadtarchiv Nürnberg, Best. F1, Nürnberger Chroniken, Nr. 59.

entailed the destruction of considerable amounts of church property.[4] Yet in many of the areas in which Lutherans took over medieval churches, the visual environment of worship remained virtually unchanged. This chapter draws in particular on evidence from Nuremberg, the first imperial free city to adopt the Lutheran faith (1525) and an important early centre of reform. In Nuremberg's churches, as in many other churches in the predominantly Lutheran north and east of Germany, altars, altarpieces, tabernacles, roods, statues, paintings and sometimes even saints' shrines remained intact and *in situ*.[5] A variety of explanations may be advanced to account for this visual continuity: theological moderation; social conservatism; a desire to avoid alienating Catholic powers; and perhaps, by the later sixteenth century at least, a respect for artistic patrimony. This chapter argues that the 'preserving power' of Lutheranism does not, however, indicate that attitudes towards sacred space remained unchanged. The Reformers' condemnations of consecration rituals and of traditional articulations of sacred space such as processions led to a gradual shift in perception, and by the end of the sixteenth century the church had become primarily a place for communal worship and quiet prayer rather than a locus of holy power.

## I

Luther condemned the traditional consecration rituals that had set sacred space apart from profane, and argued that worship could as well be conducted in the open air as in a church. In a sermon preached in 1544 at the dedication of the Lutheran chapel in Schloß Hartenfels in Torgau, Luther stated that this was no special place, and that the Word of God could just as well be preached not here, but outside by the fountain in the courtyard.[6] For him, a true church was wherever God's word was rightly preached. The rest was, at a fundamental level, irrelevant. As he stated in his lectures on Genesis, 'it is not the stones, the construction, and the gorgeous silver and gold that make a church beautiful and holy; it is the Word of God and sound preaching'. Luther did, however, recognise the practical need for a place of assembly. There were important Old Testament precedents. Abraham, for example, had chosen a definite

[4] S. Michalski, *The Reformation and the Visual Arts: The Protestant Image Question in Western and Eastern Europe* (London, 1993), pp. 86–7.
[5] Fritz (ed.), *Die bewahrende Kraft des Luthertums* discusses examples from Nuremberg, the duchy of Mecklenburg and the bishopric of Halberstadt, and there are also equivalent survivals in Schleswig-Holstein, Niedersachsen, Sachsen-Anhalt, Sachsen, Thüringen, Brandenburg and elsewhere.
[6] J. Pelikan (ed.), *Luther's Works*, 55 vols. (St Louis and Philadelphia, 1958–69), LI, p. 337.

place to teach, pray and sacrifice 'in order that by his own example and that of his people he might lead others to the knowledge of God and to true forms of worship'.[7] In the context of contemporary society Luther emphasised the importance of communal worship – an 'orderly, public, reverent assembly' – in a properly appointed place: 'one cannot and should not appoint a special place and location for each individual, and one should not seek out secret corners to hide away, as the Anabaptists do'. Not only was this a matter of convenience – the multitude needed specific rooms and times – but also prayer was stronger and more likely to be heard when the whole assembly prayed together.[8]

This place of assembly should be consecrated through the preaching of the Word of God rather than through Catholic rituals. Luther condemned the pope and his followers, saying that in sprinkling churches and liturgical vessels to make them holy they imitated Moses' example in ape-like fashion, but their actions found no justification in the Word of God.[9] In his Torgau sermon Luther emphasised that preaching and prayer consecrated the church: 'In order that it may be rightly and Christianly consecrated and blessed, not like the papists' churches with their bishop's chrism and censing, but according to God's commandments and will, we shall begin by hearing and expounding God's word, and then . . . call on him together and say the Lord's prayer.' He substituted prayer for the censer used by the Catholic bishop: 'now that you, dear friends, have helped to sprinkle with the true holy water of God's word, take hold of the censer with me, that is, seize hold upon prayer, and let us call upon God and pray'. Just as consecration was achieved through sermons and prayers rather than through meaningless rituals, desecration would result from false preaching, not from the violation of sacred space. Luther asked his congregation to pray that God 'may keep his house pure, as it is now, God be praised, consecrated and sanctified through God's word, that it may not be desecrated or defiled by the devil and his lies and false doctrine'.[10]

Luther's attitude to the cemetery, another important sacred space in the pre-Reformation tradition, also reflected his concern for order and reverence. As Craig Koslofsky has pointed out, the doctrine of justification by faith alone made the notion of burial in consecrated ground, as close as possible to a locus of holy power, irrelevant. In 1527 Luther wrote that he 'would rather be laid to rest in the Elbe or in the forest' than in Wittenberg's disordered churchyard.[11] Yet just as he recognised

---

[7] *Ibid.*, II, pp. 333–4.    [8] *Ibid.*, LI, pp. 337–8.
[9] *Ibid.*, XII, pp. 359–60.    [10] *Ibid.*, LI, pp. 333–4 and 353–4.
[11] C. Koslofsky, *The Reformation of the Dead: Death and Ritual in Early Modern Germany, 1450–1700* (Basingstoke, 2000), p. 46.

the value of churches as places of assembly for worship, Luther also acknowledged the need to set aside a particular place (preferably outside the city walls on medical grounds) for burial: 'a cemetery rightfully ought to be a fine quiet place, removed from all other localities, to which one can go and reverently meditate upon death, the Last Judgment, and the resurrection . . . Such a place should properly be a decent, hallowed place, to be entered with trepidation and reverence.' The cemetery should serve the living, inspiring devotion in those who went there.[12]

## II

Luther's condemnations of consecration rituals and of traditional understandings of sacred space were reflected in early Lutheran church ordinances, guidelines drawn up for the administration of new churches. The 1533 church ordinance that Andreas Osiander wrote for Nuremberg and Brandenburg contained, for example, no references at all to consecration rituals for churches, graveyards or liturgical objects, and this silence was typical.[13] Other documents that sought to define the Lutheran position condemned Catholic consecration rituals as superstitious. The section on human traditions in the Schmalkaldic Articles, drawn up by Luther in discussion with other theologians in 1536, ridiculed the baptism of altar stones and bells as foolish and childish products of the pope's bag of tricks. It was equally disparaging about the blessing of lights, palms, herbs and other sacramental objects.[14] Descriptions of church ceremonies indicate that new Lutheran churches were often opened with minimal ritual, in line with this condemnation of consecration and with the example set by Luther at Torgau. There might be a sermon, as at Torgau, and songs or prayers. Such evangelical observances might also accompany the taking into use of new altars, pulpits and fonts. By the later seventeenth century, however, when renewed building work followed the end of the Thirty Years War, there is evidence for an increase in the use of solemn processions as part of the dedication ceremony. These processions were justified using biblical precedents, and though they had some affinities

---

[12] *Ibid.*, pp. 46–7.

[13] E. Sehling (ed.), *Die evangelischen Kirchenordnungen des* XVI. *Jahrhunderts* 16– vols. (Leipzig, 1902–11; continued by the Institut für evangelisches Kirchenrecht der evangelischen Kirche in Deutschland, Tübingen, 1963– ), XI, pp. 140–205; P. Graff, *Geschichte der Auflösung der alten gottesdienstlichen Formen in der evangelischen Kirche Deutschlands* 2nd edn., 2 vols. (Göttingen, 1937), I, p. 401.

[14] Deutscher Evangelische Kirchenausschuß (ed.), *Die Bekenntnisschriften der evangelisch-lutherischen Kirche* 9th edn (Göttingen, 1982), pp. 461–3.

with their Catholic equivalents, they never, as far as we know, included the sprinkling of holy water, an essential part of the Catholic rite.[15]

Where consecration rituals survived or were revived they were purified by the removal of superstitious, pre-Reformation elements such as the use of the aspergillum. Despite this, attitudes towards the use of church space remained somewhat ambiguous. There was a need to maintain decorum, to enforce reverential behaviour, even though theologians asserted that church space was not especially sacred. In his 1959 study of Catholic survivals in Lutheran church orders, Ernst Zeeden argued that Lutheran authorities were concerned about what he described as the desecration or profanation (*Entheiligung*) of cultic space.[16] A church order of 1612 from Danzig, for example, imposed penalties for fighting and fornication inside the city's large Marienkirche. It also stated that those who took piglets, pigs, baskets of fish, meat and other burdens through the church in the mornings or at other times during sermons or vespers were liable to have their wares confiscated. This Marienkirche numbered amongst its employees a *Mistführer*, charged with keeping the church and churchyard clean, a *Hundepeitscher*, who chased dogs from the church before and after the sermon, and a *Steckenknecht*, who was responsible for ensuring that local children did not run and make a noise in the church and church-yard.[17] While such orders appear, as Zeeden suggests, to echo Catholic concerns about the defilement of sacred space, it seems likely that the authorities' primary concern was with disruption rather than defilement. The fact that the Danzig church order, and others, focused their atten-tion on misbehaviour *during* church services suggests that their primary concern was to ensure the uninterrupted preaching of God's word.[18] Like Luther himself, they also wished to set aside a place for peaceful prayer: children were to be disciplined in the Marienkirche in Danzig 'so that in the church it is always . . . quiet, and the people therein can make their prayers in peace'.[19]

The need to provide a suitable environment for preaching and prayer also exercised a decisive influence on the appearance of Lutheran churches. It would be a mistake, as Paul Graff pointed out, to assume that pre-Reformation churches were all about the administration of the mass while post-Reformation churches were all about the preaching of

---

[15] Graff, *Geschichte der Auflösung der alten gottesdienstlichen Formen*, I, pp. 401–3.

[16] E. W. Zeeden, *Katholische Überlieferungen in den lutherischen Kirchenordnungen des 16. Jahrhunderts* (Katholisches Leben und Kämpfen im Zeitalter der Glaubensspaltung, 17, Münster, 1959), p. 79.

[17] Sehling (ed.), *Die evangelischen Kirchenordnungen*, IV, pp. 201, 216–17.

[18] Amberg's city council also tried to stop people taking shortcuts through the church during the sermon and during communion. Zeeden, *Katholische Überlieferungen*, p. 82.

[19] Sehling (ed.), *Die evangelische Kirchenordnungen*, IV, p. 217.

sermons.[20] Medieval churches, particularly those belonging to the mendicant orders, had assigned a prominent place to the pulpit. And conversely Lutheran churches tended to retain altars for the celebration of the Eucharist. In his *German Mass*, published in 1526, Luther stated that ideally the altar should be moved, and the priest should face the people as Christ had undoubtedly done at the Last Supper. He emphasised, however, that this change could 'await its own time', and in fact Lutheran churches very rarely acquired communion tables like those that replaced altars in the churches of adherents of Reformed Protestantism.[21] Lutherans did, however, privilege the pulpit. Where Lutherans took over medieval churches altars were removed in order to improve the congregation's visual and aural access to the pulpit. With the same objective in mind, pews were added or relocated and galleries were sometimes constructed. Lutheran churches also emphasised the unity of church space, eliminating the functional division between nave and choir, which had previously served to delineate a hierarchy of sacredness. The chapel at Schloß Hartenfels at Torgau, the earliest surviving example of Lutheran ecclesiastical architecture, had no side chapels and no choir screen. The pulpit was on the north side, visible from almost everywhere, and galleries ensured that as many people as possible had good access to the sermon. Other churches built to serve Lutheran communities, for example the one at Joachimstal in Bohemia (1534–40) or the later one at Freudenstadt in the Schwarzwald (1601–9), showed the same concern for unified space and the preaching of God's word.[22]

For Lutheran commentators, church furnishings were not simply utilitarian. A church must, of course, contain the right furnishings – an altar, a font and a pulpit – for the performance of the liturgy. But in his sermons on Genesis Luther stated that altars and pulpits 'were built not only to meet a need but also to create a solemn atmosphere'.[23] In a similar vein a general recess from 1638 from Prussia ordered that all of these things should be made if not already present, so that the church did not look like a barn.[24] Images also continued to adorn Lutheran churches.

[20] Graff, *Geschichte der Auflösung der alten gottesdienstlichen Formen*, I, p. 92.
[21] Pelikan, *Luther's Works*, LIII, p. 69. For an image of Lutheran pastors distributing communion from an altar see Lucas Cranach the Younger, 'Two kinds of preaching – the evangelical', illustrated in R. W. Scribner, *For the Sake of Simple Folk: Popular Propaganda for the German Reformation* (Oxford, 1994), p. 202 or the illustrations in A. Marsch, *Bilder zur Augsburger Konfession und ihren Jubiläen* (Weißenhorn, 1980).
[22] H.-R. Hitchcock, *German Renaissance Architecture* (Princeton, 1981), pp. 101–4 on Torgau, p. 89 on Joachimstal and pp. 331–2 on Freudenstadt. For a discussion of Lutheran church architecture see A. Spicer, 'Architecture', in A. Pettegree (ed.), *The Reformation World* (London and New York, 2000), pp. 505–20, at pp. 507–11.
[23] Pelikan, *Luther's Works*, I, p. 95.     [24] Graff, *Geschichte der Auflösung*, p. 99.

Pre-Reformation statues and altarpieces were sometimes removed because of the danger of idolatry, but were replaced by new images depicting biblical themes, Reformers and key tenets of the Lutheran faith, for example those produced by the Cranach workshop for Saxon churches during the 1530s and 1540s. Luther of course defended the didactic value of art, and in his 1525 tract *Against the Heavenly Prophets in the Matter of Images and Sacraments* he also recognised the spiritual value of religious imagery: 'whether I will or not, when I hear of Christ an image of a man hanging on a cross takes form in my heart, just as the reflection of my face naturally appears in the water when I look into it'.[25] Such tolerant attitudes towards ecclesiastical art meant that Lutheran worship was often conducted in a rich visual environment.

The official Lutheran attitude may have been that churches were no more than spaces set aside for worship, that altars were simply convenient places for the distribution of communion, that graveyards were quiet places and that images were merely tools for the instruction of simple folk; none of these places or objects were especially sacred. Yet if elements, at least, of consecration rites remained, if attempts were still made to enforce reverential behaviour, and if the appearance of churches was largely undisturbed, is it likely that popular attitudes towards scared space changed? Leaving images and shrines in churches was perhaps especially dangerous, and Luther's more radical contemporaries certainly recognised this danger. Huldrych Zwingli was especially sensitive to the association between place and idolatry. In his *Answer to Valentin Compar* (1525) he wrote that the 'danger here is that everything which is in the church becomes from that moment on so great and holy in our eyes that we think it cannot be touched, so dear has it become'.[26] Paintings and statues in churches induced, he believed, an immediate religious response, whereas those outside churches were less potent. Two images of Charlemagne, the legendary founder of the city of Zürich and of her Great Minster, provided a case in point: 'we have had two Charlemagnes: the one in the Great Minster, which was venerated like other idols, and for that reason was taken out; the other, in one of the church towers, which no one venerates, and that one was left standing, and has caused no annoyance at all'.[27] Calvin also acknowledged the importance of location: he was prepared to countenance the preservation of at least some religious images in homes, but required churches to be completely cleansed of idols.[28] Margaret Aston argues that English iconoclasts likewise targeted

[25] Pelikan, *Luther's Works*, XL, pp. 99–100.
[26] Quoted in C. Garside, *Zwingli and the Arts* (New Haven and London, 1966), p. 167.
[27] Quoted in Garside, *Zwingli and the Arts*, p. 150.
[28] Michalski, *The Reformation and the Visual Arts*, pp. 70–1.

ecclesiastical rather than domestic imagery because 'it was recognized that particular attitudes belonged to particular places, and habits of reverence that started at the church door might be forgotten at the market place'.[29]

It seems that in some cases at least, the fears of these more radical Protestant reformers were fully justified. The ability of Lutheran theologians to undermine traditional understandings of divine presence and divine power, to secularise the world, was brought into question by the work of Bob Scribner. His research demonstrated 'a consistent attitude towards the world in which especially sacred places had certainly not disappeared'. Scribner pointed, for example, to six evangelical churches in eastern Franconia where the practice of pilgrimage refused to die out, and to the persistence of certain forms of Rogation Day procession, intended to mark out the boundaries of sacred space.[30] His article on incombustible images of Luther demonstrated that belief in image miracles remained a part of Lutheran cosmology into the eighteenth century.[31] Paul Graff documented the survival of the custom of adorning images on feast days; the Leipzig theological faculty decided to abolish it in 1665, for example, because although it was in itself not offensive, it provoked men to Catholic thoughts.[32] In the same year the theological faculty also prohibited the custom of genuflecting before the altar, lest it gave rise to the 'superstition' that the altar was particularly sacred.[33] A case study using evidence drawn from Nuremberg will enable us to assess how typical such cases were, and to determine whether Lutheran attempts to transform traditional practices and beliefs were as ineffectual as they suggest.

## III

In Reformation Nuremberg all forms of benediction were discontinued. The preliminary Lutheran order introduced into both of the city's parish churches in 1524 referred to them as 'fools' works'.[34] An anonymous

[29] M. Aston, *England's Iconoclasts* (Oxford, 1988), p. 404.

[30] R. W. Scribner, 'The impact of the Reformation on daily life', in G. Jaritz (ed.), *Mensch und Objekt im Mittelalter und in der frühen Neuzeit: Leben – Alltag – Kultur*, Österreichische Akademie der Wissenschaften Philosophisch-Historische Klasse Sitzungsberichte, vol. 568 (Vienna, 1990), pp. 315–43 at p. 326; R. W. Scribner, 'Magic and the formation of Protestant popular culture', in R. W. Scribner, *Religion and Culture in Germany 1400–1800*, ed. L. Roper (Leiden, Boston and Cologne, 2001), pp. 323–45 at p. 327.

[31] R. W. Scribner, 'Incombustible Luther: the image of the reformer in early modern Germany', *P&P* 110 (1986), 38–68.

[32] Graff, *Geschichte der Auflösung*, p. 100.       [33] *Ibid.*, pp. 284–5.

[34] Stadtarchiv Nürnberg, Rep. E1, Familienarchiv Spengler, Nr. 47, fol. 2r–fol. 2v: 'Es sind auch abgestelt, alle anndern Ceremonien als zu Lichtmess das wachs weyhen . . . Palm

list of ceremonies that had been transformed or abolished, dating from 1527, stated that: 'water, salt, wax, palms and *Fladen* [Easter cakes] are no longer blessed, because they have all been consecrated before through the Word of God as his creations, which were made for the good of mankind'.[35] God had bestowed his blessing on all creation, and his power could not be invoked at the behest of man. As we have seen, Nuremberg's leading theologian, Andreas Osiander, eliminated all consecration rituals from the church ordinance that he prepared for Nuremberg and neighbouring Brandenburg in 1533.

The city's principal churches were adapted for preaching.[36] The Sebalduskirche and the Lorenzkirche, the two parish churches, were already reasonably well suited to Lutheran worship: their hall-like choir areas had originally been intended to provide light-filled, open spaces, and had never been enclosed behind rood screens (see plate 3.2). Some alterations were nonetheless required to accommodate the Protestant emphasis on preaching the Word of God. In July 1542 the city council ordered the removal of three altars in the Sebalduskirche because they 'get in the way of the people hearing the word of God and in front of them the preacher cannot be seen or heard well'.[37] It is likely that several of the Lorenzkirche's sixteen medieval altars were also destroyed at this time. There is no contemporary report to this effect, but a chronicle written by Wolfgang Lüder (1551–1624), deacon at the Sebalduskirche, states that two altars, namely the St Kilian altar beside the pulpit and the Holy Cross altar on the column opposite it, were destroyed during the night in October 1543.[38] Two altars and a freestanding image were also removed from the former Benedictine church of St Egidien, and four altars in the

---

fladen, Aur, kass, flaisch, fewer, wurz, hailltumb weisen, die umgebung zu des hailligen fronleichnambs tag, mit dem sacrament wein segnen [etc.]. Solhes alles und yedes wird kains mer gesegnet oder geweyhet Sonnder alles fur Narrenwerck gehalten . . .'

[35] G. Pfeiffer (ed.), *Quellen zur Nürnberger Reformationsgeschichte. Von der Duldung liturgischer Änderungen bis zur Ausübung des Kirchenregiments durch den Rat (Juni 1524 – Juni 1525)*, Einzelarbeiten aus der Kirchengeschichte Bayerns, 45 (Nuremberg, 1968), p. 444.

[36] On the fate of the city's numerous cloister churches and chapels see G. Seebass, 'Mittelalterliche Kunstwerke in evangelisch gewordenen Kirchen Nürnbergs', in Fritz (ed.), *Die bewahrende Kraft des Luthertums*, pp. 34–53 at pp. 45–8.

[37] T. Hampe (ed.), *Nürnberger Ratsverlasse über Kunst und Künstler im Zeitalter der Spätgotik und Renaissance*, 2 vols., Quellenschriften für Kunstgeschichte und Kunsttechnik des Mittelalters und der Renaissance, N. F. Bd. 11 and 12 (Vienna and Leipzig, 1904), I, Nr. 2664.

[38] Staatsarchiv Nürnberg, Nürnberger Handschriften, Nr. 46, fol. 434v. W. Haas, 'Die mittelalterliche Altaranordnung in der Nürnberger Lorenzkirche', in H. Bauer, G. Hirschmann and G. Stolz (eds.), *500 Jahre Hallenchor St Lorenz zu Nürnberg 1477–1977* (Nuremberg, 1977), pp. 63–108 at p. 87 suggests that the Marian altar and perhaps the Conrad altar were also destroyed at this time.

Plate 3.2 Johann Ulrich Krauss (after Johann Andreas Graff), *Interior of the Lorenzkirche*, engraving 1685. © Germanisches Nationalmuseum, Nuremberg.

Heilig-Geist-Spital were dismantled.[39] The Frauenkirche (see plate 3.1), the chapel built in the 1350s on Nuremberg's main market square at the

---

[39] C. C. Christensen, 'Iconoclasm and the preservation of ecclesiastical art in Reformation Nuremberg', *Archiv für Reformationsgeschichte* 61 (1970), 205–21, at 219. See also Seebass, 'Mittelalterliche Kunstwerke', p. 44.

behest of Emperor Charles IV, was turned into a Protestant preaching hall in 1525. Again, several altars were removed, and by the end of the sixteenth century the church had also acquired galleries and pews facing the pulpit.[40]

Other than these accommodations to Protestant preaching, the overall appearance of Nuremberg's sacred spaces changed little over the course of the sixteenth century. We have seen that Luther believed that church furnishings – altars and pulpits – should remain in order to create a solemn atmosphere, and that his attitude towards religious imagery in general was a lenient one. Yet in Nuremberg the preservation of pre-Reformation furnishings and images undoubtedly pushed at the limits of legitimate Lutheran tolerance. Altars, altarpieces, statues, sacrament houses and even saints' shrines survived intact and *in situ*. Andreas Osiander was adamant in his prescription that only images depicting biblical facts or true events from the lives of model Christians should be allowed to remain.[41] Yet in 1600 Nuremberg's churches still contained numerous paintings and statues of non-scriptural subjects, for example the Holy Kindred, the coronation and assumption of the Virgin, the rosary and even the Virgin of Mercy, an iconographic theme whose intercessory connotations had been explicitly condemned by Luther.[42] Indeed only one image is known to have been removed specifically because it continued to provoke idolatry: a 'Mariapild' (probably a richly adorned statue of the Virgin Mary) in the Frauenkirche, taken away in October 1529 at the behest of the city council.[43] One other concession was made to Lutheran concerns: Veit Stoß's brightly painted sculpture of the angelic salutation, which in the pre-Reformation period had been concealed in a fabric covering for most of the year and exposed to view only on feast days, was now kept permanently covered. Tradition records that this was done at the behest of Andreas Osiander himself.[44]

---

[40] A. Würfel, *Diptycha Cappellae B. Mariae* (Nuremberg, 1761).

[41] G. Müller and G. Seebass (eds.), *Andreas Osiander d. Ä: Gesamtausgabe*, 10 vols. (Gütersloh, 1975–97), II, p. 287.

[42] B. Heal, 'A woman like any other? Images of the Virgin Mary and Marian devotion in Nuremberg, Augsburg and Cologne c.1500–1600', PhD thesis, University of London (2001), pp. 183–4.

[43] Hampe (ed.), *Nürnberger Ratsverlassse*, I, Nr. 1729. For a discussion of the Marian statues in the Frauenkirche see Heal, 'A woman like any other?', p. 60.

[44] Johannes Nas' satirical defence of the Catholic faith, *Centuria: das antipapistisch eins und hundert* (Ingolstadt, 1567), contains what is probably the earliest surviving report of this sculpture's condemnation by a Lutheran preacher, said in later sources (e.g. A. Würfel, *Diptycha Ecclesiae Laurentianae* (Nuremberg, 1756), p. 17) to be Osiander himself. See J. Grimm and W. Grimm, *Deutsches Wörterbuch*, 16 vols. (Leipzig, 1854–1954), vol. IV.1.v, col. 1986–9.

In the Lorenzkirche perhaps the most remarkable survival was Adam Kraft's spectacular stone sacrament house, commissioned in 1493 and completed in 1496. After the Reformation the Eucharist was no longer reserved, and the sacrament house therefore lost its chief function.[45] At almost twenty metres high it nonetheless continued to dominate the choir area, and even retained the grille behind which the body of Christ had previously been displayed.[46] In the Sebalduskirche the shrine of St Sebald (plate 3.3) likewise survived despite the abrogation of its original function. The gold and silver reliquary shrine dates from the late fourteenth century, and its cast-bronze canopy was created in 1508–19 by Peter Vischer the Elder and his sons. The cult of St Sebald blossomed in the years immediately preceding the Reformation: his feast day was celebrated with great ceremony, and his shrine was an important focus of pilgrimage. While St Sebald's feast day was abolished after the institution of the Reformation his shrine, which had for decades provided a key point of access to divine power, remained undisturbed.[47]

Evidence from Nuremberg suggests that outside as well as inside a city's Lutheran churches there could be some remarkable survivals. Bob Scribner argued that Germany's physical landscape was 'confessionalized', and that travellers would have been able to deduce the religion of a region's inhabitants from the presence or absence of religious monuments: 'thus, as one passed through Franconia, the sudden absence of roadside image shrines betrayed that one had passed from a Catholic into a Protestant area'.[48] Marc Forster likewise associates crucifixes and statues of saints with Catholic identity in his study of baroque southwest Germany, and argues that 'they may have had a special resonance in places where Catholics came into direct contact with Protestants'.[49] Yet in Nuremberg itself, and therefore probably also in its surrounding territory, there was apparently no attempt to remove religious statues from the everyday environment. In 1855 a local librarian published a description of Nuremberg's surviving medieval house signs. He counted forty showing the Virgin Mary and knew of another six that were no longer

---

[45] Christensen, 'Iconoclasm', 218.

[46] On Kraft's sacrament house see C. Schleif, *Donatio et Memoria: Stifter, Stiftungen und Motivationen aus der Lorenzkirche in Nürnberg* (Munich, 1990), pp. 16–75. On German sacrament houses in general see A. Timmermann, 'Staging the eucharist: late gothic sacrament houses in Swabia and the Upper Rhine. Architecture and iconography', PhD thesis, University of London (1996).

[47] F. Schnebögl, 'Sankt Sebald in Nürnberg nach der Reformation', *Zeitschrift für bayerische Kirchengeschichte* 32 (1963), 155–72.

[48] Scribner, 'The impact of the Reformation', p. 318.

[49] M. Forster, *Catholic Revival in the Age of the Baroque: Religious Identity in Southwest Germany, 1550–1750* (Cambridge, 2001), p. 73

Plate 3.3  Peter Vischer the Elder and sons, *The Tomb of St Sebald*, 1508–1519, Sebalduskirche, Nuremberg.

in existence, as well as some of other saints.[50] Both before and after the Reformation, the day-to-day life of Nuremberg's citizens was conducted beneath the watchful eyes of numerous images of the Virgin Mary and other saints.

[50] G. W. K. Lochner, *Die noch vorhandenen Abzeichen Nürnberger Häuser* (Nuremberg, 1855).

Such images remained in place in Nuremberg for a number of reasons. As we have seen, Lutheran reformers tended to adopt a moderate position with regard to religious art. Osiander was no exception: in a report submitted to Nuremberg's council in 1526 he acknowledged that images could serve as 'writing and reminders for the peasants'.[51] The saints whom many of the surviving images depicted could, according to Osiander, provide Christians with valuable examples of right belief and conduct.[52] The city council also had more mundane concerns. Like every other elite ruling body, it was determined to prevent unsupervised iconoclasm: to permit the destruction of images would have been to encourage the infringement of property rights in other contexts.[53] Political circumspection also influenced the council's thinking. In Nuremberg, as in some other Lutheran territories, the preservation of pre-Reformation images helped to demonstrate religious and political moderation.[54] Nuremberg had no wish to alienate the Catholic emperor who guaranteed both its political security and its economic prosperity, and it is therefore scarcely surprising that the council proceeded as cautiously as possible with regard to religious reform. Finally, aesthetic appreciation may have encouraged the preservation of certain monuments. As early as 1538 an English visitor commented that Nuremberg's churches were full of images that were regarded as 'ornaments of the church': the images were no longer part of the liturgy, but were valued for their decorative functions.[55] The treatment afforded to Veit Stoß's angelic salutation perhaps provides the best proof of local patrician pride in Nuremberg's artistic heritage. Kept permanently covered after 1529 the sculpture nonetheless remained in place and was well maintained: it was cleaned in 1590 and regilded in 1612. In 1614 a poem was written in its honour and it was lowered and removed from its covering several

---

[51] Müller and Seebass (eds.), *Andreas Osiander d. Ä*, II, p. 287.

[52] Andreas Osiander, *Zwo Predig. Eine von den heiligen / wie man sie ehren sol. Die ander / vonn Verstorbnen / wie man f<sup>e</sup>ur sie bitten sol* (n.p., 1547), fol. 2v: 'Dan[n] wiewol uns Gottes wort / in der heiligen Schrifft / gn<sup>o</sup>ugsam und reichlich lehret / was wir thun und lassen sollen . . . Dannoch bed<sup>e</sup>orffen wir / umb unserer schwacheyt willen / auch guter exempel / und fürbilde / der hellige[n] / und geist reichen leute / darin[n] wir eben dasselbig sehen / das uns Gottes wort lehret / von denen wir lernen / und denen wir nachfolgen solle[n] / damit wir unser leben unstr<sup>e</sup>afflich unnd Christlich füren.' For a general discussion of the role of saints in Lutheran theology, see R. Kolb, *For All the Saints: Changing Perceptions of Martyrdom and Sainthood in the Lutheran Reformation* (Macon, Ga, 1987).

[53] Christensen, 'Iconoclasm', 212.

[54] S. Michalski, 'Die Ausbreitung des reformatorischen Bildersturms 1521–1537', in C. Dupeux, P. Jezler and J. Wirth (eds.), *Bidersturm: Wahnsinn oder Gottes Wille?* (Bern, 2000), pp. 46–51, at p. 50.

[55] J. S. Brewer, J. Gairdner and R. H. Brodie (eds.), *Letters and Papers, Foreign and Domestic, of the Reign of Henry VIII*, 36 vols. (London, 1862–1932), XIII, part 1, no. 935, 5 May 1538. I am grateful to Peter Marshall for bringing this letter to my attention.

times during the seventeenth century for the benefit of visiting Catholic dignitaries.[56]

Given this remarkable continuity in appearance, one could be forgiven for thinking that Nuremberg's ecclesiastical and secular spaces scarcely changed at all as a result of the Reformation, and that Lutheran citizens worshipped in a visual environment that was practically identical to that of their Catholic forefathers. This was not so: while furnishings remained, there were important transformations in the ways in which ecclesiastical space was used. Before the Reformation certain practices had served to articulate a hierarchy of sacredness, both inside and outside the city's churches. The *Mesnerpflichtbuch* (a book describing the sexton's duties) for the Lorenzkirche records, for example, that lamps were maintained before altars, and on feast days before important sculptures such as Adam Kraft's sacrament house and Veit Stoß's angelic salutation. They were also placed before statues and paintings, and statues might, in addition, be clothed or otherwise adorned.[57] The church's altarpieces were kept closed for most of the time, each being opened only on prescribed feast days.[58] The *Mesnerpflichtbuch* also prescribed other ways in which the church's altars were to be prepared for such festivals: specific antependia were to be hung out and treasures – reliquaries and silver statuettes of saints – were to be placed on the altar on which mass was to be celebrated.[59] The traditional theological justification for such adornment, reaffirmed at the Council of Trent, was that the honour shown to an image of a saint passed to its prototype, but in practical terms these actions served to demonstrate the sacredness of the church, to mark it out as a special place, and to mark certain points within it – generally altars and images – as particularly holy.[60]

Processions, both inside and outside churches, served the same purpose. In addition to small processions at different times in the church's prayer cycle – for example at vespers – a number of major processions were held regularly in pre-Reformation Nuremberg. On the morning of the feast of Corpus Christi solemn processions with the sacrament departed from both parish churches and went through the city's streets. In Nuremberg there were also other sacrament and relic processions during

---

[56] R. Kahsnitz (ed.), *Veit Stoß in Nürnberg: Werke des Meisters und seiner Schule in Nürnberg und Umgebung* (Munich, Germanisches National museum, 1983) p. 203.

[57] Heal, 'A woman like any other?', pp. 44–6.

[58] For a comprehensive account of which retables were opened on which days see Haas, 'Die mittelalterliche Altaranordnung', pp. 93–107.

[59] A. Gümbel (ed.), *Das Mesnerpflichtbuch von St Lorenz in Nürnberg vom Jahre 1493*, Einzelarbeiten aus der Kirchengeschichte Bayerns, 8 (Munich, 1928).

[60] On Trent see G. Scavizzi, *The Controversy on Images from Calvin to Baronius* (New York, 1992), pp. 70–8.

the year. On the 19 August the silver shrine containing St Sebald's relics was carried around the church of St Sebald by members of the city council, and devotees approached it in the hope of obtaining preservation or relief from illness. On Wednesday of the week before Whitsun the relics of St Deocarus were processed around the Lorenzkirche. There were also rogation processions with relics and crosses, which, as Scribner argued, 'marked out boundaries as a form of sacred space', and occasional intercessory processions in times of political or socio-economic crisis.[61] Such processions were a visible manifestation of the holiness of the city.[62]

These articulations of sacred space stopped at the Reformation. Reformers were no longer willing to tolerate practices that honoured particular saints through their images and relics and called on them as intercessors, or that purported to offer salvation through good works. An anonymous description of the city's Reformed liturgy dating from 1527 stated that the provosts in both parish churches had suppressed the public processions and pilgrimages in which saints, intended merely as examples of belief and love, had wrongly been made into intercessors and replaced Christ, the only true mediator.[63] In his 1530 defence of the Augsburg confession Osiander condemned those who tried to serve God through pilgrimage, through donations, through having images made and through burning lights rather than through paying attention to His Commandments.[64] In Lutheran Nuremberg altarpieces were probably still opened and closed in a cycle that reflected the liturgical seasons and the purified calendar of saints' feast days.[65] But the practices that had, during the pre-Reformation period, served to honour certain images and indicate their significance as loci of sacred power were discontinued: altarpieces and statues were no longer illuminated by numerous lamps and candles; statues were no longer adorned.[66] Nuremberg's Corpus Christi procession was stopped in 1524. Criticism of the excesses of the St Sebald procession

---

[61] On Nuremberg's processions see K. Schlemmer, *Gottesdienst und Frömmigkeit in der Reichsstadt Nürnberg am Vorabend der Reformation* (Würzburg, 1980), pp. 261–76. R. W. Scribner, 'Symbolizing boundaries: defining social space in the daily life of early modern Germany', in Scribner, *Religion and Culture in Germany*, pp. 302–22 at p. 307.

[62] K. Militzer, 'Collen eyn kroyn boven allen steden schoyn: Zum Selbstverständnis einer Stadt', *Colonia Romanica: Jahrbuch des Fördervereins romanische Kirchen Köln e.V.* 1 (1986), 15–32 at 21.

[63] Pfeiffer, *Quellen*, p. 444.

[64] Müller and Seebass (eds.), *Andreas Osiander d. Ä.*, IV, p. 73.

[65] Seebass, 'Mittelalterliche Kunstwerke', p. 44.

[66] Heal, 'A woman like any other?', p. 49. Note that in some Lutheran areas, for example Prussia, it was forbidden to light candles before images of saints displayed in churches or in homes. A. Zieger, *Das religiöse und kirchliche Leben in Preussen und Kurland im Spiegel der evangelischen Kirchenordnungen des 16. Jahrhunderts* (Cologne and Graz, 1967), p. 81.

led to the imposition of limitations in 1523 and its final abolition in 1524. The Deocarus procession was held for the last time in 1523.[67]

All of this added up to a substantial transformation in the way in which the environment of worship was signposted. As Eamon Duffy has argued in the context of the English Reformation, the actions that had accompanied traditional devotions had been an essential part of their existence. When the lights before statues were extinguished and their adornments were removed, their cults went into decline. In Duffy's words, the images 'dwindled from presences to not much more than furniture'.[68] A similar process occurred in Nuremberg and elsewhere in Lutheran Germany: altars, shrines and images were stripped of the trappings of idolatry. No longer presented as conduits of divine power, they became little more than a backdrop for Lutheran worship.

Whether this transformation in use was sufficient to alter traditional perceptions of sacred space is, of course, difficult to say. The nature of Nuremberg's criminal sources makes it impossible to trace cases of conflict about religious belief and practice. Few interrogation records survive, and the compendia in which cases were summarised for the benefit of the council were concerned almost exclusively with executions for robbery and violence.[69] For Nuremberg, as for most German cities, church visitation records deal only with rural parishes. Given this paucity of records of conflict, the most one can say is that the persistence of idolatrous notions of sacred space and sacred power was not, apparently, an issue for the city's key preachers. Osiander's surviving Nuremberg sermons make no reference to continuing idolatry, and it does not feature amongst the abuses reported to the city council by Veit Dietrich, preacher at the Sebalduskirche, during and after Nuremberg's 1543 Imperial Diet. In a sermon preached later the same year during an outbreak of plague Dietrich did feel the need to remind his congregation of the dangers of seeking intercession from the saints, but he located this abuse firmly in the past: 'We all know / what idolatry there *was* in the time of the papacy.'[70]

In Nuremberg's rural hinterland the Reformers' attempts to transform popular belief concerning sacred images and sacred spaces were less uniformly successful. It comes as no surprise to find that the pace of religious

---

[67] Schlemmer, *Gottesdienst und Frömmigkeit*, pp. 265–70.
[68] E. Duffy, *The Voices of Morebath: Reformation and Rebellion in an English Village* (New Haven and London, 2001), p. 105.
[69] Staatsarchiv Nürnberg, Nürnberger Amts- und Standbücher Nr. 209 and Nr. 221; see T. Hampe, *Die Nürnberger Malefizbücher als Quellen der reichsstädtischen Sittengeschichte vom 14. bis zum 18. Jahrhudert*, Neujahrsblätter der Gesellschaft für Fränkische Geschichte, 17 (Bamberg, 1927).
[70] My italics. B. Klaus, *Veit Dietrich. Leben und Werk*, Einzelarbeiten aus der Kirchengeschichte Bayerns, 32 (Nuremberg, 1958) pp. 221–2.

change was slower in the countryside, where the progress of Lutheran indoctrination varied according to the degree of central supervision and the ability of local pastors.[71] Around Nuremberg the reformers' difficulties were compounded by the disruption of the second Margrave's War (1552–5), which destroyed some of the good practices that had been introduced over the preceding three decades and slowed the further extension of the Reformation.[72] In 1560–1 Nuremberg's city council sent out a commission, led by two theologians, to visit the parishes of its rural territory. The commissioners were charged with examining the religious knowledge and practice and the general morality of both pastors and their congregations. As the work of Bob Scribner, Scott Dixon and others leads us to expect, the records that the commissioners produced contain evidence of the persistence of superstitious and improper beliefs and practices, from apotropaic magic to blasphemy and failure to attend communion. The commissioners also found occasion to complain about the abuse of ecclesiastical space: in Gräfenburg the pastor was requested to fence the churchyard to prevent pigs and cows from walking there, in Gräbern the sexton was likewise reprimanded for allowing his cattle to roam the graveyard, and in Altdorf the commissioners told the congregation to stop misbehaving in the churchyard and gallery during services.[73]

Continued belief in images and places as loci of sacred power also featured. In the village of Hüll near Betzenstein the local pastor presented the commissioners with a memorandum detailing a cult based around two statues, one of St Martin and one of the Virgin. According to this memorandum, idolaters persisted in processing around the altar ('umb den altar gehen') and in genuflecting, praying and making offerings before the images. The commissioners decreed that the image of the Virgin should be replaced with a crucifix (a decree that was apparently not put into effect), and that the statue of St Martin should be removed.[74] In the village of Rasch near Altdorf 'old wives from the countryside' burnt candles and genuflected before an image of the Virgin located behind the church, in Tennenlohe a richly clothed image of the Virgin was the focus of parishioners' idolatry.[75] In the neighbouring village of Eltersdorf

---

[71] See for example J. M. Kittelson, 'Success and failure in the German Reformation: the report from Strasbourg', *Archiv für Reformationsgeschichte* 73 (1982), 153–75 and C. S. Dixon, *The Reformation and Rural Society: The Parishes of Brandenburg-Ansbach-Kulmbach, 1528–1603* (Cambridge, 1996).

[72] G. Hirschmann (ed.), *Die Kirchenvisitation im Landgebiet der Reichsstadt Nürnberg 1560 und 1561: Quellenedition*, Einzelarbeiten aus der Kirchengeschichte Bayerns, 68 (Neustadt a. d. Aisch, 1994) p. 19.

[73] *Ibid.*, pp. 107, 117, 189.    [74] *Ibid.*, pp. 131–2, 141.

[75] *Ibid.*, pp. 182, 245, 256. On the Hüll and Rasch cults see also E. Roth, *Volkskultur in Franken*, 3 vols. (Bamberg and Würzburg, 1990–2000), I, pp. 256–8.

commissioners were forced to remove an image that was a persistent focus of idolatrous veneration from its privileged position on the church's altar to the sacristy, a place accessible only to church officials, and local custodians were reprimanded for burning too many candles in the church on feast days.[76] The commissioners also recorded a few cases of supposedly Lutheran individuals who refused to give up going on pilgrimage. Stefan Rummer's wife, from Rasch, was accused, for example, of having repeatedly participated in a popular pilgrimage to the parish church in Trautmannshofen in the Upper Palatinate that took place annually on the feast day of Mary's birth.[77]

Should these cases be taken as an indication of the widespread survival of traditional notions of sacred space? I would argue not. Nuremberg's territory covered approximately 1,200 square kilometres. The commissioners could have visited a total of seventy-six parishes, but by limiting their purview to those parishes where the city held both territorial jurisdiction (*Landesherrschaft*) and the right of patronage (*Kirchenpatronat*), and by excluding parishes where there was no incumbent pastor, they reduced this number to fifty-seven.[78] Of course, the commissioners only saw the cases of abuse that were brought to their attention – there may well have been others that went unnoticed. Given this proviso, out of the fifty-seven parishes visited, only four showed serious evidence of the persistence of idolatrous practices. Some extenuating circumstances may be invoked to account for the persistence of idolatry in these four parishes: Hüll and Tennenlohe were filial churches, churches without their own pastors to direct the sustained efforts necessary to eradicate deeply held beliefs; Hüll and Rasch were also on the very edge of Nuremberg's territory, Hüll next to the Catholic bishopric of Bamberg and Rasch next to the relatively recently Protestantised Upper Palatinate. The testimony of local residents concerning the cult at Hüll suggests that it was maintained partly through contact with neighbouring communities.[79] There was also a generational issue: in Rasch it was 'old women' who genuflected before the altar and image behind the church and in Tennenlohe it was 'especially' the elderly who persisted in idolatry.[80] This supports Elizabeth Roth's assertion that the main caesura for the ending of pilgrimage to evangelical churches was the second half of the sixteenth century, when the generation for whom this practice had been customary since childhood died out.[81] Where Lutheran churches had their own pastors and were successfully isolated from the subversive influence of neighbouring

[76] Hirschmann (ed.), *Die Kirchenvisitation*, pp. 245, 258–9.
[77] *Ibid.*, pp. 183, 190–1. For another case (Hiltpoltstein) see p. 69.
[78] *Ibid.*, pp. 18–9.    [79] *Ibid.*, p. 139.    [80] *Ibid.*, pp. 182, 256.
[81] Roth, *Volkskultur in Franken*, I, p. 269.

Catholic communities, belief in the sacred power of images and spaces gradually died out under the Reformers' tutelage.

The evidence from Nuremberg demonstrates the 'preserving power' of Lutheranism. The appearance of the city's ecclesiastical spaces changed hardly at all over the course of the sixteenth century. Altars, altarpieces, statues, sacrament houses and even saints' shrines remained intact and *in situ*. We should not assume, however, on the basis of this continuity in appearance and of evidence from visitation records and other isolated cases of conflict, that outside theological circles understandings of sacred space remain largely unaltered. Thanks to the Lutheran Reformers, notions of sacred space were no longer articulated verbally or visually as they had been in the past. Consecration and benediction rituals stopped, and after 1525 images, altars and relics were not illuminated with votive candles, richly adorned or carried in solemn processions. They were no longer presented in ways that emphasised their value as points of access to divine power. It seems likely, judging by the relative scarcity of references to conflict over sacred spaces and images in the visitation records, that this transformation in use led to a gradual shift in perception. In Nuremberg, and elsewhere in Lutheran Germany, changes in the way in which the environment of worship was signposted enabled the majority of Lutherans to assimilate successfully the sacred topography of Catholicism and, as Ulrich Krauss' 1696 engraving of the Frauenkirche (plate 3.1) demonstrates, images and altars became little more than a backdrop for the performance of the Lutheran liturgy.

# 4 Places of sanctification: the liturgical sacrality of Genevan Reformed churches, 1535–1566

## Christian Grosse

To understand how the Reformed viewed the relationship between place and 'sacred' one must first reconstruct the Reformed definition of 'sacred', but to do so entails addressing the considerable historiographical legacy of the nineteenth and early twentieth centuries. This legacy, which particularly found a set form in the thoughts of Max Weber, still establishes in contemporary minds the idea of the Reformation as a major factor in a process of desacralisation. Although this idea often continues to determine the way in which the Reformation is seen, historiography now reacts against the simplifications that it implies by demonstrating that the Reformed understanding of what 'sacred' constitutes is still a largely unresolved problem.[1] In questioning these Weberian ideas, Natalie Z. Davis stressed, in a study where the issue of place was of particular importance, that the Reformation had not merely assimilated the sacred and transcendent but had redefined the way in which this sanctity had to be 'present in the world'.[2] The way was thus opened for a re-examination that still continues to the present day. In the light of this historiographical debate,

I would like to thank Ronald Wilkens for translating the text and the Fondation Ernst and Lucie Schmidheiny for their grant towards this. I am also grateful to Irene Backus and William A. McComish for reading the translated text. I also wish to thank Isabelle Brunier for her guidance on the financial archives of Geneva which made up for my ignorance of the technical vocabulary of sixteenth-century building, as well as for reading this chapter.

[1] Alain Cabantous, for example, thinks that the writings of Jean Calvin 'évacuent non seulement la sacralité du bâtiment, mais aussi celle du culte, voire de la plupart des sacrements'; they 'permettent aux premiers théologiens réformés de conforter le sacré comme catégorie éphémère, singulière, peut-être aléatoire, s'effaçant derrière la spiritualité', *Entre fêtes et clochers. Profane et sacré dans l'Europe moderne. xviie–xviiie siècle* (Paris, 2002), pp. 58–9. For another reaction, see R. W. Scribner, 'Perception of the sacred in Germany at the end of the Middle Ages', 'The impact of the Reformation on daily life', 'Magic and the formation of Protestant popular culture in Germany', 'The Reformation, popular magic, and the "Disenchantment of the world"', in his *Religion and Culture in Germany 1400–1800*, ed. L. Roper (Leiden, Boston and Cologne, 2001), pp. 85–103, 275–301, 323–45, 346–65.

[2] N. Z. Davis, 'The sacred and the body social in sixteenth-century Lyon', *P&P* 90 (1981), 59. For her, the Calvinists 'thought in terms of a new measure, redefining how the holy should be present in the world'.

this chapter seeks to show that the liturgical conversion of the churches inherited from the Middle Ages, carried out by the Genevan Reformation from 1535 onwards, was not just a process of desacralisation, but rather the response to a desire to rearrange the formal 'presence of the sacred in the world'. Such an approach must first determine, at least in general outline, the Reformed conception of the 'sacred', in order subsequently to show how this concept was reflected in the theology and, especially, in the liturgical organisation of the place of worship.[3]

In order to grasp the meanings that the 'sacred' might have had for the faithful of Geneva, we must start by identifying its use in the documents that encompassed the religious devotion and instruction of the Genevan people: the liturgical formula (*Form of Prayers and Ecclesiastical Songs*, 1542) and the *Catechism of the Church of Geneva* (1542).[4] In these documents, 'holy' and 'sacred' are most frequently used as adjectives and appear to be used interchangeably ('thy holy Gospel' or 'thy sacred Gospel').[5] The first, however, is more common than the second. Essentially, there were three forms of use. 'Holy' was – apart from the divine being himself in his Trinity ('thy holy name', 'thy holy Spirit', and Jesus as 'the holy [saint] bread from heaven') – that which came directly from God: the divine word ('thy holy [saint] Commandments', 'thy holy doctrine', 'thy holy Gospel', 'his holy promises') and the sacraments ('his holy communion', 'this holy sacrament'). It is to be noted in this respect that both the liturgy and the Catechism insist on the fact that the holiness of the Holy Communion demands particular ritual protection: thus the liturgical formula of excommunication warns the excommunicated 'that they must abstain from this holy table for fear of polluting and contaminating the sacred viands'.[6] Primarily, therefore, these texts associate

---

[3] The systematic study of the usage adopted by reformed theology of such categories as 'sacré', 'sainteté', 'pureté', 'pollution', to which they associated those of 'décence', 'dignité' and 'honnêté' has not yet to my knowledge been carried out. Here we shall limit ourselves, therefore, to a rapid indication of a certain number of approaches.

[4] *Tracts Containing Treatises on the Sacraments, Catechism of the Church of Geneva, Forms of Prayer, and Confessions of Faith. By John Calvin*, ed. H. Beveridge (Edinburgh, 1849), pp. 33–99, 100–28.

[5] This equivalence is general in the sixteenth century: Cabantous, *Entre fêtes et clochers*, p. 22; D. Julia, 'Sanctuaires et lieux sacrés à l'époque moderne', in André Vauchez (ed.), *Lieux sacrés, lieux de culte, sanctuaires. Approches terminologiques, méthodologiques, historiques et monographiques* (Rome, 2000), p. 245. 'Sacred' becomes distinct from 'holy' only through its uses by the historians of religion: Philippe Borgeaud, 'Le coupe sacré/profane. Genèse et fortune d'un concept "opératoire" en histoire des religions', *Revue de l'Histoire des Religions* 211 (1994), 387–418.

[6] *Tracts*, p. 120. The Catechism echoes these words from the liturgy: '*S*. But in the Supper the minister ought to take heed not to give it to any one who is clearly unworthy of receiving it. *M*. Why so? *S*. Because it cannot be done without insulting and profaning the Sacrament', *Tracts*, p. 93.

holiness with the divine, that is to say with something that is separated from the temporal world. Thus, during a sermon, Jean Calvin reminded his audience that the '*Holy word of God* implies that our Lord Jesus Christ, as Mediator, must be separated from the common ranks of men'.[7] This definition of the sacred corresponds to that which the historiography has generally considered to be typically Reformed. At the same time, however, the above-mentioned texts reveal that a form of contact with this transcendent holiness remains possible. The particular ritual protection demanded for the celebration of Holy Communion is indeed an indication that during this celebration there is communication with this holiness. From the Reformed point of view, the divine service – and in particular the sacraments – therefore establishes a link between the believers and the sacred.

Holiness adopts at least two other forms in this context. The Apostles' Creed, recited during each service, requires the faithful to affirm that they believe in 'the Holy Church' and in the 'Communion of saints'. Mindful of clarifying every word in the Apostles' Creed, the catechism explains that the expression 'Holy Church' denotes all of those 'whom God has chosen'; that is to say all those that he 'forms to holiness and innocence of life'.[8] A form of holiness resides therefore in the social reality, in so far as there is a group of human beings whose election has set them apart from other men. Submerged in society as a whole, but difficult to identify because of the impenetrable nature of the divine decrees, this group possesses a holiness that is more virtual than acquired: 'But is this holiness which you attribute to the Church already perfect?' continues the catechism; 'Not yet, that is as long as she has her warfare in this world', replies the pupil, who adds that 'she always labours under infirmities, and will never be entirely purged of the remains of vice, until she adheres completely to Christ her head, by whom she is sanctified'.[9] Thus social reality shelters a kind of incomplete holiness that remains to be perfected.

Finally, holiness also takes on a moral meaning in designating a whole body of behaviour. In the prayer for intercession, the minister prays that the Church may serve its God 'with all holiness and honesty', or for the clergy to bring back the 'wretched sheep' in order that 'they may increase in righteousness and holiness every day'. By the Eucharistic exhortation, the Church commits itself to 'live henceforth holily and according to God'.[10] Through these texts and those of the catechism, holiness appears to be an objective rather than a condition. In the temporal world it is

---

[7] G. Baum, E. Cunitz and E. Reuss (eds.), *Joannis Calvini Opera quae supersunt omnia*, 59 vols. (Berlin, 1863–1900), XLVI, col. 739.
[8] *Tracts*, p. 51.    [9] *Ibid.*    [10] *Ibid.*, pp. 102, 120.

unattainable but it suggests itself in the form of 'propriety', 'dignity' and 'honesty'.

The liturgy and catechism indicate that the concept of holiness is considered more in relation to time than to place. Indeed, Jesus' Ascension precludes its localisation. The catechism is very clear on this point: 'Did he [Jesus] ascend so that he is no more on earth?' asks the master. 'He did', replies the pupil, 'for after he had performed all the things which the Father had given him to do, and that were for our salvation, there was no need of his continuing longer on earth.' 'But', asks the master, 'did Christ, in going to heaven withdraw from us, so that he has ceased to be with us?' 'Not at all', asserts the pupil, 'he has engaged to be with us to the end of the world.' 'When we say he dwells with us, must we understand that he is bodily present', continues the master. 'No', concludes the pupil, 'the case of the body which was received into heaven is one thing; that of the virtue which is everywhere diffused is another.'[11] Present in the world not as a material and localised reality, but as a 'virtue', divine holiness animates a process of sanctification. In that sense, it exists within time. It represents an ideal towards which Christians are inclined by detaching themselves from the world and renouncing their passions. In this respect, the theological writings of Jean Calvin are more explicit. He admits a form of holiness in human beings that exists precisely through the link that unites them with their God.[12] It is this link that commits them to the way of holiness: 'We are consecrated and dedicated to God', writes Calvin, 'in order henceforth no longer to think, meditate or act except for his glory. For it is not permissible to utilize a sacred thing for a profane purpose'.[13] The Christian therefore constitutes – together with the Church and the act of worship that it celebrates – one of the ways in which the sacred is present in the world. Just as the holiness of the Church is never perfect, however, the achievement of holiness by humankind here on earth is unattainable. The process of sanctification can only be completed after the final judgement: 'only the beginning of this sanctifying can appear here; the end and accomplishment of it will be completed when Christ, the holy of holies, has filled it with all His holiness'.[14]

The elements of this summary definition of the Reformed conception of holiness are to be found in Jean Calvin's pronouncements on the subject of places of worship. His views on the subject, which are rare and

[11] *Ibid.*, pp. 48–9.
[12] 'Quand nous oyons qu'il est fait mention de la conjonction de Dieu avec nous, il nous doit souvenir que le lien d'icelle est saincteté', *Institution de la religion chrétienne*, 5 vols. (Paris, 1953–63) III, VI, 2.
[13] *Ibid.*, III, VII, 1.   [14] *Ibid.*, IV, VIII, 12.

far from verbose, essentially transfer holiness from its inscription in space to the faithful and their Church. In a frequently cited passage, he warns his readers very clearly against considering churches as 'real dwelling-places of the Lord', and not to attribute 'any secret holiness' to them. The rejection of any localisation of holiness is thus clearly asserted. Substituted for the sacralised conception of the place of worship was a vision of the believer himself as being the real place for communication with the divine: 'For if we are the real temples of the Lord, we must pray to him within ourselves if we wish to invoke him in his real temple.'[15] This idea is resumed in the catechism and numerous sermons that stress that Christians, in so far as they are 'sanctuaries and temples' of the divine, ought to protect the holiness with which they are invested: 'If we wish to have a horror of profligacy, we must adopt this principle that our bodies are temples of the Holy Spirit. Therefore those who have to do with such pollution drive away God and banish him from themselves, and profane the temple in which his majesty resides.'[16] The meeting of Christians for the purposes of worship also invests the place with a divine presence, which is both spiritual and social, but by virtue of a promise, as recalled by the liturgy: 'We have been told by [Jesus] and by his apostles to assemble ourselves together in one place in his Name, with the promise that he will be present with us.'[17] It is precisely in its functional dimension, as a place where Christians are assembled around their God, that the temple, according to Jean Calvin, finds its true justification: 'Since God has ordered all his people to pray together, it is also necessary that temples be assigned for this purpose.'[18] In the Reformed terminology, moreover, the word 'church' more rarely designates the place of worship (for which the word 'temple' is used) than the meeting of the faithful for communicating with the deity, in accordance with the instruments he instituted for this purpose: preaching and sacraments.[19]

From the functional perspective and especially from that of worship adopted by Jean Calvin, there came about progressively within the

---

[15] *Ibid.*, III, XX, 30.
[16] *Calvini Opera*, XXVII, col. 407; XLIX, col. 624. See also, *Tracts*, p. 65.
[17] According to Bernard Reymond, 'l'espace liturgique est formé de toute la communauté célébrante'. Similarly Bernard Roussel recalls that for Calvinists 'le *lieu* de la cène, ce n'est pas un édifice, mais l'assemblée des fidèles'. B. Reymond, 'Les chaires réformées et leurs couronnements', *Etudes Théologiques et Religieuses* 74 (1991), 47; B. Roussel, '"Faire la Cène" dans les églises réformées du royaume de France au seizième siècle (ca. 1555–ca. 1575)', *Archives de Sciences Sociales des Religions* 85 (1994), 105; *Tracts*, p. 101.
[18] *Institution*, III, XX, 30.
[19] W. Richard, *Untersuchungen zur Genesis der reformierten Kirchenterminologie der Westschweiz und Frankreich, mit besonderer Berücksichtigung der Namengebung* (Bern, 1959), pp. 72–85.

Reformed discourse a requalification of the liturgical place through the concept of holiness. Agostino Mainardo (*circa* 1487–1563), in his *Anatomie de la messe et du messel*, arrived at this requalification by defining the act of consecration. For him, 'the object that is consecrated remains the same as it was at first, and does not change at all in its substance: it is only dedicated, or rather assigned, to some holy and sacred purpose'. Since they are destined for the divine service, both the temple and the Christian must be considered as consecrated. It is their purpose, as a place of communication with a divine presence, which confers this character upon them. 'A house is consecrated to God when it is assigned and ordered to some holy usage, such as for preaching the holy word, administering the Sacraments and for public prayer. Thus a man is consecrated to God when he is dedicated and assigned to the sacred purpose of his service, which is a holy thing.'[20] According to Rudolf Wirth (1547–1626), a Zurich theologian, the *raison d'être* of temples also resides in their purpose as places of worship accommodating 'the Word [of God], his sacraments, the presence of his Spirit, and his gifts and the communication of his Grace'. It is its use for the purpose of worship that determines the rules governing its construction.[21] This redefinition of the Reformed position concerning places of worship that re-established the idea of holiness, was officially rendered subsequently by the Helvetic Confession, drawn up by Heinrich Bullinger and adopted by the majority of the Reformed Churches of Switzerland, including that of Geneva in 1566. Recalling the conviction of its adherents that 'God never dwells in temples built by the hands of men', this confession adds that 'places dedicated to God and to his worship *are not profane, but holy* because of God's word and the use of holy things to which they are devoted'; in consequence, 'those who frequent them must converse in all modesty and reverence, remembering that *they are in a holy place*, in the presence of God and his holy Angels'.[22] On two occasions, therefore, this doctrinal declaration of the Swiss Reformed Churches affirms unambiguously the holy character of the places of worship. There is no doubt that this constitutes a step away from the positions held by Jean Calvin.

The second Helvetic Confession bore witness to the fact that, within a Reformed discourse highly engrossed in denouncing as superstitious

---

[20] *Anatomie de la messe et du messel* ([Geneva], 1557), pp. 167–8.
[21] R. Hospinianus (Rudolf Wirth), *De origine, progressu, usu et abusu templorum, ac rerum omnium ad templa pertinentium* (Geneva, 1681), p. 41. On Rudolf Wirth, see R. Bodenmann, '"Que penser des Catholiques?" Enquête menée dans les écrits du protestant Rudolf Wirth (1547–1626)', in G. Bedouelle and F. Walter (eds.), *Histoire religieuse de la Suisse. La présence des catholiques* (Paris, 2000), pp. 141–58.
[22] O. Fatio (ed.), *Confessions et catéchismes de la foi réformée* (Geneva, 1986), p. 289.

the localisation of the divine within the material world, a reflection on religious edifices as liturgical places nevertheless progressively developed. This reflection succeeded in restoring to these buildings a specifically Reformed connotation of sacrality, by making it dependent – not upon the building as such – but upon both the people who meet there and the liturgical acts performed there. In the light of this doctrine, it is the act of worship that takes place there that distinguishes the temple from every other edifice: it becomes consecrated as a place dedicated to the divine service. Remaining very close to this definition, the theologian Bénédict Pictet even went as far as confining the sacred character of the temple to the duration of the service celebrated there.[23] Contrary therefore to the generally held ideas, the Reformation did not completely reject the idea of holiness being present in the world. In its conception of the place of worship, the sacred is coincident with the liturgical communication that the Church maintains with its God. To gain a full understanding of this concept one must therefore view it in relation to the use made of these buildings by the Reformed.

The first places of worship used by the evangelical activists between 1532 and 1535 in Geneva were profane: large rooms within private houses, a garden beyond the city walls and, more exceptionally, a public place.[24] Some witnesses have provided details of the way in which these places were arranged in order to embrace these religious services. Thus we know that during the first evangelical communion celebrated in Geneva, on 10 April 1533, the preacher stood 'near a table'.[25] Assembling more than fifty persons, including many women, in a garden not far from one of the city gates, this 'inaugural' communion had already adopted a disposition that would subsequently be recognised as typically Reformed.[26] There is every reason to believe that the piece of furniture

---

[23] 'On doit regarder les lieux, où se font les Assemblées Chrétiennes, comme saints, par rapport à l'usage auquel ils sont destinez, et cela seulement pendant le tems, qu'ils sont employez à cet usage', *Dissertation sur les temples, leur dédicace et plusieurs choses qu'on y voit, avec un sermon* (Geneva, 1719), p. 299.

[24] The term 'réformé' only appeared at the end of the 1540s. Militants for the evangélical cause preferred at first to call themselves 'évangélistes' or 'évangéliques' (Richard, *Untersuchungen*, pp. 8–60); V. van Berchem, 'Le premier lieu de culte public des évangéliques à Genève', *Bulletin de la Société d'Histoire et d'Archéologie de Genève* 3 (1912), 312–40; V. van Berchem, 'Une prédication dans un jardin (15 avril 1533). Episode de la Réforme genevoise', in *Festschrift Hans Nabholz* (Zurich, 1934), pp. 151–70; *Registres du Conseil de Genève*, ed. E. Rivoire, V. van Berchem and F. Gardy, 13 vols. (Geneva, 1900–40), XII, p. 184.

[25] Berchem, 'Une prédication', p. 166; A. Froment, *Les actes et gestes merveilleux de la cité de Genève* (Geneva, 1854), p. 48; Jeanne de Jussy, *Le levain du calvinisme ou commencement de l'hérésie de Genève*, ed. Adolphe-Charles Grivel (Geneva, 1865), p. 64; M. Roset, *Les chroniques de Genève*, ed. Henry Fazy, Georg et Cie (Geneva, 1894), pp. 168–9.

[26] I have adopted the 'inaugural' designation from Roussel, 'Faire la Cène', p. 102.

near to which the preacher was standing was actually a communion table and that the place of worship was indeed orientated towards the two ways of communication with the divine: the Word and the Sacraments. This arrangement probably represented a desire to break with the Christian concept of the relationship between the sacred and the place dating back to medieval times, for during this rather 'rustic' celebration the preacher was at pains to remind his audience that, from an evangelical point of view, churches were not 'houses of God'.[27]

A little less than a year later, the services of the evangelical community were moved to within the walls of the city, in a house recently acquired by a local noble, a citizen of Bern. Witnesses inform us quite precisely of the manner in which the building was arranged for celebrating the divine service. According to one of these, on the occasion of a baptism celebrated in February 1534, more than 300 persons attended,

in a large room, which . . . had been lengthened . . . and had, at the said place, some seats made expressly for accommodating those who came there to listen to the sermons . . . Preaching there was by a person named Viret, seated upon a higher seat than the others, and beside him sat two men, one here and the other there, who were heard to be called [Guillaume] Farel and [Antoine] Froment, also preachers.[28]

This description provides two features of the arrangement of the first liturgical places. Firstly, in mentioning that the place of worship had the appearance of a 'room', it indicates that the assembly occupied a single place comprising a sole liturgical centre. Secondly, it mentions the presence of 'seats'.[29] These two facts show that the evangelical service, which was then still partly clandestine, was held in some sort of fairly spacious auditorium. The presence of seats underlines the function of the room as a place of communication with the divinity through his word as expounded by the preachers, and clearly distinguishes this place from the medieval churches, which, as we shall see below, had only a restricted number of seating places.

Shortly after the services had been transferred to this venue, the evangelicals arrogated to themselves by force a public place of worship, but unfortunately we do not know how it was adapted for liturgical purposes.[30] This first victory, establishing the official existence of a dissident Church in Genevan society, accelerated the process of spiritual

---

[27] Berchem, 'Une prédication', p. 167.
[28] *Procès de Baudichon de la Maison Neuve, accusé d'hérésie à Lyon, 1534* (Geneva, 1873), pp. 112–13.
[29] *Ibid.*, p. 111.
[30] Berchem, 'Le premier lieu de culte', 22–3; *Registres du Conseil*, XII, pp. 493–5.

conversion by new religious ideas and the transformation of the places of worship. The final adoption of the Reformation, accomplished in several stages – from the official interdiction of the Mass, on 10 August 1535, to the confirmation of this decision by the assembly of the citizens (General Council) on 16 May 1536 – took place within the context of an icono-clastic celebration, during which the evangelical party finalised its victory by converting the places of worship.[31] The churches were systematically emptied of their liturgical furnishings; in particular the altars and the images, but the utensils, vestments and liturgical decorations were also removed.[32] At first, apart from the destruction, few changes in the city's churches appear to have been made in adapting them to the new form of worship. Once the place had been freed of most of the 'papist super-stitions', it was considered sufficient to 'cleanse' these churches.[33] Very early on, communion tables were certainly a part of the furnishing of the buildings converted to the new cult. At the end of the 1530s, city officials started reorganising the churches that were retained for celebrat-ing divine services. On 18 March 1539, when neither Calvin nor Farel were in Geneva, the authorities ordered – as proposed by the ministers – the restoration of these buildings and their equipment with 'whatever was necessary'. Among other items lacking in the temples, this decision mentioned benches.[34] Shortly afterwards, work began on the temple of La Madeleine with the construction of a stone pulpit, which was rapidly completed and placed in the middle of one of the longitudinal walls of the edifice.[35] The same period most probably saw the installation of benches, and certainly of new stained glass bearing the arms of the city in the temple windows.[36] During the summer of 1541, the authorities decided to undertake work in the cathedral of Saint-Pierre: demolishing the rood screen separating the choir from the nave, moving the canons' stalls within the choir, and installing a new pulpit.[37]

---

[31] *Registres du Conseil*, XIII, pp. 281–2, 576–7; C. Eire, *War Against the Idols. The Reformation of Worship from Erasmus to Calvin* (Cambridge, 1986), pp. 122–51.

[32] *Registres du Conseil*, XIII, pp. 279–386; M. Roset, *Les chroniques*, pp. 200, 214–15; Jussy, *Le levain*, pp. 152–5; Froment, *Les actes*, p. 144; P. Geisendorf, *Les annalistes génevois du début du dix-septième siècle. Savion- Piaget -Perrin. Etudes et textes* (Société d'Histoire et d'Archéologie de Genève, 37, 1942), pp. 443–8; L. Mottu-Weber, 'Dans les coulisses de la réforme: les recettes extraordinaires du trésorier Pertemps, 1535–1536', *Revue du Vieux Genève* 17 (1987), 4–10.

[33] Archives d'Etat de Genève (hereafter AEG), Finances M23bis, fol. 85v.

[34] AEG, R. C. 33, fol. 50v.

[35] AEG, R. C. 33, fol. 367v; Finances P4, 7 Feb. 1540; C. Martin, 'La restauration du temple de la Madeleine', *Genava* 2 (1924), 170.

[36] AEG, Finances P4, 6 Jan. 1540, 16 Jan. 1540.

[37] C. Charles, *Stalles sculptées du XVe siècle. Genève et le duché de Savoie* (Paris, 1999), pp. 59–62; AEG, R. C. 35, fols. 245, 301.

When Calvin returned to Geneva, the appearance of the Genevan temples, and especially those of La Madeleine and the cathedral, had undoubtedly greatly changed. It is possible that benches had been installed everywhere. This requirement did not manifest itself again thereafter. Although the medieval churches of the Geneva diocese were not without this furnishing, their presence was far from being commonplace.[38] On his return, Calvin was able to observe an important change in this respect, but there still remained a lot to be done. For two years, however, the priorities were more towards the institutional reorganisation of the Church than the adaptation of the temples to the new form of worship. In particular, a new parish structure was instituted. The seven parishes of the medieval city were replaced in November 1541 by three parishes centred on the temples of Saint-Gervais, La Madeleine and Saint-Pierre.[39] From 1543 until 1547, there was a systematic transformation of the temples within the town and the dependent villages of Geneva.

The first works concerned the cathedral. The decision taken on 29 August 1543 to construct a pulpit in Saint-Pierre provided the initial impulse to this campaign.[40] It makes clear that the project for installing a pulpit adopted two years earlier had not been implemented. The new pulpit, constructed in 1543, backed against a pillar at the crossing of the transept, in what had formerly been the choir when the rood screen stood there.[41] These works continued in 1544, particularly the covering over of the images and decorative items with a uniform coating of white paint.[42] The furnishing of the cathedral was also changed. Since the city officials assigned themselves the duty of attending services regularly 'in order to set a good example for people to go to the sermon', a part of the cathedral was reserved for them.[43] From December 1546 to

---

[38] Although the aim of the diocesan ecclesiastical authorities in the fifteenth century was to remove benches from the churches, a number of exceptions were accepted, especially for the nobility and aged or sick people. In this way benches came to be installed in La Madeleine in the mid-fifteenth century, except in the central part of the nave. L. Binz, 'Un évêque italien réforme les bancs d'église du diocèse de Genève (1443–1446)', in M. Fol, C. Sorrel and H. Viallet (eds.), Chemins d'histoire alpine. Mélanges dédiés à la mémoire de Roger Devos (Annecy, 1997), pp. 49–57.

[39] This new parish structure was made official by the ecclesiastical ordinances adopted on 21 November 1541. Registres de la Compagnie des Pasteurs de Genève, ed. J.-F. Bergier, R. M. Kingdon et al., 13 vols. (Geneva, 1964–2001), I, p. 5.

[40] AEG, R. C. 37, fol. 207.

[41] W. Deonna, 'Le mobilier de la cathédrale Saint-Pierre à Genève', Genava 28 (1950), 53–5.

[42] AEG, R. C. 38, fol. 187v, 6 May 1544. Images and decorations in the cathedral were not however completely suppressed at that time; further whitewashing took place in 1556 and in 1643. AEG, R. C. 52, fol. 163; W. Deonna, 'Cathédrale Saint-Pierre de Genève. La peinture', Genava 29 (1951), 56–87.

[43] Sources du droit du Canton de Genève, ed. E. Rivoire and V. van Berchem, 4 vols. (Aarau, 1927–35), III, p. 470.

October 1547, certain former canons' stalls were moved to this part of the cathedral in order to form a body of seating reserved for the Geneva authorities.[44]

In Saint-Gervais, similar works to those in Saint-Pierre were undertaken. The desire expressed by the authorities in 1543 to carry out important changes at first remained almost transient.[45] Despite a new initiative in this direction in 1544, the works did not commence until 1546, following the intervention of Calvin.[46] Within a year, a new replacement pulpit together with a canopy was installed, the former pulpit was then offered to the parishioners of a nearby village. The new pulpit was placed against a pillar, situated (as in La Madeleine) in the middle of the longitudinal part of the temple.[47] The gravestones were removed and the ground covered with flooring, the walls were partly whitewashed and the stalls were laid out in four rows against one side of the former choir and to the right of the preacher. They were intended, as in Saint-Pierre, for the authorities.[48] The former chapels facing the new pulpit and those to the left and right of it were transformed to accommodate benches, while the others were closed or converted into waiting rooms.[49] At the same time, La Madeleine temple underwent further alterations. In 1545, city officials recorded that it risked becoming a ruin and so instigated repairs. The walls were systematically whitewashed, the stained glass repaired, the façade resurfaced and repointed, and a chapel possibly blocked off. This work continued until November 1547.[50]

By 1548, therefore, the three parish temples of the city had essentially acquired the structures and general appearance that they were to keep during the whole of the *ancien régime*. Later on, only two events occurred

---

[44] AEG, Finances P5, 7 Apr. 1547, May 1547, 29 Sept. 1547, 15 Oct. 1547, 2 Nov. 1547; Deonna, 'Le mobilier', pp. 65–6; Charles, *Stalles*, pp. 84–5, 139.

[45] AEG, R. C. 38, fol. 14v; Finances M27, fol. 144v, 02, fol. 81; N. Schätti, 'Le temple réformé (XVIe–XVIIIe siècle)', in A. Winiger-Labuda *et al.*, *Les monuments d'art et d'histoire du canton de Genève*, II: *Genève, Saint-Gervais: du bourg au quartier* (Bern, 2001), p. 144.

[46] AEG, R. C. 38, fol. 187v; 41, fol. 89.

[47] AEG, Finances P5, 18 Dec. 1546, 21 Dec. 1546; Schätti, 'Le temple réformé', p. 146.

[48] AEG, R. C. 41, fol. 257v; Finances P5, 31 Dec. 1546, 4 Jan. 1547, 5 Jan. 1547, 27 Jan. 1547, 5 Feb. 1547. In 1566, the authorities ordered the covering over of the parts that had not been done in 1547. AEG, R. C. 61, fol. 8v. The temple was then whitewashed again in 1584, 1690, 1691, 1719 and 1773. A. Guillot, *Le temple de Saint-Gervais à Genève. Notice historique* (Geneva, 1903), pp. 39, 42; Schätti, 'Le temple réformé', p. 144, fn. 249). Charles, *Stalles*, pp. 139–41.

[49] Schätti, 'Le temple réformé', p. 145.

[50] AEG, R. C. 39, fol. 120; 40, fol. 358v; AEG, Finances M30, fols. 17, 20, 21, 28v, 42v, 60, 66, 68v, 69, 76v, 80v, 97v, 99, 99v, 101v; Finances P5, 17 Sept. 1546, 22 Dec. 1546, 17 Sept. 1547, 21 Sept. 1547, 29 Sept. 1547, 2 Nov. 1547, 11 Nov. 1547. The temple was again whitewashed in 1611 (*Registres de la Compagnie des Pasteurs*, XI, p. 62 and n. 86).

to disturb significantly their new equilibrium: in 1549, cupboards were placed near the pulpits in all three temples in order to house the baptismal and marriage registers kept by the pastors; and then, from the mid-sixteenth century, and more frequently in the following century, a series of galleries, sometimes two-storied as at La Madeleine, served to increase the available seating but at the same time changed the spatial dynamics of the interior area of the temples.[51] The adaptation of the Geneva country churches to the new form of worship began at the same time as in the city but took longer to achieve, for in 1555, Calvin was still recording that these buildings were in need of repair.[52] The transformations were sometimes carried out at the behest of those who were in charge of the parishioners, such as the village guards of the village of Jussy, who in 1544 requested 'that a pulpit be constructed for them'.[53] Generally speaking, four objectives determined the works: whilst the upkeep of these buildings remained a high priority, the contribution of the Reformation essentially concerned the erection of new pulpits, and the installation of benches and new bells in these churches to call the faithful to worship.[54]

At the end of this vast campaign, the appearance of Genevan temples was fundamentally transformed. Although the Genevan Reformers continued to occupy the churches constructed for other forms of worship than their own, they subverted their significance in a decisive way, thus creating 'a situation of tension between the architectural symbolism of the building and the major goal of the cult that would henceforth evolve there'.[55] The changes they had made to these buildings – at variance with the structures that organised them – made explicit their new religious identity and bore witness to a new relationship with the sacred. The external crosses that identified the churches as holy places had disappeared for the most part by 1537.[56] In 1556, lightning had struck near the

---

[51] AEG, R. C. fol. 290v; Deonna, 'Le mobilier de la cathédrale', 53.

[52] AEG, R. C. 49, fol. 178v.

[53] *Registres du Consistoire de Genève au temps de Calvin*, edited by T. A. Lambert, I. Watt, and W. McDonald, 3 vols. (Geneva, 1996–2004), I, p. 313.

[54] Thus, in 1544, the authorities ordered that the parishioners of the village of Vandœuvres should be given 'a pulpit for the sermon'. The same year, the minister of the village of Jussy complained of the passivity of his parishioners, whom he had asked to 'fere fayre une chayre'. This pulpit eventually came, in 1546, from the temple of Saint-Gervais. There was also a request for a pulpit for the village of Lancy in 1547. AEG, R. C. 36, fol. 117; 38, fol. 337; 39, fol. 53v; 40, fol. 202v; 41, fol. 242; 42, fol. 55; 61, fol. 137v.

[55] B. Reymond, *L'architecture religieuse des protestants: histoire – caractéristiques – problèmes actuels* (Geneva, 1996), p. 52. The construction of new temples only started in the seventeenth century, and at first concerned only the villages surrounding Geneva. A new temple was not built in the city until 1715. W. Deonna, 'Les arts à Genève, des origines à la fin du XVIIIe siècle' *Genava* 22 (1942), 321–2.

[56] AEG, R. C. 30, fol. 247v; Geisendorf, *Les annalistes*, p. 476.

belfry of Saint-Pierre causing a large fire, and was seen as a divine warning 'that it was shameful for such a cross, as mark or sign of papal devilry, to be left there'. The event provoked a new move to suppress the crosses that still dominated certain temples.[57] In the early 1560s, these edifices demonstrated by the absence of this sign on their belfries the Reformed desire to break with the 'idolatrous' religion. The arms of the city, which henceforth sometimes decorated the stained-glass windows, also served to indicate their new identity. Instead of appearing as separated from the profane world, they were assimilated to the community that celebrated the divine service there. They indicated that the *corpus christianum* was at one with the *corpus politicum*.

Within the churches, the disappearance of the altars, statues and reliquaries, as well as most of the painted images and tombs signified that the temple was no longer considered as a holy place with greater proximity to the divine.[58] And the ritual behaviour corresponded to these architectural features. As Bernard Roussel pointed out, the Reformed churches are not protected by any entry or exit rites.[59] 'And if someone offers up a prayer on entering the church', related Antoine Cathelan a Catholic observer, 'he is pointed to, made fun of, and held to be a Papist and idolatrous.'[60]

One of the most striking characteristics of the new appearance of the Genevan churches lay in the extreme simplicity of their decors. 'When

[57] AEG, R. C. 51, fol. 255v. The chronicler, Michel Roset, reiterated this interpretation: 'Chacun disoit que Dieu avoit faict cest œuvre voulant purger ceste Eglise de telz reliquas', *Les chroniques*, pp. 387–8.

[58] Burial inside churches were reintroduced in Geneva and in the Vaud region from the seventeenth century onwards. It was in response to the needs for social distinction and for revering the memory of certain people. But this custom was not without its problems, such as the erection in 1659 of a partition in front of the tomb of the duc de Rohan, in order to stop people from praying there (W. Deonna, 'Cathédrale Saint-Pierre de Genève. Les monuments funéraires', *Genava* 29 (1951) 132–8). On this subject, see also M. Engammare, 'L'inhumation de Calvin et des pasteurs genevois de 1540 à 1620. Un dépouillement très prophétique et une pompe funèbre protestante qui se met en place', in Jean Balsamo (ed.), *Les funérailles à la Renaissance* (Geneva, 2002), pp. 271–93; M. Grandjean, *Les temples vaudois. L'architecture réformée dans le Pays de Vaud (1536–1798)* (Lausanne, 1988), pp. 509–26. For comparison see A. Spicer, '"Defyle not Christ's kirk with your carrion": burial and the development of burial aisles in post-Reformation Scotland', in B. Gordon and P. Marshall (eds.), *The Place of the Dead. Death and Remembrance in Late Medieval and Early Modern Europe* (Cambridge, 2000), pp. 149–69; A. Spicer, '"Rest of their Bones": fear of death and Reformed burial practices', in W. G. Naphy and P. Roberts (eds.), *Fear in Early Modern Society* (Manchester, 1997), pp. 167–83.

[59] B. Roussel, 'Comment faire la cène? Rite et retour aux écritures dans les églises réformées du royaume de France au XVIe siècle', in C. Patlagean and A. Le Boulluel (eds.), *Les retours aux écritures, fondamentalismes présents et passés* (Paris, 1993), p. 198.

[60] A. Cathelan, *Passevent Parisien respondant à Pasquin Rommain. De la vie de ceux qui sont allez demourer à Genève, au pais jadis de Savoye: et maintenant soubz les Princes de Bern, et se disent vivre selon la reformation de l'évangile, faict en forme de dialogue* (Paris, 1556), fol. 15v.

[the Papists]', recalls Jean Calvin, 'enter our temples, they are so astonished that they are completely taken aback or feel they have entered a
new world. What? (they say) a Church without any pictures.'[61] Uniformly
coated with whitish distemper, the walls of these temples probably bear
no inscription dating back to before the seventeenth century, when walls
started to carry verses from the Bible and the Ten Commandments.[62]
This lack of decoration can be seen as the expression of a new aesthetic, as
recognised by Lee Palmer Wandel.[63] This aesthetic is based upon the idea
that it is through the simplicity of his Word and his Sacraments that the
divine 'majesty' communicates with Christians. Any addition of human
origin, tainted with sin, obscures and necessarily soils this communication. Simplicity, the central value of this aesthetic, is thus associated with
the notion of purity. For Guillaume Farel, as for Calvin, worship based
on preaching and the celebration of the Sacraments constitutes the sole
ornament that may adorn the temples:

And that the Church [writes the former] be adorned and decorated by Jesus
Christ and his word according to the Gospels and the holy Sacraments. This
great sun of justice Jesus Christ and his evangelical light have naught to do with
our smoking flames, our tapers and candles. May the true sermon ordained by
God manifest this light, together with the holy Sacraments in their simplicity, and
let that serve us as sole magnificence.[64]

Similarly Calvin recalled:

When I consider to what purpose the temples are dedicated and ordained, it
appears to me a thing unseemly to their sanctity to display there any other images
than those which God has consecrated with his word, and which bear his true
imprinted mark. I mean the Baptism and the Holy Communion of the Lord,
together with the ceremonies.[65]

Here again is the idea that holiness does not reside in the places where
worship takes place, but in the worship itself. Shared by all Reformed
sensibilities, this aesthetic of simplicity is built into a dogmatic affirmation
by the second Helvetic Confession, according to which

---

[61] *Calvini Opera*, XLIX, col. 613.
[62] The temple of the village of Jussy bears a verse from Psalm 119 on one of the partition
walls. In 1639, the displaying of a table of the decalogue was envisaged for all the country
temples. AEG, Cp. Past. R. 8, fol. 383; C. Bonnet, 'L'église de Jussy', *Genava*, new series,
25 (1977), 87. On the internal decor in the temples of the Vaud region, see Marcel
Grandjean, *Les temples vaudois*, pp. 367–74, 429–49, 527–32.
[63] L. P. Wandel, *Voracious Idols and Violent Hands. Iconoclasm in Reformation Zurich, Strasbourg, and Basel* (Cambridge, 1995), pp. 194–5. On the 'chromoclasme' of the protestants, see M. Pastoureau, 'La Réforme et la couleur', *Bulletin de la Societé de l'Histoire du
Protestantisme Français* 138 (1992), 324–42.
[64] G. Farel, *Du vray usage de la croix de Jesus Christ* (Geneva, 1865), p. 157.
[65] *Institution*, I, XI, 13.

. . . must be cast far from Christian temples and places of worship, all pomp and excess of clothing and ornament, all pride and all that is unseemly and contrary to humility, discipline and Christian modesty. Thus, according to the confession, the true ornamentation of the temples lies not in ivory, gold, and precious stones: but in frugality, temperance, piety and all the virtues of those who are in the Church.[66]

But the uniform whiteness of all the decor adopted by the Reformed temples does not only reflect a properly Reformed aesthetic, it also fulfils a definite liturgical function. The ornamental profusion characteristic of the 'papists' is seen indeed as distracting the attention of the faithful rather than helping them to concentrate. 'This external brilliance of the temples', points out Rudolf Wirth, 'hinders devotion and distracts the eye and mind of those who see it from spiritual thoughts.'[67] The absence of decoration, however, contributes to drawing the attention of the faithful towards what is said and done during the service. 'Be thy eyes fixed upon [the pastor], in order to be more attentive to the preaching of the word of God', is the recommendation of a preparatory treatise for the communion in the seventeenth century.[68] For Calvin as well, the effect of this lack of ornamentation was to concentrate all the attention on the service: 'our eyes must be so attentive [to it], and all our senses have such a predilection for it that there is no longer any question of craving an image created by the imagination of man'.[69] By avoiding the production of the slightest visual stimulation, the bare walls compel the faithful to see no other image than that produced by the service, in particular the Sacraments, as 'visible signs'.[70] Far from expressing the idea of the remoteness and abstract character of the divine, as noted for example by Susan Karant-Nunn, the sober decor therefore constitutes a liturgical device destined to engage the faithful in a spiritual process.[71] Inducing a form of ascetic liturgical communication with the divine, it must lead them to seek within

---

[66] Fatio (ed.), *Confessions et catéchismes*, pp. 289–90. See, for example, Ludwig Lavater, *Die Gebräuche und Einrichtungen der Zürcher Kirche. Erneut herausgegeben und erweitert von Johann Baptist Ott* (Zurich, 1987), p. 35.

[67] Wirth, *De origine*, p. 39.

[68] J. de Focquembergues, *Le voyage de Beth-el, ou les devoirs de l'ame fidele en allant au temple* (Geneva, 1665), p. 17.

[69] *Institution*, I, XI, 13.

[70] Calvin, 'souligne à plusieurs reprises l'aspect proprement iconique du sacrement. Celui-ci est "signe visible", "forme visible", "parole visible". . . . Le sacrement est donc iconique, il est une image au sens plein, symbolique, du terme; il est le prototype de toute image'; J. Cottin, *Le regard et la Parole. Une théologie protestante de l'image* (Geneva, 1994), pp. 296–7.

[71] S. Karant-Nunn, *The Reformation of Ritual. An Interpretation of Early Modern Germany* (London, 1997), p. 191.

the assembly and its act of worship an attestation of a real but spiritual divine presence. In this sense, it is a means of contributing to the process of spiritual elevation that underlies the progress of the Reformed liturgy, and which culminates during the celebrations of the Holy Communion, in the exhortation to the *sursum corda*, the elevation of hearts that the minister invokes just before the communion: 'Let us raise our hearts and minds on high, where Jesus Christ is, in the glory of his Father, and from whence we look for him at our redemption. And let us not amuse ourselves with these earthly and corruptible elements which we see with the eye, and touch with the hand, in order to seek him there, as if he were enclosed in the bread or wine.'[72] Thus the whitewashed Genevan temples clearly reflect a Calvinist conception of communication with the holy; instead of being mediatised by material reality, it is inscribed in time, like a process of elevation and sanctification.

The new manner of structuring space and the general orientation that it gives to religious buildings also profoundly changes their meaning. A place which had been subdivided into a multitude of chapels and altars that attracted a similar number of private devotions gave way to a unified space converging around a single centre of worship. This spatial levelling reflects a unified ecclesiastical society where, with the disappearance of all confraternities, religious sociability has no other field of expression than the family circle and parish assembly. What is more, this egalitarian place has eliminated the separation between the choir and the nave, marked sometimes – as at Saint-Pierre – by the rood screen.[73] By thus eliminating the distinction between a sacred order and a profane order, it reflects the 'Christianity without clerics' adopted by the Reformation.[74] The abolition of the former ecclesiastical order was particularly evident at Saint-Pierre; the congregation there, following the removal of the rood screen and the rearrangement of the stalls, occupied the area taken up by the choir of the church prior to the Reformation.

Furthermore, instead of the lengthways perspective characteristic of churches where the high altar represented the vanishing point, an arrangement 'in width' was employed, directed towards a liturgical centre.

---

[72] *Tracts*, pp. 121–2.

[73] There had not been a rood screen at the church of Saint-Gervais since the early fourteenth century, and it appears that there was no longer a rood screen in the church of La Madeleine either. P. Broillet and N. Schätti, 'Les remaniements de l'église paroissiale au début du xive siècle – La reconstruction de l'église paroissiale (après 1431–après 1449)', in Winiger-Labula *et al.*, *Genève, Saint-Gervais*, p. 115; Martin, 'La restauration du temple de la Madeleine', p. 169; C. Bonnet *et al.*, *Eglise de la Madeleine. Genève* (Geneva, 1992).

[74] Roussel, 'Faire la Cène', p. 108–9.

Henceforth, it was the relation between the pulpit and the benches that structured the area. For all observers, but also for the Genevan reformers themselves, this relationship formed the characteristic feature of the new arrangement of the temples. 'It is just like the interior of a college or school; benches everywhere and a pulpit in the middle for the preacher', noted Antoine Cathelan in the 1550s.[75] Théodore de Bèze, for his part, underlined how faithfully these temples reflected the simplicity of the primitive Church, for these contained 'just a pulpit and lots of chairs and benches'.[76] On communion days, two communion tables, arranged 'close to the pulpit', completed this furnishing.[77] The place of worship was therefore organised as an area of communication oriented towards the centre of gravity represented by the sermon and the Holy Communion.

This spatial arrangement was especially directed towards ensuring the best possible listening conditions for the largest number of participants.[78] The installation of canopies and benches in the form of an amphitheatre served the same purpose. But the answer also lay in enforcing disciplinary surveillance during the divine services in order to impose silence. According to Jean Calvin, the 'correct policy' for ensuring the unimpeded progress of these services included, among other things, 'the silence needed when harkening to the Word'.[79] Regulations for country churches legalising this discipline stipulated that 'during the sermon, everyone shall listen intently and not engage in any dissolute or scandalous behaviour'.[80] In circumstances where silence was difficult to ensure – as witness the repeated complaints of the ministers – the benches were intended to impose upon the faithful an ascesis of listening to what was happening during the service. Constrained to remain motionless and silent, they were placed in that very attitude of obedience and renunciation that the liturgy required of them before participating in the communion: 'Our Lord', it recalled, 'has given us this desire and affection to renounce our own desires, to follow righteousness and his holy commandments.'[81] The whitewashed walls of the temples, as well as the benches, therefore fulfilled a real liturgical purpose: they constituted just so many technical devices for assisting the faithful in an effort to forget themselves in order to ascend towards the divine.

[75] Cathelan, *Passevent Parisien*, fol. 15.
[76] *Le passavant de Theodore de Beze: épître de Maître Benoît Passavant à Messire Pierre Lizet où il lui rend compte de sa mission à Genève et de ses conversations avec les hérétiques* (Paris, 1875), pp. 56–7.
[77] *Registres de la Compagnie des Pasteurs*, I, p. 9.     [78] Reymond, 'Les chaires', 39.
[79] *Institution*, IV, X, 29.     [80] *Registres de la Compagnie des Pasteurs*, I, p. 15.
[81] *Tracts*, pp. 120–1.

The lay-out of the benches in the Genevan temples and the way in which the faithful were distributed also gave meaning to the temple. The deployment 'widthways' did not imply that the pulpit faced the benches, it was on the contrary integrated into the auditorium created by them. They not only faced it but also surrounded it on both sides, and since the pulpit in every temple backed onto a pillar and therefore advanced a little into the nave, some of the benches were actually distributed behind it. Thus the pulpit did not form one side of the devotional area, but its very heart.[82] This arrangement had a liturgical significance as it essentially reflected within the area of worship the divine promise, recalled in the liturgy, according to which Christ would be 'in the midst' of those who assembled to pray for him. Although not holy in itself, the Reformed liturgical scene was laid out in such a way as to convey the belief that during the services the faithful were gathered around a divine spiritual presence.[83]

Within the temple, the faithful enjoyed a relationship of spiritual equality with this 'milieu'. Calvin thus reminds the faithful in one of his sermons 'that concerning our Salvation, and concerning the Holy Kingdom of God, which is spiritual, there is neither distinction nor difference between man and woman, between servant and master, between poor and rich, great and small'.[84] Being at one with Christ, the worshipping congregation represented a local and temporal expression of a Church society that brought together all the disciples of Christ. Here was a highly communal dimension that the temple underlined, for in surrounding the pulpit, the faithful sat facing one another. Their looks not only converged towards the minister, but also encompassed the whole body of this Church of which they formed a part.

At the same time, however, this Church also existed as a social reality, and Calvin did not fail to stress this point. In the same sermon, he continued: 'Nevertheless, if there is to be some degree of order between us . . . A man in his house must instruct his children, and they must be subject to him. The servants must also recognise their degree and condition, and employ themselves in what they are called upon to do.'[85] The

---

[82] This disposition was different from the 'schéma organisationnel type' of the Reformed temples that emerged at the end of the sixteenth century, where the pulpit 'apparaît plutôt comme un élément appartenant thématiquement au côté du quadrangle choral occupé par le bancs des anciens'. In this 'quadrangle', it was the communion tables and the baptismal fonts that constituted the 'centre architectonique de l'édifice et non la chaire'. Reymond, *L'architecture*, pp. 142–7.

[83] According to Lee Palmer Wandel, the Zurich iconography of the communion also suggested the presence of Christ amidst those gathered around the communion table, 'Envisioning God: image and liturgy in Reformation Zurich', *SCJ* 24 (1993), 39.

[84] *Calvini Opera*, XLIX, col. 719.     [85] *Ibid.*

categories and functions that structured this social reality also organised the distribution of the faithful in the temple, and the men were separated from the women, who were seated in the temple with the youngest children. In front of the pulpit, according to Anthoine Cathelan, were 'the lowest benches for the women and young children and higher ones all around to seat the men'.[86] Up to 1545, there was no indication of an order having been introduced in the seats occupied by the men. But the decision taken by the authorities that year to allot reserved seats in Saint-Pierre and Saint-Gervais inaugurated a process in the course of which the same privilege was granted to other persons occupying public offices, as well as to representatives of the Church.[87] By the end of this process, the congregation who were seated in these temples found themselves strictly surrounded. In the apse at Saint-Pierre, for example, the authorities occupied the stalls that rose in tiers above the floor of the former choir; opposite and behind the pulpit were seated the ministers and the elders. In 1542, in addition to these reserved seats, other places were added near the pulpit intended for individuals that the Consistory compelled to attend in order to benefit from the preaching or as a penance for their sins.[88]

This spatial division was partly a response to the supervisory requirements. It enabled the congregation to be placed under the surveillance of the civil and ecclesiastical authorities, whilst conferring on the latter a certain prestige. But it also confronted the assembly with an order presented by the liturgy as divinely ordained. After having recalled the promise that Christ would be found 'in the midst' of those who prayed in his name, the minister first prayed 'for all princes and noblemen . . . and in particular for the nobility of this City'. The prayer specified that God had 'committed [to them] the regulation of [his] justice' in order that 'recognising Jesus Christ in true Faith . . . to be the King of kings, and Lord of lords', they 'shall seek to serve and exalt his Reign'. The authority of the rulers was thus both justified by divine intention, and limited and oriented in a Christian way. The minister then prayed 'for all those that [God had] ordained as Pastors to [his] faithful'. In this case also, he evoked the divine source of their function, its limit and its orientation

---

[86] Cathelan, *Passevent Parisien*, fol. 15.
[87] AEG, R. C. 53, fol. 36; 55, fol. 77v; 63, fol. 27v; 69, fol. 75; 79, fol. 43v; *Registres de la Compagnie des Pasteurs*, VI, p. 14.
[88] *Registres du Consistoire*, I, p. 22; AEG, R. C. 67, fol. 198; 68, fol. 69v; R. C. 72, fol. 113v; Jur. Pen. A, no. 2, fol. 61; PC1ère série no. 1552. See also A. Spicer, '"Accommodating of Thame Selfis to heir the Worde": preaching, pews and Reformed worship in Scotland, 1560–1638', *History* 88 (2003), 411–16.

(God has 'committed [to them] the custody of souls and the dispensation of [his] holy Gospel' in order that they shall 'always [have] this resolve, that all the poor erring and lost sheep shall be recovered and delivered to our Lord Jesus Christ, the Good Shepherd'). Lastly, the minister prayed for 'all mankind in general' and especially mentioned within this common category, 'those whom [God] visits and punishes, by the cross and tribulation'. That is to say, among others, the penitents who had been granted a place near the pulpit, and those who were 'gathered here', that is the congregation of worshippers before whom he was officiating. By addressing to God a particular request for each of these categories, the liturgical prayer was ordering Christian society according to the different 'vocations' of divine origin. And this order could be read by each participant in the service according to the way this society was seated in the temple.

Thus the distribution of the faithful in the temple produced a simultaneous representation of the two levels of reality in which the worshipping congregation was involved: a temporal society divided into social categories, but also a spiritual society, united in a relation of equality with the divine. There was a tense relationship between these two levels. Based on a common belief in Christ and on the charity that arose from this link, the spiritual society in reality constituted the ideal towards which the temporal society must be inclined. The entire process of the liturgy resembled a pledge by the body of worshippers to pursue this ideal. Before taking the communion, the faithful undertook to ponder whether he 'puts his trust in the mercy of God' and whether 'he truly intends and resolves to live in concord and brotherly charity with his neighbours'.[89] In a sermon delivered on a day of Holy Communion, Pierre Viret reminded his congregation that 'when we come to communicate with the Sacraments, we come to commit ourselves publicly in a desire to serve and obey our God'.[90] In this way, the liturgical space enrolled the congregation of worshippers in a process of sanctification.

It can be asserted overall that the Reformed organisation of the Genevan churches closely echoed the liturgical requirements. Both the place of worship and the conduct of the divine services aimed at producing the same effects. In accommodating communication with the divine, they signified that the latter was really present among those assembled for the purpose of worship. Together, therefore, they clearly combined to

---

[89] *Tracts*, p. 120.
[90] C. Schnetzler *et al.*, *Pierre Viret d'après lui-même. Pages extraites des œuvres du Réformateur* (Lausanne, 1911), p. 199.

bring the worshipping congregation into the presence of the holy. In so doing they conveyed a specific perception of this presence, not as a local reality, but as a spiritual and internal reality, to be sought in the faith as well as in the liturgical texts and in the scene that the cult produced. It thus committed the faithful to an effort at elevation and self-renunciation. In this sense, the Reformed temple was less a holy place than a privileged venue for sanctification.

# 5 'What kinde of house a kirk is': conventicles, consecrations and the concept of sacred space in post-Reformation Scotland

*Andrew Spicer*

The introduction of the Scottish Prayer Book in 1637 was the culmination of a series of liturgical measures that changed the religious practices of the Kirk of Scotland during the early seventeenth century. The opposition that the Prayer Book faced meant that it soon became a symbol for the wider discontent towards the crown and its ecclesiastical and religious policies. It gave rise to the National Covenant, which was signed the following year, which condemned Roman Catholic errors, asserted the freedom of the Kirk of Scotland from civil control, defended the traditions of the Reformed Church and rejected the recent religious innovations of the Stuart monarchs. In this attack upon the policies of the Crown, the impact of liturgical change and developments in sacramental theology upon the parish churches of Scotland has been overlooked. For with the changes in religious practice, there also came a fundamental re-evaluation of sacred space and the sanctity of a church, which had by the later 1630s polarised opinion within the Kirk. It is this changing perception of the sanctity of the church in post-Reformation Scotland, which was intimately linked with the liturgical and religious changes of the early seventeenth century that provides the focus for this chapter.

Following his accession to the English throne in 1603, James VI had pursued a policy which sought to establish liturgical uniformity within his three kingdoms, a policy which was also actively pursued by his son Charles I. The Stuart monarchs were not seeking to 'Anglicise' the Scottish Kirk but to bring about a convergence or establish congruity in the patterns of worship of the two Churches.[1] In particular the kings favoured the more ceremonial and reverential form of worship in the English Book of Common Prayer rather than that established by the Book of Common Order, which had been adopted at the Scottish Reformation.

---

[1] J. Morrill, 'A British patriarchy? Ecclesiastical imperialism under the early Stuarts', in A. Fletcher and P. Roberts (eds.) *Religion, Culture and Society in Early Modern Britain* (Cambridge, 1994), pp. 220–1, 231, 233.

Furthermore, while the Book of Common Prayer laid out an established and mandatory form of service, the Book of Common Order, although used in most churches, was not similarly prescribed and allowed wide variations in religious practice.[2] James had demonstrated his support for the Anglican liturgy through the use of the Book of Common Prayer in his Chapel Royal at Holyrood in 1617. Similarly the English service had been used in 1633 at Charles' coronation in Holyrood Abbey and at Sunday worship in St Giles' Kirk in Edinburgh, provoking consternation amongst the Scots. Although James had attempted to encourage the use of the English Prayer Book, it was not until after Charles' visit to Scotland that it came to be used regularly in the Chapels Royal, university chapels and the Scottish cathedrals.[3]

Between 1614 and 1621, James instigated a series of religious reforms in Scotland, including the revision of the liturgy and introducing forms of religious observance and practice which had fallen into disuse at the Reformation.[4] These latter measures culminated in the Five Articles of Perth which were presented to the General Assembly of the Kirk and accepted under duress in 1618. The Articles authorised a rite of confirmation, permitted the private administration of the two Sacraments of baptism and communion, the celebration of holy days – in particular Christmas and Easter – and most controversially that the congregation should kneel to receive communion from the minister rather than being seated at a table as had become the custom in Scotland.[5] The Articles of Perth therefore represented an elevated view of the Sacraments and ceremonial, which was at odds with the established forms of worship in post-Reformation Scotland that focused on the preaching of the Word of God.

The religious policies of James VI were revived by his son Charles and it was during the 1630s that the move towards a more ritualised and sacramental liturgy reached its peak with the Book of Canons issued in 1636 and the Scottish Prayer Book introduced the following year. Although James' programme of reform had been shelved after the Perth Articles, sacramental theology had become increasingly polarised between the views of Patristic Reformed theologians and the Presbyterian divines. It was the views of the former, who viewed the Sacraments as instruments of grace and took an elevated view of the sacramental rites, which

---

[2] D. Calderwood, *The History of the Kirk of Scotland*, 8 vols. (Edinburgh, 1842–9), VII, pp. 246–7; J. Row, *The History of the Kirk of Scotland*, ed. D. Laing (Wodrow Society 4, 1842), p. 362.

[3] G. Donaldson, *The Making of the Scottish Prayer Book of 1637* (Edinburgh, 1954), pp. 39–40, 42–3.

[4] *Ibid.*, p. 31.

[5] On the Perth Articles, see I. B. Cowan, 'The Five Articles of Perth', in D. Shaw (ed.), *Reformation and Revolution* (Edinburgh, 1967), pp. 160–77.

were reflected in the liturgical changes of the 1630s. The development of
this sacramental theology paralleled developments in England which were
expressed liturgically in the ceremonial and ritual of Laudianism.[6] The
canons and the rubrics in the Scottish Prayer Book reflected this sense of
'Laudian piety', particularly with regard to the appearance and furnishings of the church which should be imbued with the 'beauty of holiness'.[7]
The rubrics for the administration of the Lord's Supper, stated that 'The
holy Table, having at the Communion time a carpet and a fair white
cloth upon it, with other decent furniture meet for the high mysteries
there to be celebrated, shall stand at the uppermost part of the Chancel or
Church.'[8] The language of the service emphasised that the communicants
in receiving the bread and wine, were recipients of the Body
and Blood of Christ, which brought with it overtones of some form of
eucharistic sacrifice.[9]

Opponents of the liturgical changes condemned the innovations, one
pamphlet stated that 'In the pretended Communion it hath all the substance and essentiall parts of the Masse, and so brings in the most abom-
inable Idolatrie that ever was in the world.'[10] The attacks of Presbyterian
divines saw the liturgical changes as evidence of the 'English ceremonies
obtruded on the Church of Scotland' and identified the bishops who
introduced them as 'Canterburians' (reflecting the perceived origins of
these ideas) who had sought to introduce a Roman Catholic view of
the sacraments.[11] The Glasgow Assembly in 1638 denounced the Prayer
Book as 'nought bot the Mass in English, brought in by the craft and violence of some two or three of the Bishops against the mind of all the rest,
both Church and Statesmen'. The liturgical practices associated with it
were included in the charges made against the bishops by the Assembly.
John Maxwell, Bishop of Ross was denounced as 'a publick reader in his
house and cathedral of the Englishe liturgie; that he was a bower at the
altar, a wearer of the cope and rotchett', while David Lindsay, Bishop of
Edinburgh was accused of being 'a presser of the late novations, a urger

[6] B. D. Spinks, *Sacraments, Ceremonies and the Stuart Divines. Sacramental Theology and Liturgy in England and Scotland, 1603–1662* (Aldershot, 2002), pp. 88–106.
[7] *Ibid.*, pp. 95–6; P. Lake, 'The Laudian style: order, uniformity and the pursuit of holiness in the 1630s', in K. Fincham (ed.), *The Early Stuart Church, 1603–1642* (Basingstoke, 1993), pp. 164–74.
[8] Donaldson, *Making of the Scottish Prayer Book*, p. 183. See also 'Canons and constitutions ecclesiastical . . . for the government of the Church of Scotland', in *The Works of the Most Reverend Father in God, William Laud D. D*, ed. W. Scott and J. Bliss, 7 vols. (Oxford, 1853), v, p. 600.
[9] Spinks, *Sacraments, Ceremonies and Stuart Divines*, pp. 96–8.
[10] G. Gillespie, *Reasons for Which the Service Booke, Urged Upon Scotland Ought to Bee Refused* (Edinburgh, 1638).
[11] Spinks, *Sacraments, Ceremonies and Stuart Divines*, pp. 98, 102, 105.

of the liturgie . . . a bower to the altar, a wearer of the rotchet . . . an elevator of the elements at consecration'.[12]

The impact of the crown's religious policies has tended to be seen principally in liturgical terms, but this highly sacramental and ceremonial form of worship had an important spatial dimension, which was reflected in the ecclesiastical architecture of the early seventeenth century.[13] In 1617, James had ordered the refurbishment of the royal chapel at Holyrood for his first visit to Scotland since his accession to the English throne. The alterations brought the chapel into line with the English Chapels Royal, and prepared it for the use of the Anglican liturgy during the royal visit. The scheme included the erection of an organ, pews as well as statues of the apostles and evangelists carved by English craftsmen and shipped from London.[14] The religious policies were closely linked by their opponents with the revival of the Scottish episcopate by the king, and so it is perhaps no coincidence that the early seventeenth century saw the restoration of a number of Scottish cathedrals.[15] At the Reformation, only those cathedrals which had also served as parish churches were retained for worship, the remainder were abandoned thereby reconfiguring the sacred topography of the kingdom. The size of those cathedrals which remained often exceeded the liturgical needs of the Reformed parish church and so the buildings were radically altered, by creating an auditory space within part of the building, while other parts of the structure – such as the choir at Aberdeen and Brechin, the nave at Kirkwall – fell into disuse. Following the revival of the episcopate, there was a steady restoration of the cathedrals. A eulogy to Patrick Forbes, Bishop of Aberdeen lauded the fact that:

His first and foremost care, was for the House of God; and especiallie of the Cathedrall Church, where he did reside, aedifying, and repairing the ruines thereof, and furnishing it with ornamentes convenient; and which had lyen waste and desolate since the Reformation.[16]

---

[12] *The Letters and Journals of Robert Baillie*, ed. D. Laing, 3 vols. (Bannatyne Club 73, 1841–2), I, pp. 15–16, 160, 161.

[13] D. Howard, *Scottish Architecture from the Reformation to the Restoration, 1560–1660* (Edinburgh, 1995), pp. 188–94.

[14] *Accounts of the Masters of Works for the Building and Repairing of Royal Palaces and Castles*, ed. J. Imrie and J. G. Dunbar, 2 vols. (Edinburgh, 1957, 1982), I, pp. xxi–xxii, lxxxvi–lxxxvii, 441; P. E. McCullough, *Sermons at Court. Politics and Religion in Elizabethan and Jacobean Preaching* (Cambridge, 1998), p. 29; S. Thurley, 'The Stuart kings, Oliver Cromwell and the Chapel Royal, 1618–1685', *Architectural History* 45 (2002), 240–2.

[15] See A. Spicer, '"Laudianism" in Scotland? St Giles' Cathedral, Edinbugh 1633–39 – A Reappraisal', *Architectural History* 46 (2003), 97–9.

[16] D. Lindsay (ed.), *Funerals of a Right Reverend Father in God. Patrick Forbes of Corse, Bishop of Aberdene* (Aberdeen, 1635), pp. 64–5; A. A. Munro (ed.), *Records of Old Aberdeen* (New Spalding Club 20 1899), p. 54.

This programme of rebuilding included the burgh church of St Giles in Edinburgh, which had been subdivided for secular and religious uses at the Reformation but following its elevation to a cathedral in 1633, the internal walls were removed to re-establish it as a single building. The work on St Giles began firstly with the restoration of the east end of the new cathedral, following a plan of the choir of Durham cathedral.[17] Elsewhere the cathedral-rebuilding programmes similarly focused attention on the east end of the church. At Whithorn, the floor level at the east end was raised at this date to create an altar enclosure, while the work undertaken at Iona concentrated on repairing the choir of the ancient cathedral.[18] Although the evidence is fragmentary, the work undertaken on the cathedral choirs serves to underscore the liturgical measures of the period which emphasised the importance of the Sacrament. The architectural consequences of this religious policy can be seen even more clearly in the private chapel erected by Archbishop John Spottiswoode 'after the decent English form' at Dairsie in Fife.[19] The communion table at the east of the church was separated by 'a glorious partition wall, with a degrie ascending thereto, dividing the bodie of the kirk fra there queir'.[20] By emphasising the importance of the east end, a clear distinction was being made between the choir where the Sacrament was consecrated and the remainder of the church where the congregation gathered.

These architectural developments gave a spatial dimension to the emergence of a more ritualised and ceremonial liturgy in Scotland.[21] Concomitant with these developments in sacramental theology was a change in the perception of sacred space and the holiness of ecclesiastical buildings. The Articles of Perth had imposed the practice of kneeling to receive communion, the Book of Canons and the Prayer Book introduced further measures which emphasised the need for reverence in church and a sense of 'Laudian' piety, which combined to increase the aura of holiness and sanctity appertaining to the worship of God.[22] Although the canons

---

[17] Spicer, '"Laudianism" in Scotland?', 99–102, 104–5.

[18] G. Donaldson and C. A. Ralegh Radford, 'Post-Reformation church at Whithorn', *Proceedings of the Society of Antiquaries of Scotland* 85 (1950–52), 121; Royal Commission for the Ancient and Historical Monuments of Scotland, *Argyll: An Inventory of Monuments*, 7 vols. (Edinburgh, 1971–92), IV, pp. 52, 78, 94, 149.

[19] D. MacGibbon and T. Ross, *The Castellated and Domestic Architecture of Scotland*, 5 vols. (Edinburgh, 1887), V, p. 155.

[20] *Ecclesiastical Records. Selections from the Minutes of the Synod of Fife, MDCXI–MDCLXXXVII*, ed. G. R. Kinloch (Abbotsford Club 8, 1837), pp. 129, 141.

[21] For a broad survey of the spatial impact of Reformation theology, see F. MacDonald, 'Towards a spatial theory of worship: some observations from Presbyterian Scotland', *Social and Cultural Geography* 3 (2002), 61–80.

[22] 'Canons and constitutions ecclesiastical', pp. 596–7, 599–601; Donaldson, *Making of the Scottish Prayer Book*, pp. 183, 184, 189, 195, 200.

only related to behaviour during the service, the reverence and sanctity which the measures inculcated came by extension to apply to the place of worship itself. This wider view of the church as a sacred space was starkly evidenced by the actions of David Lindsay, Bishop of Edinburgh in the face of the protests which greeted the introduction of the Scottish Prayer Book in 1637. The Bishop 'stept into the Pulpit . . . intending to appease the tumult by putting them in minde that the place in which they then were was holy ground, and by intreating them to desist from that fearfull and horrible profanation of it'.[23]

By seeing the cathedral as holy ground which could be profaned, Lindsay reflected a belief in the sanctity of the church which was at odds with the theologies of the Protestant Reformation. The Reformers had rejected the notion that a particular place was more holy than another, and had dismissed the efficacy of sanctifying rites. In his *Institutes of the Christian Religion*, Calvin had argued that places of worship did not by

> any secret sanctity of their own make prayers more holy, or cause them to be heard by God. But they [temples] are intended to receive the congregation of believers more conveniently when they gather to pray, to hear the preaching of the Word, and at the same time to partake of the sacraments . . . But those who suppose that God's ear has been brought closer to them in a temple, or consider their prayer more consecrated in the holiness of the place, are acting in this way according to the stupidity of the Jews and Gentiles. In physically worshipping God, they go against what has been commanded, that, without any consideration of place, we worship God in spirit and in truth.[24]

Calvin went further to denounce the Roman Catholic claims about the sanctity of their churches, by arguing that they were like the Jews and the Temple,

> for the Lord nowhere recognizes any temple save where his Word is heard and scrupulously observed. So although the glory of God sat between the cherubim in the sanctuary, and he promised his people that this would be his abiding seat; when the priests corrupt his worship with wicked superstitions, he moves elsewhere and strips the place of its holiness. If that Temple, which seemed consecrated as God's everlasting abode, could be abandoned by God and become profane, there is no reason why these men should pretend to us that God is so bound to persons and places.[25]

---

[23] [W. Balcanquhal], *A Large Declaration concerning the late tumults in Scotland* (London, 1639), p. 23.

[24] J. Calvin, *Institutes of the Christian Religion: 1536 Edition*, trans. F. L. Battles (Grand Rapids, 1986), p. 73. The wording is slightly different in the later editions of the *Institutes*. J. Calvin, *Institutes of the Christian Religion*, ed. J. T. McNeill, 2 vols. (Philadelphia, 1960), II, p. 893.

[25] Calvin, *Institutes*, II, pp. 1043–4.

A similar view to that of Calvin was taken by Heinrich Bullinger who argued that: 'a church is large and big enough, if it be sufficient to receive all that belong to it; for the place is provided for men, and not for God'. He went on to denounce the Catholic power to consecrate a religious building, arguing that a church is not hallowed or consecrated 'with the rehearsing of certain words, or making of signs and characters, or with oil, or purging fire'.[26]

While the Swiss Reformers denounced the intrinsic holiness of a place, in practice it was much more difficult for the Reformed Church to enforce this understanding of a desacralised place of worship. This was especially true in countries like Scotland where the Kirk had taken over the existing parish churches for Reformed worship. These churches had been purged of the religious imagery, fixtures and trappings associated with the mystery of the mass and sacraments, and the interiors reorganised as an auditory space for the preaching of the Word of God. Other religious buildings had been rendered redundant by the Reformation. The *First Book of Discipline* therefore ordered that 'all monuments and places of the same [idolatry] as Abbeyes, Monkeries, Frieries, Nonries, Chappels, Chanteries, Cathedrall Churches, Chanonries, Colledges, others then presently are parish churches or schooles to be utterly suppressed in all bounds and places of the Realme'.[27] None the less on the ground the Kirk found it much more difficult to overcome the traditional beliefs associated with sacred sites. In some cases, the very location of the parish churches reflected their sacred heritage, particularly where churches had been associated with places of pilgrimage or were sited on remote islands associated with the Celtic saints who had founded them.[28] Even where churches and chapels had been abandoned and deemed idolatrous at the Reformation, the authorities still had to combat the continued perception of these places as holy sites. The kirk session at Elgin had repeated difficulty in preventing members of the congregation from frequenting the ruined cathedral church which had been abandoned at the Reformation in favour of the parish church. In 1615 it ordered 'that nane within this congregatioun hant the Chanonrie kirk to ther prayeris seing the prayeris ar daylie red in this kirk wher the trew word is preitched and the sacramentis celebrat, and therfor that ilk ane keip the publict meittings the tyme

---

[26] H. Bullinger, *The Decades of Henry Bullinger*, ed. T. Harding (Parker Society, Cambridge, 1849–52), IV, p. 499.

[27] *First Book of Discipline*, ed. J. K. Cameron (Edinburgh, 1972), p. 94.

[28] J. Dawson, 'Calvinism and the Gaidhealtachd in Scotland', in A. Pettegree, A. Duke and G. Lewis (eds.), *Calvinism in Europe, 1540–1620* (Cambridge, 1994), p. 243; R. Fawcett, *Scottish Architecture from the Accession of the Stuarts to the Reformation, 1371–1560* (Edinburgh, 1994), pp. 222–4.

of preitching and prayeris and nocht to go to ther avin privat prayeris in the Chanonrie kirk wnder pain of xl s'. In spite of this injunction the kirk session continued to reprimand people who 'haunted' the cathedral ruins and in 1641 was again forced to reiterate its warning against those 'that goes to the Chanrie kirk to there pretendit devotions'.[29] Even when the kirk session was able to ensure attendance at the parish church, it had to contend with the reverent behaviour of some members of the congregation who 'vses the superstitious becking [bowing]' after prayers in the parish church.[30] Beyond the town, the kirk session punished those who went 'to the idolatrous places of the chappell at Speyside' which was associated with a holy well.[31] Other kirk sessions and presbyteries were similarly exercised by those who frequented chapels, holy wells or shrines, in spite of an Act of Parliament in 1581 against 'the dregges of idolatrie yitt remaine in diverse parts of the realme, by using pilgrimages to some chappells, wels, croces, and such other monuments of idolatrie'.[32]

Before the Reformation, the sanctity of a church was seen to provide protection and lend weight to some secular activities carried out under its roof, so that it was common for churches to be used for swearing of oaths, concluding business deals and even for storing money.[33] The belief in the inherent value of agreements made in church continued after 1560, business deals continued to be struck on the site of former altars; St Catherine's altar in the ruins of St Andrews cathedral, for example, continued to be the site for the redemption of debts into the 1570s. Even some kirk sessions seemed to believe that statements made under oath in a church had greater veracity than those made elsewhere.[34] The tradition

---

[29] *The Records of Elgin, 1234–1800*, ed. W. Cramond, 2 vols. (New Spalding Society 27, 1903; 35, 1908), II, pp. 71, 137, 144, 169, 193, 238.

[30] *Ibid.*, II, p. 71.    [31] *Ibid.*, II, pp. 97, 202.

[32] *Selections from the Records of the Kirk Session, Presbytery and Synod of Aberdeen*, ed. J. Stuart (Spalding Club 15, 1846), pp. 110–11; *Stirling Presbytery Records, 1581–1587*, ed. J. Kirk (Scottish History Society, 4th series 17, 1981), pp. xxxiv–xxxv, 4, 115–6, 120, 128, 130, 132–7, 139–40, 144, 147, 149–51, 154–5, 161; *Visitation of the Diocese of Dunblane and Other Churches, 1586–1589*, ed. J. Kirk (Scottish Record Society, new series 11, 1984), pp. 3, 12, 41–2; *Acts and Proceedings of the General Assemblies of the Kirk of Scotland*, ed. T. Thomson (Bannatyne Club/Maitland Club 81, Edinburgh, 1839–45), pp. 462, 721, 1120; *The Acts of the Parliaments of Scotland, 1124–1707*, ed. T. Thomson and C. Innes, 12 vols. (London, 1814–75), III, pp. 212–13. On holy wells see the forthcoming work of Alexandra Walsham and her chapter in this volume.

[33] D. McKay, 'Parish life in Scotland, 1500–1560', in D. McRoberts (ed.), *Essays on the Scottish Reformation, 1513–1625* (Glasgow, 1962), p. 109.

[34] D. McRoberts, 'The glorious house of St Andrew', in D. McRoberts (ed.), *The Medieval Church of St Andrews* (Glasgow, 1976), p. 82; M. Todd, *The Culture of Protestantism in Early Modern Scotland* (London, 2002), p. 332.

of burial within the church (or former religious buildings), despite the repeated attempts by the Kirk to outlaw the custom, was probably one of the clearest expressions of the continued belief in the intrinsic sanctity of a consecrated site.[35]

The continuance of popular beliefs and practices relating to sacred sites was in spite of the attempts made by the Reformed Church to redefine and establish a new understanding of the nature and sanctity of the kirk. The Kirk of Scotland had in the *First Book of Discipline* sought to suppress 'idolatry' so that 'Christ Jesus be truely preached and his holy sacraments rightly ministered'.[36] As preaching was the means by which God communicated with his people, the ministers were the 'servants and ambassadors of the Lord Jesus' and 'whosoever heareth Christ's ministers, heareth himself, and whosoever rejecteth and despiseth their ministry, rejecteth and despiseth Christ Jesus'.[37] Therefore the congregation was in the presence of God when they gathered in church for worship. The Kirk's directions for places of worship reflect a dual concern that they should 'appertaineth to the Magestie of God as unto the ease and commodity of the people'.[38] It gave orders that the parish churches should be repaired and furnished for 'the quiet and commodious receiving of the people' as well as being concerned whether the 'unseemliness of the place' would bring 'the word of God and ministration of the Sacraments' into contempt.[39] For similar reasons the Kirk argued that 'we think it neither seemly that the Kirk appointed to preaching and ministration of the Sacraments shall be made a place of buryall'.[40] The line of argument pursued by the Kirk reflected theological developments on the continent, which defined a church as being made holy through its use rather than possessing an inherent sanctity of its own. Bullinger, whose *Decades* circulated in Scotland, had argued that the temple or church was the place where the Word of God was heard and the Sacraments were administered, but 'the place of itself is nothing holy; but because these holy things are done in that place, in respect that they are done there, the place itself is called holy'.[41] This was later expressed in the second Helvetic

[35] A. Spicer, '"Rest of their bones": fear of death and Reformed burial practices', in W. G. Naphy and P. Roberts (eds.), *Fear in Early Modern Society* (Manchester, 1997), pp. 168–74; A. Spicer, '"Defyle not Christ's kirk with your carrion": burial and the development of burial aisles in post-Reformation Scotland', in B. Gordon and P. Marshall (eds.), *The Place of the Dead. Death and Remembrance in Late Medieval and Early Modern Europe* (Cambridge, 2000), pp. 149–69.

[36] *The First Book of Discipline*, p. 94.

[37] *Ibid.*, p. 102. See T. H. L. Parker, *Calvin's Preaching* (Edinburgh, 1992), pp. 35–47.

[38] *First Book of Discipline*, p. 202.     [39] *Ibid.*, p. 202.     [40] *Ibid.*, p. 201.

[41] Bullinger, *Decades*, IV, p. 500; D. Shaw, 'Zwinglian Influences on the Scottish Reformation', *Records of the Scottish Church History Society* 22 (1986), p. 126.

Confession which was adopted by the Kirk in 1566 and reaffirmed in 1638.[42]

These arguments about the sanctity of a place of worship, that it was made holy through the services performed there rather than due to any inherent sanctity of its own or established by an act of consecration, was reflected in the sermons and writings of several Scottish ministers. Robert Pont defined all things that had been set apart from common use – whether it be man, beast, land, inheritance etc. – and which were intended for religious purposes, as 'most holy unto the lord'. While such 'things dedicate to the holy service of God, for maintenance thereof . . . in their own nature may be counted common and profane, like to others earthly possessions, yet in so far as they are annexed to holy uses, and can not be separate with-out the decay thereof, they may well be called and ought to be repute holy'. Although the sermons were principally concerned with what Pont saw as the sacrilegious appropriation of church property and teinds, the imputation of his arguments also reflected the view that churches through their use for divine worship were holy places.[43]

The question 'what kinde of a house a kirk is' was studied more closely by one minister in the early seventeenth century, William Birnie. Using biblical texts he concluded firstly that it is an 'Architectural delineation of the Lords Passover parlour' which according to Mark's Gospel was described as 'in dimension to be high and large; next in apparel to be comely prepared; and last, for that time at least particularly consecrate to the Passover use'. The kirk was, therefore, the place where the congregation assembled for worship and so should be large enough to hold them. Secondly, it was to be 'fit for contemplation of Gods promised presence there' although this was to be kept within the bounds of Christian simplicity. Finally a kirk must be 'an oratory or house of prayer', and thereby intended solely for the worship of God. Birnie concludes that 'under these three conditions (to wit, of amplitude, ornacy, and unprostituted chastity to any other use . . .) but specially the last, it becomes a Kirk'.[44] Birnie's threefold analysis of what defined a church concentrated on its dedication to the service of God and like his contemporaries did not ascribe to it an inherent sanctity of its own.

A reflection of the changing attitudes towards sacred space can be seen in the observations made by David Lindsay, later Bishop of Edinburgh,

[42] A. Cochrane (ed.), *Reformed Confessions of the Sixteenth Century* (London, 1966), p. 289; *Acts and Proceedings of the General Assemblies*, p. 90.

[43] R. Pont, *Against Sacrilege, Three Sermons Preached by Maister Robert Pont an Aged Pastor in the Kirk of God* (Edinburgh, 1599).

[44] W. Birnie, *The Blame of Kirk-Buriall, Tending to Persvvade Cemiteriall Ciuilitie* (Edinburgh, 1606), ch. 17.

on the nature of places of worship in his treatise defending the Articles of Perth, published in 1625. Scripture, he argued, had stated or implied all that was necessary for worship and salvation, but it did not state the place, time, or manner of worship and so this was the responsibility of the Church. Alongside the marginal heading 'Their power in consecrating places' Lindsay reflected that the Jews had built synagogues 'for their ordinaries meetings on the sabbath to prayer and reading the Law' but the 'Tabernacle and Temple' had been built by God. As man is no longer to worship God on the mountain or in Jerusalem, it is left to the Church to determine what is 'most expedient to be observed and done for the honour of God and edification'. While he recognized the importance of worshipping God in spirit, Lindsay went on:

Let all things be done decently, and in order, to make choice of a place convenient, within the bounds of each Parish, for the meeting of the faithful to perform all the points, and parts of Gods worship: and this place being built, and dedicated to the worship of God may not be condemned, neglected or profaned, but frequented and kept for religious uses. Not that we esteem that there is any more holiness in it, then in another place, or that Gods presence, and so his worship is annexed more to that place then to another, but to the end religious service may be performed decently, and in order, this is done.[45]

Although Lindsay accepted that while it was true that worship was no longer tied to a particular place, he went on to reassert the view that the place of worship was made holy through the services performed within it.[46] None the less, his understanding of the sanctity of a place of worship was subtly different from that put forward by Pont and Birnie that a church is hallowed purely by religious use. Lindsay argued that 'some places were made holy, by annexing to them a peculiar worship instituted by God, which lawfully could not be performed in another place, such were the Tabernacle and the Temple' but 'other places were holy for their use only, being dedicated to the service of God, but they had not the service so appropriated to them, as that it might not be performed in another place, and such were the Jewish synagogues and the Christian churches'.[47] Places were therefore holy 'either by some inherent qualitie of holynesse, or by consecration of them to holy uses'. He pursued this argument further:

---

[45] D. Lindsay, *A Treatise of the Ceremonies of the Church* (London, 1625): 'To the pastors and ministers of the Church of Scotland'.

[46] 'Worship stands in certaine actions, which must bee performed in some convenient place, as Prayers, Supplications, Intercessions, Thanksgivings, and Praises; wheresoever these actions are performed, in these places God must bee worshipped; and if the blessed Sacrament bee an action of that kinde, in it God must bee worshipped, and in the place where it is celebrated', *A Treatise*, p. 96.

[47] *Ibid.*, pp. 17–18.

the consecration of things to holy uses for policie, as for maintayning religion, or for order, and decency to be observed in the worship of God, is not onely God's prerogative, but a priviledge, and liberty granted by him to the Church; for example to build and consecrate places to be Temples.[48]

Lindsay's understanding of sacred space reflects the extent to which attitudes in Scotland had begun to change with the development of more sacramental forms of worship, as well as reflecting the more familiar 'Laudian' piety south of the border. Lindsay's argument that a kirk is 'dedicated to the worship of God' by the Church, is particularly interesting in view of the charges which were later levelled against him.

In practical terms, it was the actions and definitions of sacred space by the kirk sessions which emphasised the sanctity of the church rather than theological debate. In the past, the Catholic Church had issued statutes forbidding 'games or secular courts in sacred places' or for the reconciliation of the church after 'the shedding of blood or of sexual seed'.[49] The authorities after the Reformation, reacted similarly against those who urinated against the church walls or the behaviour of dogs inside the church.[50] The language of the kirk sessions in such instances was similar to that of their medieval predecessors, that those responsible for the offence had defiled or profaned the church. This attitude was clearly reflected in a case relating to Glasgow cathedral which came before the presbytery in 1603. Their minutes recorded

the great and horrible profanation committed and done be some godless and wicked persons within the parish kirk of Glasgow . . . to wit, how that the said persons have taken away three iron stenchoris [bars] of the glasnit door of the said kirk, and entered in the said kirk, and has ruggit away the cloth fixed to the pulpit of green stemmyne and iron that held the basin for the water to baptism; and how shamefully and filthily they did pollute the said kirk be their excrements quhairwith the formes were defiled, that God would revile the said persons in the owen time to underlie their condigne punishment.[51]

The language of the presbytery serves to emphasise the spiritual importance with which the church was imbued, but the actions of the perpetrators are also interesting. Their behaviour was more a desecration of a place of worship, than an act of vandalism, which again has implications

---

[48] *Ibid.*, p. 28.
[49] *Statutes of the Scottish Church, 1225–1559*, ed. D. Patrick (Scottish History Society 54, 1907), pp. 40, 42, 56, 76–7.
[50] Todd, *Culture of Protestantism*, p. 327.
[51] 'Extracts from the Registers of the Presbytery of Glasgow from November 1597 to December 1600', in *Miscellany of the Maitland Club*, ed. J. Dennistoun and A. Macdonald, 2 vols. (Maitland Club 25, 1833–4), I, pp. 401–2.

for understanding the way in which the church was popularly perceived.[52] In a much wider context, the Kirk's attempts to prohibit the interment of the dead inside churches, which had spurred Birnie to publish his pamphlet in 1606, reflected their concern about what was appropriate for a place of worship, regarding the custom as an abuse which defiled or profaned the building.[53] Similar attitudes were reflected in the penalties enacted for the punishment of those who committed bloodshed in kirks or kirkyards, through which parliament believed that 'the houss of the lord and his sanctuary is not fre but filthely pollutit and defylit'.[54]

In the years after the Reformation, the sanctity of the kirk was also reflected in the names assigned to it by the Protestants, such as 'God's house', a 'temple', a 'house of prayer and spiritual exercise'.[55] An equally bold statement is sculpted on the cartouche over the door of the Tron Church in Edinburgh: 'This building the Citizens of Edinburgh have consecrated to Christ and His Church. In the Year 1641.'[56] The bishops, responding to the charges levelled against them by the Glasgow Assembly, recognised that it had gathered 'for the removing of those evils wherewith the Church is infested, and for settling that order which becommeth the house of God'.[57] By 1638, however, the development of a more sacramental and ceremonial liturgy had polarised attitudes within the Kirk towards the sanctity of places of worship. In parts of Scotland, particularly the southwest, the borders and around Edinburgh, ministers and congregations had reacted against these developments and some radicals began to meet for worship in places other than the parish churches. In contrast to those who forsook the churches, the Glasgow Assembly denounced David Lindsay as 'a consecrator of churches' and Adam Bellenden, the Bishop of Aberdeen, for having 'consecrat the chapell of ane infamous woman, the Ladie Wardhous'.[58] The consecration of churches for worship and the apparent abandonment of parochial

---

[52] See N. Z. Davies, 'The rites of violence', in her *Society and Culture in Early Modern France* (Oxford, 1987), pp. 152–87.

[53] See Spicer, 'Rest of their bones', pp. 168–72; Spicer, 'Defyle not Christ's kirk with your carrion', pp. 149–51.

[54] *Acts of the Parliaments of Scotland*, III, p. 544. See M. F. Graham, 'Conflict and scared space in Reformation-era Scotland', *Albion* 33 (2001), 371–87.

[55] Todd, *The Culture of Protestantism*, p. 327.

[56] ÆDEM HANC CHRISTO ET ECCLESIÆ SACRARUNT CIVES EDINBURGHENSI ANNO MDCXLI. J. Gifford, C. McWilliam and D. Walker, *The Buildings of Scotland: Edinburgh* (London, 1984), p. 174. See also J. M. Mackinlay, *Ancient Church Dedications in Scotland* (Edinburgh, 1910), pp. 47–8.

[57] Balcanquhal, *Large Declaration*, pp. 248–9.

[58] Baillie, *Letters and Journals*, I, pp. 160, 161.

worship, represented the two extremes and opposing attitudes towards sacred space in early seventeenth century Scotland.

Although extra-parochial worship may have emerged out of the evangelical preaching of men such as Robert Bruce and John Welsh in the southwest during 1590s, it was the Perth Articles that prompted widespread religious dissent and opposition to the crown's religious policies.[59] While the private administration of the Sacraments provoked discontent, it was a measure which was intended to be used in exceptional circumstances and as part of the Kirk's ministry to the sick, rather than being a revival of private masses as its opponents suggested. The greatest reaction and public unrest was provoked by the injunction to kneel to receive communion, rather than being seated as was the custom in the Kirk of Scotland.[60] The congregation should kneel, it was argued, because 'we are commanded by God Himself that when we come to worship Him, we fall down and kneel before the Lord our Maker; and considering withal that there is no part of divine worship more heavenly and spiritual than is the holy receiving of the blessed body and blood of our Lord and Saviour Jesus Christ'.[61] Kneeling was an appropriate posture in which to reverence God and to receive the elements which symbolised Christ's sacrifice. Opponents of the policy attacked it as being idolatrous and in a petition to parliament, ministers described it as being 'a gesture invented and ordained onlie by Antichrist, more than 1,300 years efter Christ as the principal external worship of their breaden God'.[62]

One of the most vociferous opponents of the Five Articles was David Calderwood whose tract *Perth Assembly* provided a detailed refutation of the practices enjoined upon the Kirk. The arguments he advanced also had implications for the understanding of the sacred nature of a place of worship. In his attack upon kneeling, he argued that:

It is true, likewise, that God directed his people under the Law to bend and bow themselves toward the Ark, and the Temple wherein the Ark was, and the Mountains whereon the Temple was situate: partly least that rude people should turne their worship another way; partly because of his promise to heare them when they should pray towards the Temple, or the Ark; partly because of the singular maner of his presence in the Ark: he was said to dwell between the Cherubines, the Ark is called his foot-stoole and sometime the face and glory of the Lord. It is reason where God is present after an extraordinary maner, as when he first spoke out of the bush, and the cloud, that adoration be directed to the place of his extraordinary presence.

---

[59] L. E. Schmidt, *Holy Fairs. Scottish Communions and American Revivals in the Early Modern Period* (Princeton, NJ, 1989), pp. 22–7.

[60] Cowan, 'The Five Articles of Perth', pp. 66–8, 174–6; *First Book of Discipline*, p. 91.

[61] *Acts of the Parliaments of Scotland*, IV, p. 596.

[62] Calderwood, *History of the Kirk*, VII, p. 480.

Calderwood went on to argue that:

> The Sacramental elements have neither the like presence, the like promise, nor the like commandement. Worship is tyed no longer to any certaine thing or place on earth . . . Adoration is tyed in the new Testament to the manhood of Christ, the true Ark and propitiatory.[63]

The argument that worship is no longer tied to a particular place was made even more explicit in his attack upon the principle of private communion. Calderwood was mainly concerned about the administration of the Sacraments not taking place in public rather than the location of the service. He argued that:

> The Sacraments are not tyed to the materiall Kirkes made of dead stones but the Kirkes made of lively stones. If therefore the congregation bee in a woode, a house, or a Cave, the Sacraments may bee ministred in a house, a woode or a cave. But then the Sacraments are ministred, not in private but in publick because they are ministred in the sight of the whole congregation.[64]

Reflecting some years later on the celebration of communion at the bedside of the sick, Calderwood argued that his opposition was not because he believed that 'the place of it selfe disgraceth the action, but the paucitie of the communicants. If the congregation were assembled in a barne, or any like capacious place through want of a church, the action might be celebrated with no lesse grace.'[65] Calderwood's arguments therefore challenged the perception of a church as a sacred place, and it was in response to these arguments that David Lindsay formulated his statements on the holiness and dedication of churches for worship.

The controversy provoked by the Perth Articles was not merely an intellectual debate amongst the Scottish divines, the measures proved to be difficult to implement and large numbers boycotted services which enforced kneeling. At Easter 1619, a concerted effort was made to enforce kneeling, and in Edinburgh the Chancellor, President and other Lords of the Secret Council and Session conformed albeit 'with the shedding of teares of greefe'.[66] In spite of this attempt to demonstrate official support for the measures, some members of the administration absented themselves from communion, as also did the Provost of Edinburgh who had been recently knighted by Charles I. Opposition was more widespread amongst the citizens of Edinburgh who were reported 'to leave the ports in hundredths and thousands, to the nixt adjacent kirks' where they could

---

[63] [D. Calderwood], *Perth Assembly* (Leiden, 1619), p. 51.    [64] *Ibid.*, p. 97.
[65] [D. Calderwood], *A Re-examination of the Five Articles Enacted at Perth* (no place, 1636), p. 237.
[66] Calderwood, *History of the Kirk*, VII, pp. 359–60.

receive communion 'efter the old form'.[67] In subsequent years, attendance at services where communion was administered in its traditional form, meant the 'auditorie of the kirks of Edinburgh became rare and thinne'.[68]

Although the measure provoked widespread discontent, most dissidents only absented themselves from communion services or attended churches where the measures were not enforced. More radical opponents of the religious policies chose to gather in private conventicles for worship instead. Two Edinburgh merchants, John Mean and William Rig were vociferous opponents of the Articles, and were charged for their absence from communion and subsequently for receiving it from suspended ministers after the old manner. Mean and Rig were seen by the authorities to be the ringleaders in the organisation of private conventicles.[69] They met in private houses and elsewhere 'to heare from intruding ministers, preachings, exhortations, prayers and all sorts of exercises'. It was alleged that those who gathered in these conventicles, called themselves congregations and held their meetings at the same time as the services in the parish church.[70] Through their opposition to kneeling and the formation of conventicles, the Edinburgh dissidents challenged the notion of the parish church as the sole place of worship.

Religious dissent was not confined to Edinburgh, private prayer meetings spread through the southwest of Scotland during the 1620s and 1630s, led by dissident ministers such as Robert Blair and John Livingstone.[71] The evangelical preaching of these ministers led to a religious revival in the region; it was reported that during David Dickson's ministry at Irvine 'few Sabbaths did passe without some evidently converted, and some convincing proofes of the power of God accompanying his word'.[72] Characteristic of this religious revival was preaching outdoors to large crowds and extended services lasting several days. In June 1630, Livingstone preached for several hours to a crowd of five hundred people in the drizzle at a communion service at Shotts. The event has been seen as the precursor of the protester mass communions

[67] *Ibid.*, VII, pp. 359–60; W. McMillan, *The Worship of the Scottish Reformed Church 1550–1638* (London, 1932), pp. 178–82; G. B. Burnet, *The Holy Communion in the Reformed Church of Scotland, 1560–1960* (Edinburgh, 1960), pp. 77–85; P. H. R. MacKay, 'The reception given to the Five Articles of Perth', *Records of the Scottish Church History Society* 19 (1975–77), 185–201.

[68] Calderwood, *History of the Kirk*, VII, p. 458.

[69] D. Stevenson, 'Conventicles in the Kirk, 1619–37. The emergence of a radical party', *Records of the Scottish Church History Society* 18 (1972), 101–3.

[70] Calderwood, *History of the Kirk*, VII, pp. 611–4.

[71] Stevenson, 'Conventicles in the Kirk', 103–8.

[72] R. Fleming, *The Fulfilling of the Scripture, or, An essay shewing the exact accomplishment of the Worde of God* (no place [1669]), p. 143.

of the 1650s, but it was also indicative of the spread of the dissident sacramental meetings during the 1620s and 1630s.[73] Although these radicals
did not completely abandon the kirks, these mass gatherings like the
conventicles represented a radical departure from the idea of the parish
church as the single place dedicated for worship.[74]

This opinion was reflected in the statements made by the radical ministers concerning the place of worship. Robert Bruce, who was present at
Shotts, had argued earlier in *Sermons upon the Sacraments* that Reformed
worship was not tied to a particular place; in criticising the mass he
claimed that it was not necessary for 'the consecration of the place quhere
the Messe is said'.[75] Livingstone writing shortly before his death and, in
the light of events that followed the Glasgow Assembly, commented:

It is true, that none are now Apostles, but Ministers have the same charge, that
Apostles had, to feed the Flock of Christ, and are given primarily not to any
other particular Charge, but to the Universall visible Church: few Apostles or
Apostolicke Men had either such Churches and Pulpits to preach in, or a setled
maintenance . . . he is to remember that the ministrie is his main imployment and
that at his admission he engadged befor God to be diligent and faithful therin.
Some have preached out of prison windowes; some have converted their keepers.
It were to be wished, that a Minister in all places, in all company, at all times,
were about somewhat of his Masters work.[76]

The sentiments expressed by Bruce and Livingstone in part represented
a return to the early days of the Scottish Reformation, where the godly
had gathered in the fields or at mercat crosses to hear the preaching of
men such George Wishart, who himself had expressed the view that the
church was merely a convenient place for the congregation to assemble.
Perhaps ironically it was the clandestine sacramental meetings presided
over by Knox and other ministers in noble or lairdly houses during the
1550s, which were at odds with the view of the early seventeenth-century
radicals. Even at the time such services would have been deemed irregular
by Calvin, but the problem was less to do with the location than whether
a godly congregation of believers had been properly constituted.[77] Interestingly this distinction was reflected in the 1630s by David Dickson

[73] Schmidt, *Holy Fairs*, pp. 21–2, 28–9; Fleming, *Fulfilling of the Scripture*, p. 144.
[74] D. Stevenson, 'The Radical Party in the Kirk, 1637–45', *JEH* 25 (1974), 136–7.
[75] R. Bruce, *Sermons upon the Sacrament of the Lord's Supper* (Edinburgh, 1591).
[76] J. Livingstone, *A Letter Written by that Famous and Faithful Minister of Christ Mr John
Livingstoun unto his Parishioners of Ancram in Scotland* (Rotterdam, 1671), p. 11.
[77] See A. G. Ryrie, 'Congregations, conventicles and the nature of early Scottish Protestantism', *P&P* (forthcoming). I am grateful to Dr Ryrie for the opportunity to read
this paper in advance of publication; M. H. B. Sanderson, *Ayrshire and the Reformation.
People and Change, 1490–1600* (East Linton, 1997), pp. 65–68, 80; Shaw, 'Zwinglian
Influences', 132.

and Alexander Henderson who condemned the practice of private baptism and communion because they were not administered publicly which could lead to them being profaned. The ministers went on to argue that the Sacraments ought to 'be ministred in the ordinarie meetings of God's people' but emphasised that they did not see the Sacraments as being confined 'unto places of materiall kirks, which wee adde, lest any should thinke, that wee entertaine any superstitious conceat of places'.[78]

The private conventicles, outdoor preaching and mass communions of the radical ministers in the southwest brought into question the whole concept of sacred space. In doing so, they not only challenged the prevailing religious policy but also conflicted with the traditions of the Reformed Kirk. In 1561 *The First Book of Discipline* had condemned those who 'minister, as they suppose, the true Sacraments in open Assemblies; and some idiots . . . [that] dare counterfeit in their house, that which the true Ministers doe in open Congregations'. Furthermore the General Assembly in 1581 had ruled against the administration of the Sacraments in private places.[79] The significance of the church as a place of public worship was reasserted in the services of consecration conducted by Bishops Bellenden and Lindsay, which emphasised the sanctity of the church and represented a further development in the highly sacramental theology of the early seventeenth century in Scotland.

To an extent the emergence of services of consecration parallels developments in the other British kingdoms. There are forty-seven known consecrations of churches and chapels in England between 1600 and 1640, twenty of which took place during the 1630s.[80] Furthermore the Synod of Dublin, which met in 1634, ordered that 'As so often churches are newly built, where formerly there were not, or Churchyards appointed for burial, they shall be dedicated and consecrated.'[81] There was considerable variation in the form of service employed by the English bishops, but the language tended to emphasise the significance of the church as the house of God. The liturgy devised by Lancelot Andrewes for the

[78] D. Dickson and A. Henderson, *The Ansvveres of Some Brethren of the Ministerie to the Replyes of the Ministers and Professours of Divinitie in Aberdeene concerning the Late Covenant* (no place, 1638).

[79] *First Book of Discipline*, pp. 204–5; *Acts and Proceedings of the General Assemblies*, pp. 524–5. These were both arguments that had also been used by Calderwood to attack the articles on private baptism and communion, *Perth Assembly*, p. 96.

[80] J. Wickham Legg (ed.), *English Orders for Consecrating Churches in the Seventeenth Century* (London, 1911), pp. 318–23. See A. Spicer, '"God will have a house": defining sacred space and rites of consecration in early seventeenth-century England', in A. Spicer and S. Hamilton (eds.), *Defining the Holy: Sacred Space in Medieval and Early Modern Europe* (forthcoming).

[81] *Constitutions, and canons ecclesiastical, treated upon by the Archbishops and Bishops, and the rest of the clergy of Ireland and agreed upon by the Kings Majesties licence in their synod begun and holden at Dublin, Anno Domini* 1634 (Dublin, 1685), p. 26.

consecration of the Jesus Chapel at Peartree near Southampton in 1620, proved to be the most influential and was employed on a number of occasions, and may have been used by William Laud at the consecration of St Katherine Cree in 1631.[82] This stated that the church was 'an habitacion for thee, and a place for us to assemble and meete together in, for the observacion of thy divine worship, invocation of thy great name, reading, preaching and hearing Thy heavenly Word, administering thy most holy sacraments, above all in this place, the very gate of heaven upon earth'. The liturgy called upon God to accept 'this for thine owne house for ever; and bycause holiness becometh thine house for ever, sanctifie this house with thy glorious presence, which is erected to the honour of thy glorious name' and 'Let thine eye be open towards this house night and day: Let thine eares be readie towards the prayers of thy children, which they shall make to thee in this place; and lett thy heart delight to dwell here perpetually.'[83]

While orders of service survive for the consecration of several English churches and chapels, considerably less is known about the service or instances of consecration in Scotland. Although the circumstances surrounding the two known Scottish consecrations remain rather sketchy, some account of the bishops' actions can be established through the accusations which were levelled against them. Bellenden was criticised for having 'consecrat the chapell of ane infamous woman, the Ladie Wardhous', presumably some time after his translation to Aberdeen in the autumn of 1633.[84] One Thomas Mitchell gave evidence to the Glasgow Assembly

that he was present by accident when he [Bellenden] did consecrate a chapel, the chapel being richly hung, and all the rest of it. The lady came in, and gave him a catalogue of the things that are within, which she had wrought with her own hands, and desired that they might be dedicated to God and so delivered the key to the bishop, who went in and preached a sermon of consecration, and baptized a child, and then went to their feasting. His text was upon Solomon's dedication of the temple.[85]

The chapel was probably erected at Tillyfour in Aberdeenshire, the seat of the Leslies of Wardhouse. Although little of the original castle remains, a rebuilding programme had been undertaken after Sir John Leslie of Wardes had been created a knight baronet of Nova Scotia in 1625. When Leslie died in November 1640, according to the contemporary historian

---

[82] Legg (ed.), *English Orders*, p. 338.
[83] *Ibid.*, p. 57; *The form of consecration of a church or chappel. And of the place of Christian buriall. Exemplified by the R. R. F. in God Lancelot late Lord-Bishop of Winchester, in the consecration of the chappel of Jesus in the foresaid dioceses* (London, 1659), pp. 25–7.
[84] Baillie, *Letters and Journals*, I, p. 161.
[85] *Records of the Kirk of Scotland containing the Acts and Proceedings of the General Assemblies*, ed. A. Peterkin (Edinburgh, 1838), p. 171.

John Spalding he 'was buried in his own chapel at Tillyfour, where never Laird of Wardis was buried before, and himself being the last Laird of Wardis was first buried there'.[86] Leslie's wife, Elizabeth Gordon, was the daughter of John Gordon of Newton, a Roman Catholic who had steadfastly refused to conform to the Reformed faith. Leslie and his wife had both been summoned to appear before the presbytery of Aberdeen in 1601 for their failure to receive the Lord's Supper. Their repeated evasion and unwillingness to conform led to them being excommunicated by the presbytery.[87] The bishop's consecration of the chapel is perhaps surprising but suggests that the family might have come to accept the sacramental forms of worship being pursued by the crown.

The charges made against Bishop David Lindsay relate to the newly built church of South Queensferry; George Dundas reported to the Glasgow Assembly that he 'saw him dedicat a kirk after the popishe maner'.[88] The burgh of South Queensferry lay within the parish of Dalmeny, but the corporation sought the convenience of their own place of worship within the town and, with the approval of the commissioners and the bishop, a new parish was subsequently formed.[89] A 'goodly and commodious kirk' was 'well erectit' within the burgh of South Queensferry and was consecrated by Lindsay on 13 August 1635. A unique but damaged account of the service is given in the kirk session records:

Mr David Lindsay, second bishop of Edinburgh came to the above named town of Queensferry for the consecration of the newly erected church there. And for admitting Mr Robert Gib[son] Minister thereof being the first man that was presented to that place. After the said Mr David his entry in the town he went up the way towards the doors of the kirk which were then locked. There met him Robert Daulling and Robert Hill. Then present baillies . . . accompanied with all honest men of the town. The said Mr [David Lindsay] demanding the baillies(?) and the rest of the company to what end they had built that house. They replied only to the glory [of God] and for his worship and in token thereof They did render [to him the key]. This being done and doors made open the said bishop [went to?] . . . the pulpit and thereafter prayer consecrated and following . . . made choice of his text forth of set forth [sic] to the consecration of the house and next the promiss . . . said Mr Robert. Sermone being ended, two children were baptized . . . after the said Mr David bishop descended to . . . before the

---

[86] Royal Commission for the Ancient and Historical Monuments of Scotland, Canmore Database, NMRS Number: NJ61NE 7.00, NJ61SE 21; J. Spalding, *Memorialls of the Trubles in Scotland and in England, AD 1624–AD 1645*, 2 vols. (Spalding Club 21, 23, 1850–51), I, p. 357; Colonel Leslie, *Historical Records of the Family of Leslie from 1067 to 1868–9*, 3 vols. (Edinburgh, 1869), III, pp. 285–90.

[87] National Archives of Scotland (hereater NAS), CH2/1/1 (unfoliated); *The House of Gordon*, ed. J. M. Bulloch, *et al.* 3 vols. (New Spalding Club 26, 33, 39, 1903, 1907, 1912), III, pp. 289–90.

[88] *Records of the Kirk*, p. 170.     [89] NAS, GD75/719.

Plate 5.1 South Queensferry, Old Parish Church. (Crown Copyright: Royal Commission on the Ancient and Historical Monuments of Scotland.)

pulpit there he did demand forth of the books of orders such and such questions as concerned the admission of the said Mr Robert Gibson. Which finished he received the imposition of hands. Last of all the Sacrament of the Lord's Supper was celebrated . . . ended and psalms sung the Company then there convened for [the] said work was dismissed.[90]

The partial accounts of these consecrations indicate some striking similarities in the ways the services were conducted and in both cases they hark back to the rituals of the pre-Reformation Church. In both cases the bishops entered a building which had been locked, in being handed the key the owner or founder symbolically surrendered the building to the Church before it could be consecrated for public worship. The celebration of the mass was central to the medieval rite of consecration, but only at South Queensferry does it seem that the Lord's Supper was administered although in both churches the Sacrament of baptism was

---

[90] NAS, CH2/689/1, fol. 1. The spelling has been modernised and contractions extended in this transcription.

performed.[91] The rituals as far as can be discerned also have striking parallels with those used south of the border. In particular the bishops seem to have consecrated various church furnishings, such as the pulpit at South Queensferry or those in the list given to Bellenden at Tillyfour. The perambulation of the church building, blessing the pieces of furniture or particular places in the church, was not part of the medieval ritual but dated from the liturgy devised by Lancelot Andrewes.[92] While it was not unusual to include a baptism as part of the service of consecration, an ordination was exceptional but not without precedent. The consecration of the chapel at Peterhouse, Cambridge, in 1633 by the Bishop of Ely at the instigation of the master of the college, Matthew Wren, included communion, baptism and ordination.[93] The details about the rituals employed by Bellenden and Lindsay are too fragmentary for any firm conclusions to be reached about the orders of service that they used, but none the less there was a striking similarity with the Anglican liturgies of consecration.

The emergence of rituals of consecration during the 1630s, reflected the extent to which attitudes towards sacred space had evolved by the early seventeenth century. The definition and understanding of sacred space in post-Reformation Scotland had been contradictory; the Kirk attempted to deny the sanctity of a particular church and site, deeming such beliefs to be superstitious or idolatrous, but simultaneously strove to ensure that church buildings were dedicated solely for religious purposes and treated accordingly. This apparent contradiction reflected the emergence within Reformed theology of the concept that a church was sanctified by its use rather than through the rites of man or some inherent sanctity of its own. The religious policies of the early seventeenth century prompted a rethinking of what was meant by sacred space, and served to polarise attitudes within the Church. The development of a highly sacramental theology and liturgy, was reflected in the greater reverence expected during religious services. To a degree, the thought of some Scottish divines paralleled the culture of Laudianism south of the border, which saw a church as being the place where God's presence on earth was more intense, literally the house of God. The furnishings, decoration and ornamentation of the building should ensure that the building glowed with 'the beauty of holiness'.[94] The restoration of the Scottish cathedrals and construction of chapels such as Dairsie reflected this reappraisal of religious buildings. While the highly sacramental theology of the Scottish divines drew upon Patristic scholarship, the consecration of churches was a return to

---

[91] Legg (ed.), *English Orders*, pp. xxi–xxix.     [92] *Ibid.*, p. xxxii.
[93] *Ibid.*, pp. xxxiii, 128, 349.     [94] Lake, 'The Laudian Style', pp. 164–5.

the traditions established in the Early Church. This perception of sacred space was markedly at odds with the views of the radical Presbyterians, who not only opposed the implementation of the crown's religious policies but began to meet outside the kirk in private conventicles or open-air assemblies. In so doing, the radicals not only rejected the parish church as the place for worship but also challenged the contradictions in the Kirk's interpretation of sacred space.

## 6    Psalms, groans and dogwhippers: the soundscape of worship in the English parish church, 1547–1642

### John Craig

Did sacred space exist in Protestant England and did it exist for Protestants? A primary concern of English Protestantism was to rid particular people, places and things of sanctity and sacred power. The priesthood of all believers and the abolition of shrines, pilgrimages and relics transformed the holy. The parish church was stripped of its altars, images, and ornaments. Walls were whitewashed, stained glass imagery gave way to clear panes, rood screens were dismantled, images of saints were blotted out or defaced and parish clergy were even told to take home what remained of the consecrated bread for their own use. Yet the church itself remained a consecrated building with a consecrated churchyard with worship services led by an ordained clergyman whose words were invested with new power as learned, godly preaching was proclaimed the chief means of salvation. The focus on the word is a reminder that sacred space encompassed more than the visible or the tangible; there was an important aural or acoustic dimension, little studied by historians. How did the changing soundscape of worship affect early modern conceptions of the sacred? If sacred space existed for English Protestants, it was found pre-eminently in the place and sounds of worship, as the word was preached, the Sacraments administered, prayers prayed and psalms were sung. Through these actions, sacred space came to be articulated not merely in visible and tangible ways but through the very sounds of worship. Perhaps because, both prior to the Reformation and long afterwards, the requirement for parishioners to participate in weekly worship was so constant and unremarkable helps to explain why the character of weekly services has been so little explored by social and ecclesiastical historians. Here is a subject which has been much debated and analysed from the perspective of liturgical change and official formularies, but we

I wish to thank Richard Boyer, Patrick Collinson, Robert Goheen, Beat Kümin, Joy Parr and Alexandra Walsham for their comments on an early draft of this chapter from which I greatly profited. I would also like to thank the audiences in Warwick, Cambridge, San Antonio and York for their interest and response.

know relatively little about the sounds of worship, how those sounds were shaped and controlled by the people, or the extent to which they defined sacred space.[1]

There were any number of sounds in an Elizabethan parish service, from the expected voices of minister, parish clerk and congregation, the ringing of church bells, in some parishes the music of an organ or the chanting of the litany, to the less looked for elements of feet shuffling, people talking, snoring, walking, pew doors banging and dogs barking. Voices, sounds, noises – all of these were controlled by the church, or better, the Elizabethan and Jacobean church *sought* to control the varied sounds of parish worship, to distinguish between the acceptable and unacceptable, the reverent and the disturbing. Within the relationship between ecclesiastical authority and local practice, this chapter looks briefly at three aspects of the sounds of worship: the singing of metrical psalms, the spontaneous or studied exclamations of sighs and groans and the presence and noise of dogs.[2]

## I    Psalms and psalm singing

The churchwardens' accounts of a number of London parishes in the sixteenth century record that many parishes, first in the late 1540s and again, or for the first time in the early 1560s, purchased psalters, song books, psalm books and occasionally ballads. The parish of St Botolph Aldersgate in 1560 bought 'v songe bokes' for 20 pence and five psalm books for

---

[1] H. Davies, *Worship and Theology in England from Cranmer to Hooker, 1534–1603* (Princeton, 1970); H. Davies, *Worship and Theology in England from Andrewes to Baxter, 1603–1690* (Princeton, 1975); H. Davies (ed.), *The Godly Kingdom of Tudor England, Great Books of the English Reformation* (Wilton, Conn., 1981); F. Proctor and W. H. Frere, *A New History of the Book of Common Prayer* (London, 1911); F. E. Brightman, *The English Rite* (London, 1914); H. Gee, *The Elizabethan Prayer Book and Ornaments* (London, 1902). Considerations of space preclude a full discussion of the term soundscape and of the ways in which historians have sought to approach past sounds. The following works have proved particularly helpful: P. Burke, 'Notes for a social history of silence in early modern Europe', in *The Art of Conversation* (Cambridge, 1993), pp. 123–41; J. Parr, 'Notes for a more sensuous history of twentieth-century Canada: the timely, the tacit and the material body', *The Canadian Historical Review* 82 (2001), 720–45; B. Smith, *The Acoustic World of Early Modern England* (Chicago, 1999); B. Truax, *Acoustic Communication* (Norwood, NJ, 1984). Discussions with Elizabeth Clogg, doctoral student at Simon Fraser University currently working on 'The organ and religious change in early modern England', have proved most helpful.

[2] These three aspects have been chosen partly because they emerge from an examination of various sets of parish accounts and partly because they interest me. They do not constitute a full examination of the sounds of, and at, worship which might well include the sounds produced by the weather, or of moving the communion table or of birds trapped in the building, a point I owe to Beat Kümin.

5 shillings.[3] In the same year, the parish of St Stephen Walbrook bought 'a service book with the psalter and the homilies', another psalter and two psalm books, while the parish of St Mary Woolnoth spent 16 pence for 'ii psalme bookes in myter for the churche'.[4] According to an inventory of 1567, the parish of St Margaret Pattens possessed among other books, 'a psalter bocke in prose, 3 in myter' and 'i other boke wherin is contaynyd the psalmus in prose and also in myter with homilies'.[5] Between 1547 and 1570, various London parishes purchased 'six bokes of david salter for the church use in englysh', 'iiii salme books of Awstyne', 'v Jenova bokes', 'vi balletes of the pater noster and the tenn commaundementes', 'two psalters and two books of Jeneva psalms' and such examples might easily be multiplied.[6]

These London parishes were taking the initiative to provide for and equip the parish congregation in the singing of metrical psalms. In general, churchwardens' accounts distinguish the prose psalter with the terms 'psalter', or 'one psalm book in prose', which meant the psalms that were read aloud or chanted by the minister and parish clerk, from the metrical versions of the psalms, which were referred to as 'psalm books', 'psalm books in meter', 'Jeneva psalms', or even '2 psalm books covered with black and clasps to them contayning the singing psalms'.[7]

At first, these purchases sat uneasily with the authorities. The Elizabethan injunctions of 1559 tolerated congregational singing without explicitly enjoining it or making it an integral part of the service. The relevant injunction read:

And that there be a modest and distinct song, so used in all parts of the common prayers in the church, that the same may be as plainly understood, as if it were read without singing. And yet, nevertheless, for the comforting of such that delight in music, it may be permitted, that in the beginning, or in the end of common prayers, either at morning or evening, there may be sung an hymn, or such like song, to the praise of Almighty God, in the best sort of melody and music that may be conveniently devised, having respect that the sentence of the hymn may be understanded and perceived.[8]

Congregations exceeded this permission and incorporated metrical psalms, not just one but several, and sung by the whole congregation,

[3] Guildhall Library London (hereafter GL) MS 1454/65.
[4] GL MS 593/2, fol. 44r and MS 1002/1A, fol. 96r.    [5] GL MS 4570/2, p. 452.
[6] GL MS 2596/1, fol. 98v (St Mary Magdalen Milk Street); MS 4570/2, pp. 3–4, 12 (St Margaret Pattens); MS 42411/1, p. 69 (St Ethelburga the Virgin Bishopsgate).
[7] GL MS 4956/2, fol. 132v; MS 2596/1, fol. 124r; MS 1002/1A, fol. 96r; MS 4409/1, fol. 5v.
[8] W. H. Frere and W. M. Kennedy (eds.), *Visitation Articles and Injunctions of the Period of the Reformation*, 3 vols. (London, 1910), III, p. 23.

both morning and evening, in their weekly services. Where the crown granted permission for one hymn or song, congregations interpreted this more generously. Indeed metrical psalmody so eclipsed parish choirs that by 1580, both organs and choirs were virtually non-existent in the parish church.[9] Psalms were sung generally before and after sermons as William Harrison in his description of parish worship makes clear.[10] Despite the opposition from some bishops such as Thomas Bickley of Chichester who in 1586 was asking with obvious disapproval whether or not ministers 'endeavour to have the parishioners say service and sing psalms in prose and metre with them in Church', it is clear that by the mid-1570s, the Church no longer opposed popular practice. In a series of occasional services, such as the Accession Day service and the services ordered following the earthquake of 1580, the Church incorporated and enjoined the singing of specific metrical psalms.[11]

Participation in singing must have been limited to those who had committed the psalms to memory or who were literate enough to read from a psalm book, but by the 1630s, some parishes were making a further concession to popular singing in the practice of lining-out. In 1636, Matthew Wren, Bishop of Norwich, wanted to know

if any psalms be used to be sung in your church, before or after the sermons (upon which occasion only, they are to be allowed to be sung in churches) is it done according to that grave manner (which first was in use) that such doe sing as can reade the psalmes, or have learned them by heart, and not after that uncough and undecent custome of late taken up, to have every line first read and then sung by the people?[12]

Was this practice of lining-out a clerical concession to popular illiteracy and lay desire for all to sing, or a clerical initiative to ensure maximum participation? However interpreted, it speaks of a desire, whether clerical or lay, for greater participation in psalm singing.

---

[9] N. Temperley, *The Music of the English Parish Church* (Cambridge, 1979), pp. 39–76; B. Kümin, 'Masses, morris and metrical psalms: music in the English parish, *c.* 1400–1600', in F. Kisby (ed.), *Music and Musicians in Renaissance Cities and Towns* (Cambridge, 2001), pp. 70–81. The parish of Ludlow was a notable exception: A. Smith, 'Elizabethan church music at Ludlow', *Music and Letters* 49 (1968), 108–21.

[10] W. Harrison, *The Description of England*, ed. G. Edelen (Ithaca, 1968), p. 34.

[11] W. P. M. Kennedy (ed.), *Elizabethan Episcopal Administration* (London, 1924), III, pp. 214–15. W. K. Clay (ed.), *Liturgies and Occasional Forms of Prayer set forth in the reign of Queen Elizabeth* (Cambridge, 1847); Temperley, *Music of the English Parish Church*, pp. 46–8.

[12] K. Fincham (ed.), *Visitation Articles and Injunctions of the Early Stuart Church*, 2 vols. (Woodbridge, 1998), II, pp. 148–9.

Here is an underrated and underexplored aspect of the spread, internalisation and popularity of Protestant practice – a tale which owes something to clerical aspirations and courtly verse, the efforts of Thomas Sternhold and John Hopkins and the experience of the Marian exiles – but even more to the popular public response to these rhyming verses set to common and popular tunes. It would be hard to underestimate the popularity of singing metrical psalms and as difficult to estimate the influence these verses had upon popular Protestantism at the parish level.[13]

But why did metrical psalm singing prove so popular? That it did so is incontestable as any survey of churchwardens' accounts will demonstrate; parishes throughout England purchased psalm books for parish use. Bishop Jewel, famously in 1560, wrote to Peter Martyr of the impact of congregational singing saying that the

people are everywhere exceedingly inclined to the better part. Church music for the people has very much conduced to this. For as soon as they had once commenced singing publicly in only one little church in London, immediately not only the churches in the neighbourhood, but even distant towns, began to vie with one another in the same practice. You may now sometimes see at Paul's Cross, after the service, six thousand persons, old and young, of both sexes, all singing together and praising God.[14]

Nicholas Temperley has argued that psalm singing became popular simply because people loved to sing. The tunes were popular and the verse form was simple.[15] But perhaps part of the delight lay in the very sound itself. Produced by 100, 200, or 500 (even Jewel's 6,000!) male and female voices singing in unison or in parts and in the vernacular, this was a powerful, public experience, producing a sound that only the louder sounds of the acoustic landscape of early modern England – thunderclaps, cannon blasts and bells – could beat.[16]

---

[13] R. Zim, *English Metrical Psalms: Poetry as Praise and Prayer 1535–1601* (Cambridge, 1987); Temperley, *Music of the English Parish Church*, pp. 7–76; H. Davies, *The Worship of the English Puritans* (Glasgow, 1948), pp. 162–81. See also the discussion of the emergence of the Bay Psalm Book of 1640 in T. D. Bozeman, *To Live Ancient Lives* (Chapel Hill and London, 1988), pp. 139–50.

[14] J. Ayre (ed.), *The Works of John Jewel*, 4 vols. (Cambridge, 1845–50), IV, pp. 1230–1.

[15] Temperley, *Music of the English Parish Church*, p. 46. See also I. Green, '"All people that on earth do dwell, Sing to the Lord with cheerful voice": Protestantism and music in early modern England', in S. Ditchfield (ed.), *Christianity and Community in the West, Essays for John Bossy* (Aldershot, 2001), pp. 148–64.

[16] The inclusion of female voices is often commented upon. In 1616, Thomas Harrab, a Catholic controversialist, observed of psalm singing in England, 'here all sing, boyes, wenches, woemen and all sorts'. T. Harrab, *Tessaradelphus, or the foure Brothers* (London, 1616), sig. E3v. I owe this reference to Arnold Hunt. Cf. Temperley, *Music of the English Parish Church*, p. 43; Smith, *The Acoustic World of Early Modern England*, pp. 49–95.

## II     Groaning in prayer

Where psalm singing was primarily a collective activity performed in public, groaning in prayer was primarily the activity of individuals and of private piety. The context for these groans was prayer, both public and private and the fact that the Reformers taught that true prayer was spirit-led.[17] Martin Bucer's first point about prayer was that 'we pray in the Spirit' and Jean Calvin contrasted those who 'do mumble up prayers without any musing of the mind on them' with the godly 'who must take heed that they never come into the sight of God to ask anything but because they do both boil with earnest affection of the heart, and do therewithal desire to obtain it of him'.[18] William Tyndale, a little earlier had stressed the affective and spirit-led aspects of prayer: 'Prayer is a mourning, a longing and a desire of the spirit to God ward, for that which she lacketh: as a sick man mourneth and sorroweth in his heart'.[19] These men were not saying that praying with forms or prayer books inevitably quenched the spirit, but in stressing the spirit-led nature of true prayer, the Reformers made the nature of true prayer central to their understanding of Reformed worship. Thus George Foxley in his 1639 analysis of prayer, *The Groanes of the Spirit or the Triall of the Truth of Prayer* 'endeavoured to cleare by proper and distinct notes the true being of Prayer from all Semblances of prayer'. Foxley argued that 'Prayer is not a naturall acquired ability . . . it consisteth not in words, though they be ornat, or well set forth with seeming holynesse, but in powring out of the heart by sighes and groanes inexpressible'.[20] Inexpressible perhaps but also 'unpressible' as Foxley continued to elucidate:

By these unpressible grones is meant the vehemency or fervency of Prayer, being the work of the spirit, which worketh after an unspeakable manner in the hearts of all that pray: this is that wrestling that prevaileth with God: this is that which

---

[17] See G. F. Nuttall, *The Holy Spirit in Puritan Faith and Experience* (Oxford, 1946), pp. 62–74; Davies, *Worship of the English Puritans*, pp. 98–114 and the useful survey by R. Williams, 'Lessons from the prayer habits of the Puritans', in D. A. Carson (ed.), *Teach us to Pray* (Exeter, 1990), pp. 272–85. The subject of prayer in early modern England is both immense and largely neglected. But see J. Maltby, *Prayer Book and People in Elizabethan and Early Stuart England* (Cambridge, 1988); S. Arnoult, '"Spiritual and sacred publique actions", the Book of Common Prayer and the understanding of worship in the Elizabethan and Jacobean Church of England', in E. J. Carlson (ed.), *Religion and the English People 1500–1640, New Voices, New Perspectives*. Sixteenth Century Essays and Studies 45 (Kirksville, Mo., 1988), pp. 25–47.

[18] Cited in G. Rupp, 'Protestant Spirituality in the First Age of the Reformation', in G. J. Cuming and D. Baker (eds.), *Popular Belief and Practice* (Cambridge, 1972), p. 161.

[19] H. Walter (ed.), *Doctrinal Treatises and Introductions to Different Portions of the Holy Scriptures by William Tyndale* (Cambridge, 1848), p. 93.

[20] G. Foxley, *The Groanes of the Spirit or the Triall of the Truth of Prayer* (Oxford, 1639), 'To the reader', pp. 7–8.

stirreth up a man to lay hold on God; this is that which layeth violent hold on him whom the soule loveth; this was the practice of our Saviour Christ, who in the daies of his flesh offered up prayers and supplications with strong cryes and teares.[21]

Although the godly were more than conscious of the 'darkness of their understanding, the weakness of their memories, the perverseness of their wills, the deadness of their affections' and the way in which they were troubled with idle thoughts in prayer, Foxley encouraged his readers to consider the means of attaining the sense of the Spirit in prayer through a mixture of spiritual exercises and practical advice. It is in this context that he speaks briefly of 'a habit of holy ejaculations' which he described as 'holy breathings' which like 'ayre, keepe and cleare the fire upon the hearth, whereby sense is kindled, when thou settest upon the worke'.[22]

Prayer, in this light, takes on a more dynamic and more audible aspect than historians perhaps have tended to consider. It would appear that early modern English piety among the godly in particular, took to heart Christ's example of praying with 'strong cryes and teares' and the scriptural promise that the 'Spirit itself maketh intercession for us with groanings, which cannot be uttered' and developed a manner of praying that both sought to attain a sense of the spirit and that displayed the presence of the spirit in fervency and sincerity. Praying with groans was possibly a widespread practice.[23] Simeon Foxe related how his father, the famous martyrologist John, often prayed with audible groans.[24] When the godly Suffolk gentlemen, Sir Robert Jermyn and Sir John Higham, rejected the slander that they were Puritans, it was with the claim that they were those who knew what it was to 'groan over their sins'.[25] And the prayer meetings held in the small market town of Mildenhall, Suffolk, in the summer months of 1584 by the zealous Thomas Settle, were said to be so loud that 'the noise might be hard to the furtherside of the streate'.[26] All of which suggests that in some circles of parish worship, perhaps especially where the godly were in control, the experience of worship might be considerably more noisy, or more interactive, than has been associated with the service defined by the crown.

---

[21] *Ibid.*, p. 34.    [22] *Ibid.*, pp. 22, 177.

[23] The key text is Romans 8: 26. The Geneva Bible has 'maketh request for us with sighs, which cannot be expressed'. See also Hebrews 5: 7.

[24] He speaks of the 'vehement groans he mingled with his prayers, being heard by some that were neer the place'. *The Second Volume of the Ecclesiasticall History: Containing the Acts and Monuments of Martyrs* (London, 1641), sig. B2. I owe this reference to Thomas Freeman.

[25] BL, Lansdowne MS 33, no. 67.

[26] Lambeth Palace Library, Carta Misc., XII, 19, fol. 2r.

But where psalm singing appears to have been genuinely popular, eclipsing the musical alternatives of choirs and organs, groans proved a more contentious matter. There was a fine line between the sounds of the godly and the sounds of the demented. Not all groaning was evidence of the spirit's leading. How might one distinguish the involuntary groan from the voluntary simulation, the performative fake? Job Throkmorton was convinced that the prayers of William Hacket, the pseudo-messiah of 1591, so peppered with 'groanings and murmurings', were sure proof of his insanity.[27] And in 1556, the Marian martyr, John Careless, wrote disparagingly to Thomas Jackson, a fellow prisoner but Free-willer, of the active and noisy way in which the Free-willers sought to pray in the spirit using such 'hoppinge and dauncinge and wreastlynge with themselves, such howelinge and cryeng' as Careless had never seen 'emongest men that weare well in theyre witt', practices which he likened to the priests of Baal on Mount Carmel.[28]

Satirists of the godly were quick to pick out the sound of fervent prayer as marks for their scorn. The best known of these comes from the poison pen of Richard Bancroft who in setting down the 'plattforme of a precisians Sermon' satirised both the sermon and its 'acceptacion'. The preacher's long and extempore prayer 'ended with an applaudite', and a similar response concludes the sermon, 'which beinge ended the chief gentlemen in the place beginning with a groaning, but yet with a loud voice, crieth most religiously Amen. And then the whole companye of that sect followe, Amen, Amen.'[29] Bancroft was describing services he had attended in one of the parish churches in Bury St Edmunds in the early 1580s. Fifty years later, another observer of those same services would speak of how the sermon was punctuated by 'the weomens sighes and the mens hauchins [hawkings]'.[30]

There is some evidence from the 1620s that preachers sought to restrain some of these sounds. In 1629, Arthur Lake stressed that 'retirednesse is most fit for passionate and affectionate Prayers' and that 'many things may beseeme us in private, which in publicke are not fit; the teares of the eyes, the sobs of our tongues, the beating of our breasts; the interruptions of our affections, the prostration of our persons, the villifying of our-selves, expostulations with God, and such like', which 'modesty will stifle in

---

[27] A. Walsham, '"Frantick Hacket": prophecy, sorcery, insanity, and the Elizabethan puritan movement', *Historical Journal* 41 (1998), 37. I owe this reference to Alexandra Walsham.

[28] BL, Additional MS 19,400, fol. 62v. I owe this reference to Thomas Freeman.

[29] A. Peel (ed.), *Tracts Ascribed to Richard Bancroft* (Cambridge, 1953), pp. 71–2.

[30] Cited in P. Collinson, 'Lectures by combination: structures and characteristics of church life in 17th-century England', *Bulletin of the Institute of Historical Research* 48 (1975), p. 208.

company'.[31] And a few years earlier, Daniel Featley constrasted public and private devotion, observing that 'the afflicted soule, which sometimes stealeth a groane, and fetcheth a sigh in the Church, offers up often prayers with strong cries at home . . . Publike makes more noise but private (for the most part) hath a deeper channell.'[32]

These examples push us to consider not only the participatory nature of prayer but also the way in which men and women listened to sermons. John Donne, in an undated sermon preached at St Paul's, spoke of how listeners in the early Church were far from passive:

> all that had been formerly used in Theaters, *Acclamations* and *Plaudites*, was brought into the *Church*, and not onely the vulgar people, but learned hearers were as loud, and as profuse in those declarations, those vocall acclamations, and those plaudites in the passages, and transitions, in Sermons, as ever they had been at the Stage, or other recitations *of their Poets or Orators.*[33]

Donne pointed out that the same custom had been observed in other places 'where the People doe yet answer the Preacher, if his questions be applyable to them, and may induce an answer, with these vocall acclamations, "Sir we will, sir we will not"', a practice which was not far from his experience with English audiences who made 'those often periodicall murmurings and noises . . . when the Preacher concludeth any point'. Donne complained about the time lost to these 'impertinent Interjections' and that 'many that were not within distance of hearing the Sermon will give censure upon it according to the frequencie or paucities of these acclamations'.[34] There is more to explore here – evidence that people wept, groaned, or urged the preacher on in his discourse – and as the literature on sermons in early modern England grows apace, so too do we need to attend to the way in which people listened, how they heard and how they responded.[35] Rather than groups of sober and reverent men, women and children listening with a kind of hushed awe, should we rather be thinking of participatory, audible and emotional responses not far removed from the later tent meetings or of the interactive models of

---

[31] Arthur Lake, *Sermons* (London, 1629), sig. 3M5r. I owe this reference to Arnold Hunt.

[32] Daniel Featley, *Ancilla Pietatis* (London, 1626), sig. B2v. I owe this reference to Arnold Hunt.

[33] E. M. Simpson and G. R. Potter (eds.), *The Sermons of John Donne*, 10 vols. (Berkeley and Los Angeles, 1962), x, p. 132.

[34] *Ibid.*, pp. 133–34. Cf. the case of John Doughty, rector of Lapworth, Warwickshire, who allegedly complained that 'turning and tossing over the leaves of the Bible is a disturbance to the congregation' cited in Robert Hudson, *Memorials of a Warwickshire Parish* (London, 1904), p. 157.

[35] For an excellent discussion of these matters, see A. Hunt, 'The Art of Hearing', unpublished PhD thesis, University of Cambridge, 2001.

worship found in the black communities of the United States?[36] Recasting parish services in this more audible, emotional, even noisy context raises again the ecclesiastical insistence upon what constituted due reverence within the confines of sacred space and leads to a consideration of one solution to this problem in the emergence of the office of the dogwhipper.

## III    Dogs and dogwhippers

Dogs were invariably present during parish services. This may be inferred from sixteenth-century churchwardens' accounts which record the small amounts of money paid by the parishioners to individuals known as dogwhippers. In 1536, the parish of Culworth in Lancashire purchased whips for dogs and in 1542, the parish of Ludlow, Shropshire spent 8 pence on 'whipping dogs out of the church'.[37] The parishes of St Nicholas, Warwick, Staplegrove in Somerset, Bray in Berkshire and East Dereham in Norfolk all employed dogwhippers.[38] At the parish of St Peter Mancroft in Norwich in the 1580s, the dogwhipper was paid 4 shillings for his year's work and the entry read 'paide to the driver out of the dogges for his whole year'.[39] Elsewhere, we find the parish of All Saints Pavement in York buying dog whips in 1568 and references to dogwhippers in Stanford in Berkshire in 1567, Leverton, Lincolnshire in 1572, Cheddar in Somerset in 1612, the parish of St Laurence, Reading in 1649 and the parish of Boyton in Cornwall in 1682.[40] A dog whip was still to be seen in the vestry of Baslow in Derbyshire in the 1920s – a stout ash stick with a three-foot long lash – and dog tongs which enabled one to take firm hold of reluctant dogs can be seen in the Welsh parishes of Clynnog Fawr in north Wales and Llanynys near Denbigh as well as the Herefordshire parish of Clodock.[41] Such examples might easily be multiplied.

---

[36] W. Cross, *The Burned-Over District: the Social and Intellectual History of Enthusiastic Religion in Western New York, 1800–1850* (Ithaca, 1950). Cf. the experience of Scottish Eucharistic piety in L. E. Schmidt, *Holy Fairs Scottish Communions and American Revivals in the Early Modern Period* (Princeton, 1989).

[37] J. C. Cox, *Churchwardens' Accounts from the Fourteenth Century to the Close of the Seventeenth Century* (London, 1913), p. 308.

[38] *Ibid.*, p. 309, Norfolk Record Office (NRO), PHI 608.

[39] NRO, PD 26/71, fol. 22r.

[40] York: Borthwick Institute, Y/ASP F14/2, expenses 1568; Stanford: Berkshire Record Office D/P 118/5/1; Leverton and Cheddar: cited in E. C. Ash, *Dogs: Their History and Development*, 2 vols. (London, 1927), I, p. 117; Reading: Berkshire Record Office, D/P 97/5/1, p. 167; Boyton: Cornwall Record Office, DDP 16/5/1, expenses 1682.

[41] Cox, *Churchwardens' Accounts*, pp. 307–8.

But what did these dogwhippers actually do? The answer at first appears obvious as the churchwardens' accounts from Ludlow (1542) make clear; they were whipping dogs out of the church.[42] But why were these dogs being whipped? To whom did they belong? And where were they before they were whipped?

Keith Thomas implies that dogwhippers were employed to prevent dogs from entering the church and to remove those that succeeded, although he concedes that 'some pets came to church in spite of the opposition of Tudor bishops'.[43] Rather than this antagonistic view of dogs and parish churches, it seems probable that many dogs, and not just pets, accompanied their owners to church. The evidence for their presence in the weekly worship services can be inferred from a variety of sources.

Dogs were ubiquitous in early modern England.[44] We know this from travellers' comments and might also infer it from the number of proverbs about dogs.[45] The very number of dogs and their variety were seen as displaying a hierarchy that resembled the social order of English society. John Caius in his celebrated tract of 1570 *De Canibus Britannicis* described something of this hierarchy in which the hunting dogs – hounds, bloodhounds and greyhounds – were the dogs of princes and noblemen.[46] Wealthy women often had their lap dogs.[47] Mastiffs were bred for bear- and bull-baiting and also served as butcher's dogs. Spaniels were used in hunting with hawks; kitchen dogs turned the spits in large ovens or drew water and a variety of dogs served other purposes seen in their names: defending dogs, tie dogs, terriers and tinker's curs.

The argument that dogs commonly accompanied men and women to church services, should not be confused with any sentimental notions we might hold towards dogs or dog ownership. It is clear that the term 'dog', when applied to humans, was taken as a serious insult. When the churchwardens of the parish of Highworth in the diocese of Salisbury took down the altars on 12 December 1550, their actions so incensed John Boller, a yeoman parishioner, that he lost his temper: 'Wher for doo you pull downe theis aulters? A dog commanded thee to do this and thow

---

[42] *Ibid.*, p. 310; the entry reads 'for whipping dogs out of the church'.

[43] K. Thomas, *Man and the Natural World* (London, 1983), pp. 112–13.

[44] *Ibid.*, pp. 101–9; M. Jenner, 'The great dog massacre', in W. G. Naphy and P. Roberts (eds.), *Fear in Early Modern Society* (Manchester, 1997), pp. 51–3.

[45] M. P. Tilley, *A Dictionary of the Proverbs in England in the Sixteenth and Seventeenth Centuries* (Ann Arbor, Mich., 1950), pp. 163–70. See especially: 'to love it as a Dog loves a whip'.

[46] Thomas, *Man and the Natural World*, pp. 55–6.

[47] Katherine Stubbes, wife of Philip, had a 'Puppie or Bitch' which she 'loved well' and which would sleep with the couple in their bed. Philip Stubbes, *A Christal Glasse for Christian Women* (London, 1591), sigs. A4v–Br.

hast no more authoritye to doo this than hath a dogg'. The resulting Star Chamber case described his language as 'opprobrious, detestable and despiteous . . . lewd, seditious and pernicious'.[48] And as Mark Jenner has shown, early modern urban authorities slaughtered dogs and cats in their hundreds whenever an outbreak of the plague threatened.[49] On 15 May 1607, John Noyes wrote from London to his wife in Calne in Wiltshire, having heard that the 'sickness increaseth in Calne', and gave advice to 'serve God with reverence and feare, call upon him both early and late' and counsel concerning contact with any that are infected, which included the stark advice to 'kepe in youre dogge, or knocke him in the heade'.[50] Alongside the affection of Katherine Stubbes for her lap dog was a more common and brutally hard-nosed attitude towards dogs.[51]

If Tudor bishops were opposed to dogs in churches we might expect this view would readily be found in visitation articles and injunctions.[52] I have found only two bans on dogs in churches and both concern cathedrals rather than parish churches. Archbishop Holgate's injunctions for York Minster in 1552 spoke of the necessity of vergers expelling 'beggars, other light persons and dogs forth of the said Church', but it would be unwise to read all dogs into this piece of regulation.[53] In 1577, John Whitgift drew up injunctions for the cathedral in Worcester, one of which read that the

Dean and chapter shall forthwith take order that the beadsmen or the sextons beginning of the senior shall weekly and successively see that the Cathedral church is kept clean: and that in the time of public service or of sermons there be no walking, talking, crying or playing of children, or fighting or brawling of dogs; that from henceforth they refrain to walk or talk or to suffer their children or dogs to come or to be brought to church to the hindrance of the preacher and auditory, as they will answer to the contrary according to the statutes provided against disturbers of Divine service and of the preacher.[54]

A quick reading of this injunction might support the view that children and dogs were no longer permitted to attend public service or sermons in Worcester cathedral, but this is not, I think, what Whitgift meant. His quarrel was with noise and behaviour – with children's games and

---

[48] PRO, STAC 3 5/77.    [49] Jenner, 'The great dog massacre', pp. 44–61.
[50] A. S. M., 'John Noyes of Calne', *Wiltshire Notes and Queries* 4 (Devizes, 1905), p. 422.
[51] Stubbes, *A Christal Glasse for Christian Women*, sigs. A4v–Br. Stubbes relates how his wife Katherine in a fit of remorse for a lack of hospitality utterly rejects her bitch 'which in her life time she loved well', beating the 'filthie Cur' away from her bed and refusing to look upon it.
[52] Akin to the ban on doves or on dogs in colleges: Frere and Kennedy (eds.), *Visitation Articles*, II, pp. 77, 319; III, pp. 136, 188, 320.
[53] Frere and Kennedy (eds.), *Visitation Articles*, II, p. 318.
[54] Kennedy (ed.), *Elizabethan Episcopal Administration* II, p. 68.

dogfights – with those matters that hindered the preacher and auditory. This was no bar for quiet children or submissive dogs. And Whitgift's injunction of 1577 is the closest one can get to Tudor opposition to dogs.

To be sure, the ecclesiastical injunctions and interrogatories from this period speak repeatedly of the importance of reverence during divine service. The people were to abide soberly and orderly, they were not to talk or babble, walk or jangle or play the fool. They were not to molest, unquiet or grieve the minister with noise, brute cries or clamours. They were not to suffer children to disturb divine service. More positively they were enjoined to hear attentively, reverently, devoutly, to be in quiet attendance, to hear, mark and understand.[55] Thomas Bentham in the diocese of Coventry and Lichfield in 1565 put some teeth into these injunctions with the order that the clergy and churchwardens were to choose some eight, six or four of the most

> substantiall and honest men in the parish, who being charged upon their corporal oaths and having white rods in their hands, shall have authority to see good order kept in the church: they shall first gently admonish them and if they will not be reformed so, then two of the honestest men aforesaid shall lead them up unto the chancel door and set them with their faces looking down towards the people for the space of one quarter of an hour.[56]

The practice seems not to have caught on as this was never again enjoined in any other diocese, but the very use of this modest shaming ritual, reflects a more widespread assumption of the need for quietness and reverence during public services.

It is not until the early seventeenth century that ecclesiastical authorities specifically attacked the practice of taking dogs into church services. In 1611, Samuel Harsnett, Bishop of Chichester, enjoined his clergy to 'let no man bring dogs into the church by reason of the filthiness, which is known often to occur'.[57] In 1636, Matthew Wren, Bishop of Norwich, asked whether the churchwardens

> were carefull to take speciall order that no dogs be at any time suffred to come into the church, to the disturbance of the divine service and the polluting of the Christian congregation. And doe any of the inhabitants (of what condition soever)

---

[55] Frere and Kennedy (eds.), *Visitation Articles*, III, pp. 93, 106, 266, 380; Kennedy (ed.), *Elizabethan Episcopal Administration*, I, p. cxix; II, pp. 45, 60, 68, 95–6, 119, 126; III, pp. 142, 230. G. Bray (ed.), *The Anglican Canons 1529–1947* (Woodbridge, 1998), pp. 189, 287–9 for the canons of 1571 and 1603 respectively concerning lay behaviour during service.

[56] Frere and Kennedy (eds.), *Visitation Articles*, III, p. 168. See also a similar if less explicit injunction for the diocese of St Asaph of 1561, pp. 112–13.

[57] Cited in Ash, *Dogs: Their History and Development*, I, p. 117.

or of their company, bring their hawkes into the church, or usually suffer their dogs of any kind to come with them thither to the prophanation of the house of God and his holy worship.[58]

We should not be surprised to find these men, with their concern for the sacredness of church buildings and the beauty of holiness inveighing against the filthiness and pollution of dogs.[59] Yet the statements of Harsnett and Wren stand in stark contrast to the silence from their Tudor predecessors and Stuart contemporaries. And despite their strictures, their opposition was helpless in the face of the long-established custom of taking dogs to church both among the wealthier and the poorer sort of people. In 1734 in *A choice drop of seraphic love*, Robert Poole was complaining about the same practice:

Remember the Sabboth day to keep it holy and carefully attend the worship of God. But bring no Dogs with you to Church – these Christians surely do not consider where they are going when they bring Dogs with them to the Assembly of Divine Worship – disturbing the Congregation by their Noise and Clamour. Be thou careful I say, of this scandalous Thing, which all ought to be advised against as Indecent.[60]

Ecclesiastical injunctions and clerical complaints could do little in the face of popular practice.

Most Tudor and Stuart clergymen preferred to let sleeping dogs lie. They had no quarrel with dogs attending worship services provided their behaviour was in keeping with the emphasis placed upon good order and reverence. The condition was all important and is attested to over and over again. The very few presentments that can be found concerning dogs in churches all involve other aspects of reverence, noise or neighbourliness. The reason why Mary Knights of Blythburgh in Suffolk was presented to the church courts in 1597 had little to do with the fact that she brought her mastiff with her to church, and everything with that fact that this particularly unpleasant dog prevented other people from being able to sit, and then as if, aware of the slightness of the charge, the churchwardens

---

[58] Fincham (ed.), *Visitation Articles*, II, p. 148.

[59] This is reminiscent of the stance of the Russian Orthodox Church which regarded dogs as unclean beasts. See G. Scheidegger, *Perverses Abendland, barbarisches Russland: Begegnungen des 16. und 17. Jahrhunderts im Schatten kultureller Missverstandnisse* (Zurich, 1993), pp. 59–63. I owe this reference to Julia Mannherz.

[60] Cited in Ash, *Dogs*, I, p. 118. Eighteenth and nineteenth century examples from Canada can be found in P. Moogk, *La Nouvelle France. The Making of French Canada – A Cultural History* (East Lansing, Mich., 2000), p. 259 and A. Brooks (ed.), *Religion and Rural Ontario's Past* (University of Guelph, 1980), p. 20.

added, 'she also useth to chide and braule in the church'.[61] The York-shirewoman who, in 1632, while the minister was delivering communion 'did dangle a dog on her knee and kiss him with her lips' was presented for behaving irreverently not because she had a dog with her but because her actions were deemed inappropriate in the context of receiving communion.[62] Similarly the Cambridgeshire man who was presented in 1593 for bringing his dog into the parish church offended because his dog was wearing bells and this disturbed the congregation.[63] Deportment, reverence and noise, not dogs per se, were the issues at stake.

The argument is both furthered and given a twist by a brief examination of the Laudian injunctions to place the communion tables at the upper end of the chancel and to enclose the same within decent rails. As is commonly known, a primary reason given for railing in the table was to keep off dogs. Archbishop Laud's injunctions of 1635 for Chichester diocese ordered that tables 'shalbee rayled in with a decent rayle, to keepe of dogs and to free it from all other pollutions'.[64] Richard Montagu, Bishop of Norwich asked in 1638 not only whether 'dogs were kept from coming to besoil or profane the Lord's table' but also whether the communion table were 'enclosed and ranged about with a rail of joyners and turners work, close enough to keep out dogs from going in and profaning that holy place, from pissing against it, or worse'.[65] These concerns corroborate the argument that dogs were generally permitted access to the church.

The Laudian twist is that the desire for rails to avoid the pollution of dogs helps to explain more about the role of the dogwhipper. One wonders why dogwhippers were not used by parish authorities as a sufficient reason to oppose the railing of communion tables. The silence on this score perhaps was a grudging admission that lapses in controlling dogs had occurred and that the famous tales of dogs causing offence – such as the 'very ill incident' on Christmas day 1638 in the town of Tedlow, in which a dog 'came to the Table and took the loaf of bread prepared for the Holy sacrament in his mouth and ran away with it', or of another dog that leaped upon a cleric as he was genuflecting, need not have been

---

61  J. F. Williams (ed.), *Diocese of Norwich, Bishop Redman's Visitation 1597* (Norfolk Record Society, 18 (1946)), p. 127. There is a similar case in 1619 from the parish of St Mary Dover: Canterbury Cathedral Archives, Act book I. 9. 14, fol. 259v. I owe this last reference to Professor R. H. Helmholz.

62  Thomas, *Man and the Natural World*, p. 113.     63  *Ibid.*, p. 113.

64  Fincham (ed.), *Visitation Articles*, II, p. 108.

65  *Ibid.*, p. 195. Matthew Wren ordered that rails be constructed in one of the Norwich churches 'reaching from the north wall to the south wall, near one yard in height and so thick with pillars that dogs may not get in'. Bodleian Library, Tanner MS 68, fol. 33r.

the fabrications of pro- or anti-Laudian factions, but genuine, bizarre lapses from the norm.[66] If railing in communion tables was seen as a way of securing things sacred for sacred uses, it was also a concession to the custom of bringing dogs into the church. Viewed this way, one might argue that the Laudian Church, unable or unwilling to bar dogs from church, adapted by railing off a sacred space within the church to keep the dogs at bay. The argument, at one level is absurd, failing to take account of the theological and ceremonial ideas behind the Laudian altar policy, but fear of dogs and the fear of pollution remained in spite of the rails.[67] In 1673 in Wells cathedral, the chapter argued that 'as for the rails before the altar, we conceive that if they be taken any lower, every dog will leap over them'.[68] How much of this was real and how much was rhetoric is perhaps impossible to determine.

The argument that dogs routinely accompanied their owners to church is further supported by the art from the period although in general one must travel to France and the Low Countries to obtain this support. There is the famous painting of the Huguenot assembly in Lyons in the temple called Paradis of 1564 in which a dog is depicted sitting quietly whilst a sermon is being preached.[69] Many of the views of church interiors painted by Dutch artists such as Hendrik van Vliet, Emmanuel de Witte and Pieter Saenredam in particular depict dogs in churches. Over and over again in the churches of Haarlem, Alkmaar, Utrecht and elsewhere, Saenredam depicted dogs sitting quietly, sniffing about, playing with children, attending workmen or mixing with the people.[70] Nor was this particular to the Reformed countries. The Moroccan Muslim, al-Hajari who visited France and the Netherlands in the early seventeenth century describes how freely dogs had access to the churches of St Jean de Luz in the south of France: 'When a worshipper has a dog or dogs, then they arrive at church before their owner while nobody sends them

---

[66] Cf. the first incident as recorded in Christopher Wren, *Parentalia or Memoirs of the Family of the Wrens* (London, 1701), p. 76; PRO SP 16/388/41; Bodleian Library, Rawlinson MS D 1480 fol. 118. The second type of story is reminiscent of the anecdotes found in the Marprelate tracts and that formed part of the debate over vestments. Marprelate relates how Dr William Turner trained his dog to snatch off the corner cap worn by a visiting bishop. W. Pierce, *The Marprelate Tracts 1588, 1589* (London, 1911), p. 86. See also Ash, *Dogs*, I, pp. 117–18.

[67] K. Fincham, 'The restoration of the altars in the 1630s', *Historical Journal* 44 (2001), 919–40 highlights the extensive literature on this subject.

[68] C. Estabrook, 'In the mist of ceremony: cathedral and community in seventeenth-century Wells', in S. Amussen and M. Kishlansky (eds.), *Political Culture and Cultural Politics in Early Modern England* (Manchester, 1995), pp. 153, 161 n. 146.

[69] B. Reymond, 'D'ou le temple Paradis (1564–1567) tenait-il son modele?', *Bulletin de la Societe de l'Histoire du Protestantisme Francais* 145 (1999), 266.

[70] *Catalogue Raisonné of the works by Pieter Jansz. Saenredam* (Utrecht, 1961).

away'.[71] John Gipkyn's 1616 painting of a sermon at Paul's Cross depicts a seated auditory outside St Paul's. In the foreground a dogwhipper is in the act of whipping a dog who has just jumped up against an older man sitting in the back row.[72]

Incidental details also attest to the access dogs had to church space. A controversy about a desk in the chancel of the parish church of Ilam in Staffordshire, disclosed that the desk was placed 'so highe unto the glasse wyndowes as that contynually dogges thereby clymyd up unto the glasse wyndowes and brake the same', much to the annoyance of the lay rector.[73] An ugly case from the parish of Stocksbury in Kent in 1561 involving one George Brysto who misbehaved in church and reviled his minister with irreverent and threatening words revealed that the trouble began during a Sunday service in which Brysto, 'being in the middle part of church did play with a dog when the curate was in the pulpit reading of the paraphrases of the gospel, and the curate rebuked him of it'.[74] When lightning struck the parish church of Anthony in Cornwall in 1640, the only fatalities were two dogs, one 'at the feet of those who were kneeling in the Chancell to receive the Sacrament', and the other outside the church at the 'Bell-free doore'.[75] The conclusion must be that Tudor and Stuart ecclesiastical authorities, whilst stressing reverence and railing off sacred space, were unwilling to take an officious stand against the custom and practice of dogs coming with their owners and remaining quietly in the parish church at time of divine service.

On dogs and dogwhippers, therefore, the older view of that remarkable antiquarian, John Charles Cox, is essentially sound. He wrote:

In days long prior to a dog tax, dogs abounded in great numbers and almost every cottager possessed one to aid in fetching his cow or a few sheep from the common. They were often in the habit of attending church with their masters, from the squire downwards. To regulate their behaviour and to remove the unseemly, almost every parish possessed a modestly paid official termed the dog whipper. The absurd suggestion has been printed by several would be folklorists and repeated in a Hertfordshire volume in 1912, that the custom of taking dogs to

[71] P. S. Van Koningsveld, Q. Al-Samarrai and G. A. Wiegers (eds.), *Ahmad Ibn Qasim Al-Hajari, Kitab Nasir Al-din Ala 'L-Qawm Al-Kafirin* (Madrid, 1997), p. 122.

[72] M. MacLure, *Register of Sermons Preached at Paul's Cross, 1534–1642*, revised by J. P. Boswell and P. Pauls (Ottawa, 1989), p. 4.

[73] PRO STAC 3 1/15.

[74] Cited in D. Cressy, *Travesties and Transgressions in Tudor and Stuart England* (Oxford, 2000), p. 145. See also the account of the Dean of Lichfield, George Boleyn, 'being at another time in the pulpit hearing his dog cry, he out with his text – 'Why, how now? Ho, can you not let my dog alone, there? Come, Spring! Come Spring!' in the Marprelate tract *The Protestatyon*: Pierce, *The Marprelate Tracts 1588, 1589*, p. 417.

[75] *The Voyce of the Lord in the Temple* (London, 1640), p. 10. I owe this reference to Alexandra Walsham.

church was introduced by the Puritans to show their contempt for the sacraments and for old fashioned reverence. This is ridiculous, for entries as to dogwhippers occur in pre-reformation accounts and at the present time dogs attend mass in out of the way chapels in Ireland; I have myself seen fine wolf hounds crouching behind the shepherds in churches of the French Pyrenees.[76]

The earliest example, however, of a dogwhipper that Cox cites comes from the parish of Culford in 1536 and what Cox misses in his indignant spluttering at the absurdities of would be folklorists is the way in which the sixteenth century witnessed the growth of this office. Throughout the sixteenth century, no doubt as a result of the emphasis upon preaching sermons and attending to the word, there was a greater awareness of the need for abiding 'soberly and quietly'. At the same time, as rood screens were taken down, access to the chancel was now made easier for both parishioners and their dogs. Dogwhippers emerged as the solution not only to the problem of dogs barking, fighting, pissing or defecating in the nave or elsewhere, but also as a means of enforcing punitive control over sacred space within the parish church. The only contemporary description of dogwhippers in action comes from the pen of John Foxe who wrote that if the people of England did not cease to act 'so doggish and currish one to another, the Lord lacketh not his dogstrikers to whip us'.[77] Dogwhippers then, were minor parish officials paid to maintain a level of quietness, control and decorum among the dogs in the nave, whipping them either into submission or out of the church.[78] It is not surprising that by the mid-seventeenth century in a number of parishes, the dogwhipper had become a kind of petty parish policeman, waking sleepy hearers, disciplining children, whipping dogs, controlling persons, behaviour and space within the post-Reformation parish church.[79]

## IV    Conclusion

Like the use of psalms and groans, the employing of a dogwhipper was clearly an initiative of the parish. Nowhere was the office required by

---

[76] Cox, *Churchwardens' Accounts*, p. 307.

[77] John Foxe, *Actes and Monuments* (London, 1583), preface. See also the punishment inflicted on Lance in William Shakespeare, *Two Gentlemen of Verona*, act 4, scene iv.

[78] It is possible that churchwardens and sidesmen themselves took on these duties. In 1611, when John Whighton of Whitstable in Kent was discovered in an alehouse 'in the time of service and sermon time and being admonished to come unto the Church by the churchwardens and sidesmen, he refused saying he would not follow a company of dog whippers'. A. Hussey, 'Visitations of the Archdeaconry of Canterbury', *Archaeologia Cantiana* 27 (1905), p. 227.

[79] The parish of St Nicholas, Warwick in 1578 paid 16d to John Whettley 'for looking to the children and for whyppynge of the dogges'. Warwickshire Record Office DR 87/1, expenses 1578.

ecclesiastical authorities, yet everywhere these minor officials were spring-
ing up, attesting to the knowingness of parish authorities in the face of
ecclesiastical pressure for due reverence during parish services. The creative response of many parishes was to grant authority to a fellow parishioner to whip and discipline unruly dogs from the church, which practice
reflected both their own concern for quietness and order during services
and their recognition of the community's custom of taking their dogs with
them where they went.

Herein lie the seeds of an important argument not only about the
accommodations made by Tudor and Stuart churchmen but about the
characteristics of an emerging popular Protestantism whose initiatives
were expressed in the singing of paraphrased psalms put to popular tunes,
in the audible responses to preaching and prayer, in the insistence that
their dogs might have access to the nave and in the local solution to
the shared concern for order and reverence during the time of divine
service that arose in the person of the dogwhipper. The worship of the
Reformed church worked. Perhaps it did not meet the exacting standards
insisted on by the godly, but the varied caricatures of the services, preachers and parishioners of the Reformed church have overlooked the ways
in which Elizabethan and Jacobean services were shaped by the people.
Such accommodations are evidence of the resilient popularity of parish
worship.[80]

A final instance raises the problem of what constituted reverence and
what constituted a disturbance. The case moves us away from the parish
church and back into the much larger space of the cathedral.[81] In 1634,
William Laud drew up twenty-nine articles inquiring into the state of
affairs in Salisbury cathedral, in which the final question asked 'if you
know any other offence or crime committed by any of this church contrary
to the statutes and laudable customes of the said church or canons and
constitutions of the Church of England, wee require you by vertue of

---

[80] The classic statement belongs to Keith Thomas: 'the tone of many Elizabethan congregations seems to have been that of a tiresome class of schoolboys', in *Religion and the
Decline of Magic* (London, 1971), p. 162. Cf. Davies, *Worship and Theology in England
from Cranmer to Hooker*, p. 213: 'now that the Anglican services were set off by so little
ceremony and symbolism, church attendance must have been excessively dull'. See also
A. Tindal Hart, *The Man in the Pew, 1558–1660* (London, 1966), pp. 128–32.

[81] Cathedrals are paradoxical spaces, both sacred and secular and the larger dimensions
of cathedral naves permitted or encouraged activities perhaps less commonly found in
parish churches. St Paul's Cathedral had its walkers and it is clear that many respectable
citizens of Canterbury regarded the nave of the cathedral as a suitable place to walk, talk,
perhaps smoke their pipes, especially on rainy days, thoughts I owe to Professor Patrick
Collinson. See his chapter 'The Protestant cathedral, 1541–1660', in P. Collinson, N.
Ramsay and M. Sparks (eds.), *A History of Canterbury Cathedral* (Oxford, 1995), and
pp. 177–8 in particular.

your oath to present it'.[82] Even though the dean and chapter drew up a detailed response to Laud's inquiries, John Lee, the prebendary of Calne, with no small axe to grind, drew up his own response and in answer to the final article of inquiry gave the following report on noise and deportment in the cathedral:

> Men, both of the better and meaner sort, mechanicks, youths and prentises do ordinarily and most unreverently walk in our church in the tyme of divine service and within hearing of the same, with their hats on their heads. I have seen them from my seat (and not seldom) so walking or standing still, and looking in upon us when we have been on our knees at the litany and the commandments. I earnestly and humbly desire some effectual course may be taken for redress. As also for the ordinary trudging up and down of youths and clamours of children, to the great disturbance of the preachers in their sermons. The vergerers and other officers have had a charge to look to this: but to little or no purpose. Dr Barstow, Dr Hinchman and myself have been fayne to rise and go out of our seats to see and stay the disorders. But I never (to my uttermost remembrance) saw Barfoot the vergerer (who sits in my sight) to ryse at the greatest noyse.[83]

John Lee clearly disliked being stared at as a kind of tourist attraction and it is not impossible that Barfoot the verger was severely deaf, but it is also possible that where the prebendary saw disorder, the vergerer did not. Akin to Keith Wrightson's discussion of differing concepts of order, the evidence causes us to ask whether the soundscape of parish church and cathedral embraced two concepts of reverence and noise, disturbance and sound?[84] And if this is right then perhaps part of the story of the collapse of the Caroline church can be found in the way in which Laud's ceremonial policies were all but tone deaf to the more popular concept of parish sounds and reverence.[85]

---

[82] 'Archbishop Laud's visitation of Salisbury in 1634', *Wiltshire Notes and Queries* 1 (1893), pp. 10–23.

[83] *Ibid.*, p. 122.

[84] K. Wrightson, 'Two concepts of order: justices, constables and jurymen in seventeenth-century England', in J. Brewer and J. Styles (eds.), *An Ungovernable People: the English and their Law in the 17th and 18th Centuries* (London, 1980), pp. 21–46.

[85] It is worth noting that Archbishop Laud kept cats and a giant tortoise but no dogs, a reference I owe to Diarmaid MacCulloch.

# 7     A microcosm of community: burial, space and society in Chester, 1598 to 1633

## Will Coster

The English parish church has emerged as the focal point of three branches of historical study. The first is that of religious history, which has increasingly turned to the experience of devotion in the interior of the church or chapel.[1] Second, there has been a growing acknowledgement among social historians that the church was the centre of the community in both town and village.[2] Finally, there is the burgeoning historiography of death and burial, which has reminded us of the centrality of the church as the place where the living interacted with the departed.[3] Just as different forms of historical enquiry meet within the parish church, so the different elements of religious and social life encountered each other there. In modern terminology, it was both sacred and secular space. It was also often the ultimate earthly resting-place, where death, at a stroke of his scythe, created an unavoidable equality and unity.

However, the same divisions of hierarchy, sex and age that dominated in life can be seen in the utilisation of space for burial. Sanctity did not simply permeate the church and there were gradations of the sacred. In the medieval church the high altar, side altars and shrines were seen as centres of a series of circles of holiness that radiated out through the building and up to the churchyard wall. This boundary finally marked

---

I would like to thank Margo Todd and Peter Marshall for commenting on this chapter.

[1] See C. Haigh, 'The recent historiography of the English Reformation', in C. Haigh (ed.), *The English Reformation Revisited* (Cambridge, 1987), pp. 19–33; E. Duffy, *The Stripping of the Altars, Traditional Religion in England 1400–1580* (New Haven and London, 1992).

[2] K. French, G. G. Gibbs and B. Kümin, 'Introduction', in their (eds.), *The Parish in English Life 1400–1600* (Manchester, 1997). See also the incisive assessment in S. Hindle, 'A sense of place? Becoming and belonging in the rural parish 1550–1650', in A. Shepard and P. Withington (eds.), *Communities in Early Modern England* (Manchester, 2000), pp. 96–114.

[3] The starting point is P. Ariès, *Western Attitudes Towards Death: From the Middle Ages to the Present* (Baltimore, 1974) and his *The Hour of Our Death* (Harmondsworth, 1983). For recent work on England see D. Cressy, *Birth, Marriage and Death: Ritual, Religion and the Life-Cycle in Tudor and Early Stuart England* (Oxford, 1997); R. A. Houlbrooke, *Death, Religion and the Family in England 1480–1750* (Oxford, 1998); V. Harding, *The Dead and the Living in London and Paris, 1500–1670* (Cambridge, 2002); P. Marshall, *Beliefs and the Dead in Reformation England* (Oxford, 2002).

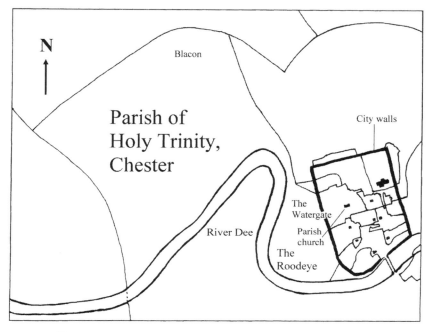

Figure 7.1  Map of the parish of Holy Trinity, Chester.

off the consecrated burial ground from that of the external and profane world. Inevitably such gradations of sanctity were employed to
reflect the concerns of the living.[4] This chapter considers the ways in
which the spatial dimensions of burial mirrored these concerns by focusing on the pattern of interment in one particular parish in the city of
Chester.

Holy Trinity in Chester is unusual in having a parish register that
allows us to understand burial practice in considerable detail between
1598 and 1633. As can be seen in figure 7.1, the parish was based on a
medieval church close to the centre of the city, but expanded out beyond
the Watergate, encompassing the low-lying meadow of the Roodeye in the
curve of the River Dee and stretched out to include most of the manor
of Blacon to the west. Consequently, parishioners included not only
urban craftsmen, sailors, traders and local dignitaries, but also prominent
local gentlemen, yeomen and agricultural labourers. Chester, capital of a

[4] C. P. Grave, 'Social space in the English medieval parish church', *Economy and Society*
18 (1989), 297–322. On the early modern period see C. Marsh, '"Common Prayer" in
England 1560–1640: the view from the pew', *P&P* 171 (2001), 66–94; C. Marsh, 'Sacred
space in England, 1560–1640: the view from the pew', *JEH* 53 (2002), 286–311.

palatinate and a major port with a cathedral church, was the crossroads of a number of different societies. Thus, the parish church could only serve as a centre of community if it could create a unity between these disparate or disruptive elements.

The fact that the parish registers record the places of burial may be an indication of the nature of these problems and of the pressure created by an expanding population and the higher rates of mortality that are found in many early modern urban centres.[5] Vanessa Harding, focusing mainly on London, has made extensive and insightful use of parish registers and other materials to illuminate patterns and practices of burial.[6] This work differs not only in the location of the community under study, but in a focus on what these factors reveal about the sanctity of space, an investigation possible because of the comprehensiveness of the sources for Holy Trinity, Chester.

The original parish registers for the period under consideration have been lost, but a local antiquarian Randle Holme copied part of them, which together with the bishop's transcripts has preserved this rich vein of data.[7] There are 787 burial entries for the period between the opening of the register in 1598 and the death of John Totty, the last clerk to record details of locations, in March 1633/4. Of these, some 742 include indications of the place of burial. From 1532 onwards the churchwardens' accounts (also copied by Holme) provide numerous insights into the fabric and structure of the church.[8] Working with this information, this chapter examines the utilisation of space within the church and how this was reproduced in burial, the degree to which burial practice can be seen as reflecting social and communal structures and how this situation may have changed as a result of fundamental pressures on the early modern parish community.

[5] C. Galley, *The Demography of Early Modern Towns: York in the Sixteenth and Seventeenth Centuries* (Liverpool, 1998); W. Coster 'Popular religion and the parish register', in French, Gibbs and Kümin (eds.), *Parish Life in England*, pp. 94–111.

[6] V. Harding, '"And one more may be laid there": the location of burials in early modern London', *London Journal* 14 (1989), 112–29 and her 'Burial choice and burial location in early modern London', in S. Bassett (ed.), *Death in Towns, Urban Responses to the Dying and the Dead, 100–1600* (Leicester, 1992), pp. 119–35. Most studies rely heavily on preferences expressed in wills, rather than records of burial, particularly important are D. Beaver, '"Sown in dishonour, raised in glory": death, ritual and social organisation in Northern Gloucestershire', *Social History* 17 (1992), 389–410 and D. Cressy, 'Death and the social order: the funerary preferences of Elizabethan gentlemen', *Continuity and Change* 5 (1989), 99–119. It was not possible to use the wills for Holy Trinity, Chester in this way because of problems of identifying those from within the parish.

[7] L. M. Farral (ed.), *The Parish Register of the Holy and Undivided Trinity in the City of Chester 1532–1837* (Chester, 1914) (hereafter *PRHT*).

[8] J. R. Beresford (ed.), 'The churchwardens' accounts of Holy Trinity, Chester, 1532 to 1633', *Journal of the Chester and North Wales Architectural, Archaeological and Historic Society* 38 (1951), 95–172.

# I          The utilisation of space within the church

It is widely acknowledged that the medieval geography of interment reflected the topography of sanctity within the parish church.[9] However, given the removal of many of the sites of sanctity in the church during the Reformation, and the general condemnation of the idolatry of the concept of consecration that followed, it remains an open question as to how much the places of interment in late-sixteenth- and early seventeenth-century England reflected the church as the locus of the holy and to what degree burial had been transformed into a social institution, indicating purely status. David Cressy has noted that 'proximity to the altar and location within the chancel or aisle still mattered for social reasons' and Vanessa Harding observes that 'the social value of a hierarchy of burial location survived its spiritual rationale', and has raised the point that these survivals suggest that a large part of the medieval utilisation of space already had important social significance.[10] However, Chris Marsh sees the pattern of position within the post-Reformation church as still reflecting 'sacred space'.[11] We can only understand the significance of these patterns of behaviour if we are first cognisant with the physical and mental structures of space within the church.

The existing building of Holy Trinity in Chester, now the guildhall, and its surrounding environment, bear very little resemblance to the church of the late sixteenth and early seventeenth centuries. The south aisle and west end of the medieval red sandstone building were reconstructed from the ground in the late seventeenth century, the north aisle was extended in the late eighteenth century, along with other major modifications and the whole building was razed to its foundations and rebuilt in 1865. In the same period the churchyard was reduced, extended, reduced again and built upon.[12] Moreover, the street outside the church has been widened

---

[9] Cressy, *Birth, Marriage and Death*, pp. 456–69; C. Daniell, *Death and Burial in Medieval England 1066–1550* (London and New York, 1998), pp. 97–115.

[10] Cressy, *Birth, Marriage and Death*, p. 461; Harding 'Burial choice and burial location', p. 131. See also V. Harding, 'Choices and changes: death burial and the English Reformation', in D.Gaimster and R. Gilchrist (eds.), *The Archaeology of Reformation 1480–1580* (Leeds, 2003), 386–98.

[11] Marsh, 'Sacred space in England', 311.

[12] Chester, Cheshire County Record Office (hereafter CCRO), EDP 70/2 Parish bundle, Holy Trinity Chester, 1865–70; P1/143 Folder of Misc. Notes; P1/147 Article of agreement on enlargement of church, 1774; P1/149 Estimate of costs of enlargement of church, 1774; P1/151 Sketch of improvements, 1774; P1/152 Plan of improvements,1774; P1/153 Plan of gallery, 1774; P1/154 Certificate of allotment of new pews and plans, 1778; P1/156 Faculty for building new vestry, 1798; P1/176 Faculty, 1865; P1/308 Articles of agreement to enlarge churchyard by pulling down parsonage house, 1771. On the plans for the restored church see, 'A brief abstract of the proceedings of the society', *Journal of the Architectural, Archaeological and Historical Society of Chester* 11 (1864), 378–80.

Churchyard

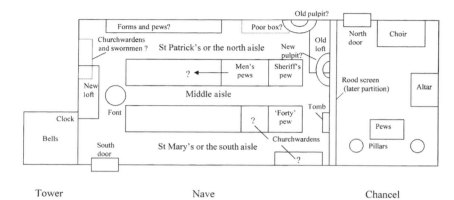

Figure 7.2  Plan of the church of Holy Trinity, Chester.

and the frontage of the church has been shifted back away from the road. The past denizens of this parish could never have anticipated these transformations, but they do mean that many who achieved church burial are now outside and many of those outside have been moved within. As a result of all these changes, it is only because of the survival of the parish register and churchwardens' accounts that we are able to reconstruct the building of this period.

These records reveal that before the mid-sixteenth century Holy Trinity contained at least two chantry chapels: that of St Mary in the south aisle and of St Patrick in the north. There is no reference to the Mary chapel in the later register, but, except in two instances, the north aisle continued to be referred to as 'St Patrick's Aisle' and one case as 'St Patrick's Chapel'.[13] While in many churches the cult of the Virgin tended to be the first to be revived in the reign of Mary, in this parish the only side altar for which we have evidence of restoration is that of St Patrick in the north aisle, which was made or topped with alabaster and painted in 1558.[14] We cannot be certain, but this suggests that the north aisle had enjoyed greater status and devotion than the south.

As can be seen in figure 7.2, at least by the late sixteenth century the main body of the church was divided by two sets of pews into three aisles: St Patrick's to the north, a middle aisle and finally, what had been St Mary's aisle, along the southern wall. At the 'lower', west end of the

[13]  Farral (ed.), *PRHT*, pp. 89, 93, 95.
[14]  Duffy, *Stripping of the Altars*, p. 563 and Beresford, 'Churchwardens' accounts', 122.

middle aisle was the font, near the main (south) door, clock and the bells in the tower. At the 'higher', east end, connecting the chancel to main body of the church, was a rood screen, purchased in 1536, and a loft made in the following year.[15] From the mid-sixteenth century Holy Trinity underwent the same process of the reordering of space for Protestant worship that was seen throughout the realm. The rood screen was neglected, but not destroyed in the reign of Edward VI, and evidently became a renewed focus of piety in the reign of Mary, being cleaned in 1556/7 and repaired in 1559, when the images of Mary and John were repainted.[16] After the archiepiscopal visitation of 1571 it was taken down and replaced with inelegant sounding 'bords, nayles, etc'.[17] References to the loft continued in both registers and churchwardens' accounts, but in 1577 a new 'loft' was raised in the lower part of the church, probably near the clockhouse and almost certainly a gallery to create additional seating. At a cost of only 4 pence this cannot have been very ornate, which may explain why a new and more elaborate gallery was built in 1605. The fact that at the same time the 'partition' between the church and chancel was repainted suggests that it had been moved back close to its original position.[18] This is the first indication of a change from a destructive or functional process towards a positive re-ordering and beautifying of space within the church in a way appropriate to Protestant worship, part of what has been called a neglected 'building revolution' that gained momentum towards the end of Elizabeth's reign and reached its apogee in the reign of Charles I under the direction of Archbishop Laud.[19]

Along these lines, the pulpit, a characteristic feature of the medieval parish church, but now the totemic symbol of 'the Word', had evidently been at the higher end of the north aisle, and may have been part of the loft, but a new one had replaced it, or been added, probably in a more central location, in 1608.[20] Also in this area from 1566 was another symbol

---

[15] Beresford, 'Churchwardens' accounts', 109–10.

[16] *Ibid.*, 119, 123.      [17] *Ibid.*, 127.

[18] *Ibid.*, 129, 140 for the implication that this loft was near the clock. The replacement needed two pieces of Irish timber, fourteen fir planks, holes in the walls (presumably for the nine ten-foot joists and fifty spars), plus other odd bits of wood and labour: amounting to a sum probably more than £2.

[19] D. MacCulloch, 'The myth of the English Reformation', *Journal of British Studies* 30 (1991), 13.

[20] Location of the pulpit is based on references to the Wever family, buried in the 'ile under the pulpit' in 1599, 1601 and 1604, but in the 'north ile' in 1623, while the first reference to the 'old' pulpit in the parish register is from 1611, see, Farral, *PRHT*, pp. 66, 68, 70, 89 and 78. However, the burial of Thomas Wever in 1628 was 'under the pulpit where Mr P'son Hoppwood redeth service', suggesting that the old pulpit was still in use, *PRHT*, p. 92. There is no reference to the old pulpit being removed and when the new one was built in 1608, the old had just been given a cover and gilded. In 1656 the parishioners complained that many lacked seats because the pulpit had been

of Protestant virtues that had been adapted from medieval precedents, the poor box. From 1612 this sat on a table that bore the injunction to 'remember the poor'.[21] By the time of the opening of the burial register, the chancel contained at least one set of pews, with an open space, effectively another aisle, to the south side. From 1549 the altar had been replaced by a communion table, which was used as the point of reference for one burial. In the chancel was another door, possibly close to a set of seats for the choir, which probably led out to the churchyard to the north where the majority of burials would have taken place.

Within the main body of the church we know that there were a number of tombs and monuments. There is a reference to 'the great marble stone set w[th] brasse by the chancell in the body of the church', probably the tomb to Henry Gee, three times mayor of Chester who died in 1545, which was mentioned in the churchwardens' accounts in 1551 and was apparently removed from the church in the renovations of 1865.[22] A monumental brass was set up for Richard Clyve who died in 1572 and another monument for Ellen Hicks, wife of Clement Hicks, gentleman and the chief searcher of the Ports of Chester and Liverpool, reflecting in a small way the revival of the practice of erecting memorials that has been much noted for this period.[23] The register contains very little information about the positioning of burials within the churchyard. There was a path, stone wall and gate and at least one 'tomb', that of Mr William Massy, alderman, whose status and several instances where it was used as a reference point, suggest that it was a substantial private family monument of stone.[24]

Burials cost money and the place of burial played a large part in determining that cost. Payments of laystalls, sums of money due to the churchwardens for burial, in the period between 1532 and 1592, varied between 4 pence for children (who were probably buried in the churchyard), to 4 shillings and 4 pence for burials in the north or south aisles.[25] A

---

moved, strengthening the argument that a more central location was being used that had previously been occupied by seating, but it is possible that the pulpit had been moved yet again, see CCRO, P1/145, Folder. The location of the poor box is suggested by the burials of the Hand family, two of which were in this area, but one of which was 'nere the poore mans box', see, Farral (ed.), *PRHT*, pp. 70, 78, 87 and 94.

21  Beresford, 'Churchwardens' accounts', 124, 148. A reference to money found in the box in 1536 may refer to a figurative box, 109.

22  Farral (ed.), *PRHT*, pp. 83, 721; Beresford, 'Churchwardens' accounts', 113.

23  *Ibid.*, pp. 717–18. On memorials in general, see J. Finch, 'A reformation of meaning: commemoration and remembering the dead in the parish church, 1450–1640', in Gaimster and Gilchrist (eds.), *The Archaeology of Reformation*, pp. 437–49.

24  Massy was buried before the opening of the register in 1598 and his wife was buried in his tomb in 1600; see Farral (ed.), *PRHT*, p. 67.

25  *Ibid.*, pp. 713–18.

memorandum in the churchwardens' accounts, dated 1618, underlined the greater prestige of the two aisles by outlining a fee of 6 shillings and 8 pence for burial of an adult and 4 shillings for a child. Burials between the partition that separated the chancel from the main body of the church and the churchwardens' seat were to cost 5 shillings for adults and 3 shillings and 4 pence for children. Burial in the main body of the church back from the churchwardens' seat cost 3 shillings and 4 pence for an adult and 2 shillings and 6 pence for a child.[26]

There is little doubt that burial within the church partly reflected seating patterns and the desire to be placed close to or below where individuals had sat, where their ancestors had participated in divine service and where their relatives and descendants would do so in the future.[27] We know that Holy Trinity had pews before 1532 when the churchwardens' accounts begin, as in that year old forms were sold off and new ones built.[28] From this point, pews were some of the most regular expenses to appear in the accounts, indicating a continual process of the reorganisation of space within the church. Although in most churches pews were assigned on the basis of family or property, there were other systems, particularly in a civic setting, that could apply.

In Holy Trinity, Chester, we know that there had been a seat, located in the south aisle (presumably at the higher end) that had been reserved for the civic dignitaries who were members of the parish, known after the council of forty as the 'forty seat', or 'alderman's forme', which had evidently fallen out of use before 1628.[29] As late as 1640 there was an attempt to rebuild this seat in a grander style to encourage the civic leaders to return, but it in the meantime it had probably been used by the most prestigious remaining members of the parish. A seat used by the two churchwardens was said in 1608 to be 'in the higher south ile', probably just behind that of the aldermen or actually in the south aisle and in 1612 they evidently moved to a new 'wainscot form' under the loft.[30] A seat was set aside for the two swornmen who supported the churchwardens, which in 1612 was given a new door with hinges and a desk.[31] A seat also seems to have been reserved for the sheriff of the county, probably at the high end of the north aisle, just below the old pulpit.[32]

[26] Beresford, 'Churchwardens' accounts', 171.

[27] A situation that predated the Reformation. See Duffy, *Stripping of the Altars*, pp. 331–2 and R. Dinn, '"Monuments answerable to men's worth": burial patterns, social status and gender in late Medieval Bury St Edmunds', *JEH* 46 (1995), 248.

[28] Beresford, 'Churchwardens' accounts', 108.     [29] Farral (ed.), *PRHT*, p. 93.

[30] *A Cheshire Sheaf* (3rd series), 46 (1951), 1; Farral (ed.), *PRHT*, pp. 76, 95; Beresford, 'Churchwardens' accounts', 148.

[31] *Ibid.*     [32] See the references to the Hand family in n. 21 above.

The most intriguing references are in 1627 to a burial 'at uper end of the men's seat on north side', and in 1632 to a burial 'at higher end of the mens seates on north side'.[33] The need to distinguish the higher end of these seats suggests that there was more than one form and therefore that there was a significant element of sexual segregation in the church. There is no suggestion that there were any general women's seats in the church and for the men to be on the north side was contrary to usual practice, whereby they sat on the right facing the altar. However, as Margaret Aston has noted, where there were exceptions to this pattern, they were often connected to the gendered location of medieval chantry chapels.[34] This seems to fit for Holy Trinity where we know that St Patrick's chapel was to the north and St Mary's to the south. In the register there are a number of references to the ownership (or occupation) of particular pews, but only in a dozen cases is it possible to be certain of the location of these seats. Two pews were stated to belong to men; one of these was in the north aisle and one in the south. Of the ten pews belonging to individual women only four were in the south aisle. This small sample indicates that at least some women were sitting to the north, so any gendered pews were probably for young men to sit in and were therefore part of the tendency observed by Paul Griffiths to constrain the youths of English parishes.[35] The ownership of pews was more often ascribed to women than to men and it is possible that the men usually sat together and the women were distributed across the church. The churchwardens' accounts contain frequent references from 1607 to fees paid for women's kneeling places or pews, all of one shilling. Since no man appears to have paid for his own pew, it seems likely that these were in some sense inherited or connected to property, but those of women had been allocated by the church and were evidently maintained at the user's expense. This suggests that what was occurring was similar to the process observed by Nick Alldridge for the neighbouring parish of St John, for which a plan of 1638 shows that prominent citizens had two pews, one for themselves and one for their wives, often some distance away. A little lower down the social scale young men were segregated, but changes on the plan show that once they married and formed their own households they would move to sit with their wives. This fluidity goes a long way to explaining the intricacies of burial within the church.[36] These were matters of considerable importance in

---

[33] *Ibid.*, 91, 96.

[34] M. Aston, 'Segregation in the church', in W. Sheils and D. Wood (eds.), *Women in the Church*, SCH 27 (1990), pp. 223–94, especially, p. 280.

[35] P. Griffiths, *Youth and Authority, Formative Experiences in England 1560–1640* (Oxford, 1996), pp. 104–5.

[36] N. Alldridge, 'Loyalty and identity in Chester Parishes', in S. J. Wright (ed.), *Parish, Church and People Local Studies in Lay Religion, 1350–1750* (London, 1988), p. 94.

the parish of Holy Trinity, not least to the parish clerk, who, according to a memorandum of 1601 in the churchwardens' accounts, was to be given the profits from the allocation of forms.[37] This also suggests why in 1622 a map was drawn up to record the allocations of seats, which sadly has not survived.[38]

As Chris Marsh has recently underlined, in early modern England pews were frequently places where concepts of community and good neighbourliness broke down and several such cases are extant from Holy Trinity.[39] In 1568 the churchwardens were keen to establish that when Mr Richard Clyve, esquire, set up a pew for his family in St Patrick's aisle it would only be granted until he and his wife left the parish or died.[40] Similarly, a disagreement between John Shaw and Mrs Gyttones in 1575, led to the mayor underlining the authority of the churchwardens to decide these issues and denying the right of parishioners, 'to clayme me any forme or kneelinge place as p[ertainin]g to them or by reason of their howses'.[41] Thus the churchwardens were operating a complex spatial system that encompassed conflicting principles of status, office holding, property ownership, gender and age, which seems to have needed continual refinement and reinforcement.

## II    The geography of church burial

This complex pattern meant that the prestige of space did not simply radiate out from the site of what had been the high altar at the east end. Of thirty-two people indicated to have been buried in the chancel or near the north door, nineteen (59 per cent) were stated to have been of gentry status, but this group also included a yeoman, five brewers and a haberdasher. This was a prestigious position, but not reserved only for the social elite. Results are even more mixed in the 'liminal' zone between the chancel and the main body of the church, where of twenty-eight persons for whom we have status descriptions only two (7.1 per cent) were of gentry status and they included, among the many varied trades, a husbandman and even a labourer. Similar results are evident for the nineteen burials at the lower end of the church or near the font, which included only two members of the gentry and reached down the social scale to include another labourer. In contrast, of those twenty-two

---

[37] Beresford, 'Churchwardens' accounts', 138.     [38] *Ibid.*, 159.
[39] Marsh, 'Sacred space in England', 308–11.
[40] This reference and the later debate over lost seating where the new pulpit had been placed suggest there may have been some seats, perhaps temporary, along the north wall.
[41] Beresford, 'Churchwardens' accounts', 126.

individuals described as buried in the higher end of the main body of the church, three were styled 'Sir' or 'Esquire', fifteen were of gentry status, two related to higher clergy, one an alderman and the most humble a yeoman. This strongly suggests that the Reformation had carried out a revolution in the understanding of sanctity within the parish church as it appears that the location of the designated pews for aldermen and sheriffs were the greatest influence on spatial prestige in the church, rather than the high altar and that, as some historians have concluded, medieval ideas of sanctity had given way to those of social status within the church. However, before the Reformation these positions would have been closest to the side altars, which would have been in the east ends of the two aisles and therefore this pattern may tell us more about the residual impact of the cult of saints over the significance of the high altar.

The tendency for families to be buried together magnified the social distinctions of space, loading certain areas of the church with the elite and others with those of lower status. The connection between burial and kinship was often explicitly made in the register. In May or June 1626 Robert Boydle, a shoemaker residing in the neighbouring parish of St Oswald, had been buried in St Patrick's aisle, in Mrs Bromfield's seat, 'w[th] his ancestors'.[42] Examining family groups for which we have several entries, it is possible to see some clustering of burials. For example, between 1628 and 1631 Mr Thomas Drinkwater, ironmonger and member of the city council, his father and three children were all buried in the chancel. This pattern meant that a relatively wide circle of kin could be buried together, as was the case in 1608/9 when John Bruyn, junior, esquire of Stapleford had his son and namesake buried in the higher south aisle on 21 December. On the following 19 March, his sister was buried 'nere to her nephew aforesaid'.[43] However, there are some cases where members of a family were buried in a variety of locations. For example, Mr William Aldersey, who was a merchant and justice of the peace, had a pew in Holy Trinity, but was prestigious enough to be buried in the cathedral. Two male relatives of his were buried in neighbouring St Werburgh's church and another female relative (perhaps his mother) in St John's. His son Hugh was buried in the chancel of Holy Trinity, while William's wife and two daughters were interred in the churchyard. Such a pattern was unavoidable in the urban social elite, who had loyalties that crossed parish boundaries. These circumstances were also a product of the bilateral nature of English kinship, judging descent to be from both parents, which meant that a person might be entitled to burial in two parishes, or two places within a parish church. Older children were

---

[42] Farral (ed.), *PRHT*, p. 91.     [43] *Ibid.*, p. 77.

often noted as being buried under or near the pews of their mothers (in twenty-nine instances) or grandmothers (in two cases). In the case of Mary Evans daughter of Thomas Evans, sailor, on 17 February 1632 she was buried 'in her aunt Sara Howes seat'.[44] These cases may have been part of a trend suggested by archaeological evidence for less segregation on the basis of age in post-Reformation burial.[45]

The impulse to share the grave of a deceased spouse was very strong, as can be seen in the case of Mrs Anne Barnes, whose body was returned to the parish to lie beside that of her late husband Rowland Barnes on 10 April 1612, although she had evidently moved to St Peter's parish some time before.[46] Similarly, on 20 September 1627, Mr Clement Kickes, gentleman, was buried in St Patrick's aisle, in his first wife's grave.[47] More extremely, on 20 September 1611, the widow of Mr John Cotgrave, who had moved to Hampshire forty years earlier to live with her daughter, Lady Eleanor Savage, had her bones brought into Holy Trinity to be buried in the south aisle beside her husband who had died some sixty years before.[48] The problem of where individuals would be buried when they had been joined to more than one marriage partner was always resolved by interment with the first spouse. This can be seen in the case of Anne Dod, wife of the evidently still living Mr Hugh Dod, gentleman and scrivener of St Peter's, who nevertheless, on 13 September 1610 was interred beside her late first husband Dr Reynolds in Holy Trinity.[49]

The topography of burial shadowed the complex organisation of space within the English parish church. We can see that the principles of status, gender and kinship all played a major part in determining the patterns of burial within the church and although these had a relationship to the patterns of sanctity within the later medieval church, they did not simply reflect these patterns. What remains to be seen is the degree to which these factors determined the distinction between burial within the church and churchyard.

## III    Sanctity and exclusion

In the late medieval period, as Chris Daniell has put it, 'the perimeter of the churchyard was a boundary between the Christian and the non-Christian in death'.[50] This distinction was underlined by the use of the

---

[44] *Ibid.*, p. 95.
[45] R. Gilchrist, '"Dust to dust": revealing the Reformation dead', in Gaimster and Gilchrist (eds.), *The Archaeology of Reformation*, pp. 399–414.
[46] Farral (ed.), *PRHT*, p. 79.
[47] *Ibid.*, p. 91.    [48] *Ibid.*    [49] *Ibid.*, p. 78.
[50] Daniell, *Death and Burial in Medieval England*, p. 103.

churchyard for communal gatherings.[51] There is considerable anecdotal evidence from elsewhere that the same ideas survived the Reformation.[52] Among the excluded were the executed, suicides, those that died suddenly or by accident, excommunicates, strangers to the parish, women who died in childbirth or unchurched, and most obviously children who were stillborn and therefore unbaptised, all of whom could have been seen as contaminating the sanctity of the churchyard.[53]

There are no instances of the burial of executed felons in the register, but there was one clear instance of the burial of a suicide. Probably around midnight on 23 May 1609, William Kennyough, a labourer, took himself outside and 'did hange himselph in his backyd. on an elder tree'. Nevertheless, after the coroners had examined him he was buried in the churchyard.[54] Similarly, the idea that those dying from accidental causes were excluded from churchyard burial can be dismissed. The River Dee accounted for five deaths, two of which were in boating accidents and one, that of John Longe, a soldier, who was buried on 14 July 1599, occurred when he was bathing.[55] Most dramatically, on 10 July 1610, John Brookes, the mason who had pointed the steeple of Holy Trinity and those of several other local churches, broke his neck falling from steps by the church. He, like all the others who suffered such accidents, was buried in the churchyard.[56]

The problem of the burial of recusants has been noted by a number of historians.[57] When, as was often the case, they were significant members of the community, there was a social dysfunction created by the law that stated that they should have been excluded from 'Christian' burial. In most parishes it was normal to give them burial in the churchyard and this seems to have been the case in Holy Trinity. One couple, Katherine and William Liverpool, a joiner, are noted as recusants in the register. She was buried in the churchyard on 11 February 1614/5 and he on 30 January 1629, as was often the case, 'at night'.[58]

All parishes faced the problem of strangers who died within their boundaries and had to be found a place of burial. In a busy port this

---

[51] D. Dymond, 'Gods disputed acre', *JEH* 50 (1999), 464–97.

[52] See, J. Cox, *The Parish Registers of England* (London, 1910), pp. 107–8.

[53] *Ibid.*, pp. 103–6.

[54] Farral (ed.), *PRHT*, p. 77. One case, that of a twelve year-old girl, Ellen Parry who 'drowned herself' may also have been a suicide, but the implication is unclear. She was buried in the churchyard, 13 June 1619, see Farral (ed.), *PRHT*, p. 85.

[55] *Ibid.*, p. 66.     [56] *Ibid.*, p. 81.

[57] J. A. Bossy, *The English Catholic Community 1570–1850* (London, 1975), pp. 140–4; Cressy, *Birth, Marriage and Death*, 465–6; Houlbrooke, *Death, Religion and the Family*, p. 336.

[58] Farral (ed.), *PRHT*, pp. 82, 93.

problem was likely to be particularly acute. The difficulty here was not one of inclusion, as much as finding a fitting place among the complex map of family and social status that underlay the church and churchyard. Only twenty-one persons were identified in the register as 'strangers' or were clearly indicated as coming from another city or country. They ranged in status from paupers to rich merchants and in origins from Cheshire to the Netherlands, with the largest group of six coming from Ireland. Most, unsurprisingly, were buried in the churchyard, like Ellen Owen, described as 'an Anglesey girle', on 2 March 1622/3, having died at Ellen Browne's house.[59] Some strangers were of considerable status and this was reflected in their place of burial within the church, much as if they had been local residents. These included on 17 July 1623 Garrat Symons, 'a Dutchman & marchant of Ansterdam who brought a hope laden w^{th} malt'. His status was underlined by the sermon preached by the minister John Hopwood.[60] The most humble to make it within the building was Evan ap Rees, evidently a Welshman, and described as a 'yeoman and stranger', who died at John Askew's house and on 6 October 1610 was buried 'in the church nere the north dore'.[61] One case from 1608 shows the extreme concern over having a good burial: 'Upon the 22 Aug. a stranger called John came out of Ireland and dyed at Widow Griffeth house was bur. in ch. Yard. He left 54^{s} 6^{d} & his clothes to John Harp ironmonger & the sayd widow Griffeth to see him well buried. Jo. Harps wife payd all charges.' When such provision was not forthcoming the churchwardens had the unpleasant duty of raising a special collection.

There is some evidence that women who died in childbirth, or between childbirth and the ceremony of churching (which normally took place around twenty-eight days after birth), were considered as impure and even as objects of danger.[62] There were, however, a number of cases where women died in childbirth and were buried in the churchyard of Holy Trinity, like that of Jane Kenndek, on 27 June 1602.[63] Most interesting is the case of Priscilla, the wife of Mr William Ince, merchant, who was buried between two pillars on the south side of the chancel on 3 July 1627, the same day, we are told, that her daughter was baptised and given the name Priscilla. This strongly suggests, not only that the mother was unchurched, but also the ways in which the custom of naming after

[59] *Ibid.*, p. 88.    [60] *Ibid.*    [61] *Ibid.*, p. 78.

[62] P. Crawford, 'The construction and experience of maternity in seventeenth-century England', in V. Fildes (ed.), *Women as Mothers in Pre-Industrial England* (London, 1990); K. Thomas, *Religion and the Decline of Magic, Studies in Popular Beliefs in Sixteenth- and Seventeenth-Century England* (London, 1971), pp. 59–61; Cressy, *Birth, Marriage and Death*, pp. 197–229 and W. Coster, 'Purity, profanity and Puritanism: the churching of women 1550–1700', in Sheils and Wood, *Women in the Church*, pp. 377–87.

[63] Farral (ed.), *PRHT*, p. 69.

godparents could be suspended to produce a memorial and a sense of renewal, which implies nothing but regard for women who died in the travails of childbirth.[64]

I have argued elsewhere that there is evidence of a shift in attitudes following the Reformation from regarding children who died before baptism as contaminated by original sin (and therefore potentially damned) to being born innocent.[65] Very young children were being buried in the churchyard of Holy Trinity by the early seventeenth century. For a number of infants, like a child of Randle Ince who was placed in the churchyard on 6 February 1605/6, we are told that they died when they were born or were 'still born'.[66] In the case of one of the children of Thomas Drinkwater, who was buried with his family in the chancel on 11 March 1637/8, we are specifically told that the child died before it was baptised.[67] Similarly, the wife of Richard Crachley, brewer, was 'delivered of tow girles at one birth who dyed before they were babtized' and were buried in the churchyard on 13 June 1619.[68]

In a number of cases these children were not buried with their families, or even in a separate grave, but in a grave with an unrelated individual who happened to have died around the same time. This was the case with a daughter of Christopher Howle a sailor, whose unnamed daughter was interred on 6 April 1599 'in the grave w[th] Mr Rogerson', and whose entry appears immediately before for the same day.[69] Similarly, on 19 October 1610, Rafe son of Issac Warmington, tailor, was buried in the same grave as Elizabeth Totty, wife of Henry Totty, hooper.[70] Such practices would no doubt confuse an archaeologist who might, logically, assume some relationship between the two occupants of the same grave. Putting infants in already open graves would have saved effort and money and this was almost certainly what occurred in 1599 when 'Henry, a yong youth borne in London came out of Ireland & dyed in Piers Hughes stable', was buried on the same day, 10 August, and in the same grave as Widow Crier.[71] These factors could be taken to indicate that, unlike older children, there was little imperative to place infants in close proximity to their families, perhaps reflecting a lack of attachment between parents and new-born children. A more interesting question is why the relatives of a respectable or even highly prestigious individual might agree to have an unrelated

[64] W. Coster, *Baptism and Spiritual Kinship in Early Modern England* (Aldershot, 2002), pp. 178–82.

[65] W. Coster, '"Tokens of innocence"': infant birth, baptism and burial in early modern England', in B. Gordon and P. Marshall (eds.), *The Place of the Dead. Death and Remembrance in Late Medieval and Early Modern Europe* (Cambridge, 2000), pp. 266–87.

[66] Farral (ed.), *PRHT*, p. 74.

[67] *Ibid.*, p. 92.    [68] *Ibid.*, p. 85.    [69] *Ibid.*, p. 65.

[70] *Ibid.*, p. 78.    [71] *Ibid.*, p. 66.

infant placed in the grave of their kin. This fits with hints collected in the nineteenth century that having an infant in a grave might be, as one Devonport man put it, 'a sure passport to heaven for the next person buried there': to put it another way that the innocence of the young might be considered beneficial to the adult dead.[72]

We do not know who was excluded from burial, because this information was not recorded in the parish register, but it is clear that almost no one category appears to have been excluded absolutely. It could therefore be argued that the parish churchyard was reflective of a highly inclusive community, perhaps indicating a post-Reformation re-evaluation of the utilisation of space for burial, but a counter-claim might be that the strength of a community is partly indicated in its sense of difference and that a failure to exclude suggests a lack of sense of neighbourhood. The situation in regard to inclusion and exclusion in an urban parish, even one like Holy Trinity that took in a large slice of agricultural land, is complex, since the options for burial outside the graveyard, or at a crossroads, were likely to be limited. For these reasons the distinction between church and churchyard burial may have been more significant in this context and therefore a better guide to membership of the community.

## IV    Community, burial and social change

The churchyard was most likely to be the location of the burials of those on the margins of society. Of eleven persons described as poor or paupers in the register for whom we have a place of burial, only one, Katherine Peterson, on 1 April 1616, was buried in the church, probably near members of her family under the loft.[73] Similarly, of ten children described as illegitimate, all were buried in the churchyard. Part of the memorandum of 1612 in the churchwardens' accounts directed that the bodies of the poor should not be buried in the church until the end of the year and then only if space was available.[74] This may have been a response to increasing pressure on space within the church. The evidence of laystalls between 1532 and 1592 suggests that an average of between three and four individuals were buried in the church every year. The burial registers indicate that for the period 1598 to 1633 it was between eight and nine. In 1547 some ninety-one persons were assessed for payments to the church at Easter, but in 1633, 152 persons were included in the assessment, suggesting a population rise from around 430 persons to 720, although it

[72] Coster, 'Tokens of innocence', pp. 266–87. Quotation from W. Henderson, *The Folklore of the Northern Counties of England and the Borders* (London, 1838, repr. Wakefield, 1973), p. 6.

[73] Farral (ed.), *PRHT*, p. 83.    [74] Beresford, 'Churchwardens' accounts', 171.

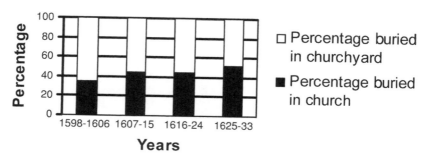

Figure 7.3 Graph of the ratio between church and churchyard burials at Holy Trinity, Chester, 1598–1633.

is certain that no assessment of the period included all the householders in the parish.[75] Given an expanding population and increasingly full churches, it seems logical to expect that a growing proportion of parishioners would have been buried in the churchyard, as has been found in other parishes in the early seventeenth century.[76] However, as figure 7.3 shows, in fact the proportion of burials in church rose across this period. From 1598 to 1606 it was 35 per cent, but by 1625–33 it had risen to 52 per cent. This could be taken to indicate a number of factors, including an increasing emphasis on the significance of the physical church building particularly associated with the policies championed by Archbishop Laud, which may have raised the prestige of the church through a process of beautification and re-sacralisation.[77]

However, the opening years of the register happened to be a period when the ravages of plague were particularly severe in Chester. Between January 1604 and January 1606 some eighty-four individuals were identified as victims. Of these, only three were buried in the church, among them the first victim, Alice, the daughter of James Hand, a husbandman from Blacon, and the reason for her death 'was not known to the p'ish till she was buried'.[78] If we exclude all of the identified plague victims, some 64.4 per cent of burials were in the church in the period 1598–1606, a notably higher proportion than for later periods. Similarly, in 1610 there was a less severe (and probably less carefully recorded) outbreak of

---

[75] *Ibid.*, 11–12, 168.

[76] C. Gittings, *Death, Burial and the Individual in Early Modern England* (London, 1984), pp. 140–1.

[77] P. Lake, 'The Laudian style: order, uniformity and the pursuit of the Beauty of Holiness in the 1630s', in K. Fincham (ed.), *The Early Stuart Church, 1603–1642* (London, 1993) and J. Fielding, 'Arminianism in the localities', in the same work.

[78] Farral (ed.), *PRHT*, p. 70.

plague, which may well have reduced the proportion of church burials in this period. As we might anticipate, the proportions of the population of the parish being buried in the church was generally falling in the first part of the seventeenth century, but these patterns could be severely disrupted by the outbreak of infectious disease.

It was the fear of contagion associated with plague that disrupted the normal patterns of everyday life. Victims were moved out of the city, usually to separate plague cabins, but the register indicates that most were brought back for burial in the churchyard. It is possible that a large plague pit was dug in the yard, but these are probably less common than often assumed and if so, at least some individuals were evidently being buried away from it.[79] For example, on 12 January 1604/5 Mr Rowland Barnes, mercer, was buried 'next to William Massey's tomb'.[80] By its nature, plague often destroyed entire families and it is evident that where this was the case they tended to be buried together within the churchyard, as can be seen with the unfortunate Stevenson family. William Stevenson, a joiner, was the first to be carried away by the plague and was buried on 9 January 1604/5 in the churchyard. His wife Elizabeth and family had evidently been moved to the plague cabins and when Elizabeth died a few days later she was buried in the churchyard 'nere her husband'. On 1 February 1604/5 Margaret, their daughter, who also died at the cabins, was buried 'by her father & mother'.[81]

The reluctance to bury plague victims within the church meant a disruption of the normal patterns of burial. The family of Thomas Fletcher, alderman and justice of the peace was devastated by the plague. He lost three daughters in 1605, all of whom were buried in the churchyard of Holy Trinity, but when he died in 1607 he was buried, as befitted his status, in the south aisle near the alderman's seat.[82] Similarly, the more socially humble John Hutchens, tailor, had lost three sons in the outbreak of 1605, all of whom were placed in the churchyard, but his daughter Jane, who died in the same year, not from the plague but from a long-term illness, was buried at the end of her grandmother's form and another daughter Alice, who died in 1615 was buried at the end of her mother's pew. When John Hutchens himself was buried in 1622, it was in the lower end of the body of the church.[83] It seems that, for those who might expect church burial, plague could create not only a separation

---

[79] V. Harding, 'Burial of the plague dead in early modern London', in J. A. I. Champion (ed.), *Epidemic Disease in London* (Centre for Metropolitan History Working Papers Series, no. 1, 1993), pp. 53–64.
[80] Farral (ed.), *PRHT*, p. 71.          [81] *Ibid.*
[82] *Ibid.*, pp. 72–3, 75.          [83] *Ibid.*, pp. 71, 73, 82, 87.

in life, but also in death. It might be argued that this indicates a lack of concern among parents for their offspring, who, dying later, chose to be buried inside the church, rather than with their children outside, but it is worth noting that John Hutchens' wife, Jane, was buried in the churchyard on 24 February 1611/2.[84] We do not know if this was close to her children who had died five years before, but it is possible that here the burial arrangements divided marriage partners between two groups of graves so that they could enjoy a partial reunion in burial.

The disruption to normal patterns of burial and the imperative for interment in family groups, was, nevertheless, balanced by some evidence that the church was also becoming more exclusively the preserve of the elite of the parish.[85] In the periods 1598–1606, and 1607–15, even if we exclude those burials identified as the victims of plague, only two out of sixteen and three of twenty-five burials, respectively, of members of the families of those identified as gentlemen or local office holders were buried in the churchyard, meaning that in both cases 87.5 per cent were buried in the church. However, in the period 1616–24 thirty-three of thirty-six (92.6 per cent) and for 1625–33 all members of this group were buried in the church. This suggests that the pattern of elite burial in church, strongly marked towards the end of the sixteenth century, became almost universal in the early seventeenth century. Unfortunately, it is not possible to discern whether there was a corresponding pattern of other social orders being more firmly excluded from the church. The crafts and trades that predominated in the parish do not provide a reliable guide to status and produce erratic figures. Husbandmen and yeomen, whose designations carry clearer hierarchical implications, disappeared from the records after 1606 and 1625 respectively. This disappearance of the small landholder is of course, a reminder of a much-noted social phenomenon.[86] Notably, burial in the churchyard was almost universal among the labourers and their families that proliferated in this period in place of the small landholders. This evidence can only be suggestive, but it is possible that an increasingly divided society may have been marked in burial by the walls that partitioned the church from the churchyard and the inner circle of sanctity and community from the outer circle of consecrated ground.

---

[84] *Ibid.*, p. 79.
[85] K. Wrightson and D. Levine, 'Death in Wickham', in J. Walter and R. S. Schofield (eds.), *Famine, Disease and the Social Order in Early Modern Society* (Cambridge, 1989), pp. 163–5 for comments on changes to the 'communal culture of death'.
[86] K. Wrightson, *English Society 1580–1680* (London, 1982), pp. 137–8, 173–80.

# V    Conclusion

The processes behind burial in the early modern parish church were highly complex, shadowing the patterns of seating, which themselves could be the result of negotiation between competing principles of status, age, gender, place and family. These distinctions were further sharpened by the pattern of local office-holding, which reinforced the standing and claims to space of some members of the local elite. The Reformation had clearly re-ordered the structure of sanctity within the church, but perhaps it is best to say that there was a residual pattern of holiness, an echo of the sanctification of an earlier era, that was reflected in seating and in behaviour regarding burial within the church.

The churchyard provided a less exclusive burial place, but one that the presence of at least one family tomb strongly suggests was not disdained by all of higher social status. This provided an outer circle of community; it was the best that could be hoped for as a resting place for those on the margins of parish life, including the poor, illegitimate and those that died of infectious disease. As a rising population and continuing high death-rate raised the pressure on urban populations, it was perhaps inevitable that burial in the church would be increasingly reserved for the social elite. For most individuals in early modern England, the parish church remained the centre of both religious devotion and communal identity, but this was a community increasingly divided between a small elite and a growing commonality. As a result of this widening breach, in death there was an increasing significance to burial in the inner or outer circles of sacred space.

# 8    *Apud ecclesia*: church burial and the development of funerary rooms in Moldavia

*Maria Crăciun*

During the early modern period, a special funerary room developed in the churches of Moldavia which was unique and without parallel in the Orthodox world.[1] Burial inside churches was not in itself new to the Christian tradition and was popular in the Eastern Church, but it had generally taken place in separate chapels or even in specially built churches. Where a tomb chamber existed, for example in the rock-cut churches of Cappadocia, it was usually a distinct room, leading off the nave or *narthex*.[2] In Moldavia, this funerary room developed not as an addition adjacent to the building, but as part of the main structure of the church located between the nave and the sanctuary. This chapter explores the reasons for the emergence of a special funerary room and the functions it had, stemming from a new definition of sacred space in the context of the multiconfessional environment of late medieval and early modern Moldavia. This could provide insight into alternative ways of understanding sacred space, linked in significant ways to an early Christian tradition and yet receptive to western developments of the later Middle Ages.

This special funerary room was not a feature of the earliest religious buildings in this country which were mostly single-naved Romanesque or Gothic churches with a *basilica* plan. The burial chamber in fact tended to appear in churches with a *trefoil* or *pseudo-trefoil* plan. The church in this case consisted of a *bema* or sanctuary (which contained the altar), a *naos*, a *narthex* and sometimes an *outer-narthex*. To this basic plan an extra room was added, between the *naos* and the *narthex*, which communicated with both these spaces through low portals (figure 8.1). This planimetric solution was adopted in the early fifteenth century (archaeological investigation has indicated the presence of funerary rooms at Bistriţa (1408), Probota (1465) and Putna (1466–9) followed by Neamţ (1497)) and its

---

[1] T. Sinigalia, 'L'église de l'ascension du monastère du Neamţ et le problème de l'espace funéraire en Moldavie aux xvᵉ et xvɪᵉ siècles', *Revue Roumaine d'Histoire de l'Art. Série Beaux Arts* 25 (1998), 22.
[2] L. Rodley, *Cave Monasteries of Byzantine Cappadocia* (Cambridge, 1985), pp. 201, 227.

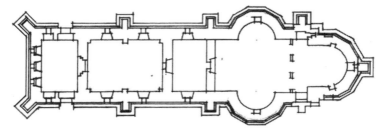

Figure 8.1 Plan of the church at Neamţ after Grigore Ionescu.

implementation has been associated with the Gothic–Byzantine synthesis in Moldavian church architecture.

Because of its uniqueness, the burial chamber has received significant attention and several attempts have been made to account for its appearance. It has first of all been suggested that the burial chamber developed out of the model of the church that used to be placed on top of the graves to emphasise the protective role of the institution.[3] On the other hand, reasons for the development of the burial chamber have been considered structural, for instance the enlargement of the *narthex* in order to accommodate more graves.[4] The emergence of this special funerary space was further explained as a manifest veneration for an important founder, buried close to the place where the liturgy was held, but still avoiding burial in the *naos*, a space which, according to ecclesiastical law should not come into contact with the dead.[5] Some authors were more concerned with the social aspects involved in this development and the political context for it. The burial chamber was thus understood as a space which isolated the tombs of the founders and separated the *naos*, reserved for the prince and clergy from the *narthex*, reserved for the boyars and courtiers.[6] Finally, the emergence of the funerary room has been accounted for through the implementation of external influences, such

---

[3] G. Balş, 'Bisericile lui Ştefan cel Mare', *Buletinul Comisiunii Monumentelor Istorice* 18 (1925–1926), 103, 241–4; G. Balş, 'Bisericile şi mănăstirile moldoveneşti din veacul al xvi-lea (1527–1582)', *Buletinul Comisiunii Monumentelor Istorice* 21 (1928), 268.

[4] D. Năstase, 'Despre spaţiul funerar şi arhitectura moldovenească', *Studii şi Cercetări de Istoria Artei (Seria Artă Plastică)* (hereafter *SCIA*) 14 (1967), 201–8; V. Vătăşianu, *Istoria Artei Feudale în Ţările Române*, i (Bucharest, 1959), p. 310; G. Ionescu, *Istoria Arhitecturii în România*, i (Bucharest, 1963), pp. 253, 278–9.

[5] P. Henry, *Monumentele din Moldova de Nord de la origini până la sfârşitul secolului al xvi-lea. Contribuţie la Studiul civilizaţiei moldave* (Bucharest, 1984), pp. 119–20.

[6] C. Nicolescu, 'Arta în epoca lui Ştefan cel Mare. Antecedentele şi etapele de dezvoltare ale artei moldoveneşti din epoca lui Ştefan cel Mare', in M. Berza (ed.), *Cultura moldovenească în timpul lui Ştefan cel Mare* (Bucharest, 1964), pp. 339–41; I. D. Ştefănescu, *L'évolution de la peinture religieuse en Bucovine et en Moldavie depuis les origines jusqu'au xix siècle* (Paris, 1928), p. 33.

as from Serbia.[7] In Serbia, eschatological and dynastic concerns have led to an original architectural structure (which comprised the tomb itself, located in the niches flanking the lateral apse, where stone sarcophagi were placed on top of crypts) and an appropriate iconographical programme.

Perhaps a more convincing explanation would take into account both religious and political considerations and suggest that the burial chamber developed out of a need to create a special space with a funerary function and that this stemmed from a new understanding concerning sacred space, which highlighted both dynastic and spiritual messages. This chapter explores the ways in which the elite of Moldavia, especially the princes made burial in the church a part of their religious experience and gradually refined their definition of burial space, which evolved towards the insertion of a burial chamber between the *naos* and *narthex*. In trying to answer the deceptively simple question: why was this well-defined and clearly delineated burial space necessary, one is compelled to consider the channels of communication between the laity and the divinity, and the functions of this space in staging the relationship with the sacred. The chapter examines the changes in attitudes to sacred space and burial within the church highlighted by this development and their various and often complex determinations, ranging from the social to the religious. Finally, I argue that the presence of a room with a special funerary function in the plan of the Moldavian churches owed its emergence to a variety of social and religious factors, which were significantly informed by Moldavia's contact with the Catholic Church in the neighbouring kingdoms of Hungary and Poland.

Initially an outpost of the Hungarian kingdom, Moldavia emerged as a principality during the fourteenth century when an autonomous political structure was established by nobles, who had crossed the mountains from the county of Maramureş in north-eastern Hungary and renounced their feudal allegiance to the monarchy. The most prominent noble, Bogdan, recorded in Hungarian documents as 'our notorious infidel' established himself as the ruler of the territory, integrating the pre-existing social and political structures of these lands.[8] The prince was defined by his title as an owner of land 'dominus' but also as a military ruler 'voievod'. Although

---

[7] Sinigalia, 'L'église de l'ascension', 22; E. Cincheza Buculei, 'Programul iconografic al gropniţelor moldoveneşti (sec. xvi)' in M. Porumb (ed.), *Artă Românească, artă europeană. Centenar Virgil Vătăşianu* (Oradea, 2002), p. 86.

[8] Ş. Papacostea, *Geneza statului în Evul Mediu Românesc. Studii critice* (Cluj-Napoca, 1988), pp. 33–65, 76–96, 131–50; Ş. S. Gorovei, 'Poziţia internaţională a Moldovei în a doua jumătate a veacului al xiv-lea', *Anuarul Institutului de Istorie şi Arheologie (Iaşi)* 16 (1979), 187–219.

he deemed himself 'avthentis', ruling by the grace of God ('din mila lui D-zeu') he was actually a vassal of the Hungarian and later of the Polish king.[9] Moldavia had both a traditional landowning elite, which existed prior to the founding of the state and an elite which had become upwardly mobile through its military role and who largely depended on endowments from the prince to consolidate its patrimony. These were received from the ruler in exchange for military service and their input into the mechanisms of government.[10] The nobility of Moldavia, as one knows it from fifteenth to seventeenth century documents, belonged to the Eastern Orthodox Church, which shaped its religious experience. But the piety of the Moldavian elite did not develop in isolation and it was therefore not completely free of influence from neighbouring, mostly Catholic kingdoms, such as Poland and Hungary. The fact that Moldavia, first received western Christianity and initially had a Catholic ecclesiastical organisation, the fact that members of the ruling dynasty and of the elite continued to belong to the western Church, all may have had some impact on the religious experience of the Moldavian Eastern Orthodox laity.[11] Both the archaeological evidence, the presence of the sacristy to the north of the altar in the plan of the church at Cuhea[12] and the dedication of the church to St Stephen of Hungary[13] suggest that Bogdan (the founder of the Moldavian ruling dynasty) and his family may have adopted Catholicism while still in Maramureş. The favouring of Catholicism by Laţcu, Margaret and Petru II, although hotly debated in the secondary literature, is supported by documentary evidence and suggests a strong Catholic influence on religious life in fourteenth-century Moldavia.[14] Emphasising

---

[9] G. I. Brătianu, 'Caracterul constituţional al domniei', in *Sfatul Domnesc şi Adunarea Stărilor în Principatele Române* (Evry, 1974), pp. 17–47; Papacostea, *Geneza*, p. 132.

[10] G. I. Brătianu, 'Stările şi Adunările lor în Moldova până la 1700', in *Sfatul Domnesc*, pp. 155–214. Papacostea, *Geneza*, pp. 133–5, 137.

[11] Ş. Papacostea, 'La fondation de la Valachie et de la Moldavie et les Roumains de Transylvanie: une nouvelle source' *Revue Roumaine d'Histoire* 17 (1978), pp. 402–7; Papacostea, *Geneza*, pp. 59–63, 128; G. Moisescu, *Catolicismul în Moldova până la sfârşitul veacului* XIV (Bucharest, 1942), pp. 32–3.

[12] R. Popa and M. Zdroba, *Şantierul arheologic Cuhea. Un centru voievodal din veacul al* XIV-lea (Baia Mare, 1966), pp. 35–8. R. Popa, *Ţara Maramureşului în veacul al* XIV-lea (Bucharest, 1970), p. 226 argues that the presence of the sacristy only suggests that the church copied existing churches in the area and is not relevant for the religious affiliation of the founder. He also argues that the space was used as a burial chamber, suggesting that a western building had been adapted to the needs of the Romanian Orthodox nobility.

[13] I. Mihaly, *Diplome maramureşene din secolele* XIV–XV (Sighet, 1900), p. 505; R. Popa, 'Biserica de piatră din Cuhea şi unele probleme privind istoria Maramureşului în secolul al XIV-lea', *SCIA* 17 (1966), 515, 521–2 argues that this does not mean it was necessarily a Catholic church.

[14] Papacostea, *Geneza*, pp. 52–8, 62–3, 83, 115, 119, 124–5, 128; C. Rezachievici, *Cronologia domnilor din Ţara Românească şi Moldova 1324–1581 vol. I secolele* XIV–XVI (Bucharest, 2001), pp. 420, 431, 444–5, 449–50.

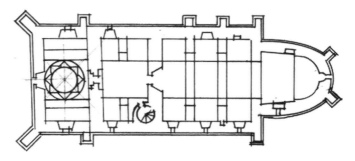

Figure 8.2  Plan of the church at Rădăuţi, after Grigore Ionescu.

the rift with the Hungarian kingdom, the Moldavian princes made Eastern Orthodoxy the official religion of their country and established an Orthodox bishopric in Moldavia, affiliated to the Patriarchate of Constantinople.[15] Contacts with Catholicism continued to flourish, aided by the presence of missionaries.[16]

If one examines the emergence and development of these funerary spaces one notices that the burial chamber only appeared in churches which were monastic princely foundations and only in churches which had a *trefoil* plan.[17] An investigation of the reasons for this may shed some light on the process itself. From an architectural perspective, the emergence of the burial chamber shows a close link between funerary rooms and the *trefoil* plan of the churches. Previously, when the plan of the church was a *basilica*, burials mostly tended to take place in the nave, or within an enlarged nave, for instance at Rădăuţi (figure 8.2) and Giuleşti.[18] Once the Byzantine *trefoil* plan was adopted burials tended to be in the *narthex*, the *outer-narthex* and, eventually in the special burial chamber.[19] Although the existence of the tomb room can be archaeologically

[15] N. Iorga, 'Condiţiile de politică generală în care s-au întemeiat bisericile româneşti în veacurile xiv–xv' *Analele Academiei Române*, 2nd series, 35 (1913) 387–411; C. Marinescu, 'Infiinţarea Mitropoliilor în Ţara Românească şi în Moldova' *Analele Academiei Române* ii, 2, (1924), 247–68; Papacostea, *Geneza*, pp. 120, 124, 129,134.

[16] Papacostea, *Geneza*, p. 116; Moisescu, *Catolicismul în Moldova*, pp. 92–5.

[17] L. and A. Bătrâna, 'O primă citorie şi necropolă voievodală datorată lui Ştefan cel Mare: mănăstirea Probota', *SCIA* 24 (1977), 218; Sinigalia, 'L'Église de l'ascension', 19, 29; Cincheza Buculei, 'Programul', p. 86; V. Puşcaşu, *Actul de Ctitorire ca fenomen istoric în Ţara Românească şi Moldova până la sfârşitul secolului al xviii-lea*, (Bucharest, 2001), pp. 100, 125–8; L. Bătrâna, A. Bătrâna, 'Contribuţia cercetărilor arheologice la cunoaşterea arhitecturii din Moldova în secolele xiv–xv', *SCIA* 45 (1994), 159.

[18] Năstase, 'Despre spaţiul funerar şi arhitectura moldovenească', 200–2; Bătrâna, 'Arhitectura', p. 155.

[19] Năstase, 'Despre spaţiul funerar şi arhitectura moldovenească', 202; Bătrâna, 'Arhitectura', p. 155.

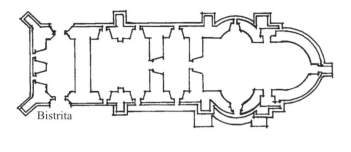

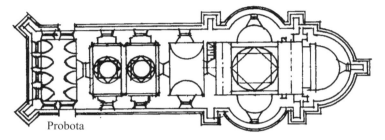

Figure 8.3 Plan of the church at Bistriţa after Ioan Bălan; plan of the church at Probota after Vasile Drăguţ.

proven at Bistriţa, a church which had a rectangular layout with a longitudinal development,[20] the other churches where it first emerged, which had already adopted the *trefoil* plan (Probota, Putna and Neamţ) suggest that the emergence and development of the burial chamber was closely connected or at least contemporary with the more definite contacts with the Byzantine Empire and a stronger Orthodox influence in Moldavia (figure 8.3).[21] Moreover, it seems that the idea of the funerary room appeared when the western plan of the church was abandoned in favour of the eastern one. A comparison between the *basilica* church (Rădăuţi, Giuleşti) and the *trefoil* plan church (Vorniceni, Volovăţ) suggests that, initially in the churches registering Balkan influences burials had to take place in the *narthex* rather than the nave.[22] The interesting development is that when princes started to be buried in *trefoil* plan churches, beginning with Alexandru cel Bun at Bistriţa, the burial chamber emerged. However, the idea of the funerary room was not a Byzantine one. It thus becomes necessary to explore why the princes instituted this major

---

[20] *Ibid.*, pp. 158–9.    [21] Puşcaşu, *Actul*, p. 94.
[22] Bătrâna, 'Arhitectura', pp. 155–6.

readjustment in terms of burial, rejecting the Byzantine tradition of interment in the *narthex* while fully adopting the plan of an eastern church.

Burial in the nave and even the choir area was very much in the tradition of the western Church and suggests that, as concern shifted from the burial *ad sanctos* to burial *apud ecclesia*, the preferred burial place was near the altar or near the statues of major intercessors, like the Virgin.[23] On the other hand, in the Byzantine Empire burials were more likely to take place in the *narthex* or in special funerary chapels, or even churches built as funerary spaces within a monastery (a famous example being the *parekklesion* of the Chora (Kariye Djami) monastery at Constantinople).[24] The *narthex*, which was used for burial rites and had a relevant iconographical programme was generally used for the interment of ordinary mortals, while emperors tended to be laid to rest in specially built churches, like the *parekklesion* of Fethiye Camii, the central chapel of the Pantoktrator monastery (Zepek Camii) and the chapel built by the empress Theodora, wife of Michael VIII Palaiologos next to the church of the Virgin of the monastery of Lips.[25] As Moldavia was exposed to both western and eastern influences it is more difficult to determine the exact origin of customs regarding burial location. However, archaeological findings suggest that the earlier tradition of burial in the nave came from Maramureş with Bogdan and his followers. Thus, the church at Giuleşti (built at the end of the fourteenth century), which functioned as a necropolis had twenty graves within the monument itself (many of them of teenagers and children, emphasising the role of family necropolis), thirteen of which were in the nave.[26]

Consequently, while Catholic influence was still strong in Moldavia burial tended to take place in the nave, but once the Orthodox impact became more powerful the *naos* ceased to be accessible for burial and interments would have to take place in the *narthex*. In these circumstances, the burial chamber appears, almost like a reaction of the princes, who continued to want a burial place near the sanctuary, reflecting notions of sacred space, which was defined in terms of proximity to the

---

[23] P. Ariès, *L'homme devant la mort* (Paris, 1977), pp. 37–96 argues that the change from burial *ad sanctos* to burial *apud ecclesia* was gradual, culminating at the beginning of the fifteenth century. E. Borsook, *Messages in Mosaic. The Royal Programmes of Norman Sicily (1130–1187)* (Oxford, 1990), pp. 69–70.

[24] Sinigalia, 'L'église de l'ascension', 22.

[25] T. F. Mathews, *The Art of Byzantium* (London, 1998), p. 135. Rodley, *Cave Monasteries*, pp. 127, 178, 181, 183, 188, 189, 192, 207, 208; D. Mouriki, 'The iconography of the mosaics', in C. Mango (ed.), *The Mosaics and Frescoes of St Mary Pammakaristos (Fethiye Camii) at Istanbul* (Washington DC, 1978), pp. 69–70.

[26] Puşcaşu, *Actul*, p. 129; Bătrâna, 'Arhitectura', pp. 147–8, 153, 155.

altar. The orientation of an Orthodox church is east to west, its sanctity increases as one moves from the entrance to the sanctuary. Visually, the sanctuary or *bema* (which housed the altar) was cut off by the *templon* or *iconostasis*, which gradually became more opaque as the sacred nature of the liturgy was emphasised and the ceremony itself reduced to a series of appearances, delineating two performance areas within the church: the *bema* (for the more sacred part) and the central area of the *naos*. The *narthex* was clearly the less sacred space, destined for those who did not have access to the sanctified area, penitents, catechumens and women. As has already been noted this was also the place of the dead, where burial and commemoration services were normally conducted.[27] In an Orthodox church, burial in the sanctuary area was out of the question and interment in the *naos* frowned upon.[28] The special funerary room thus becomes a compromise between a wish to adhere to church tradition and the desire to be buried in what was deemed a more sacred space. Funerary rooms were a feature of the *trefoliate* church and thus linked to the rejection of the Catholic tradition of burial (in the nave or choir area) and the acceptance of eastern Orthodoxy, while at the same time retaining the idea of proximity to the altar (which burial in the nave had accommodated and interment in the *narthex* had denied).

This attitude tends to suggest that the prince wished to benefit from a special burial place, within the church itself and having a sacred location. In Moldavia, as elsewhere in the Christian world, burial within the church was the prerogative of the founder, whether it was defined as a right of the *Ktitor* of the eastern Orthodox Church or the *ius presentationis* practised in the west. In the Byzantine Empire, the founders of the church, the clergy, the *higumenes* of monasteries and even the laity who had endowed the church were buried within its walls.[29] This obviously has significant parallels in western Europe, where kings, bishops and abbots were equally concerned to secure the protection of the church in death.[30] The private monastery, which was a characteristic feature of the Byzantine Empire was also considered a family graveyard. Burial within the monastery church was a spiritual privilege the founder acquired for himself, although the rest of the family and his clients would also benefit

[27]  R. Ousterhout, 'The holy space: architecture and the liturgy', in L. Safran (ed.), *Heaven on Earth. Art and the Church in Byzantium* (Philadelphia, 1998), pp. 82–5, 94–7; R. F. Hoddinnot, *Early Byzantine Churches in Macedonia and Southern Serbia. A Study of the Origin and the Initial Development of Early Christian Art* (London, 1963), pp. 23, 36, 40.

[28]  E. Branişte, *Liturgica generală* (Bucureşti, 1993); E. Patlagean, 'Bizanţ secolele x–xi' in G. Duby and P. Ariès, *Istoria vieţii private* (Bucureşti, 1994), pp. 265–351.

[29]  Rodley, *Cave Monasteries*, pp. 248–9; Patlagean, 'Bizanţ secolele x–xi', pp. 265–351.

[30]  Ariès, *L'homme devant la mort*, pp. 77–83, 87–93.

from it.[31] The evidence from other eastern Orthodox realms suggests that the model forged in the Byzantine Empire was successfully implemented. A study of the Russian Church shows that burial within the sacred space of the Church itself was considered part of the religious experience of the laity.[32] In Serbia as well, monasteries were endowed by and the resting places of *zhupans*.[33] So, at first glance the burial customs of the eastern Orthodox Moldavian elite do not seem particularly novel. However, the first document from Moldavia mentioning burial in the church comes from a Catholic, the Princess Marghita, who endowed the church of the mendicant brothers of Siret, because she wished to be buried there.[34] Thus, from the very beginning, whether under eastern Orthodox or Catholic influence, the princes of Moldavia and their families would benefit from the right to be buried in the church as a consequence of patronage.[35] Princes not buried in the church are exceptions and comprise those considered unworthy of the throne or those who had renounced their faith. Thus, the burial places of Jacobus Heraklides Despotus (a Protestant) and Iliaş Rareş (a Muslim) are not known.

However, the practice of church patronage was widespread across a fairly broad social spectrum, which meant that the prince was not alone in exercising this right. Regardless of their confessional background, the landowning elite of Moldavia also wished to be buried within the church, probably reflecting the right of patronage, and in order to highlight their status as founders. From the fourteenth century and the emergence of the Moldavian principality and throughout the following two centuries the evidence, both textual and archaeological suggests that the boyars were founding numerous churches on their lands and using them as family necropolis. It has been suggested that patterns of burial within the church reflected the dynamics of power and mirrored relations between the landowning elite and the political authority. Consequently, a tendency to control patronage rights was representative of a solid political authority: during the fourteenth century and the first half of the fifteenth century there were numerous churches built under the patronage of the elite,

---

[31] S. Runciman, *The Great Church in Captivity. A Study of the Patriarchate of Constantinople from the Eve of the Turkish Conquest to the Greek War of Independence* (Cambridge, 1968), pp. 39–41.

[32] P. Buschovitch, *Religion and Society in Russia. The Sixteenth and Seventeenth Centuries* (Oxford, 1992), p. 38.

[33] P. Pavlovitch, *The History of the Serbian Orthodox Church* (Toronto, 1989), p. 39.

[34] *Documente privind Istoria României, A Moldova veacul XIV–XV*, 2 vols. (Bucharest, 1952), I, p. 1.

[35] G. Cronţ, 'Dreptul de ctitorire în Ţara Românească şi Moldova. Constituirea şi natura juridică a fundaţiilor din Evul Mediu' *Studii şi Materiale de Istorie Medie* 4 (1969), 83; M. M. Székely, 'Femei Ctitor în Moldova medievală'. *Anuarul Institutului de Istorie "A. D. Xenopol"* 32 (1995), 441–58.

while there were relatively few princely foundations,[36] whereas during the long and relatively stable reign of Ştefan cel Mare, although seventy-two churches were built, only four of them were founded by boyars and they were all important dignitaries with significant political careers.[37] This somewhat authoritarian policy, which involved placing private monasteries under the control of the prince, or alternatively the building of a new stone church on the site of an existing boyar foundation (as had happened at Dobrovăţ and Voroneţ),[38] continued until the middle of the sixteenth century (the reign of Alexandru Lăpuşneanu). After that, the political situation changed again and the role of boyars became more prominent, parallel to the weakening authority of the princes. Ultimately, between the sixteenth and the eighteenth centuries a process of consolidation of the nobility took place in Moldavia. Some boyars were candidates to the throne and some (Alexandru Lăpuşneanu, Ion Vodă, Ieremia Movilă) succeeded in occupying it. Consequently, their role in patronage increased significantly.[39]

One has to consider whether these shifting patterns in the rights of patronage had an impact on burial within the church. The evidence suggests that, on the whole it was more usual for boyars to have their own foundations and burial places in the fourteenth and early fifteenth centuries, rather than in the later fifteenth and sixteenth centuries. Very often, in this later period the boyars were buried in churches founded by the princes, which gradually filled with the graves of their clients. It would seem that authoritarian princes tended to reserve for themselves the right to found churches and to highlight their status as founders through interment in the special funerary room and an elaborate burial programme.

In this context, one has to consider where the rulers themselves wished to be buried and the symbolism of their choice. The evidence suggests that the prince would designate a certain monastery as the family necropolis, generally attempting to establish subtle links with the past and family tradition, especially with the ruling dynasty. Thus, in this quest for legitimacy, various dynastic messages were associated to the usual religious

[36] Puşcaşu, *Actul*, pp. 69–72, pp 82–83; M. Crăciun, 'Semnificaţiile ctitoririi în Moldova medievală. O istorie socială a religiei', in *Naţional şi universal în istoria românilor. Studii oferite profesorului dr. Şerban Papacostea cu ocazia împlinirii a 70 de ani* (Bucharest, 1998), p. 161; Bătrâna, 'Arhitectura', pp. 147–53.

[37] Crăciun, 'Ctitorirea', pp. 161–2; Nicolescu, 'Arta' in Berza, *Cultura*, p. 314; *DIR*, I, p. 51. Puşcaşu, *Actul*, pp. 96–9; Balş, 'Bisericile lui Ştefan cel Mare', 111, 133; C. Popa, *Bălineşti* (Bucharest, 1981).

[38] M. A. Musicescu, S. Ulea, *Voroneţ* (Bucharest, 1969); V. Drăguţ, *Dobrovăţ* (Bucharest, 1984); S. Ulea, 'Datarea ansamblului de pictura de la Dobrovăţ', *SCIA* 8 (1961), 483–5.

[39] R. Theodorescu, 'Despre câţiva "oameni noi" ctitori medievali', *SCIA* 24 (1977) 73–4, 77–9; Crăciun, 'Ctitorirea', p. 163; M. M. Székely, *Sfetnicii lui Petru Rares. Studiu prosopografic* (Iaşi, 2002), pp. 231, 300, 311, 319, 350.

ones. This was especially obvious in the case of princes who were illegitimate (Petru Rareş) or members of boyar clans with questionable claims to political authority (Alexandru Lăpuşneanu, Ieremia Movilă), as the foundation was meant to enhance the prestige and to highlight the claim to power of an 'upwardly mobile' boyar clan. The church and necropolis became the symbolic expression of the new status of the family, accompanied by an emphasis on links with a glorious past and with prestigious ancestors.[40] However, this movement to designate specific churches as princely necropolis and invest them with a complexity of dynastic and religious messages was slow in its progress and initially members of the ruling dynasty, such as Ştefan II were randomly buried in other churches as well.[41] In fact, interest in ancestors and the wish to build a family necropolis, although both determined by concern for legitimacy are not directly linked, as the latter intention was focused on posterity, the construction of a new lineage, to be included in the offer of salvation ensured by the endowment, while the former was frequently associated with the exaltation of a prestigious ancestor. It has been suggested that occasionally the bodies of ancestors had been re-interred in the elaborate tombs prepared for them in the newly built family necropolis.[42]

In trying to understand why princely foundations, although not necessarily the churches designated as the family necropolis were chosen for the insertion of a special funerary room one may be able to grasp some of the social intricacies which led to the emergence of this architectural solution. It appears that all monastic foundations, where a member of the ruling dynasty was buried eventually had a burial chamber.[43] There is consequently a social or perhaps even a political element involved in this clear demarcation between monastic princely foundations, which had funerary rooms and the foundations of the landowning elite, which did not. The explanation which has been put forth so far has highlighted the social aspect and the element of prestige involved in the princely endeavour. It has been suggested that boyars, no matter how significant they had become in the political hierarchy, had to find other means of highlighting

---

[40] Bătrâna, 'Arhitectura', pp. 145–7, 158–60, 162–3; Bătrâna, 'Probota', pp. 206, 214–19, 228. Crăciun, 'Ctitorirea', pp. 166–7; Balş, 'Bisericile şi mănăstirile moldoveneşti', 149, 152; M. Crăciun, *Protestantism şi Ortodoxie în Moldova secolului al XVI-lea* (Cluj, 1996), pp. 80–1. Sorin Ulea, 'O surprinzătoare personalitate a evului mediu românesc, cronicarul Macarie', *SCIA* 31 (1985), 14–49. Székely, *Sfetnicii*, pp. 217–19, 223–31, 234; Theodorescu, 'Despre câţiva "oameni noi" ctitori medievali', 80–1, 83–4.

[41] Sinigalia, 'L'église de l'ascension', 20, 29. Ştefan II, son of Alexandru cel Bun 1442–7 was killed by his nephew Roman and buried in the first stone church at Neamţ.

[42] Bătrâna, 'Probota', pp. 215–16; Sinigalia, 'L'église de l'ascension', 20.

[43] Bistriţa, Putna, Probota, Moldoviţa, Neamţ, Suceviţa, Slatina, Dobrovăţ. Sinigalia, 'L'église de l'ascension', 29, was unable to find a reason why Moldoviţa had a burial chamber.

their status, even in their own foundations.[44] Princes on the other hand would highlight their status by constructing a special funerary room.

If one looks at the list of princes who initiated the building of churches with funerary chambers: Alexandru cel Bun (Bistriţa), Ştefan cel Mare (Probota, Neamţ, Putna, Dobrovăţ), Petru Rareş (Probota, Humor, Dobrovăţ), Alexandru Lăpuşneanu (Slatina), Petru Şchiopul (Galata) and Ieremia Movilă (Suceviţa)[45] and considers what they had in common, one comes up with a rather interesting result. It is perhaps worthy of note that all these princes had strong dynastic concerns, were all interested in establishing links with a lineage and the ruling family of Moldavia, which was part of a construct of legitimacy. Alexandru cel Bun came to power after a difficult political situation.[46] Ştefan cel Mare's concern for lineage, manifest in his interest in historiography (he initiated the writing of the first history of Moldavia from its foundation to his own reign) and genealogy also stemmed from political difficulties, as his claim to power was contested by centrifugal tendencies in the southern part of Moldavia and the betrayal of the boyars (who probably wished to replace him), which led to mass executions after the battle of Baia.[47] The reasons of Petru Rareş, Alexandru Lăpuşneanu, Petru Şchiopul and Ieremia Movilă, who wished to legitimise their claim to the throne through an appeal to tradition largely stemmed from their fragile claim to political authority, determined either by illegitimacy or inferior status. In this context dead ancestors came to play an important role and the link with the dynasty is established through the attention bestowed on the graves of the key figures in the lineage.

An important element in marking the burial site in a church was the tombstone, accompanied by an inscription. Interestingly enough, and relevant to this argument, the first Moldavian princes were buried without tombstones. These were placed on their graves later, during the reign of Ştefan cel Mare.[48] He wished to honor the memory of his ancestors buried in the churches of Rădăuţi, Bistriţa, Probota and Neamţ, but marking the burial sites of his ancestors carried various dynastic and political messages.[49] In a similar manner Ieremia and Simion Movilă and their families were interested in their own graves.[50]

Dynastic concerns could also be expressed through images and thus the votive compositions in various churches are able to shed some light on this issue. The votive image at Dobrovăţ (built 1503–4, painted 1529)

---

[44] Puşcaşu, *Actul*, p. 100.     [45] Sinigalia, 'L'église de l'ascension', 29.

[46] Papacostea, *Geneza*, pp. 105, 136.

[47] Şerban Papacostea, *Stephen the Great. Prince of Moldavia 1457–1504* (Bucharest, 1981), pp. 20–2; Papacostea, *Geneza*, pp. 103, 141.

[48] Puşcaşu, *Actul*, p. 123.     [49] *Ibid.*, p. 125.     [50] Székely, *Sfetnicii*, pp. 234–6.

Plate 8.1  Votive image at Dobrovăț.

especially has a strong dynastic dimension (plate 8.1). Petru Rareş, who was responsible for the painting of the church[51] was interested in highlighting the connection with his ancestors, his father and his half brother, Bogdan III. Consequently, the votive image, which depicts only the men in the family, includes this princely genealogy, expressing the dynastic message in visual terms. A similar example is encountered at Suceviţa (1584/96) where, in the votive image the Princess Maria, Ieremia's mother is depicted right next to him and before his wife Elisabeta (plate 8.2). For Ieremia, the status of his mother, as a member of the ruling dynasty must have been a significant legitimising factor.[52]

It is perhaps noteworthy that votive images in Moldavia were equally concerned with human relationships as with those between the human and the divine. In most cases in the Byzantine Empire the votive images in churches depict donors interacting with the sacred and not among themselves. They are generally represented on either side of Christ or the

---

[51] Ulea, 'Dobrovăţ', p. 484.    [52] Székely, *Sfetnicii*, p. 223.

Plate 8.2  Votive image at Suceviţa.

Virgin.[53] In some churches donors are portrayed with their families and, sometimes (especially in Serbia) even with the rulers (their lords), which tends to emphasise vassalage rather than dynastic links.[54] Although such instances are not absent in Moldavia (for example at Humor) generally speaking the votive image depicts the family of the donor/founder and acts as a vehicle for complex dynastic messages. The focus is on lineage and the complex power relations within it. The inclusion in the Moldavian case of family members, ancestors as well as wives and children can be construed as an attempt to highlight dynastic links. Moreover, the women are included in these compositions in a hierarchical arrangement which owes more to genealogical concerns than to gender constructs. This is particularly interesting as in other places in the Orthodox world, while male and female donors are included in votive compositions, the men tend to be depicted on the left (the more sacred side), while the women tend to be on the right.[55]

---

[53]  Rodley, *Cave Monasteries*, pp. 54, 71, 166, 167, 200, 207, 208.
[54]  E. Kitzinger, *The Mosaics of St Mary's of the Admiral in Palermo* (Washington DC, 1990), p. 207.
[55]  Rodley, *Cave Monasteries*, pp. 71, 182, 199–200.

Consequently, the emergence of the burial chamber is framed by the right of patronage, a tradition of burial within the church, which all founders benefited from and the desire of the prince to define a special and perhaps more sacred burial space of his own. Reasons for this development, suggested in the existing literature have focused on the dynamics of power within the elite. While this largely political reasoning can not be excluded, it needs to be refined by taking into account the dynastic concerns of the rulers. This attitude could be construed as a reflection of the fact that a prince who defined himself as *avtenthis* would consider himself responsible for the collective salvation of his subjects and the principal mediator in the relationship with the sacred. The burial chamber thus became the ultimate sacred space, the realm of protective actions and intercessory prayers whose main function was to stage the relationship with the divine. In order to argue this point better it is necessary to examine the decoration of the burial chamber, to understand the reasons of people who wished to be buried in the church and to explore the choice of monastic foundations as the preferred location of funerary rooms.

It has already been suggested that the iconography of the burial chamber expresses the intercessory and protective function of that particular compartment and enhances its value as sacred space. The most interesting feature is the presence of a portrait of the deceased, a composition similar to the votive image, but with a strong funerary function, which makes it analogous to epitaphs. Such a portrait exists at Probota (built 1530, painted 1532) associated with the grave of Ion, the son of Petru Rareş. The composition is interesting, as the prayers of the donors are not addressed directly to Christ, but to St Nicholas who is the patron of the church. Similar to the more usual depiction of Christ, the saint is represented seated on a throne, wearing clerical vestments, holding the Gospel in his left hand and blessing with his right a child, who asks for his protection with both arms raised in prayer. The child is wearing princely attire and is identified by inscription as Ion.[56] This image, on the one hand tends to highlight the intercessory role of saints. The replacement of Christ with St Nicholas becomes meaningful as he is a strongly intercessory saint for the faithful of the eastern Church and tends to indicate a more personal relationship with a particular saint. On the other hand, the image emphasises the responsibility of the family for the

---

[56] S. Ulea, 'Portretul funerar al lui Ion un fiu necunoscut al lui Petru Rareş şi datarea ansamblului de pictură de la Probota', *SCIA* 6 (1959), 62; Crăciun, 'Ctitorirea', pp. 148–50. Sinigalia, 'L'église de l'ascension', 27; A. Semoglu, 'Contribution à l'étude du portrait funéraire dans le monde byzantin 14–16e siècles', *Zograf* 24 (1995), 8–11; Puşcaşu, *Actul*, pp. 47–8.

souls of the dead and can be understood as a bequest, made on their behalf. This particular composition is obviously dedicated by the parents for the salvation of Ion and they are the ones who pray to St Nicholas on his behalf, as is highlighted also by the accompanying inscription.[57] The responsibility of the family is now conveyed in both visual and textual terms.

There are similar images in the burial chamber at Humor (1530, 1535) associated with the graves of Toader Bubuiog and his wife Anastasia.[58] The portrait of the founder has a *Deesis* painted above it, while his wife Anastasia is depicted kneeling in front of the Virgin. Both representations suggest prayer for salvation.[59] At Arbore (built 1502, painted 1504, repainted 1541) there are also two compositions portraying donors, which would qualify as votive images, while only one of them, placed on the wall of the *arcosolium*, near the burial site has a clear funerary function.[60] This image has probably been commissioned by Ana, the daughter of Luca Arbore for the members of her family who had met with a tragic end, condemned for treason at the behest of Ştefan the Young. The image in the burial area only depicts the dead of the family, Luca Arbore with his wife Iuliana and his sons, Toader and Nichita, executed shortly after the beheading of their father. The other image is a more traditional votive composition in the nave.[61] There is a similar image at Râşca (1542, 1552), in a niche of the southern wall, representing *stareţ* Silvan who died in 1579.[62] Analogies with Probota are suggested by the depiction of the Virgin on the throne, flanked by two standing angels. Behind one of the angels Silvan is represented in his monastic habit, with hands lifted in prayer. The image stresses the intercessory role of the Virgin, as Silvan's prayers are addressed to her. The fact that Silvan is introduced by an angel is also interesting, as angels are meant to intercede for ascetics. At Suceviţa, the votive image is placed on the wall dividing the burial chamber from the nave.[63] But there are also two votive portraits, of Grigore Roşca and the monk Ioanichie (Ion Movilă) whose function went beyond

---

[57] Crăciun, 'Ctitorirea', p. 150.

[58] Ulea, 'Portretul' p. 65 n. 3 considers that they are funerary portraits. Sinigalia, 'L'église de l'ascension', 27, argues that the portraits in the burial chamber at Humor are funerary, while that of Petru Rareş in the nave is a votive image. Crăciun, 'Ctitorirea', pp. 150–1.

[59] Crăciun, 'Ctitorirea', p. 148; C. Peters, 'The relationship between the human and the divine: towards a context for votive images in mural painting in Moldavia and Wallachia', *Revue des Etudes Sud Est Européenes* 32 (1994), 42.

[60] V. Drăguţ, *Dragoş Coman, maestrul frescelor de la Arbure* (Bucharest, 1969), passim.

[61] Sinigalia, 'L'église de l'ascension', 29.      [62] Ulea, 'Portretul', p. 65.

[63] M. A. Musicescu, *Mănăstirea Suceviţa* (Bucharest, 1967); D. Dan, *Mănăstirea Suceviţa* (Bucharest, 1923); Nicolescu and Miclea, *Suceviţa*, p. 16.

that of a donor portrait and could be construed as funerary, especially since Ion Movilă was buried at Suceviţa.[64]

One has to first of all unravel the meaning of the image of the deceased. They are usually depicted alone, in the physical proximity of their grave. The image is thus a substitute, a true representation, which has the power to invoke the absent person.[65] But our understanding of the images is not complete if we do not also consider the divine element present. A double intercession is usually involved, as the prayers of the dead and of their families are addressed to both Jesus and the Virgin, or another saint who is able to intercede for the donor (St Nicholas at Probota, the Virgin at Suceviţa, the Virgin and St John the Baptist at Arbore). The Virgin is either the recipient of prayers or depicted next to the donor and thus interceding for him on a more immediate level. A most touching example comes from the church at Dolheştii Mari (1481), the foundation of the hatman Şendrea, where the Virgin is leading the donor by the hand.[66]

The presence of the Virgin and St John the Baptist at Arbore results in a *Deesis* composition. This, especially if included in or associated with a Last Judgement tends to remind the viewer that the purpose of intercession and of prayer is salvation.[67] The *Deesis* is in a sense an evocation of the Last Judgement and as such was often found in the apse of churches, which were used for funerary purposes, such as the crypt of the Monastery of Hosios Loukas, Bačkovo, Sarica Kilise and the chapel of the hermit Peter at Koriša in Yugoslavia.[68] The *Deesis*, seen in an eschatological context or not, tends to be easily invested with a funereal function and so is often a preferred choice for the decoration of the burial space.[69] At Humor, the fact that the tomb of the founder has a *Deesis* painted above it emphasises the idea of prayer and the protection sought through burial within the church. The imperial *Deesis*, present at Dobrovăţ and Moldoviţa (built 1532, painted 1537), is also significant for the iconography of princely foundations.[70] In the burial chamber at Dobrovăţ the scene above the entrance to the nave is a monumental *Deesis* with Jesus enthroned, depicted as high priest, the Virgin as Empress and John the Baptist. The meaning of this image is further decoded by the prayer written underneath it. The iconographical programme of the church of Şendrea comprises a *Hetoimasia*, Christ in a *Deesis* and the Ancient of

[64] Székely, *Sfetnicii*, p. 231.
[65] C. Ginzburg, 'Représentation, le mot, l'idée, la chose', *Annales* 46 (1991), 1219–30.
[66] Sinigalia, 'L'église de l'ascension', 23.
[67] Crăciun, 'Ctitorirea', pp. 152–3; Mathews, *Art of Byzantium*, p. 135.
[68] Mouriki, 'Iconography of the mosaics', pp. 58, 61–2.
[69] Rodley, *Cave Monasteries*, pp. 55, 207, 212; Mathews, *Art of Byzantium*, p. 135; Kitzinger, *Mosaics of St Mary's*, pp. 209–10; Mouriki, 'Iconography of the mosaics', pp. 58, 70.
[70] Cincheza Buculei, 'Programul', p. 87.

Days.[71] This seems to combine the Trinity, the idea of intercessory prayer and the Last Judgement. Moreover, alongside the tombstone there is an intercessory composition, an Imperial *Deesis* with St Nicholas replacing John the Baptist, as he is the patron of the church. The popularity of the *Deesis* composition can be accounted for by the fact that the Virgin and John the Baptist are the most powerful intercessors, the Virgin because she is herself exempt from sin and John the Baptist because he was saved by Christ himself in the womb of his mother. Moreover, the *Deesis* is often (at Dobrovăţ, Probota, Moldoviţa) placed among the martyrs depicted in the *Menologion*. This composition conveys complex messages, it presents princely authority as a reflection of divine authority, but the eschatological message of the prayer is in direct relation with the burial place. The Virgin, John the Baptist and all the other saints are praying for the forgiveness of the sins of the founders.[72] This extended *Deesis* might be a pictorial expression of the intercession, in the form of *Theotokion*, an invocation addressed to Christ by the Virgin, the Baptist, the apostles, prophets, bishops, and the righteous and finally by all the saints for the salvation of the deceased, which concluded the funeral service.[73]

The burial chamber at Humor contains an extended depiction of the life of the Virgin promoting incarnational theology. This has a salvific undertone as well, as the incarnation makes salvation possible. The Marian emphasis is generally introduced because of the intercessory dimension adequate for a necropolis.[74] The eschatological dimension is strongly highlighted by the inclusion in the programme of the funerary chamber of either a Last Judgement composition, or simply the *Hetoimasia* (Dolheştii Mari), but also by the depiction of the competition between the forces of good and evil for the soul of the founder. This is suggested by the struggle between Michael and the Devil over the body of Moses, which is presented at Humor. This highlights Michael's role in funerary iconography, while the issue of salvation, intercession and responsibility is also represented.[75] At Suceviţa, the life of Moses is depicted in the burial chamber presumably with a similar intention.[76]

There are a few other features that distinguish Moldavian votive images and highlight the relationship of the laity with the divine. First of all, the donors tend to be the same size as the sacred figures, which is unusual,

---

[71] Sinigalia, 'L'église de l'ascension', 26.
[72] E. Cincheza Buculei, 'Menologul de la Dobrovăţ (1529)', *SCIA* 39 (1992), 7; Cincheza Buculei, 'Programul', pp. 88–9.
[73] Mouriki, 'Iconography of the mosaics', pp. 71–3.
[74] Borsook, *Messages in Mosaic*, p. 72; H. Maguire, 'The Cycle of Images in the Church', in Safran (ed.), *Heaven on Earth*, p. 147.
[75] Cincheza Buculei, 'Programul', pp. 90–1.       [76] *Ibid.*, pp. 92–3.

as in many votive panels elsewhere in the Byzantine Empire, the donors are represented as much smaller than the sacred characters.[77] Moreover, the pose of Moldavian donors is distinctive, as they are not depicted either kneeling or performing *proskynesis*.[78] They are making an offering to Christ, but are generally shown standing, advancing towards the throne of the Saviour. Finally, many votive images, or portraits of founders involved the donor depicted with an intercessor, the Virgin or a saint, who mediated their relationship to Christ. Clearly these images emphasise saintly intercession, but the messages conveyed can be read in more subtle and more complex ways. The fact that the donors are crowned may be construed as an attempt to stress the divine source of their authority.[79]

This elaborate construction of sacred space as a stage for the relationship to the divine leads one to explore the motives of princes who wished to be buried in the church or to construct elaborate burial sites as vehicles for complex dynastic and religious messages. For instance, in the inscription at Războieni (Valea Albă) from 1496 the prince explicitly states he had built the church for the Christians who had died there, in the battle with the Ottomans (1476). The text is quite moving, as it alludes to the connection between the church and the battle site, the dramatic circumstances the church was meant to commemorate and the Christians who had died there.[80] This idea is further supported by archaeological evidence which shows that the church was built on top of a mass grave where the remnants of those fallen in battle were interred.[81] This is also a good example of the prince taking responsibility for the salvation of his subjects and presenting himself as the main channel of communication with the sacred. The inscription in the church at Reuseni (1503–4) highlights a more personal level of involvement and emphasizes the dynastic dimension.[82] The church started to be built by Ştefan cel Mare, but was finished by his son Bogdan III in 1504. The place which was chosen is laden with meaning, because Ştefan's father was beheaded there by his political rivals. The dedication of the church is also evocative, as the chosen feast is the beheading of John the Baptist. Obviously, both Ştefan cel Mare and Bogdan were concerned for the soul of their father, but they also wished to make a gesture with symbolic value for the glory of their lineage.

[77] Rodley, *Cave Monasteries*, pp. 55, 71, 156, 173, 178, 182, 198.
[78] *Ibid.*, pp. 54, 156, 166–7, 178, 182, 200; Kitzinger, *Mosaic of St Mary's*, pp. 190, 197–8.
[79] Rodley, *Cave Monasteries*, p. 73; Kitzinger, *Mosaic of St Mary's*, pp. 197, 199–200, 201–2.
[80] Balş, 'Bisericile lui Ştefan cel Mare', 75–6; Crăciun, 'Ctitorirea', p. 157.
[81] Bătrâna, 'Arhitectura', p. 167.
[82] Balş, 'Bisericile lui Ştefan cel Mare', 117; Crăciun, 'Ctitorirea', p. 157.

In order to complete the picture one still needs to explain why monastic foundations were chosen as the burial sites of the princes, as the churches where these elaborate funerary rooms would be constructed. In the early Church people requested burial *ad sanctos*. While the western Church evolved gradually towards burial *apud ecclesia*, where people wished to be buried in the nave or even the choir area, in the immediate proximity of the Sacrament or near the statues of major intercessors, burial in the eastern Church seemed to perpetuate the idea of interment *ad sanctos*.[83] Certainly, in the beginning the people who wished to be buried within the church wished to emulate the example of martyrs, but later occurrences from various places in the Orthodox realm suggest that this continued to be a major concern of the founders. For instance, in Cappadocian churches, the memorials of founders tended to be the site of hermitages, made sacred through the association with anchorites.[84] The nature of sanctity itself had obviously been redefined and the holy recluse, practising an extreme asceticism became the most respected figure, whose prayers would have the highest intercessory value. If the founder was buried in a church the community of the faithful and clergy would become responsible for his soul. If the foundation is a monastic church, the sanctity of the regular community living there and their prayers would be more effective in ensuring the salvation of the founders.[85] Thus, the responsibility for the soul of the dead is collective and shared by the founder and clergy. The family would intervene, through its endowments and prayers on behalf of the deceased, while the clergy promised to pray for them on designated occasions. The patronage of churches in itself was meant to ensure the salvation and protection of the dead in a family, the ancestors of the founder, the founder himself and, ultimately his heirs. This idea is strongly emphasised by the *pisania*, the inscription accompanying the foundation.[86] Unfortunately, the evidence does not allow one to speculate whether the move to the burial chamber meant that burial and commemoration services took place in this special funerary room rather than the *narthex* as Orthodox tradition prescribed. Starting from the assumption that the iconography of an eastern Orthodox church mirrors the liturgy,

---

[83] Ariès, *L'homme devant la mort*, pp. 37–96; Borsook, *Messages in Mosaic*, pp. 69–70.

[84] Rodley, *Cave Monasteries*, pp. 248–9; Ousterhout, 'The Holy Space', pp. 99, 105; Maguire, 'Cycle of Images', pp. 124–7; G. Vikan, 'Byzantine Pilgrims' Art' in Safran (ed.), *Heaven on Earth*, pp. 229–31, 262.

[85] Puşcaşu, *Actul*, pp. 58–9; M. Crăciun, 'Burial and Piety in Comparative Perspective. Moldavia 15th and 16th centuries', in N. Bocşan and N. Edroiu (eds.), *Studii istorice. Omagiu profesorului Camil Mureşan* (Cluj, 1997), pp. 117, 126–7, 221; Rodley, *Cave Monasteries*, pp. 248–9; Mouriki, 'Iconography of the mosaics', p. 64; Borsook, *Messages in Mosaic*, p. 53.

[86] Crăciun, 'Ctitorirea', pp. 155–6.

the expansion of an iconographical programme with funerary significance focused on the hope of salvation from the *narthex* to the burial chamber could be construed as a sign that burial and commemoration services may have taken place in this room next to the tombs of the princes.[87]

However, in Moldavia, although the prayers of the monks were deemed to be the most effective and consequently could be held to account for the choice of monastic establishments as the burial sites of princes, there is little evidence that the sanctity of a site was associated with relics. One rare example is provided by the monk Tudosie and his sister Odochia who made a donation to Voroneţ, the church they wished to be buried in. The reason for choosing this monastery was the presence of the relics of the hermit Daniil.[88] Thus it would appear that when Moldavian princes wished to be buried in the church, this was determined to a significant extent by their desire to be interred close to the altar, where the sacrifice of Christ was re-enacted and the Sacrament itself dispensed. This is suggested by the fact that, as long as the plan of the church was a *basilica* the prince wished to be buried in the nave. However, in an Orthodox church burial in the sanctuary area was impossible and even burial in the *naos* was not encouraged. The princes who still wished to be closer to the Sacrament than burial in the *narthex* allowed, devised the idea of the funerary room which communicated with the *naos*. The importance attached to the Sacrament and the liturgy is also suggested by requests for prayer. These were no longer attached to saint's days, but rather to particular days of the week, which were significant to the Christological cycle and especially the events of the Passion. Saturday, the day of the *Anastasis*, when Christ descended into hell and saved the souls of Adam and Eve, was a much favoured choice. Moreover, the founders started to request that their names be mentioned not only in the *pomelnic* of the monastery, but also while the gifts were being prepared in the *prothesis*.[89] The latter started to be decorated with an image of the *Vir Dolorum*, which is sometimes (for example at Probota) positioned above the list of founders' names (plate 8.3). It has been argued that although Eucharistic subjects are to be expected in the *prothesis* and there are a few examples, such as the figure of Christ in the Taxiarches church at Kastoria or the Communion of the Apostles in the tenth-century Koloritissa cave church

[87] Cincheza-Buculei, 'Programul', pp. 85–92.
[88] *Documente privind Istoria României, A Moldova veacul* XVI, 4 vols. (Bucharest, 1952–54), IV, pp. 57, 275.
[89] M. Crăciun, 'Piety and individual options in sixteenth century Moldavia', in M. Crăciun and O. Ghitta (eds.), *Church and Society in East Central Europe* (Cluj, 1998), pp. 319–23; *Documente privind Istoria României, A Moldova veacurile* XIV–XV, I, p. 344; *Documente privind Istoria României, A Moldova veacul* XVI, IV, p. 194.

Plate 8.3 Vir Dolorum at Probota.

at Naxos or the bust of Christ Emmanuel in the late twelfth-century Megara church, there seems to have been no continuous tradition in this respect.[90] In fact there are numerous depictions of saints in the *prothesis*.[91] This enhanced interest in the Sacrament suggests parallels with Catholic rather than Orthodox practice and reflects the western influence in the construction of sacred space in Moldavia.[92]

[90] K. M. Skawran, *The Development of Middle Byzantine Fresco Painting in Greece* (Pretoria, 1982), pp. 27–8, 175, 276; H. Belting, *The Image and its Public in the Middle Ages. Form and Function of Early Paintings of the Passion* (New Rochelle, 1990), pp. 193, 123, 126; W. Podlacha and G. Nandriş, *Umanismul picturii murale postbizantine* (Bucharest, 1985), pp. 119–23.
[91] Skawran, *Development of Middle Byzantine Fresco Painting*, pp. 159, 166, 170, 173, 176, 182; Mouriki, 'Iconography of the mosaics', p. 58.
[92] E. D. Perl, '"That man might become God": central themes in Byzantine theology', in Safran (ed.), *Heaven on Earth*, pp. 39–57.

First of all, this chapter has attempted to explain the emergence and development of the burial chamber, an original architectural solution of the Moldavian church with a specific funerary function. I have attempted to highlight the fact that, although the religious experience of the Moldavian elite was more or less circumscribable to that of the Eastern Orthodox Church in general, contacts with and receptivity to Catholic religious practice may account for some of its more original features. This development has to be understood within the framework of a policy of control over patronage, which became an increasingly coherent strategy between mid-fifteenth and the end of the sixteenth century. Although in the existing literature, political motivations have been held to account for this policy, the evidence suggests that dynastic considerations, often equatable to 'class' consciousness and ultimately the projection of the ruler as the spiritual leader of the country were equally important. Within this context specific churches tended to be designated as princely necropolis and invested with a complexity of dynastic and religious messages.

While burial in the nave was the preferred option in basilicas, after the adoption of the *trefoil* plan, the most coveted burial places were in the *narthex* and subsequently a separate burial chamber. This custom reflected the sanctity of the building and the importance of burial close to the altar. While the emergence of the burial chamber can be explained in social and structural terms, this chapter has illustrated the important eschatological and dynastic reasons for its emergence. It combined a desire to be buried close to the altar, reflecting Catholic influences, as well as consolidating or establishing dynastic associations. The burial chamber was the site of the final rite of passage and had important salvific significance. As the iconography of the funerary room illustrates, it was the place where the human and the divine interacted. The evidence suggests that this relationship is mediated by both human and divine intercessors, on the one hand, the regular clergy of the monasteries, whose duty was to pray incessantly and on the other, the saints in the *Menologion* or the two major intercessors, the Virgin and John the Baptist. Thus, concern for salvation and interest in the consolidation of a dynasty have ultimately led to the emergence of a special burial space with a specific funerary political function.

# 9　Reading Rome as a sacred landscape, c. 1586–1635

*Simon Ditchfield*

## I　Introduction – *Roma antica* versus *Roma moderna* – the missing dimension

Even as Rome was reinventing itself as the capital of the first world religion, its universal virtues of holiness and devotion were being particularised and owned by *Roman* Catholics as never before. This process centred on an investigation of unprecedented scope and thoroughness of the material and archival remains from the city's early Christian past. This enterprise entailed a fundamental change in the image of Rome: from being a spectacle itself – an impressive, if essentially static backdrop for nostalgic ruminations on past, classical Roman greatness (*Roma antica*) – to becoming a dynamic setting for spectacle – a shining model of Counter-Reformation 'best practice' as reflected in a period of ambitious new building activity, which framed and facilitated the progress of increasing numbers of pilgrims who visited the city (*Roma moderna*).[1] Within a relatively short space of time, from the publication of the first edition of the revised Roman martyrology with the historical annotations of Cesare Baronio in 1586 to the posthumous appearance of Antonio Bosio's *Roma sotterranea* in 1635 devout Romans and pilgrims visiting the city were provided with texts that not only mapped the universal saints' calendar of the Roman Catholic Church onto (and underneath) the particular physical topography of the city with unprecedented care and attention to detail, but also reclaimed for veneration the material culture of Roman Christians from the first centuries AD in such a way as to make possible a comprehensive mental (and spiritual) re-imagining of early Christian devotional practice.

The mismatch between the poetic splendour of *Roma antica* as represented in classical literature and the prosaic, even sordid reality of

---

This chapter is dedicated to the memory of Clare 'Petra' Rosser (1958–2001).

[1] For a recent, clear treatment of this idea see L. Spezzaferro, 'Baroque Rome: a "Modern City"', in P. van Kessel and E. Schulte (eds.), *Rome – Amsterdam: Two Growing Cities in Seventeenth-Century Europe* (Amsterdam, 1997), pp. 2–12.

*Roma moderna* experienced by the visitor, to use two labels which enjoyed currency throughout the early modern period, was gleefully picked up and developed polemically in the first history of Italy in English, which was published in 1549.[2] Its author, the Protestant humanist William Thomas (*c.* 1507–54), visited Rome in the Christmas of 1547 during his three-year stay in the Italian peninsula (*c.* 1545–8). Something of the sense of loss and decay he felt can be seen from the opening paragraph of his description, where he wrote:

Thinking to find a great contentation in the sight of Rome . . . did it grieve me to see the only jewel, mirror, mistress and beauty of this world, that never had her like nor (as I think) never shall, lie so desolate and disfigured that there is no lamentable case to be heard or loathsome thing to be seen that may be compared to a small part of it.[3]

He closed with a dismissive, summary account of Papal Rome, the tenor of which may be gathered by his inclusion of the proverb: 'in Rome the harlot hath a better life than she that is a Roman's wife'.[4]

By contrast, a visitor to the city later in the same century, the Catholic priest and translator of scripture, Gregory Martin (1542?–1582), left a very different, decidedly upbeat account of his time spent there (1576–8). As its title: *Roma sancta* and its division into two books, 'Concerning devotion' and 'Concerning charitie' unambiguously suggest, this work portrayed the city as a shining beacon of the Catholic Reformation.[5] For Martin: 'yea Jerusalem in maner is come to Rome' and he rejoiced in the fact that the pagan ruins of the city were neglected in favour of the Christian monuments. For him, this symbolised nothing less than:

the victorie of Christ over the Divel, of Peter over Nero, of the See Apostolicke over the earthly empyre, of Rome the spouse of Christ over Rome the whoore of Babylon.

All this enabled him to conclude: 'And thus far Rome is now nothing degenerated from Rome in old tyme shuch as the [Church] fathers have described it.'[6]

---

[2] W. Thomas, *The Historie of Italie* . . . (London, 1549; repr 1561). There is an edition with modernised spelling: G. B. Parks (ed.), *The History of Italy (1549)* (Ithaca, NY, 1963). Subsequent references are made to this more recent printing. However, an essay – 'A shorte discourse of Pilgrimage and Relycles', containing material that was also drawn upon for *Roma sancta* – did appear in a volume of his writings entitled *A Treatise of Christian Peregrination* (n.p., 1583).

[3] Thomas, *History of Italy*, pp. 20–1.    [4] *Ibid.*, p. 50.

[5] All references to the work will be made from the printed version edited by G. B. Parks, *Roma sancta (1581)* (Rome, 1969). The work remained unpublished until this date.

[6] Martin, *Roma sancta*, pp. 9–10, 11.

Sixtus V (pope, 1585–90) is associated more than anyone else with the supersession of what might be termed the 'humanist' view of the city expressed by Thomas – as a spectacle or setting for reflection on the past greatness of a civilisation – by a specifically Counter-Reformation one, in which Rome became a setting for devout spectacle, as articulated by Martin.[7] The pope's plans for the city reincorporated the spacious emptiness of the so-called *disabitato* by means not only of new streets, squares, refurbished churches and modern buildings which the pope had built or planned as conduits for pilgrims, but also through the revival of Lenten visits to the stational churches which effectively knitted together the city both within and without the walls.[8] In this way, an ordered pattern was created for pilgrims who were arriving in ever-increasing numbers since the Jubilee of 1575 to experience Rome: 'as a spectacle of fayth and good workes', to borrow Martin's evocative phrase.[9]

This contemporary awareness of the city as a place of theatre or setting *for* spectacle and procession is attested by Antonio Tempesta's famous representation of the Rome published in 1593. Here, as Tempesta explicitly states in the opening phrase of his dedication of the map to Giacomo Bosio (Antonio's uncle), the plan presents 'not the ancient city, but that which we see flourishing today under the Holy Popes'.[10] Tempesta took advantage of his chosen viewpoint, looking east, hovering over the Gianiculum, which marked the western limit of the city across the Tiber (still known today as Trastevere). Armed with a fish-eye lens of the mind that would defy even the most gifted of today's camera makers, he not only foregrounded that emblematic project of *Roma moderna* – the rebuilding of St Peter's, but simultaneously exaggerated the size of the densely populated 'Tiber bend' area of the city. In this way, Tempesta also integrated the thinly populated area of the city inside the walls – east and south of the Capitoline hill, which was known as the *disabitato*. This was largely achieved by means of downplaying the

---

[7] For a fair assessment of what these changes involved see H. Gamrath, *Roma sancta renovata: studi sull'urbanistica di Roma nella seconda metà del sec.* XVI *con particolare riferimento al pontificato dei Sisto V (1585–1590)* (Rome, 1987).

[8] See P. Ugonio, *Historia delle Stationi di Roma* (Rome, 1588). I am most grateful to Tobias Kämpf for drawing my attention to the importance of this liturgical revival for the reimagining of Rome's urban topography.

[9] Martin, *Roma sancta*, p. 8.

[10] 'Urbem non illam veterem, sed quam hodie sub Sanctis Pontificibus florentem aspicimus . . .' This map has been reprinted in loose leaf form by the Vatican Library: *Roma al tempo di Clemente VIII – la pianta di Roma di Antonio Tempesta del 1493 riprodotta da una copia vaticana del 1606*, with an introduction by Franz Ehrle (Vatican City, n.d.). See also the reproduction in book form with detailed topographical commentary, S. Borsi, *Roma di Sisto V: la pianta di Antonio Tempesta, 1593* (Rome, 1986).

latter's relative extent. Such an approach also allowed him to bring to the viewer's notice not only early Christian basilicas, several of which, such as St Giovanni in Laterano and St Maria Maggiore, were now identified topographically by relocated Egyptian obelisks, but also a number of recently built or rebuilt churches which testified to the city's religious rebirth. These included: the Oratorian St Maria in Vallicella and the Jesuit Gesù.

In this Tempesta was not only departing from previous cartographic representations of the city, (such as those by Francesco Paccioti (1557) and Mario Cartaro (1576) from the west and that by Etienne Dupérac (1577) from the east), but also from his own frescoed depiction in the map gallery of the Vatican palace, which clearly show the extent of the city within the walls that was thinly populated – a feature of Rome that was particularly noted, for example, by Montaigne in his *Travel Journal* for 1580/1.[11] Mention of Montaigne brings me to my principal theme, which is concerned with how the supersession of *Roma antica* by *Roma moderna* was accompanied by a less well-known process: the spatial and mental reappropriation of the city's early Christian past – a *Roma antica cristiana*, if you like – and how this process integrated the *disabitato* both above and below ground, inside and outside the city walls into the liturgical life of the devout. It was Montaigne who, building on the humanist trope of nostalgia defined by loss, remarked at how: 'an ancient Roman could not recognize the site of his city even if he saw it' since subsequent centuries had used classical Roman buildings as foundations for their own humble dwellings to the extent that by the late sixteenth century: 'It is easy to see that many streets are more than thirty feet below those of today'.[12] Montaigne's image of chronology expressed vertically serves my purpose as a powerful metaphor for the way in which the work of two individuals reclaimed for Roman Catholics (and *Roman* Catholics) not only a sense of the historical depth of tradition, but also added a specifically spatial dimension that testified to the antiquity and therefore legitimacy of Roman Catholic devotional practices. They are the Oratorian, Cesare Baronio and the layman, Antonio Bosio.

[11] 'La ville est, d'à cette heure, toute plantée de long de la riviere du Tibre, deçà et delà. Le quartier montueux, qui estoit le siege de la vieille ville, et où il faisoit tous les jours mille promenades et visites, est saisi de quelques eglises et aucunes maisons rares et jardins des Cardinaux'. F. Rigolot (ed.), *Journal de voyage de Michel de Montaigne* (Paris, 1992), pp. 91–2. The journal was not written for publication, which had to wait until 1774. For the maps by Paccioti, Cartaro and Dupérac see figs. 133, 136 and 137, respectively, of I. Insolera, *Roma. Immagini e realtà dal x al xx secolo* (Rome and Bari, 1980).

[12] 'Il croyoit qu'un ancien Romain ne sauroit recognoistre l'assiette de sa ville quand il la verroit . . . Il est aysé à voir que plusieurs rues sont à plus de trente pieds profond au dessous de celles d'à cette heure', *Journal de voyage*, p. 101.

## II          Cesare Baronio – reclaiming a *Roman* Catholic topography of truth

It was Cesare Baronio (1538–1607), who encapsulated more clearly than any other contemporary the excitement engendered by the rediscovery in 1578 of the so-called Catacombs of St Priscilla (which only since 1966 have been more accurately identified as 'anonima di Via Anapo')[13] when, in the second volume of his magisterial statement of the historical continuity the Roman Catholic Church professed with its Apostolic origins, the *Annales ecclesiastici*, he wrote:

We can find no better words to describe its extent and its many corridors than to call it a subterranean city . . . All Rome was filled with wonder, for it had no idea that in its neighbourhood there was a hidden city, filled with tombs from the persecutions of the Christians.[14]

For Baronio himself, however, this discovery had been long-anticipated. For not only was it a confirmation of: 'That which we knew before from written accounts . . . and see with our own eyes the confirmation of the [descriptions in] Jerome and Prudentius', but also a vindication of the topography of Oratorian devotion as embodied by the example of the congregation's founder, Philip Neri.[15] For it was Neri, who soon after his arrival in Rome in 1533 began to practise nocturnal devotions in the only catacombs which had been visited pretty well without substantial interruption since the early Middle Ages, those of St Sebastiano on the Via Appia. Then, in 1559, in a deliberate effort to provide a devout

---

[13] For a recent assessment of contemporary reactions to its discovery see V. F. Nicolai, 'Storia e topografia della catacomba anonima di via Anapo', in J. G. Deckers, G. Mietke and A. Weiland (eds.), *Die Katacombe 'Anonima di Via Anapo'. Repertorium der Malereien* (Vatican City, 1991), pp. 3–4. My thanks to Giuseppe Guazzelli for drawing this publication to my attention. Cf. G. Ferretto, *Note storico-bibliografiche di archeologia cristiana* (Vatican City, 1942), pp. 104–14. Antonio Bosio himself refers to this event, as told to him by an eyewitness, the Dominican scholar Alfonso Ciacconio, in his *Roma sotterranea* (Rome, 1632 [1635]), p. 511.

[14] '. . . quod nullo magis proprio vocabulo dixerimus prae eius amplitudine, multisque atque diversis eiusdem viis, quam subterraneam civitatem . . . Obstupuit Urbs, cum in suis suburbiis abditas se novit habere civitates, Christianorum tempore persecutionis olim colonias . . .' Cesare Baronio (and continuators), *Annales ecclesiastici*, 27 vols. (Bar-le-Duc, 1864–83; 1st edn, Rome, 1588–1607), II, an. 130, n. 2, p. 213. Cf. 'Li Cimiterij dunque sono caverne e antri, ò spelonche sotterranee, cavate nel tufo . . . con infinite strade, vicoli e rigiri simili a laberinthi oscurissimi . . . sono spaziosi e ampli in modo che ciascuno rassembra una gran città . . .' Antonio Bosio, *Roma sotterranea* (Rome, 1632 [1635]), p. 1.

[15] 'quod legebat in chartis . . . tunc plenius intellexit; quae enim de iisdem apud S. Hieronymum vel Prudentium legerat, suis ipsius oculis intuens, vehementer admirabunda spectavit'. Baronio, *Annales*, II, an. 130, n. 2, p. 213.

recreational alternative to the excesses of Carnival, Neri reinstituted the Seven Church's devotion.[16]

Those attending, who by the 1570s frequently numbered over 1,000 people, were asked to meditate on scenes from Christ's passion between each of the seven principal basilicas of early Christian Rome and sustained by means of the communal singing of *laudi* and the promise of a spare but, by all accounts, rather jolly picnic at the half-way point, usually in the park of the Villa Mattei on the Caelian hill. In this way, the universal Christian message of redemption was grafted onto the particular topography of Rome.[17] Moreover, it was a topography which included parts of the city both within and without the walls that were still substantially a wilderness for the cultivation of vegetables, the grazing of sheep and the quarrying of classical roman *spolia*. But if Neri may be said to have understood the significance for the embattled Counter-Reformation Church of the legitimising role which could be played by physical ownership of *vestigia* from such an heroic chapter of its early Christian past, it was left to his faithful lieutenant Baronio and the younger Antonio Bosio to chart and mine this promised land – *Roma sotterranea* – for the spiritual consolation of their contemporaries.

A key feature of Tridentine liturgical reform, which began with the introduction of the revised Roman breviary in 1568, was the drastic pruning of the calendar of saints' feasts in order to free up space in which to recite the ordinary, ferial office in which key passages from Scripture and patristic writings were read. According to the revised Roman Breviary, no fewer than twenty-two days in April, for example, were left free of obligation to recite particular saints' offices (though when Easter fell in that month Holy Week celebrations naturally took preference over all other feasts, whose number would therefore have been further reduced). At issue here was the need to reconcile the universal calendar with the devotions of particular dioceses, religious orders and churches. One of the key instruments adopted here was that of historical scholarship – where, when and in what circumstances had the saint or saints in question died, what

---

[16] A. Gallonio, *Vita del Beato P. Filippo Neri Fiorentino* (Rome, 1601; repr. Rome 1995), pp. 16, 18, 102, 104 (pagination is from the 1995 edn). Cf. Gamrath, *Roma sancta renovata*, pp. 128–39 and A. Cistellini, *San Filippo Neri. L'oratorio e la congregazione oratoriana: storia e spiritualità*, 3 vols. (Brescia, 1989), I, pp. 96–7.

[17] According to Pietro Focile, in his testimony at Filippo's canonisation trial given on 23 April 1610, already during Carnival in 1560 ('giovedi grasso') there were as many as 2,000 taking part. Although given Focile's age at the time of trial (seventy-five), he might well have been indulging in nostaglic exaggeration. See G. Incisa della Rochetta and N. Vian (eds.), *Il primo processo per San Filippo Neri*, 4 vols. (Vatican City, 1957–63), III, pp. 35–6. Cf. the contemporary directions of Virgilio Spada, 'Istruttioni per chi haverà la cura d'assistere al giardino, quando si dà mangiare a quelli che vanno alle sette chiese, il giovedì grasso', in C. Gasbarri, *La Visita filippina alle sette chiese* (Rome, 1947), pp. 113–30.

were the key exemplary deeds or events of their lives and where were their relics now to be found. Granted the frequent absence of hard historical data for many of those listed in the calendar, this was frequently supplemented by recourse to more purely liturgical criteria: what evidence was there for the existence of a long-standing cult of a given saint? With the aid of such tools, whose precise deployment was overseen, from 1588, by the Sacred Congregation of Rites and Ceremonies (in conjunction with the Congregations of the Index and Holy Office), Rome went a long way towards reconciling the particular with the universal, devotionally speaking.[18]

One of the highly active members of the Congregation of Rites was Cesare Baronio, whose historical notes to the revised *Roman Martyrology* of 1584, first published in 1586 and then revised again in 1589 and 1598, provided the Eternal City with an inventory that identified and located – chronologically and, wherever possible, topographically – its holy heroes.[19] Technically speaking, the Roman martyrology was a historical martyrology – which is to say, it provided not only a calendar of names and places of martyrdom arranged according to the day of their festival, but it also added summary accounts of their lives and deaths. As such, it stood in a long tradition of similar works stretching back to Bede's martyrology of *c.* AD 730. However, Baronio's edition was of unprecedented thoroughness and detail. While the nucleus of his annotations was already substantially in place in his first, 1586 edition – particularly those relating to information Baronio had gleaned from literary sources (both printed and in manuscript) – Giuseppe Guazzelli has recently demonstrated that information relating to the material remains of early Christian Rome was regularly updated right on up to the Baronian edition of 1598. For example, the entry on St Priscilla (16 January) in the second edition of 1589, contains reference to the Roman structures, identified as the *Thermae Novati*, which had only been found underneath the church of St Pudenziana as recently as 1588.[20]

---

[18] For a full consideration of this process as it relates to the cult of saints see my 'Santità e culti nel mondo della Riforma e della Controriforma (1560–1800ca)', in S. Boesch Gajano, A. Benvenuti, S. Ditchfield, R. Rusconi and F. Scorza Barcellona, *Storia della santità nel cristianesimo occidentale* (Rome, 2005) ch. 5.

[19] My understanding of Baronio's erudite elaboration of this text is heavily indebted to the ongoing research of Giuseppe Guazzelli, who is currently completing a dottorato di ricerca entitled *Cesare Baronio ed il Martyrologium Romanum: le redazione del libro liturgico e la progressiva definizione del suo contenuto alla luce dei documenti baroniani (ca. 1582–86)* at the University of Rome II 'Tor Vergata' (relatore F. Scorza Barcellona).

[20] *Martyrologium romanum* (Antwerp, 1589), p. 30–1 n. 1 (cf. *Mart. Rom.* (Rome, 1586), pp. 30–2 n. 1). These had been uncovered during the restoration of the church which had been undertaken at the behest of Cardinal Enrico Caetani and begun only the previous year (1588). Cf. *Annales*, II, ad an. 162, p. 298. (Pagination refers to the Bar-le-Duc edition, 1864.)

Likewise, Baronio was ever careful to incorporate into his annotations information relating to recent translations of relics. That best known to scholars today is undoubtedly the procession of the relics of the eunuch Christian slaves, St Nereo and St Achilleo together with that of their well-born mistress, niece of the Emperor Domitian, Flavia Domitilla (whom they converted), to Cesare Baronio's titular church, which was dedicated to the two male martyrs on 11 May 1597.[21] Described evocatively by Richard Krautheimer in his article as 'A Christian Triumph', this translation took the form of a solemn four-hour procession from the church of St Adriano ai Fori (which had originally been the Senate House), around the bottom of the Capitoline Hill to the Gesù, then back over the Capitoline, across the Forum (taking care to use and appropriate the triumphal arches of Septimus Severus, Titus and Constantine, which were specially decorated with Christian inscriptions for the occasion), before skirting the southern edge of the Palatine Hill on their way to the basilica of St Nereo and St Achilleo that was situated just across from the ruined baths of Caracalla.[22]

Although Baronio's census of the sacred was not restricted solely to Rome, an analysis of the 1598 edition reveals that there was at least one and frequently several saints martyred in the city on 226 days of the year, while the topographical index to the same edition lists 473 saints under the entry for Rome, which does not include over 1,500 anonymous saints referred to over the course of the year nor the four feasts which simply indicated 'item plurimorum' in the space where they were usually listed by name. Attentive readers (and listeners) of the *Martyrologium romanum* – whether in the privacy of their own silent devotions or at *prime* in choir – were almost daily transported back to Rome's own heroic early Christian

---

[21] See *Martyrologium romanum*, pp. 326–7 (12 May). Cf. the eyewitness account of the Oratorian Pietro Perrachione given in a letter to his coreligionist Antonio Talpa of 16 May 1597, Archive of the Congregation of the Oratory at Naples, 169, fols. 135–6. Given this archive's notorious difficulty of access, it is fortunate that the relevant part of the letter is fully transcribed in Cistellini, *San Filippo Neri. L'oratorio e la congregazione oratoriana*, II, pp. 1165–6.

[22] R. Krautheimer, 'A Christian Triumph in 1597' in D. Fraser *et al.*, *Essays in the History of Art Presented to Rudolf Wittkower* (London, 1967), pp. 174–8. Krautheimer confusingly and erroneously refers to a manuscript account by a certain Antonio 'Galliano' (Biblioteca Vallicelliana, Rome, G. 99, fols. 1r–17r). This should, of course, read, 'Gallonio' (on whom see further below). Other contemporary (or near contemporary) translations mentioned by Baronio in his edition of the Roman martyrology include those of: St Susanna caused by Cardinal Rusticucci's restoration of her church beginning in 1593 (11 August, note. c.), p. 547; St Abundius and St Abundantius to the Gesù from St Cosmo e St Damiano in 1583 (16 September, note e), pp. 635–6 and St Nemesius, St Lucilla and others translated to the church of St Maria Nuova, at the behest of Cardinal Antonio Caraffa, during the pontificate of Gregory XIII (31 October, note b), p. 742. All page references are to the Cologne, 1610 edition.

past, as they heard condensed but vivid accounts of their predecessors' steadfastness in torment.[23]

This 1584 edition of the Roman martyrology was the first to be officially endorsed by the papacy as a liturgical text of universal validity in the prefatory apostolic letter *Emendato iam*. Given the official standing of this edition, it is no surprise that Baronio took this text as the basis for his annotated edition published two years later. Guazzelli now argues convincingly that we must be prepared to consider that Baronio was already heavily involved in the drafting of the main text of the 1584 edition. This re-evaluation of the role played by the author of the *Annales ecclesiastici* in the revision of the *Martyrologium romanum* surely helps us to understand the important part played by the latter in providing historical justification for aspects of Tridentine devotional practice, which were then being contested by the Reformers. These included papal supremacy, whose apostolic origins are asserted, *inter alia*, in notes to the feasts of St Agatho (pope, 678–81) and of the *Cathedra Petri*; the veiling of religious women, whose antiquity is argued for in notes for the feast of St Flavia Domitilla; the cult of the Blessed Virgin Mary and the honour due to the Host, whose universal validity is set out in notes for the Feast of the Assumption and for the feast of St Thariscus (both celebrated on the same day).[24]

---

[23] See, for example, the entry for St Processi e St Martiniani, al 2 July: '. . . Romae via Aurelia natalis sanctorum martyrum Processi et Martiniani, qua a B. Petro Apostolo in custodia Mamertini baptizati, sub Nerone oris contusionem, equuleum, nervos, fustes, flammas, scorpionesque perpessi, novissime gladio caesi, martyrio coronati sunt'. This passage is characteristic of the bulk of entries for brevity, topographical references and the macabre catalogue of the various kinds of torture the martyr(s) in question have undergone. An analysis of the last edition of 1598 revised by Baronio (in a reprint of Cologne, 1610) shows that there were at least one and often several saints martyred in Rome on 226 days of the year (i.e. 62 per cent of the total). On average, therefore, saints martyred in Rome were celebrated two days out of three. However, these figures do not show the absolute number of Roman martyrs in relation to those martyred elsewhere, and the predominance of the former. This can be seen in the list of almost 500 saints given in the topographical index found in Baronio's revised Roman martyrology. Furthermore, this does not include anonymous saints referred to on various feast days with the phrase: 'item plurimorum' (as on 2 January, 2 March, 10 April and 24 June). Baronio included a 'De immensa martyrum multitudine elogium' on the final page of the prefatory material (p. xxxvi). This comprised quotes from the works of St Cyprian, St Gregory the Great and St Ambrose.

[24] *Martyrologium romanum* (Cologne, 1610; substantially based on the final Baronian edition of 1598), January 10 note c, pp. 35–6 and January 18 note a, pp. 54–6; May 7 note c, pp. 312–14; 15 August, notes a and c. All the themes mentioned are also indicated in the *index rerum* found at the end of the Cologne, 1610 edition. Throughout the text, Baronio frequently referred the reader in his annotations to his *Annales* for further information (even to the extent of including references to the latter in his 1586 edition, i.e. two years before the first volume of the *Annales* was even published). I am grateful to Giuseppe Guazzelli for first drawing this to my attention.

Over and above his copious annotations (which although located at the foot of the page, not infrequently visually dominated the whole, despite their smaller type), Baronio also prefaced the text of the Roman martyrology of 1586 with an extensive treatise: *De martyrologio romano*. This sought to demonstrate for the cult of martyrs what he also wanted to achieve for the whole Roman Church in his *Annales*: that practice and tradition had remained unchanged since its apostolic origins: *semper eadem*. Central to the success of this enterprise was the ability to demonstrate that the acts of the martyrs themselves had not only undergone rigorous processes of authentification by the relevant authorities soon after the events they describe, but also that those preserved in the main text of the Roman martyrology had successfully, if with no little difficulty, survived the depredations of pagan persecutors such as Diocletian.[25] Highly significant, in view of this volume's theme, is the direct link made between martyrology and the topography of the city. This was made explicit by Pope Clement I's decision in the first century AD to appoint a notary for each of the seven regions of Rome, who was made responsible for collecting and authenticating, by his very act of writing, martyrs' acts which had taken place in his area. Throughout, Baronio was at pains to demonstrate that the acts of martyrdom which followed his treatise had been preserved from the attempts of heretics to defile them and that they had always been the object of recitation and veneration by the faithful.[26] Having drawn some explicit parallels between the suffering of those listed in the Roman martyrology and those being martyred in his own day for their Roman Catholic faith, he concluded by emphasising that what he was doing did not represent any innovation, but merely restored ancient texts.[27] The publication of Baronio's successive editions of the

[25] 'Acta illa sanctorum martyrum tanta cura ac diligentia perquisita, per Notarios S. R. Ecclesiae conscripta, per Subdiaconos et Diaconos cognita, ac demum per ipos Romanos pontifices probata atque recondita . . .' *Martyrologium romanum* (Cologne, 1610), p. iv. On the following page, Diocletian's burning of so many martyrs' acts is acknowledged.

[26] Amongst the authorities cited are (in chronological order): Tertullian; St Cyprian of Carthage; St Augustine of Hippo; St Gelasius I; Gregory of Tours and St Gregory the Great. In particular, Baronio makes use of the penultimate writer's collection of stories about martyrs and the miracles their relics effected; the *Glory of the Martyrs* (citing from chs. 39, 50 and 63). I am following the chapter numbers given in the translated edition by Raymond van Dam, *Glory of the Martyrs* (Liverpool, 1988).

[27] 'Non enim (ut apparet) fuit in praesens Romanae ecclesiae institutum, novum conscribere martyrologium, sed vetus (ut diximus) ex veteribus exemplaribus restituere'. *Mart. Rom.*, p. xviii. Cf. Curzio de' Franchi, a member of the commission charged with the revision of the martyrology, explicitly stated his desire to include references to contemporary martyrs: 'Anzi vorrei che de i martiri de nostri tempi si potesse haver certa historia per honorarli anch'essi e per mostrar che in ogni tempo la chiesa santa è stata illustrata dal martyrio . . .' Biblioteca Apostolica Vaticana, *Vat. lat.* 6194, fol. 63r–v cited in Pio Paschini, *La Riforma Gregoriana del Martirologio Romano* (Monza, 1923), p. 14.

*Martyrologium romanum* therefore represents a thoroughgoing attempt to reclaim a specifically *Roman* Catholic topography of truth, in which the fragmentary, textual *lemmata* stood in for the relics themselves at *prime* or during private readings.

Something of the desired effect which the daily reading and hearing of such brief, catalogue-like evocations of martyrs' suffering was designed to have on the minds of late sixteenth-century *Roman* Catholics, may be gauged by Cesare Baronio's attempt to realise the *ecclesia primitiva* physically rather than simply metaphorically in his restoration of his titular church of St Nereo and St Achilleo carried out between 1596 and 1597.[28] Alexandra Herz has convincingly argued for a fundamental reappraisal of the quality and ambition of Baronio's work here. In contrast to Richard Krautheimer, who gives the impression that the Oratorian was essentially a pragmatist in a hurry, who unwittingly purchased 'medieval' materials in the belief that they were early Christian, and others who have implied that the poor quality of the nave frescoes he commissioned from Cristoforo Roncalli simultaneously reflects the cardinal's indigence and indifference to art, Herz suggests that Baronio displayed a sophisticated grasp of his project. To begin with, he had a thorough understanding of its vicissitudes as a church, records of whose first building went back to 337, before it was substantially rebuilt by Pope Leo III (reigned 795–816) and then restored by Sixtus IV (reigned 1471–84). Then, in his redecoration of the apse-conch, Herz shows that Baronio deliberately sought to create a painting style that predated that of Leo III's triumphal arch mosaic, thereby evoking: 'Christianity's golden age by creating a wholly new work using the ancient content, vocabulary and syntax'.[29] Next, in his decision to raise the presbytery, with a central vertical axis consisting of altar, with *confessio* and a *fenestella confessionis* directly beneath and the *ciborium* above, Baronio showed a clear dependence on the one extant model in Rome of early medieval precedent: Old St Peter's. By integrating the tomb of St Peter with the high altar, Pope Gregory I (reigned 590–604) had reasserted that basilica's identity as the *martyrium* of the apostle to whom Christ had given the keys of heaven and earth, and thereby

---

[28] For the martyrs' sufferings, see for example an entry under 12 January: 'Romae S. Tatianae martyris, quae sub Alexandro Imperatore uncis atq[ue] pectinibus laniata, bestis exposita et in ignem proiecta, sed nil laesa, gladio demum percussa, migravit in coelum'. *Rom. Mart.* (Cologne, 1610), p. 39. For an excellent account of Baronio's work on St Nereo and St Achilleo, to which what follows is indebted, see A. Herz, 'Baronio's restoration of SS. Nereo ed Achilleo and S. Cesareo de'Appia', *Art Bulletin* 70 (1988), 590–620.

[29] Baronio's probable model here was the apse mosaic at St Agata dei Goti (now lost, but certainly known to the Oratorian). Herz, 'Baronio's restoration', 610–12 (quote at p. 612).

relaunched it as a place of pilgrimage, where visitors could gain proximity to the tomb, but without getting close enough to damage the relics. As a vocal proponent of the conservation of the old nave of St Peter's during deliberations which were being undertaken at precisely this time (with the decision to demolish it finally taken by Paul V in 1605), it is perhaps natural that Baronio should have sought to recreate, and thereby preserve for posterity, such a significant model of the integration of the cult of the martyrs with celebration of the Eucharist.

In further deference to the model of Old St Peter's, Baronio had constructed a curved bench in the apse with a throne in the centre. It was from this seat that the Cardinal believed Pope Gregory had delivered his twenty-eighth homily, in which the pope had said that Nereus and Achilleus had given up the ephemeral pleasures of this life for the eternal ones of the next, before urging his audience to be more like them. In recognition and celebration of this event, the Oratorian commissioned an apse wall fresco depicting the event in contemporary, late mannerist, fully illusionistic style. Baronio's decision to go 'modern' here was evidently motivated by a desire to involve the spectator more fully in the scene depicted. This supposition is supported by the fact that the orthogonals of the composition follow those of the real church, so that the painted space becomes part of the real space. Further to bring the painted sermon to life, Baronio had the painter depict all the figures in contemporary dress. All this combined to imply that: 'Gregory's time is thus the present, and the words of his homily are as relevant today as they were around AD 600.'[30]

### III    Antonio Bosio – making fragments whole

It was precisely this attempt to abolish, or rather, transcend time that animated the work of Antonio Bosio. For him this subterranean space was not important for itself but for what signs it contained which might bear witness to the suffering and devotions of the early Christians. Even where the corridors were empty of actual bodies, it was enough simply to reflect on the martyrs' bloody end to feel one's heart fill with spiritual consolation.[31] In a very real sense, therefore, the catacombs constituted reliquaries whose contents were to be treasured (and traded) for the spiritual benefits they could bring to the faithful.[32]

---

[30] *Ibid.*, 619.

[31] '. . . oltre che, dove ancora non sono restati i corpi, le strade stesse ornate e sanctificate, col sangue de'martiri, e con i sospiri e lagrime de' fedeli, spirano santità e riempiano il cuore di tanta dolcezza spirituale'. A. Bosio, *Roma sotterranea* (Rome [1632], 1635; repr. Rome, 1998) 'al benigno lettore', p. 25* (unpaginated in original edn).

[32] This emphasis on the spiritual benefits such *vestigia* might bring, as opposed to the archaeological knowledge they might be expected to contribute, is reflected by the

When Bosio went underground, he took with him not only candles and assistants armed with shovels and pickaxes to clear his passage and paper and charcoal to record what he found, but also a head filled with an encyclopedic knowledge of the city's topography gleaned from a heady mixture of classical writings, humanist topographical studies, patristic texts, papal documents, martyrological *atti*, saints' *vitae* (both manuscript and printed) as well as the more recent works of Onofrio Panvinio and Cesare Baronio, in particular Baronio's edition of the Roman martyrology.[33] As I have argued elsewhere, this ensured a priority of text over trowel.[34] In other words, Bosio had a clear agenda before he had even set eyes on the material evidence. This agenda was informed by the belief that the catacombs had been the setting not only of the suffering, but also of the liturgical life and devotions of the early Christians.[35]

Despite the fact that the much-reproduced anteportam of *Roma sotterranea*, shows in its central panel not an act of martyrdom but one of burial and the fact that book I of the work as printed was wholly given over to the rituals relating to this act, the full extent of Bosio's preoccupation with the devotional life of the early apostolic church expressed liturgically and sacramentally as a way of justifying contemporary practice has not been fully appreciated. Undoubtedly, this is partly owing to the fact that the section where he dealt most extensively with this theme never came to be published.[36] In this part which was omitted by his editor, the Oratorian Giovanni Severano (largely for the practical reason that much of this ground had been already covered in Severano's own *Memorie sacre delle sette chiese di Roma*, 1630 to which Bosio was happy to defer),[37] Bosio drew extensively on Onofrio Panvinio's study of early Christian burial practice (*De ritu sepeliendi mortuos apud veteres christianos et eorundem coemeteriis*

---

institution, in 1669, of the Sacred Congregation of Indulgences and Relics, *Bullarium, Diplomatum et Privilegiorum Sanctorum Romanorum Pontificum Taurinensis Edito*, 25 vols. (Turin, 1857–72), XVII, pp. 805–6.

[33] The best way to reconstruct Bosio's sources is to read his punctilious marginal references in his *Roma sotterranea*, but see also the transcription of the inventory to his private library in A. Valeri, *Cenni biografici di Antonio Bosio con documenti inediti* (Rome, 1900), pp. 84–110.

[34] See my 'Text before trowel: Antonio Bosio's *Roma sotteranea* revisited', in R. Swanson (ed.), *The Church retrospective*, SCH 33 (1997), pp. 343–60.

[35] O. Panciroli, *I Tesori nascosti dell'alma città di Roma* (1st edn 1600; revised edn, Rome, 1625), 'Trattato secondo de' Sacri Cimiterii de' Santi, pp. 17–27' (pagination from revised edn). See in particular p. 18 for a summary of the belief that the catacombs witnessed the celebration of all the Sacraments.

[36] Biblioteca Vallicelliana, Rome (BVR), MS. G. 31, fols. 94r–246v. Cf. my 'Text before trowel', pp. 353–4 and n. 22.

[37] See a letter of 28 February 1629 from Bosio to Padre Cescenzi saying how he had read 'con molto gusto' Severano's book before continuing: 'Io nella mia opera di Roma sotterranea havevo messo quasi le stesse cose quali con molto mio gusto levarò rimettendomi a lui.' BVR, MS. G. 20, fol. 221r.

*liber*, 1568) in order to validate current Tridentine devotional practice by demonstrating its antiquity.[38] Indeed, the list of contents to the first book (as originally planned) of Bosio's work reads almost like a checklist of what was distinctive about Roman Catholic devotional practice: from chapter 1, on masses for the sick, to chapter 13, on funerals, the celebration of the dead and the prayers to be said and offerings to be made for their redemption.[39]

It was Bosio's learning, in combination with the illustrations of his collaborators, which did so much to establish and elucidate the iconography of early Christian martyrdom. This iconography was, to a significant degree, one of fragments. Indeed, even before descending to consideration of the particular objects he had personally seen with his own eyes, Bosio emphasised how incomplete and ruined were the remains he saw before him (plate 9.1(a)). For example, near the start of what was the most extensively described catacomb (or group of catacombs, centred on that of St Callisto on the Appian Way) in *Roma sotterranea*, Bosio wrote:

From the said year 1593, up until now we have visited this extensive and most beautiful cemetery many times; whose dimensions (as far as we can see from the remains (*reliquie*) which survive, having suffered the fate of the other cemeteries of being ruined and wrecked) make it the biggest of all we have so far seen.[40]

The link between the fragmentary state of what he found in the subterranean corridors and the fragmentary context is emphasised by his use

---

[38] For a succinct summary of what Panvinio believed, see the opening sentence of this work: 'Hominem Christianum aegrotantem presbyteros ecclesiae usque ab apostolorum temporibus visitasse, pro eo orasse, ipsius confitentis, peccata audisse et dimisisse, eucharistiam porrexisse, extremaeque unctionis sacramento donasse docent tum S. Iacobus apostolus, tum alii patres apostolorum temporibus vicini.' *De ritu*, ch. 1. Bosio's original book I follows very closely the topics of the first 16 chapters of Panvinio's work.

[39] Ch. 1 'De Visitatione Episcopi, seu Sacerdotis ad Infirmos, vel Martyrium subituros. De Missis et oblationibus pro eisdem' (fols. 95r–96r) and ch. 13 'De Exequijs et numero dierum Exequiarum, de tertia septima nona trigesima et quadragesima die. De annua Defunctorum commemoratione, et anniversarijs diebus. De Missis, precibus, oblationibus, et elimosynis pro eorum requie et redemptione' (fols. 218r–246v). Cf. ch. 3 (on confession); ch. 4 (on the Viaticum); ch. 5 (on extreme unction); chs. 6–8 (masses and prayers for the dead); chs. 9, 11 and 12 (honouring martyrs with due rites and burial).

[40] 'Dal detto anno 1593, fin'hora innumerabili volte habbiamo visitato quest'ampio, e bellissimo Cimiterio; il quale di grandezza, e di adornamenti (per quanto dalle reliquie, che restano si può comprendere, havendo egli ancora patito l'influsso de gli altri Cimiterij, d'esser rovinato, e devastato) porta il principato fra tutti, che fin'hora habbiamo veduti', *Roma sotterranea*, bk III, ch. 23, p. 195. This is the longest chapter in the whole book (pp. 195–295) and is closely followed by another catacomb which Bosio had personally visited: bk III., ch. 61: 'Delli cimiterij ritrovati dall'Autore nelle Vie Salarie, vecchia e nuova' (pp. 488–571).

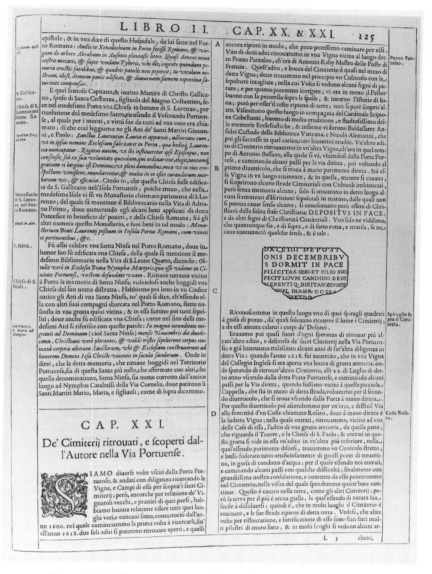

Plate 9.1(a) *Roma sotterranea*, bk II, ch. 21, p. 125. Even at its most complete, Bosio notes that the state of his evidence was imperfect, as in the case of this inscription.

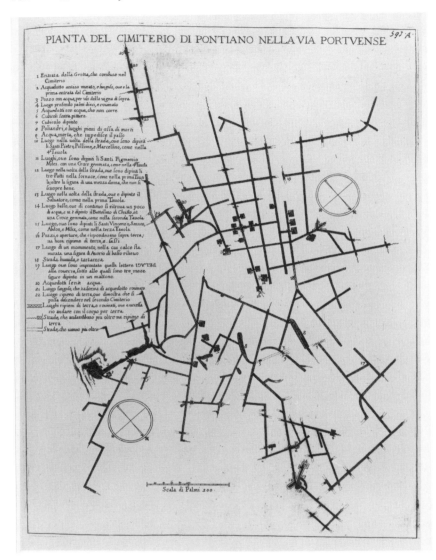

Plate 9.1(b) *Roma sotterranea*, p. 593A. Plan of the catacombs of Pontiano on the via Portense. This was one of catacombs which Bosio actually visited.

of the same word for 'relic' as for 'remains'.[41] This sense of incompleteness pervades the whole book; the sentence immediately following the above extract runs: 'As to its size, it is so extensive that we have never been able to see its full extent'.[42] He then went onto speculate how these catacombs were most probably connected to others nearby to form an extensive network (plate 9.1(b)).

Before going any further, it is important to note that owing to passages such as that quoted above – the number of illustrations throughout the book notwithstanding – *Roma sotterranea* essentially remains a monument to textual study, not to trowel-powered and candle-lit labour.[43] In fact, one might even say text *substituted* for trowel; for the majority of the catacombs included in Bosio's book (aside, principally, from his eyewitness, extended coverage of the catacombs on the Via Appia and Via Salaria mentioned above, which took up almost a third of the book), he was content to add textual references to Panvinio's outline so as to clarify the topography of early Christian burial immediately outside the walls of Rome.[44] This is in no way to denigrate Bosio's achievement, but to observe that his chief preoccupation was to clarify references to places and dates found in martyrs' acts. In this context, it is revealing to note how even where Bosio integrated eyewitness material, he ordered his criteria of inclusion not only on the basis of whether or not: 'there are to be found things which are worthy of observation' but also: 'whether it can be said that these things are mentioned in the Acts of the Martyrs'.[45] In other words, Bosio sought to facilitate the reading of and spiritual reflection upon saints' lives by helping the reader or hearer to envisage where their

---

[41] Cf. 'Queste sono le reliquie dell'iscrittioni, e Monumenti di marmo, che habbiamo ritrovate in questo Cimiterio', 'De ritu sepeliendi mortuos', p. 216.

[42] 'Quanto alla grandezza è tanto ampio, che mai di esso habbiamo potuto veder'il fine', *Roma sotterranea*, bk III, ch. 23.

[43] In addition, many of the work's illustrations were of objects, principally sarcophagi decorated in relief, which even if perhaps originally of subterranean provenance, were to be found very much above ground, more often than not, as long-standing fixtures of the city's major basilicas. See *Roma sotterranea*, bk III, ch. 23, pp. 101, 103, 155, 157, 159, 161, 181, 183, 285, 287, 289, 291, 293, 295, 317, 411, 421, 423, 425, 427, 429, 431, 571, 589 and 591.

[44] Bosio was always scrupulous in making clear to his readers which of the *circa* fifty catacombs treated in his book he had actually visited, where, in each case, he includes in the chapter title: 'ritrovati dall'Autore'. Aside from the two mentioned above, these were: the two sets of catacombs on via Portuense, Jewish and Christian (*Roma sotterranea*, bk II, chs. 21 and 22, pp. 125–43); those on Via Ostiense (bk III, ch. 10, pp. 169–70); those on Via Latina (bk III, ch. 30, pp. 301–11); those on Via La[v]bicana (bk III, ch. 37, pp. 321–95); those on Via Tiburtina (bk III, ch. 41, pp. 402–13; those on Via Nomentana (bk III, ch. 50, pp. 435–75) and those on Via Flaminia (bk III, ch. 65, pp. 576–83).

[45] 'andaremo descrivendo solamente quei luoghi, ne'quali si sono ritrovate cose degne d'osservazione' e che verisimilmente possiamo credere siano quelle parti, ch se ne fa mentione ne gli Atti de'Martiri . . .' *Roma sotterranea*, bk III, ch. 23, p. 488.

holy heroes now lay (or more usually, may have lain, before plunderers ransacked the catacombs and previous popes removed their bodies for safekeeping in the several urban basilicas within the walls where memory of their translation had recently been refreshed, for example, by Carlo Borromeo's restoration of his titular church of St Prassede, in which Pope Pasquale I had reburied numerous 'catacomb martyrs' in the early ninth century) (plate 9.2(a)).

It is within this overall awareness of the necessarily incomplete and fragmentary nature of Rome's subterranean early Christian heritage, that Bosio went on to mention (and have depicted) what he considered to be the signs of martyrdom. These consisted of: palm fronds, crowns of laurel, flames, a burning vase and a wool comb, (the latter resembling rather a sharp four-pronged fork) (plate 9.2(b)).[46] Significantly, he noted here that all of these symbols were found in a context in which the 'monuments' (for which we should read 'tombs') that remained intact were unmarked by name or title. Elsewhere, he was equally scrupulous in not arguing beyond the fragmentary evidence; many of the inscriptions reproduced in the illustrations, for example, were shown broken or incomplete. On one occasion, in his discussion of an illustrated inscription that bore a device that appeared to be a saw, Bosio dismissed the supposition that this represented the instrument of martyrdom of the person being celebrated; deferring instead to Baronio, who believed that the saw was more likely to refer to the dead person's trade (plate 9.3(a)).[47] However, when it came to more generalised rumination on the slaughter and death that he sincerely believed had taken place in these suggestively ruined and devastated corridors and cubicles, Bosio did not hold back from reading ambiguous evidence according to the heroic script of martyrdom. For example, at one point he asserted that he had found congealed blood next to a tomb, which once wet took on its vivid red colour so that it seemed to have issued freshly from a vein.[48] This charged interpretation also extended to the belief that the glass and terracotta jars which were found littered about the catacombs had once contained the precious blood of the martyrs, rather than the more likely oil originally used to treat the corpses or water needed by the burial parties (plate 9.3(b)).[49]

*Roma sotterranea* enjoyed immediate and long-lasting popularity. Although the first edition was very much a wealthy connoisseur's trophy

---

[46] *Ibid.*, p. 196. Cf. pp. 216, 217, 302 and 303.
[47] *Ibid.*, p. 433.    [48] *Ibid.*, p. 196.
[49] Some of these are illustrated: e.g. on pp. 197, 199, 201. Several had not been found by Bosio, but rather were given to him at a later date or illustrated for him.

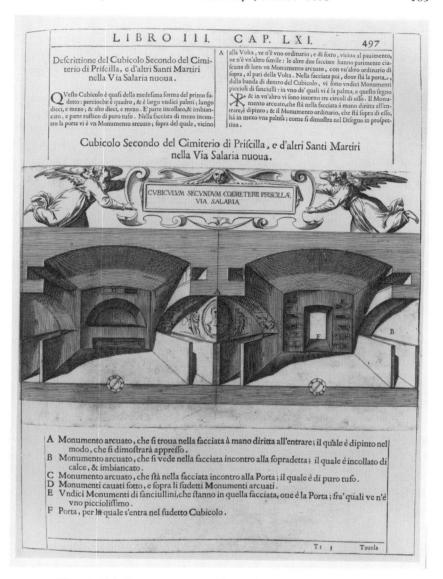

LIBRO III.    CAP. LXI.    497

Defcrittione del Cubicolo Secondo del Cimiterio di Prifcilla, e d'altri Santi Martiri nella Via Salaria nuoua.

Vefto Cubicolo è quafi della medefima forma del primo fudetto: percioche è quadro, & è largo vndici palmi; lungo dieci, e mezo; & alto dieci, e mezo. E' parte incollato,& imbiancato, e parte ruftico di puro tufo. Nella facciata di mezo incontro la porta vi è vn Monumento arcuato; fopra del quale, vicino

A  alla Volta, ve n'è vno ordinario; e di fotto, vicino al pauimento, ve n'è vn'altro fimile: le altre due facciate hanno parimente ciafcuna di loro vn Monumento arcuato, con vn'altro ordinario di fopra, al pari della Volta. Nella facciata poi, doue ftà la porta, dalla banda di dentro del Cubicolo, vi fono vndici Monumenti piccioli di fanciulli: in vno de' quali vi è la palma, e quefto fegno ℞ & in vn'altro vi fono intorno tre circoli di effo. Il Monumento arcuato,che ftà nella facciata à mano diritta all'entrare,è dipinto; & il Monumento ordinario, che ftà fopra di effo, hà in mezo vna palma; come fi dimoftra nel Difegno in profpettiua.

Cubicolo Secondo del Cimiterio di Prifcilla, e d'altri Santi Martiri nella Via Salaria nuoua.

CVBICVLVM SECVNDVM COEMETERII PRISCILLÆ VIA SALARIA

A  Monumento arcuato, che fi troua nella facciata à mano diritta all'entrare; il quale è dipinto nel modo, che fi dimoftrarà appreffo.
B  Monumento arcuato, che fi vede nella facciata incontro alla fopradetta; il quale è incollato di calce, & imbiancato.
C  Monumento arcuato, che ftà nella facciata incontro alla Porta; il quale è di puro tufo.
D  Monumenti cauati fotto, e fopra li fudetti Monumenti arcuati.
E  Vndici Monumenti di fanciullini,che ftanno in quella facciata, oue è la Porta; fra' quali ve n'è vno piccioliffimo.
F  Porta, per la quale s'entra nel fudetto Cubicolo.

Tt  3                Tauola

Plate 9.2(a)  *Roma sotterranea*, bk III, ch. 61, p. 497. Second chamber of the catacombs of St Priscilla and other martyrs on the via Salaria nuova.

pi di Santa Cecilia, di S. Marino, di S. Varo, e di altri Santi.

Grandiſſima diligenza habbiamo, fatta per tutto il tempo, che ſiamo ſtati in queſto Cimiterio, per ritrouare alcuna Iſcrittione, ò memoria notabile; dalla quale ſi poteſſe argomentare qual parte foſſe queſta del Cimiterio di Caliſto; però non vi habbiamo ritrouato mai coſa di momento; anzi ne meno alcun'Epitaffio, nel quale vi foſſe il nome di qualche Santo co'l titolo di Martire; da vno ſolo in fuori, impreſſo nella calce, in vn luogo anguſto, in queſta maniera.

┌─────────────────────┐
│   V L V A S I O      │
│   M A R T V R I.     │
└─────────────────────┘

Del quale però non ſi fà mentione alcuna ne' ſacri Martirologij; nè meno fin'hora ne hò trouato memoria ne gli Atti de' Martiri da me veduti: ſe bene non è dubbio, che molti, anzi infiniti, ve ne doueuano eſſere; però, ſecondo che li Monumenti ſi ſono aperti, ſono ancora caduti i Titoli; i quali il più delle volte erano impreſſi con lo ſtilo nella calce, che ſi poneua alla bocca della ſepoltura per fermar la tegola co'l tufo: & alle volte ancora ò nelle tegole, ò nelli marmi iſteſſi, che chiudeuano il ſepolcro: e trouandoſi in queſto Cimiterio molte ſepolture aperte, dalle quali ſi vede, che con grandiſſima diligenza non ſolo ſono ſtate leuate le oſſa, ma anco la terra iſteſſa, teniamo per fermo, che queſte doueſſero eſſer ſepolture di Santi Martiri: i corpi de' quali da' Sommi Pontefici ſono ſtati traſportati dentro di Roma; ouero da altri traſferiti altroue, quando queſti Cimiterij furono derelitti, e ſpogliati nelli tempi antichi: & all'hora parimente ſi debbero leuare i Titoli, e le Iſcrittioni de' Martiri più noti, e ſegnalati. Quindi è, che hora ſi veggono per queſto Cimiterio laſciati intatti ſolo alcuni Monumenti, che per il più ſono ſenza Titolo, e ſenza nome. Hanno però molti di loro alcuni ſegni di Martirio, ò di Chriſtianità; come Palme, Corone, Fiamme di fuoco, e Vaſi ardenti, e Pettini nella forma, che quì ci è parſo di rappreſentare.

In

Plate 9.2(b)  *Roma sotterranea*, bk III, ch. 23, p. 196. Different Christian symbols in the catacombs (detail).

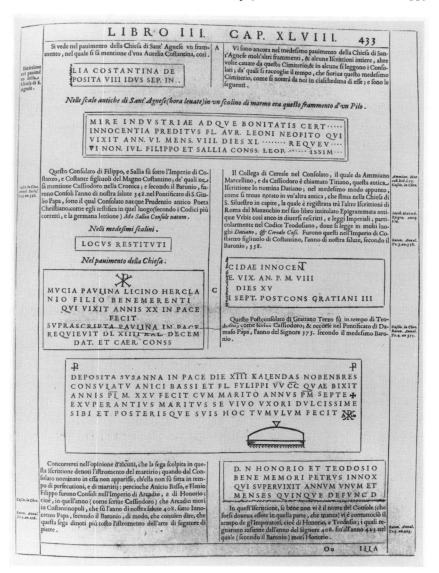

Plate 9.3(a) *Roma sotterranea*, bk III, ch. 48, p. 433. Some examples of Christian sepulchres (including the representation of what looks like a saw).

Plate 9.3(b) *Roma sotterranea*, bk III, ch. 23, p. 201. Glass and pottery vases containing the blood and ashes of holy martyrs found in the catacombs of Calixtus.

item, and only came to fruition, after years of delay, owing to direct Barberini patronage, the later editions were translated into Latin and some of them shorn of most or all of their illustrations so that they could be purchased by seminaries and reasonably prosperous convents the length and breadth of the Catholic world for the delight and instruction of their inmates.[50] Moreover, even for the vast majority who never set eyes on this work, its influence was widely felt via the authority it imparted to the iconography of martyrdom, and the terms it set even for those who disputed Bosio's interpretations. Ultimately, however, Bosio's work should be seen not as an end in itself, but in common with the other text I have endeavoured to contextualise in this chapter, as a tool to assist the faithful and, in particular, those who directed their devotions, to complete the fragmentary, material *vestigia* of this heroic chapter of Church history, with a whole understanding of the spiritual 'reality' they imperfectly represented in the present.

## IV       Conclusion – space is what space does

Ultimately, perception of time and space was not entirely dependent on physical movement. Rather, it was affected profoundly by interior disposition. Those who visited the holy city of Rome were continuously exhorted to bring with them the right attitude of mind and spirit in order to achieve nothing less than personal transformation. In the words of Gregory Martin:

> And if any where a man stand nigh to these tombes [of the martyrs], he perceaveth his sence by and by ravished with this sayd force, for the sight of the coffin entring into the hart, pearceth it, stirreth it up and moveth it in such maner, as if he that lyeth there dead, did pray with us, and were visibly present to be seen. Besides it cometh to passe, that he which feeleth him selfe so sweetly moved, is marvelous jocand, and gladsom, and being cleane altered after a sort into an other man, in such heavenlie plight departeth he out of the place.[51]

For Martin, as he next goes onto say, such material reliquie: 'striketh up the heart, and reneweth our memorie, eftsones fraile and forgetfull'. But perhaps, rather than seeing them as just places of memory, one might

---

[50] In 1650 there was published an abbreviated edition (with no illustrations); in the following year a Latin edition was printed, with additional material, edited by the Oratorian, Paolo Aringhi. This latter edition was reprinted twice – at Paris and Cologne in 1659. A German translation appeared in 1668, which was reprinted, in a shorter version, in Arnheim, 1671. The Latin edition of 1650 was republished, under papal patronage in Rome, 1710. A new, revised edition, in the vernacular and with new engravings, was prepared by Giovanni Bottari in three volumes under the title, *Sculture e pitture sagre estratte dai cimiteri di Roma* (Rome, 1737–54).

[51] Martin, *Roma sancta*, p. 27.

consider these remains as portals to a space, or rather place, in which the time between early Christian and late-sixteenth century Rome was abolished. In this way, Martin's identification of *Roma sancta* with early Christian Rome was to be realised. 'And thus far Rome now is nothing degenerated from Rome in old tyme shuch as the fathers have described it.'[52]

Laurie Nussdorfer, in a recent article, has argued convincingly for the necessity of seeing space in early modern Rome in terms which are both plural and contested.[53] In other words, there simultaneously existed different levels of space: from domestic and neighbourhood to family and institutional, in which terms such as 'public' and 'private', 'institutional' and 'patrimonial' constantly overlapped and frequently conflicted with one another. This, in turn, reflected the fact that: 'Rome was a city of diverse and independent centers of influence' to a degree that was unusual even given the fissiparous nature of early modern power networks.[54] It is within this context, I believe, that one should also consider sacred space. For the latter did not simply evolve as successive spatial imaginings of the city, each of which enjoyed a hegemonic position at any one moment, but rather co-existed with other, frequently rival, but also overlapping conceptions of the city. For example, as a counterpart to the subject of this chapter – *Roma oratoriana* – was *Roma Ignaziana*, an illustration of which was inserted into a special Antwerp edition of Pedro Ribadeneira's *Vita Beati Patris Ignatii Loyolae* (1609). It depicted the heart of the city effectively as: 'an urban theater in which the Ignatian *Opera pietatis* could be performed, with his well-trained troupe occupying center stage'.[55] In contrast to an Oratorian reading of the city (and Bosio, though a layman, was very closely linked to Oratorian circles and his magnum opus was prepared for publication by a member of the congregation, Giovanni Severano), which may be said to have privileged, above all, the *disabitato* and periphery of Rome – site of the catacombs and of early Christian churches, such as Baronio's titular church of St Nereo and St Achilleo – *Roma Ignaziana* may be seen to have placed its landmarks bang in the geographical centre of the city – as represented most dramatically by the largest single building project of the period (excluding St Peter's),

---

[52] *Ibid.*, p. 11.

[53] L. Nussforder, 'The politics of space in Early Modern Rome', *Memoirs of the American Academy in Rome* 42 (1999), 161–86.

[54] *Ibid.*, 161. Recent historiography of the city has placed much more emphasis on the heterogeneous/international nature of its population and the strategies used to contain the resultant tensions. See, for example: T. J. Dandelet, *Spanish Rome 1500–1700* (New Haven and London, 2001) and M. A. Visceglia, *La città rituale: Roma e le sue cerimonie in età moderna* (Rome, 2002).

[55] T. M. Lucas (ed.), *Saint, Site and Sacred Strategy: Ignatius, Rome and Jesuit Urbanism* (Vatican City, 1990), pp. 133–4 (cat. 71).

the Collegio Romano (together with the adjacent church of St Ignazio, whose building was underway by the end of our period). Finally, turning to what Nussdorfer describes as 'the most traumatic redrawing of Rome's urban space during the Early Modern period': the creation of the Jewish Ghetto in 1555, a recent study by Kenneth Stow has shown how by deploying a variety of 'strategies of survival' (predicated on a specifically Jewish, personal view of ritual space) its inhabitants nevertheless succeeded in maintaining, even enhancing, their 'microculture' within a spatially constricted world.[56]

Over the course of researching and writing this chapter, I have become increasingly aware of the problems of using the concept of 'space' for the early modern period. Again and again, when reading contemporary documents and books I came across 'place' (*luogo*) where, today, one might have expected 'space'. The modern Italian word 'spazio' is conspicuous by its absence (ditto for the Latin 'spatium' – 'amplitudo, -inis' is the more common substitute).[57] Indeed, in the early modern period, 'spazio' appears to have had altogether wider connotations, which related the concept not only to space but also to distance of time, place or leisure.[58] Even allowing for the clear absurdity of a self-denying ordinance that restricts one to using only concepts which might have been clearly understood by the society one is studying, I feel that one should be aware of the fundamentally anachronistic notion of considering space as in any way an abstract quality. Rather, to borrow the idea of the geographer W. J. T. Mitchell, we should approach space as he approaches landscape, as a verb rather than as a noun, 'a process by which social and subjective identities are formed'; considering 'not just what landscape [space] "is" or "means" but what it does, how it works as cultural practice'.[59] If we do so, we not only foreground the processes by which space becomes a live issue to people – more often than not owing to contestation (either real or perceived) – but also appreciate the degree to which space/place is created in the mind of the beholder. I will therefore end this account which has focused on two closely related ways of reading Rome as a sacred

---

[56] K. Stow, *Theater of Acculturation: the Roman Ghetto in the 16th century* (Seattle and London, 2001), ch. 1 (p. 50).

[57] For a thoroughgoing treatment of the word 'spazio' and its various uses over time see S. Battaglia, *Grande Dizionario della lingua Italiana*, 21 vols. (Turin, 1961–2002), xix, pp. 750–3 (in particular, section 5, p. 751). It should perhaps be noted that the then dominant Aristotelian view of the natural world did not conceive of space in the abstract, but in relation to the extension of bodies and within an overall finite world defined by the solid sphere of stars which, it was believed, encircled the earth.

[58] 'spazio, quel tempo, o luogo, che è di mezzo tra due termini', from *Vocabolario degli Accademici della Crusca*, 6 vols. (Florence, 1729–30), iv, p. 642.

[59] W. J. T. Mitchell (ed.), *Landscape and Power* (Chicago, 1994), p. 1. Cf. David Matless, *Landscape and Englishness* (London, 1998), pp. 12 and 285.

landscape with an extended quote from a document which, as well as any I know, conveys just what contemporaries believed the pilgrim to Rome should, ideally, bring with them to the holy places they visited:

When visiting these holy places . . . and in going from one church to another, from one altar to another, in order that you might feel greater charity and devotion, you should meditate on those journeys that Christ made in this world for us . . . and together with this [you should reflect on] those of the saints, whose churches and altars you will visit. Now remember with what fervour the Prince of the Apostles, St Peter, suffered his chains, prison and finally the torments of the cross . . . Let yourselves be inflamed with the love of God; that fire of the Christian religion which burned in the heart of St Lawrence, when you contemplate the memory of his martyrdom in the place where, on the gridiron, his body was roasted. With similar meditations, while you visit those holy places, you will have occasion to remember the many saints, martyrs, confessors, pontiffs and virgins; considering their lives and some of their particular actions, good deeds and martyrdom about which you will know and which the same memories of those holy places will show you.[60]

---

[60] Carlo Borromeo, 'Lettere pastorali et altre istruttioni per il Santo Giubileo (10 September-ber 1574)', in A. Ratti (ed.), *Acta Ecclesiae Mediolanensis*, only 2–4 vols. published (Milan, 1890–1900), III, coll. 511–13. For a contemporary English translation of this passage see G. Martin, *Roma sancta*, pp. 226–7.

# 10 Gardening for God: Carmelite deserts and the sacralisation of natural space in Counter-Reformation Spain

*Trevor Johnson*

In the 1590s the Spanish Discalced Carmelites began establishing so-called 'deserts' (*desiertos*) or 'wildernesses' (*yermos*) in remote rural areas, within which communities of friars could pursue eremitical vocations in emulation of the legendary practice of the primitive order on Mount Carmel. During a century or so, at least six deserts of this kind were founded in Spain and several others were established elsewhere in Europe and the New World.[1] In a practical extension of the reformed Carmelites' reassertion of apophatic spirituality, the deserts offered selected religious the opportunity to respond to the anchorite calling with a supposed authenticity and an undeniable rigour which were unsustainable in the environment of the urban convent. The leading modern scholar of the Spanish deserts, Fernando de la Flor, has seen in their establishment a 'spatial reform' which was analogous to the reform of consciences, bodies and institutions undertaken by the Carmelites and other religious orders in the Counter-Reformation era. Indeed it can be shown that a unique kind of sacred space, something rather more multi-faceted than the traditional monastery, was thereby created, especially since, in contrast to their inhabitants' simplicity of life, the hermeneutics of the deserts were as complex as their many-layered spatial configurations. On one level, such copy-cat Carmels housed, reified and made dramatically visible the radical apophasis (the 'negative way') which was so central to

I would like to record my gratitude to María Victoria González for the generous hospitality extended to me during a research trip to Salamanca while preparing this essay.

[1] The first three Carmelite deserts were founded at Bolarque (in the province of Guadalajara, 1592) at Las Batuecas (Salamanca, 1599) and Las Nieves (Málaga, 1599). There followed similar foundations in Italy at Varazze (1616), at Varese (1619), at Montevirginio in the Lazio (1649) and at Massa Lubrense on Capri (1679), in France at Virons (1641) and La Garde-Chatel (1660), in Flanders at Marlagne (1619) and Nethen (1680), in Poland at Czerna (1631), in Austria at Mannersdorf (1644), foundations in Portugal and Mexico and further deserts in Spain, of which the last was San José de la Isla (Bilbao, 1719). For brief descriptions of all the Discalced deserts, see Benoit Marie de la Sainte-Croix (Benedict Zimmerman), *Les saints déserts des carmes déchaussés* (Paris, 1927).

the fledgling reformed order's distinctive spirituality and the asceticism which was equally integral to its practice. They therefore served to vindicate the emergence of the barefoot branch and powerfully fostered its identity as an authentic recreation of the original Carmelite ideal. On a broader level, this spiritual colonisation of the natural world prompted a renewal of reflections on the relationship between nature and the holy, an engagement between two traditional symbolic discourses, which both, in their way, embraced a 'regressive utopian nostalgia' for a lost terrestrial paradise and eschatological yearnings for a paradise to come.[2] Both around and from within the deserts there emerged in the course of the seventeenth century a spiritual literature which in part seems to have celebrated the created world as inherently sacred, where the bounded yet liminal space of the desert defined and preserved an Adamic state of natural existence, a pristine *hortus conclusus*, a simulacrum not merely of Carmel but of Eden, peacefully luxuriating in abundant flora and fauna. Yet, simultaneously, the desert was also an outpost within a more troubling, post-lapsarian, pagan and even demonic nature, the latter an unbounded space in need of sacralisation through the presence and penitential regime of the holy hermits.[3] The present chapter hopes to explore this phenomenon, beginning by sketching the background of the revival of desert spirituality in Counter-Reformation Spain. Following a second section which briefly describes the deserts and the lifestyle of their inhabitants, a third part examines the importance of desert spirituality to the identity of the fledgling Discalced order, as witnessed by the latter's seventeenth-century historiography. In a fourth section, a discourse of nature and the holy arising from the context of the Carmelite deserts is

---

[2] F. R. de la Flor, 'El Jardín de Yahvé. Ideología del espacio eremítico', in F. R. de la Flor, *La península metafísica. Arte, literatura y pensamiento en la España de la contrarreforma* (Madrid, 1999), pp. 123–54, here p. 127. In what follows my indebtedness to De la Flor's scintillating interpretation of the Spanish Carmelite deserts is immense. Silverio de Santa Teresa, OCD, *Historia del Carmen Descalzo en España, Portugal y America*, VII (Burgos, 1937), chronicles the first wave of desert-foundation in considerable detail, drawing heavily on seventeenth-century histories. For a recent study of apophatic spirituality which deftly and movingly combines scholarly analysis with highly personal reflection, see B. C. Lane, *The Solace of Fierce Landscapes. Exploring Desert and Mountain Spirituality* (New York, Oxford, 1998). On apophasis see also M. A. McIntosh, *Mystical Theology* (Oxford, 1998), especially pp. 123–6.

[3] Such paradoxes of desert spirituality were not new, of course, and it is precisely their revival rather than invention which is of interest here. For an admirable study of these motifs in the writings of and about the early Fathers, including the Desert Saints, see A. G. Elliott, *Roads to Paradise. Reading the Lives of the Early Saints* (Hanover and London, 1987). Combining a chronologically broader sweep with a particular examination of this thematic cluster in Reformed Christian spirituality is G. H. Williams, *Wilderness and Paradise in Christian Thought. The Biblical Experience of the Desert in the History of Christianity and the Paradise Theme in the Theological Idea of the University* (New York, 1962).

analysed, and in a fifth section it is exemplified through the particular case of the desert of Las Batuecas.

# I

'Desert nostalgia', as Alain Saint-Saëns has shown, was not confined to the Discalced Carmelites but resonated throughout the religious culture of Golden Age Spain. The Jesuit founder, Ignatius Loyola, had wished to 'go barefoot to Jerusalem and eat nothing but grass', had lived as a hermit at Manresa and, like St John of the Cross, had for a time been attracted to the Carthusian order's semi-eremitical lifestyle. Ignatius and John were not alone. The hair shirt of the penitent was adopted by many Counter-Reformation *dévots* in imitation and emulation of the desert hermits, and along with the palm-frond tunic reappeared in representations (visual and literary) of John the Baptist, the penitent Magdalene, Mary the Egyptian, Jerome, Paul the Hermit and other Desert Saints as an increasingly popular topos of the Spanish Baroque. Juan de Castaniza failed in his ambition, in the 1590s, to establish an Iberian foothold for the Camaldolesi, although the hermitages founded by St Romulado in the late tenth century at Casentino were depicted allegorically by El Greco around this time.[4] However the Hieronymite order, which had had spectacular success in Spain since its foundation in the fourteenth century, maintained its strength for much of the sixteenth, when its aim to recreate Bethlehem in Castille attracted substantial patronage from Charles V, who had a small hermitage constructed for himself just outside the main monastic complex at Yuste, and from Philip II, who founded the monastery of the Escorial. If the Spanish Hieronymites peaked in strength under Philip II and started to decline after 1598, continuing eremitical enthusiasm could be found beyond the structures of the larger orders, in individuals and small communities subject to greater or lesser degrees of regulation.[5]

Nonetheless, it was the Discalced Carmelite reform which turned desert nostalgia into a novel spatial configuration. The creation of the deserts allowed the barefoot friars to move beyond what Saint-Saëns has termed the 'sublimated eremiticism' of the mid-sixteenth-century observance. Clearly central to the reforming tendency led by Teresa of Ávila and John of the Cross was an emphasis on asceticism, silence and contemplative prayer which took its inspiration from the anchorite tradition.

---

[4] A. Fanfani, *El Greco y Teresa de Ávila*, trans. Susana Hurtado (Madrid, 1988), pp. 68–9.
[5] A. Saint-Saëns, *La nostalgie du désert. L'idéal érémitique en Castille au Siècle d'Or* (San Francisco, 1993), *passim*.

As children Teresa and her brother Rodrigo had dreamed of becoming hermits. Mary Magdalene, Mary the Egyptian and the Desert Fathers were leading objects of Teresa's personal devotions, recommended by her to her fellow nuns. She later saw their virtues as literally embodied in her spiritual director, Pedro de Alcántara, whose emaciated flesh, she thought, resembled nothing so much as a cluster of tree roots. According to one of her nuns, such was her devotion to the penitential ideal that Teresa even contrived to die assuming the pose in which 'the Magdalene is painted'. The necessity for enclosure prevented Teresa and her nuns from doing more than dreaming of the desert, defining spaces for solitaries within their convents and encouraging the men who were not subject to the same restrictions. Teresa had hoped to recruit hermits for the male branch and indeed the first two Discalced friars who had not previously been Carmelites were anchorites, Brothers Mariano and Juan de la Miseria. The attachment of John of the Cross to the tradition is revealed in his own sojourns in hermitages and his exhortations to his brethren to do likewise: his reformed convent at Duruelo impressed Teresa for its anchorite symbols ('so many crosses, so many skulls!') and cells so small one could not stand up in them. Writing in 1591, John argued that 'the extent of the desert greatly helps the soul and the body, even when the soul is not very courageous. The Lord must wish that the soul also has its spiritual desert.' The attachment is also clear from his poetry and commentaries, even if his own 'ascent of Mount Carmel' was mystical and not literal.[6]

Teresa and John could fairly be described as 'anchorites within the city', as a later Portuguese Carmelite put it.[7] It would be left to the next generation of Discalced to develop the radical alternative of fleeing the cities and abandoning Babylon in favour of the desert.[8] Deeply beholden to the spiritual witness of Teresa and John, they were free of some of the particular pressures of institutional strife which had attended the first breakaway.[9]

---

[6] *Ibid.*, pp. 173–84. For a compelling new appraisal of John's poetic imagination, see C. Thompson, *St John of the Cross. Songs in the Night* (London, 2002).

[7] José del Espíritu Santo, *Cadena Mystica Carmelitana de los autores Carmelitas Descalzos. Por quien se ha renovado en nuestro siglo la doctrina de la theologia mystica, de que ha sido discipulo de San Pablo, y primero escritor San Dionisio Areopagita, antiguo obispo, y martir* (Madrid, 1678), preface.

[8] Of course, not all cities were 'Babylonian', although Góngora referred to Seville in such terms. Indeed, in precisely this period, some strove to remodel urban space as sacred, as in Granada, where the pious fraud of the 'Lead Books' and other mysterious relics uncovered in the 1580s and 1590s served to reinvent the identity of the city as a site of antique Christian holiness and to help obliterate the memory of its Moorish past. See A. K. Harris, 'The Sacromonte and the geography of the sacred in early modern Granada', *Al-Qantara* XXII, 2 (2002), 517–43.

[9] Limitations of space prohibit here an account of the tortuous history of sixteenth-century Spanish Carmelite reform. Regional details of initiatives up to the Discalced breakaway are

Nonetheless there was still much friction. Competition between shod and unshod orders for patronage in the foundation of new convents continued, as did jurisdictional wrangling over pastoral ministries and the right to dispense the privileges of the 'Sabbatine Bull'.[10] Against this background of pronounced inter-order rivalry, Fray Tomás de Jesús (1564–1627), future provincial of Old Castile and subsequently active in Italy and Flanders, mystical writer and promoter of the *Congregatio de propaganda fide*, conceived the idea of establishing isolated half-cenobitic, half-eremitical communities, whose lives would be governed by a return to a strict interpretation of the primitive Carmelite Rule of St Albert.[11] His 'beautiful dream' (as a twentieth-century confrère has called it) rested on five pillars: continuous prayer, strict silence, total exclusion of contact with laity, a more rigorous regime of fasting and penance than was practised even in the reformed convents and a common ground-plan for the deserts. First mooted around 1590, the scheme was initially opposed by the vicar-general of the Discalced, Nicolás de Jesús María Doria, who feared that such institutions would cream off his best friars and leave the

given in Balbino Velasco Bayon, *Historia del Carmelo Español*, I (Rome, 1990), especially pp. 137–77. For the most recent summary in English and for further references, see Thompson, *John of the Cross*, pp. 45ff and for an extended account of the period 1550–1600, J. Smet, *The Carmelites. A History of the Brothers of Our Lady of Mount Carmel*, II (Darien, Ill., 1976).

[10] The Sabbatine privilege allegedly dates from 1251 when the Blessed Virgin was said to have given the scapular to the former hermit and future prior-general of the order, St Simon Stock, in Cambridge, and to have promised that anyone dying wearing it would be spared eternal fire. The following centuries saw bulls by a number of popes, most significantly by John XXII in 1322, confirming that Mary had promised to members of the scapular confraternity that she would personally release them from Purgatory on the first Saturday after their deaths. Post-Trent, Gregory XIII renewed the Sabbatine privilege. Tomás de Jesús discussed the Bull in a short treatise on the scapular confraternity appended to his general history of the Discalced reform, in which he emphasised that the scapular promise did not depend on papal approval since it was not part of the treasury of merit at the disposal of the pope but had arisen from the special intercession of the Virgin. He admitted that this unique status had been less than well received by rival orders. Responsibilities of confraternity members included prayers for the exaltation of the faith and the extirpation of heresies: Tomás de Jesús, *Libro de la Antiguedad, y sanctos de la orden de nuestra Señora del Carmen: y de los especiales privilegios de su cofradia* (Salamanca, 1599), book 2, pp. 18–19, 49.
Narratives of miracles attributed to the Carmelite scapular were assiduously collected and reported by Carmelite historians in the seventeenth century; plentiful examples may be found in the 600-page hagiographical compendium of Fray José de Santa Teresa, *Flores del Carmelo. Vidas de los Santos de Nuestra Señora del Carmen, que reza su religion, assi en comun, como en particulares conventos* (Madrid, 1678). For a case-study of rivalry between the two Carmelite branches in seventeenth-century Antwerp, *inter alia* over administration of this indulgence, see C. Göttler, *Die Kunst des Fegefeuers nach der Reformation. Kirchliche Schenkungen, Ablaß und Almosen in Antwerpen und Bologna um 1600* (Mainz, 1996), pp. 195–212. For welcome light on the murky origins of the scapular legend, see R. Copsey, 'Simon Stock and the Scapular Vision', *JEH* 50 (1999), 652–83.

[11] J. de Jesús Crucificado, OCD, 'El padre Tomás de Jesús, escritor mistico', *Ephemerides Carmelitana* 3 (1949), 305–49.

remaining convents in the hands of the less zealous. However Tomás did receive support from influential brethren, including the rector at Alcalá, Juan de Jesús, Alonso de Jesús María (later general twice) and Francisco de Santa María (later twice provincial). Eventually Doria was persuaded to approve the proposal and set Tomás to work on the instructions which would provide the basis for later legislation on the deserts.[12] By the end of the decade the first three Spanish deserts had been founded, at Bolarque in the province of Guadalajara, at Las Nieves in Málaga and at Las Batuecas in Salamanca. Aside from the resources and wishes of their patrons, the sites were chosen for their isolation, their natural beauty, their ability to be self-sufficient and, in the case of Las Nieves and Las Batuecas, their proximity to existing sacred sites, in both cases fifteenth-century Marian pilgrimage shrines.[13]

## II

Tomás' fifth pillar, the common ground plan, was prescribed in some detail in his own legislation. Each desert was a reification of an eremitical ideal, but also a physical recreation of Mount Carmel, designed to allow friars to live as contemplative solitaries in prayer, but also to gather, just as Elijah had supposedly gathered his hermits, for collective liturgies. Their basic layout was decreed in the constitutions of 1597, 1605 and 1614.[14] At the centre of each desert was an enclosed quadrilateral compound

---

[12] Silverio de Santa Teresa, *Historia del Carmen Descalzo*, VII, pp. 320–43.

[13] The isolation conducive to uninterrupted prayer and contemplation was a crucial factor. Unsurprisingly, references to the desirability of isolated locations in the order's original rule were emphasised by contemporary commentators. As one gloss put it: 'here it [the Rule] ordains that we have our convents in wildernesses, or where they may be more appropriate for the maintenance of our profession. It is the same as saying to us that generally the locations of our convents will be in the wildernesses, in solitary places, but that if for some reason it may be convenient that they are not in completely deserted, hidden and inaccessible places, at least they may be such that they have solitude and quiet, which is necessary for the accomplishment of our obligations', Francisco de San Elias, *Commentarios, y doctrina sobre la regla primitiva de la Orden de Nuestra Señora del Carmen* (Segovia, 1638), p. 135. However, the importance of patronal inclinations and resources in determining location must not be underestimated. The site of the desert of Las Nieves, for example, was offered to the Discalced Carmelites by the local bishop who wanted them to replace a number of unregulated hermit custodians of the Marian shrine. The Carmelites took formal possession of the site in 1593 and the towns of Málaga and Ronda donated them further lands there in 1599, F. J. Rodríguez Marín and J. M. Morales Folguera, 'La sacralización del espacio rural. Las ermitas del desierto Carmelita de Ntra. Sra. De las Nieves (El Burgo, Málaga)', *Cuadernos de Arte e Iconografía* 6 (1993), 187–92.

[14] On the architecture of the deserts generally, see Luciano Patetta, *Storia e tipologia. Cinque saggi sull'architettura del passato* (Milan, 1989), pp. 203–13. On that of the Mexican desert of Los Leones see A. Bonet Correa, 'Las iglesias y conventos de los Carmelitas en Mejico y Fray Andrés de San Miguel', *Archivo Español de Arte* 145 (1964), 31–47, especially p. 36.

with chapel, cloister, cells, refectory, library, guest accommodation and ancillary buildings. The constitutions were strict on the size and proportions of the chapels, the internal arrangement of altars and sacristies and their décor, always prescribing simplicity. The cells on two or three sides of the central compound took the form of miniature houses, each comprising an oratory, bedroom and study. The constitutions of 1597 prescribed a limit of the cells to 3.25 square metres (or thirteen 'palms' in the order's own system of measurement).[15] A poem attributed to Fray Diego de Jesús describes those at El Burgo as indeed no larger than nine feet square.[16] Like a Russian doll, this compound was surrounded by the extensive space of the desert proper (that at Las Nieves covered seventy hectares, that at Buxaco one hundred), which was in turn bounded by a high perimeter wall. The desert was left in, or allowed to revert to, a wild state, aside from planting with 'cedars of Lebanon' and laying out of paths which connected the central compound to the chapels, calvaries, 'fountains of Elijah' and isolated hermitages which were scattered around it. The dedications of the latter established a sacred topography and protective pantheon which unsurprisingly privileged the saints of the Carmelite order or those associated with its traditions. In the case of Las Nieves, where the advocations are known from an eighteenth-century drawing, the titular saints included Our Lady of Carmel, the Child Jesus, Joseph, John the Baptist, Mary Magdalene, Águeda, Teresa of Ávila, Andrew, Anne, John of the Cross, Elijah, Nicholas and John the Evangelist. Only one, perched on a rocky pinnacle, seems to have lacked a saintly patron and was simply (if ominously) labelled the 'hermitage of penance'.[17]

The number of religious in each desert was capped at twenty-four. Most were to live within the cloister, but the constitutions stipulated that at least six at any one time were to be solitaries inhabiting the isolated hermitages, whilst at least four friars should be perpetual hermits, acting as examples to the rest. De la Flor has called the deserts 'asceticism-machines' and indeed the regime imposed on all their inhabitants was strict. Only brethren given to prayer and mortification were admitted in the first place and licence to enter had to be granted by the general. They had to reside for at least one year and no one, not even the prior, could leave the enclosure without the general's permission. The meat-free diet was described as the minimum to sustain life. The friars were not permitted to vacate their cells without licence: as Tomás de Jesús warned, 'the cell is rightly compared to a perpetual prison'.[18] Three hours a day

---

[15] Patetta, *Storia e tipologia*, p. 206.
[16] Marín and Folguera, 'La sacralización del espacio rural', 190.
[17] *Ibid.*, 191–2; Sainte-Croix, *Les saints déserts*, p. 150, for Buxaco.
[18] Tomás de Jesús, *Instruccion espiritual para los que profesan la vida eremitica* (Madrid, 1629), pp. 25–6.

were to be spent in communal prayer, while the isolated hermits were to pray the office at the same time as it was being said in the convent. Only books of spirituality and the Fathers could be kept.[19] Strict silence was observed and communication was through sign language (for example, 'to ask for the prior, make a Cross in the form of a benediction with the whole hand', 'to call for the razor, pass the hand over the head', 'to signal that one is going to the kitchen, make the action of beating eggs', 'to say "I don't know", shrug your shoulders'). The signing system itself was laid out in a set of 'holy customs' (as opposed to mandatory constitutions) recommended by Fray Tomás for the deserts. These also included a practice whereby on the feast of the Circumcision every friar was to choose one or two virtues which he intended to exercise with particular devotion during the forthcoming year. These virtues were then listed alongside the corresponding name on a public noticeboard in the convent.[20] Tomás de Jesús spent two separate spells at his own foundation of Las Batuecas, the first after completing his term as provincial of Old Castile, and the second after a three-year period as *definidor general*. He was summoned from the desert to take up the post of prior of Zaragoza in 1607.[21] Tomás, as a serial holder of key positions in the order, was perhaps exceptional, but his eremitical career reveals that the deserts existed in part to offer friars a space for temporary retreats from a more active role, even if, for some, residence within them was of a much longer duration.

## III

The principal justification for the establishment of the deserts was that they marked a return to the original lifestyle and identity of the Carmelite order. The deserts were the physical expression of a parallel literary campaign to vindicate the Discalced reform by placing it within a Carmelite historical tradition which viewed the order in general, and particularly now its reformed branch, as the continuation of a prophetic and eremitical past of breathtaking antiquity. Alone of the religious orders, the foundation myth of the Carmelites stressed a fictive pedigree stretching back beyond their thirteenth-century 'refoundation' all through the Byzantine centuries, through even John the Baptist and the Essenes, to the deep time of the Old Testament prophets, to Elishah and, ultimately, to Elijah, who had so dramatically clashed with the prophets of Baal on Mount

[19] Silverio de Santa Teresa, *Historia del Carmen Descalzo*, VII, pp. 333–41.
[20] Tomás de Jesús, *Instruccion espiritual*, pp. 117, 121–5.
[21] Eulogio Pacho (ed.), *Diccionario de San Juan de la Cruz* (Burgos, 2000), 'Tomás de Jesús, OCD'.

Carmel.[22] For the barefoot friars of the later sixteenth century, the recreation of the community of hermits said to have been founded by Elijah on Carmel was the fruit of an urgent desire to reconnect to this past and to renew an ascetic and mystical thread. The deserts then were an important part of a broader reinvention of a tradition, providing a visible emblem of continuity and a legitimation for the Discalced reform and the bruising process of schism associated with it.

Tomás de Jesús was clear that the reform now re-adopted by the unshod friars was in fact the 'primal state' of the religious life and represented the recovery of the true Carmelite ideal, as enshrined in the early thirteenth-century Rule of St Albert but based on much older practice, which had been mitigated for the Calced order by the papacy since the mid-thirteenth century. In his *Spiritual Instruction for those Professing the Eremitical Life*, he noted that the primitive rule was one of 'utmost perfection and rigour, including divine and most ancient institutions'. On the importance of fasting, for example, Fray Tomás explained that 'those holy desert fathers well understood this, reducing all harshness and rigour to abstinence in the quality and quantity of food'.[23] In a separate work on the order's history, published in the year of the foundation of the desert at Las Batuecas, Fray Tomás insisted that his brethren were recovering a tradition which antedated even Albert's Rule and lamented the fact that the 'carelessness' and other priorities of the medieval Carmelites had allowed their ancient Syrian origins to be forgotten.[24] The appeal to antiquity was not novel, because Elijah had been consistently portrayed by the Carmelites as their founder since the first serious attempts to chronicle the early history of the order began following its migration to the west in the thirteenth century.[25] Nonetheless the claim of Elianic descent was not only ubiquitous but seems also to have been pushed to the fore with particular insistence in seventeenth-century reformed Carmelite chronicles. Tomás de Jesús stressed that Elijah and his successors had kept the three vows of religion, that Elijah had instituted the vow of chastity and that he was the first man to vow his virginity (Mary being the first

---

[22] The tendency to 'back-date' medieval regular eremitical origins to an antique past was not peculiar to the Carmelites. The Hieronymites argued that they had been founded by St Jerome in Bethlehem, had continuously existed in some form since then and that their official establishment in the fourteenth century was therefore in fact merely a 'restoration', a view repeated by the order's leading sixteenth-century historian, José de Sigüenza, *Historia de la Orden de San Jerónimo* (Madrid, 1600), ed. Juan Catalina García (Madrid, 1907), book 1, ch. 1. The putative Carmelite origins were, however, far older.

[23] Tomás de Jesús, *Instruccion espiritual*, pp. 25–6.

[24] Tomás de Jesús, *Libro de la Antiguedad*, I, p. 1.

[25] On this theme, see the superb study by A. Jotischky, *The Carmelites and Antiquity. Mendicants and their Pasts in the Middle Ages* (Oxford, 2002).

woman).[26] Diego de Jesús María, the leading contemporary chronicler of the deserts, began his description of the foundation at Bolarque with two chapters on the lives of solitaries from Elijah to John the Baptist.[27] Francisco de Santa María began earlier still, insisting that even before Elijah a 'natural light' had disclosed to the Gentiles the importance of serving God not just in community but also as anchorites, by retreating into deserts and mortifying the flesh.[28] The cult of Elijah, whose feast was celebrated by the Carmelites on 20 July, intensified during this period. In discussing the prophet's special significance to his order, Francisco de Santa María reported Teresa of Ávila's interpretation of the vision of a Sevillian nun, Beatriz de la Madre de Dios: prior to the foundation of the Discalced Carmelites, Beatriz had sensed her vocation to the religious life on witnessing the apparition of an old, unshod friar; the latter Teresa subsequently identified as 'Our father, Saint Elijah'.[29] Unsurprisingly, tropes of traditional Carmelite exegesis, such as the identification of the refreshing, rain-bearing cloud which appeared to Elijah on Mount Carmel as the Blessed Virgin, the order's patroness (whose feast was celebrated on 16 July), were also emphasised. The little cloud was, as José de Santa Teresa put it, an 'image' or 'stamp' of the Virgin, who would 'water the earth with her graces'.[30]

No less honoured than Elijah was his eremitical descendant and mystical revenant, John the Baptist, who was enlisted by the order's historians as a monk and hermit in the Carmelite tradition. Francisco de Santa María wrote: 'besides Christ we meet Elijah, who started our journey and returned from Paradise to Earth in the person of John . . . That valiant spirit which outraged kings was once again resuscitated against them in John. The caves, the deserts, the fasts, the tears and the vigils of Carmel were revived in this great prince, proving that between such a beginning and such an end the angelic life of the prophets could not falter and that Heaven which sustains it never ceased in its movement around

---

[26] Tomás de Jesús, *Libro de la Antiguedad*, I, pp. 18ff.

[27] Diego de Jesús María, *Desierto de Bolarque, yermo de Carmelitas Descalzos, y descripcion de los demas desiertos de la Reforma* (Madrid, 1651), pp. 1–25. On the author, see C. de Villiers, *Bibliotheca Carmelitana* (Aurelianis, 1752), 2nd edn G. Wessels (Rome, 1927), I, col. 390.

[28] Francisco de Santa María, *Historia general profetica de la Orden de Nuestra Señora del Carmen* (Madrid, 1630), pp. 7–8. On the author, see C. de Villiers, *Bibliotheca Carmelitana*, I, cols. 502–3.

[29] Francisco de Santa María, *Reforma de los Descalzos*, pp. 523–5. The story recalls earlier prophetic visions in the Carmelite tradition, such as the dream attributed to Elijah's father of a gathering of men in white, taken in the fourteenth century to be a prophecy of the Carmelite order and employed as one of several justifications for its change (or reversion, as some apologists claimed) of habit to the white *cappa* from its earlier particoloured striped *pallium*: Jotischky, *Carmelites and Antiquity*, pp. 55–7.

[30] José de Santa Teresa, *Flores del Carmelo*, p. 309.

these twin poles . . . I will not call him [John] a Carmelite, although I could, but son of Elijah, prophetic monk, perpetual Nazarene and Essene by institution.'[31]

In claiming Elijah and John the Baptist as Carmelite friars *avant la lettre*, Discalced historians could further plead a confessional as well as a sectional purpose, taking as their target not simply the Calced branch but now also the new churches of the Protestant Reformation. In part their aim was to re-emphasise the role of prophecy within Catholic tradition and thereby reclaim prophetic authority from Protestant appropriation.[32] More obviously, however, by establishing the continuity of eremitical monasticism and pushing its pedigree back to the Old Testament, they hoped to refute Protestant challenges that it was a more recent (and thus discardable) invention. Specifically, they had in mind heretical opponents, including Matthias Flacius Illyricus and the Magdeburg Centuriators, who sought to use ridicule of the Carmelite claim to ancient lineage as a means of vilifying not just the order but the entire body of regular clergy along with the papal structure which had supported it.[33]

Tomás de Jesús therefore justified his revisitation of Carmelite historical origins in terms of confessional apologetics:

I determined to take up this enterprise and ascertain the truth of this history, considering that this work would bear much fruit, as much for the universal Church (since from it can be taken a great and powerful argument against . . . the heretics of our times, who with falsehood and lies claim to make a novelty of the ancient estate of the religious orders) as for her religious, since knowing that they have as an institutor and patriarch such a great man as the holy prophet Elijah, they will animate themselves to possess his zeal, to imitate his virtues and to suffer persecution and burdens as the holy prophet did. And it is no little consolation to know that they have a founder of such singular sanctity, not dead (as are those of the other orders) but living on earth.[34]

Likewise, in his *General Prophetic History* of the Carmelites, Francisco de Santa María insisted on the descent of the Carmelites from the prophets:

In our times . . . Luther and Calvin, who were consumed with undying hatred . . . have raised an army, captained by the Prince of Darkness, against the antiquity of the monks. They claim that the Church did not have them before the start of

---

[31] Francisco de Santa María, *Historia general profetica*, pp. 650–1.

[32] For suggestive theses on Protestant uses of prophecy in the period, see the essays by U. Lotz-Heumann and D. Johnson in H. Parish and W. G. Naphy (eds), *Religion and Superstition in Reformation Europe* (Manchester, 2002).

[33] Although even the Centuriators seem to have accepted that the twelfth-century Carmelites had antecedents in the 'Byzantine period', A. Jotischky, 'Gerard of Nazareth, John Bale and the Origins of the Carmelite Order', *JEH* 46 (1995), 214–36, here p. 224.

[34] Tomás de Jesús, *Libro de la Antiguedad*, p. 2.

the fourth century, when Anthony, Pacomius and other divine fathers flourished. Catholics, aided by past studies, have found them close to the time of Christ and within His own family and house. But they disagree with each other as to whether they existed under the Law. Some say not. Others with greater study and diligence have ascertained that they did and discovered that the monastic life has continued through hereditary succession, without any break, in the Order of Our Lady of Carmel.[35]

Citing Peter Canisius ('prosecuting the same intent against the heretics'), the friar focused especially on the figure of John the Baptist whose lifestyle was a 'sure indicator' of his religious and penitent life and proof that he was a monk and a hermit, indeed, as Chrysostom and Jerome had proclaimed him, a 'prince and captain of monks'.[36] John had entered the desert at a very tender age. Modern heretics, unwilling to concede that he lived an anchorite life, were interpreting John's 'wilderness' as a generic term for the mountainous region of Hebron, and thus a space of no special significance, but Canisius had refuted this 'with great erudition and eloquence'. For why would the Evangelist have written that John lived in deserts if his habitation were no different from that of his fellow citizens? And why does the Scripture speak of 'deserts' if Hebron were simply mountainous? In fact the mountains had cities and the deserts did not. Similarly, echoing a long line of medieval exegesis of the distinctive habit of the order and its Elianic and post-Elianic associations, the friar discusses the Baptist's clothing. He mocks a 'modern writer', clearly a critic of the pretensions of the Discalced, who had insisted that John wore shoes, since if he did not the Evangelist would have pointed it out. Fray Francisco suggests that on that basis, 'we would have to say that John wore a hat too . . . since the Evangelist did not mention that he did not wear such a standard garment'.[37]

The confessional dimension to the historiography of the desert tradition, penned not least by those who were most active in establishing the deserts, is proof that withdrawal from the world need not signify retreat from the big issues of the moment, but rather allowed these to be addressed with a mixture of engagement and detachment. In his 900-page treatise of 1613, *On procuring the salvation of all peoples, schismatics, heretics, Jews, saracens and other infidels*, Tomás de Jesús could write of patient missionary labours among the infidel of the east, but use too the eremites as exemplars of monasticism, the venerability and value of which had been attested by the Fathers.[38]

---

[35] Francisco de Santa María, *Historia general profetica*, prologue.
[36] *Ibid.*, pp. 656–7.    [37] *Ibid.*, pp. 684–9.
[38] Tomás de Jesús, *De procuranda salute omnium gentium, schismaticorum, haereticorum, iudaeorum, sarracenorum, caeterorumque infidelium libri XII* (Antwerp, 1613), pp. 73–7 on eremites.

**IV**

In the preface to his chronicle of the first of the deserts, that of Bolarque, Diego de Jesús María described his subject as a 'garden of delights,
which fill and satisfy', a 'mystical garden, cultivated by a superior hand
and watered by evangelical doctrine'.[39] Doña Bernarda Ferreira de la
Cerda described the Portuguese desert at Buxaco as 'a closed garden,
a flood of scents, a sealed crystalline and pure fountain, an indestruc-
tible tower, where, safe from assault, the soul tastes its loves'.[40] Garden
metaphors were certainly not new to the mystical tradition, although
it is surely significant that they were employed in force by those connected with the Discalced reappropriation of desert spirituality.[41] However, since the deserts, as physical rather than metaphorical gardens,
defined spaces of wild, untrammelled and unproductive terrain, they
departed significantly from the traditional norms of monastic gardening.[42] For the first time, perhaps, extensive natural gardens were now
offered as sites for contemplation. Asceticism-machines the deserts might
have been, but penance did not exclude appreciation of beauty, nor were
these deserts barren wastelands but landscapes teeming with life. The
frequently used term 'wilderness', in fact, captured the richness of these
spaces rather better than the more symbolically charged 'desert'. Apophasis rested on penitential purgation, but paradoxically the deserts offered
the anchorite a vast, potentially distracting world of sensual curiosity.
An aesthetic of asceticism blossomed in the context of desert spirituality
which fostered the view of this newly bounded natural space as a recovered
Eden.[43]

---

[39] Diego de Jesús María, *Desierto de Bolarque*, preface. He goes on to call Bolarque 'the
remade Carmel of our Europe, office of health, workshop of saints, Heaven of the century,
habitation of angels, region of Paradise, climate of celestial influences'.

[40] Bernarda Ferreira de la Cerda, *Las Soledades de Buxaco*, cited in De la Flor, 'Jardín de
Yahvé', p. 152. On the Portuguese desert, founded in 1628 and boasting a *via sacra*
and Calvary based on measurements specially taken in Jerusalem, see Sainte-Croix, *Les
saints déserts*, pp. 142–51.

[41] Francisco de Santa María, for example, reproduced Teresa's gardening metaphor for
the abundance of divine graces bestowed on her and her followers, a metaphor based
on the four ways of watering a garden: the burdensome method of taking water from a
well by hand, the more efficient method of waterwheel, winch and aqueduct, the even
better method of channelling water directly from a spring and finally the best method,
letting rain from heaven water all the ground, which requires no human effort at all and
leaves the plants 'happy' and the flowers 'most beautiful'. The soul is the garden and
gardener, the flowers are the virtues, the watering represents our works and those that
God performs through us. Thus the first mode of watering corresponds to those who
are at the beginning of their life of prayer, making heavy work of seclusion, reading,
gathering their thoughts and otherwise moderating their affections, Francisco de Santa
María, *Reforma de los Descalzos*, pp. 56–7.

[42] De la Flor, 'Jardín de Yahvé', p. 132.

[43] Even the ground-plans of the deserts resemble some seventeenth-century depictions of
Eden, whilst their central compounds echo contemporary reconstructions of Solomon's

This sensibility was not new. Centuries before, the prior-general, Nicholas Gallicus, had lamented the abandonment of the Carmelite order's eremitical life in the *Ignea sagitta* (1270):

> I want to tell you of the joys of the solitary life. The beauty of the elements, the starry heavens and the planets ordered in perfect harmony, invite us to contemplate infinite wonders. The birds in the sky, like angels, delight us with their melodious cadences . . . While we praise the Lord the roots of the trees grow, deep in the ground; the meadows grow green; in their own manner the bushes dance rejoicing and the foliage of the groves waves joyfully, as if clapping its hands to the rhythm of our song. Flowers of strange beauty and delightful fragrance smile in the austere solitude. The silent starlight measures the time of each day. Even the bramble and the brushwood provide shade and offer simple gifts. All our sisters the creatures strive in the solitude to fill our eyes, ears and feelings with their caresses. Their inexpressible beauty cries out in silence and invites us to praise the marvellous Creator.[44]

A striking feature of this gardening, mystical and physical, is a restraint on human intrusion into the landscape: hence the limitation of the central compound and its architectural necessaria to the smallest possible space and barest architectonic display and hence too the minimalist architecture of the outlying hermitages. Justified by asceticism, it forced the hermits to hug the landscape, appearing to be hiding in it, enveloped by it, and both physically and mystically at one with creation. We find the solitaries inhabiting peaks, clefts in rocks, caves and, perhaps most dramatically of all, trees. These arboreal hermits, in their dendritic cells, enjoyed a peculiarly intense organic lifestyle in harmony with their environment. One tree-house at Las Batuecas was described in 1664:

> the hermitage of the cork tree, so poor, so desirable and so appropriate to the desert, was completed in 1606. It does not belong to anyone, for it belongs to all. Since its trunk is alive, from that time until 1664 it has stayed green, leafy and in the same vigour, poverty and austerity as at the start. The wall, the door and the window are growing with the rest of the tree, so they have to be cut back so that the hermit's light is not blocked out.[45]

Nature here becomes the house, the adornment and the primary devotional aid. One is reminded of tendencies in the visual art of the period.

Temple. For examples of such representations, see J. Bennett and S. Mandelbrote, *The Garden, the Ark, the Tower, the Temple. Biblical Metaphors of Knowledge in Early Modern Europe* (Oxford, 1998). The paradoxical association of desert and garden was of course biblical; thus the leading Jesuit exegete of the era, Cornelius a Lapide (1567–1637), glossed Isaiah 51.3 as signifying the transformation of the world through the conversion of its peoples by the Church, prefigured by that of the desert into paradise, the 'Garden of the Lord', Cornelius a Lapide, *Commentaria in scripturam sacram*, XI (Paris, 1860).

[44] Cited in Thompson, *St John of the Cross*, p. 37. On the *Ignea sagitta*, see Jotischky, *The Carmelites and Antiquity*, pp. 79–105.

[45] Cited in De la Flor, 'Jardín de Yahvé', p. 149.

More than rustic conceits, organic forms, woody and rocky landscape and crucifixes rudely crafted from bare branches were ubiquitous in contemporary representations of the eremitical wilderness. However beyond that there is perhaps a homology between the hermit's gaze, sharpened by mortification, his intense contemplation of details of the natural world in order to perceive the divine reality beyond it, and the baroque painter's near microscopic examination of natural forms in the still-life genre which began to flourish at precisely this time.[46]

## V

The intution of the desert as meeting place of nature and the holy found its apotheosis in the symbolically almost overdetermined desert of San José del Monte at Las Batuecas, founded in 1599. The site chosen for the most famous of all the Carmelite deserts was a remote valley in the Sierra de Francia, south of Salamanca. Here a secular tradition had already arisen which mythologised the allegedly isolated, primitive, savage, pagan and even demonic identity of the region and its inhabitants. Several Golden-Age court dramatists drew parallels between a legendary early sixteenth-century colonisation of Las Batuecas, described as a 'New World' within Spain, and the simultaneous conquest of the Americas. In his comedy on the theme, written between 1604 and 1614, Lope de Vega presented 'a valley, the deepest and most isolated that nature made in the world', whose wild inhabitants were Christianised thanks to the noble missionary zeal of an ancestor of his dedicatee, the Duke of Alba.[47] Enough of this myth stuck for a late-seventeenth-century Carmelite chronicle to revel in reporting that the

strangeness and isolation of these mountains . . . had caused the opinion to spread among the nearest villages that devils lived there . . . In the more distant villages there were tales that in past times this place had been the habitation of savages and people unknown for many centuries, neither seen nor heard by anyone, people whose language and customs differed from ours, who worshipped the Devil, walked around naked and thought themselves alone in the world.[48]

---

[46] A synthesis between the two can perhaps be detected in Antonio de Pareda's 'Man of Sorrows' of 1641, now in the Prado, where the unplanned tree bark and the woodiness of the crown of thorns are worked with as much intensity as the flesh of the Redeemer. The popularity of the work, which was based on a sculpture of 1635 by Domingo de Rioja, is attested by the existence of at least two similar versions, Javier Portús Pérez, *Pintura barroca española* (Madrid, 2001), pp. 224–5. Useful reflections on the spiritual themes underscoring Spanish still-life painting can be found in W. B. Jordan and P. Cherry, *Spanish Still Life from Velázquez to Goya* (London, 1995).

[47] On the mythologising of Las Batuecas, Fernando de la Flor, *De Las Batuecas a Las Hurdes. Fragmentos para una historia mítica de Extremadura* (2nd edn, Mérida, 1999).

[48] Alonso de la Madre de Dios, *Crónica de la Reforma de los Descalzos de Nuestra Señora del Carmen* (Madrid, 1683), cited in De la Flor, *Las Batuecas*, p. 82.

The myth of the valley's savage isolation was sufficiently salient to have been recycled too by the Jesuit *litteratus*, Juan Eusebio Nieremberg, when speculating about the location of the Garden of Eden in his *Treasury of Natural Wonders* of 1629.[49]

At the same time, Tomás de Jesús and his brethren were establishing their desert in the valley and there is something of the thrill of encounter with a dangerous, if also sacred, *terra incognita* in a later Carmelite chronicle of their 'discovery' of Las Batuecas:

> Looking to the right, one saw a colossal mountain, which caused horror to the unaccustomed gaze, but which was of marvellous beauty, since besides appearing from afar to have some fine sites for the hermitages, its hills were clothed with low shrubs and trees and rich with different mountain species . . . little springs, appearing in various parts, ran down the mountain, searching for the river . . . Looking to the west, one saw inaccessible mountains, one above another, looking like a stairway to the clouds . . . One noted their size, the variety of their shapes, the multitude of forest trees, ravines made beautiful with the variety of plants, all in profound silence venerating the Supreme Majesty.[50]

Once enclosed within the hermits' perimeter, this wilderness, only partially tamed by the friars' own gardens, came to be seen as a kind of botanical Noah's Ark, in which, in the words of the seventeenth-century Carmelite nun and poet, Cecilia de Nacimiento, 'innumerable plants and flowers' were represented and protected; 'God', she wrote, 'who in the beginning wanted to create being from nothing and man from earth, in this same site and in our era for the eternal glory of His name, has disposed a new Paradise, bringing to light a second demonstration of the admirable wisdom of his friendship.'[51]

It was left to the Spanish Enlightenment, spearheaded by the local cleric, Tomás González de Manuel, to debunk the fabulist notion of a 'New World within Spain'.[52] Yet the myth of paradisiacal beauty and

---

[49] Juan Eusebio Nieremberg, *Curiosa filosofia y tesoro de maravillas de la naturaleza, examinadas en varias questiones naturales* (Madrid, 1629), p. 30. See also De la Flor, *Las Batuecas*, pp. 70–1. In this context it is of interest that the first Discalced desert, Bolarque, was also associated with a putative mysterious past, Diego de Jesús María noting that it occupied the site of a Visigothic city, long since abandoned and obliterated, *Desierto de Bolarque*, pp. 45–6.

[50] José de Santa Teresa, *Historia General de los Padres Carmelitas Descalzos* (Madrid, 1693), III, pp. 221ff., cited in De la Flor, 'Jardín de Yahvé', pp. 145–6 and De la Flor, *Las Batuecas*, pp. 63–4.

[51] The full text of Cecilia's poem, *Descripción de Nuestro Desierto de San José del Monte Batuecas*, is given as an appendix in De la Flor, *Las Batuecas*, pp. 184–91.

[52] González de Manuel set out to demolish 'this fiction of Las Batuecas', which he feared had been diffused throughout Spain, but could not resist acknowledging that the fertility and fragrance of the valley made it seem like the terrestrial paradise: T. González de Manuel, *Verdadera relacion y manifiesto apologetico, de la antiguedad de las Batuecas y su descubrimiento* (Madrid, 1693), prologue and pp. 4rff. On the author and the work, De la Flor, *Las Batuecas*, pp. 87ff.

uncontaminated exoticism survived in a secular tradition which stressed the unique flora and fauna of the region, a myth of such longevity and force that in 1857 a scientific expedition was mounted to test it. Notions of a regional exceptionalism persisted into the early twentieth century, when the adjacent valley, Las Hurdes, achieved notoriety with Buñuel's cinematic treatment of rural poverty in *Las Hurdes, Land without Bread* (1932). As De la Flor puts it, Paradise had now become Hell.[53]

## VI

The eremitical craze lasted for just over a hundred years and most of the Discalced deserts were dissolved in the eighteenth and nineteenth centuries. Throughout the period of their existence they formed and perfected many hundreds of friars in the ascetic life and, as we have seen, served powerfully to vindicate the Discalced reform movement. As manifestations of a recreated eremitical ideal, the Carmelite deserts were certainly emblematic of a broader and often overlooked aspect of Counter-Reformation monastic mentality, but to what extent did they also constitute a distinctive type of sacred space?

For the hermit perhaps the most significant space was his own body, the primary 'asceticism machine', sacralised through mortification. Secondly came the cell, long praised by the Fathers of the desert tradition, as in the line of St Basil recycled by Juan Eusebio Nieremberg in an encomium on the spirituality of the hermit: 'Oh, royal cell, God's tabernacle, tower of David, spectacle of angels, place of those who struggle valiantly!'[54] Outwards in turn from the tiny womb-like cell, where the hermit lived his life in a near permanent foetal position, a creative sacrality streamed, infusing the surrounding desert. Yet the spiritual traffic appears to have been two-way, for spiritual fecundity could be derived from the wilderness too.[55]

As 'asceticism machines' the deserts were contrived spaces, but in them human artifice cohabited with the natural in a unique way. It is perhaps no accident that their creation coincided with a crisis, not merely in Catholic monasticism, but also, and much more broadly, in the imaginative relationship between Europeans and the natural world, a shift one might say from *admiratio mundi* to *dominatio mundi*.[56] The deserts

---

[53] De la Flor, *Las Batuecas*, preface to the 2nd edn.

[54] J. E. Nieremberg, *Epistolario*, ed. N. A. Cortes (Madrid, 1945), epistola LIV, p. 186.

[55] On the hermit's cell as spiritual womb, Elliott, *Roads to Paradise*, p. 107.

[56] This vast theme may be approached through P. Findlen, *Possessing Nature: Museums, Collecting, and Scientific Culture in Early Modern Italy* (Berkeley, Los Angeles and London, 1994); see also T. Leinkauf, *Mundus combinatus: Studien zur Struktur der barocken Universalwissenschaft am Beispiel Athanasius Kirchers SJ* (1602–1680) (Berlin, 1993), especially pp. 35–129.

showed that nature could still be wondered at, interpreted symbolically and seen as pointing to the unknowable Creator. The very uselessness of the deserts in conventional terms, their abandonment of any directly productive exploitation of nature, allowed each to glow as an unstained space, a simulacrum of a lost paradise closed off against the prevailing proto-capitalistic secular values of production and commerce.[57] This was precisely their spiritual utility, creating a domain in which by approaching nature in the raw a closer relationship with the divine might be achieved. Of the unbounded ancient desert, St Basil had written: 'Oh wilderness! Death of vices, life of virtues! . . . You are the Ladder of Jacob, for you take men to Heaven and you send angels to help them. Oh wilderness! Proud flight from the world which persecutes us . . . repudiation of sin, prison of bodies, liberty of souls!'.[58] Teresa of Ávila, glimpsing a prefiguration of the later deserts in the deportment of the Carmelite friars at Villanueva de la Jara, had recorded: 'this house is in a desert . . . as the friars went bare-foot with their poor homespun capes I was overwhelmed . . . [they] seemed to inhabit this landscape like sweetly smelling white flowers, and I thank God that I saw them thus'.[59] Here the harmony was complete: poetically and spiritually the hermits had become the desert. And it could be argued that the fusion of holy person and sacred space was indeed the ideal to which these baroque Eden projects aspired.

[57]  De la Flor, 'Jardín de Yahvé', p. 127.
[58]  Nieremberg, *Epistolario*, epistola LIV, pp. 186–7.
[59]  Saint-Saëns, *La nostalgie du désert*, p. 183.

# 11 Holywell: contesting sacred space in post-Reformation Wales

*Alexandra Walsham*

Today the declining industrial and market town of Holywell in Flintshire is still the destination of thousands of visitors and pilgrims. Annually on 22 June Roman Catholics from across the country assemble to celebrate the summer feast of St Winefride or Gwenfrewi, a seventh-century virgin decapitated by Caradoc, a local prince enraged by her pious resistance to his lustful advances, but miraculously restored to life by her uncle St Beuno, who reunited her severed head with her body. According to the legend, a fountain sprang up where her head initially fell. Each year hundreds of people bathe in the waters of this ancient holy well in the hope that they may be cured of chronic and terminal illnesses: its reputation for thaumaturgic healing has earnt it the epithet 'the Lourdes of Wales'. Undoubtedly the pattern of devotional practice and ritual now associated with this site is in large part a consequence of its reinvention in the nineteenth century. Against the backdrop of Victorian romanticism and Catholic emancipation, Holywell was remodelled in the image of emerging shrines on the continent. A papal indulgence was granted, a hospice erected, a convent of nuns established to care for the sick, and plans drawn up for a substantial basilica. Pilgrims came in ever increasing numbers: in 1895 alone 30,000 votive candles were lit at the well and the local railway company collected some 96,000 tickets at the station in the three years between 1894 and 1896.[1]

Unlike Lourdes, however, Holywell has a continuous documented history as a place of pilgrimage since the Middle Ages. The tradition of spiritual journeying to this sacred spring can be dated from written records to the twelfth century, the period from which the first extant life of the saint

The research for this chapter was undertaken during the tenure of a Leverhulme Research Fellowship. I express my gratitude to the Trust for facilitating my work on holy wells and healing springs and thank Patrick Collinson and Andrew Spicer for comments on earlier versions.

[1] J. F. Champ, 'Bishop Milner, Holywell, and the cure tradition', in W. J. Sheils (ed.), *The Church and Healing*, SCH 19 (Oxford, 1982), esp. pp. 162–4. On Lourdes, see R. Harris, *Lourdes: Body and Spirit in the Secular Age* (Harmondsworth, 1999).

by Robert, abbot of Shrewsbury, survives, but it probably stretched even further back into the pre-Conquest era. Remarkably the shrine weathered the storm of the Protestant Reformation, remaining a focus for penitential fervour, festive sociability, and medical expectation long after the theological and liturgical upheavals of the 1530s, 40s and 50s. Almost uniquely, it survived a process in which Catholics were literally displaced from the sacred spaces in which they had worshipped and prayed for many centuries and deprived of cathedrals, churches and shrines traditionally revered as receptacles and touchstones of the holy.

This chapter traces the survival and transformation of Holywell against the backdrop and in the aftermath of these religious ruptures. It treats the site not as curious relic or fossil of the medieval past, but rather as an emblem of the complex cultural changes which were a byproduct of the advent of Protestantism, as a symbol of an ongoing struggle to control points of access to supernatural power, to redefine the boundaries between the sacred and the profane, and to harness and refashion British history and heritage. It also proceeds from the assumption that Holywell cannot be detached from the wider sacralised landscape of which it was an integral part – from the dense matrix of wells, stones and trees venerated before Christianity reached these islands but gradually assimilated by it.[2] A careful reassessment of the evidence may cast new light on the nature and impact of the Counter-Reformation in Wales and offer fresh insight into the processes by which early modern Britain adapted to the dramatic ideological changes of the sixteenth century and eventually became a Protestant nation.

## I

For the purposes of this discussion, it is not necessary to enter into the long-running debate about whether or not St Winefride was a post-Conquest fabrication – a saint created by Latin writers intent upon investing the religious innovations of the eleventh and twelfth centuries with the sanction of the past. Suffice it to say that her earliest *vitae* are a function of the new impulse towards hagiographical production which accompanied the reorganisation of the Welsh Church during this period and the eclipse of native monasticism by a new wave of foreign foundations. Appropriated and reshaped by the Anglo-Norman invaders of Wales, the cult of St Winefride successfully made the transition from regional to national and international status in the course of the later Middle Ages. Her relics were translated from their resting place in Gwytherin to the Benedictine abbey

---

[2] See F. Jones, *The Holy Wells of Wales* (Cardiff, 1992).

of St Peter and St Paul in Shrewsbury in 1138 and by 1398 her major festival on 3 November was extended to the entire province of Canterbury. Liturgies in her honour were incorporated in official breviaries; a confraternity in her name was established at Shrewbury towards the end of the fifteenth century; copies of her life proliferated in Latin and English; and Welsh bards like Tudur Aled composed many *cwydd* or poems in praise of Gwenfrewi.[3]

Her well, meanwhile, remained a dependency of the nearby Cistercian house at Basingwerk, to which Pope Martin V granted the right to sell indulgences in 1427.[4] This marked the beginning of the apotheosis of the shrine, which thereafter enjoyed the patronage of nobility and royalty. In 1439 Isabella, Countess of Warwick, bequeathed a gown of russet velvet to adorn the image of the saint on feast days and it was endowed with a chaplain by a succession of fifteenth-century kings, several of whom graced it with their presence. Henry V undertook the fifty-mile journey from Shrewsbury to Holywell on foot in 1416, possibly to give thanks for the victories at Harfleur and Agincourt, and Edward IV also made a personal pilgrimage to the shrine sometime after 1461. In the late 1490s, the well chapel was rebuilt in the fashionable Perpendicular style by Lady Margaret Beaufort, mother of Henry VII, for whom William Caxton had prepared the first printed edition of St Winefride's life in 1485. Embellished with bosses in the vaulting bearing the arms of the house of Tudor as well as those of Catherine of Aragon, it appears that by the early sixteenth century the shrine had become nothing less than a dynastic icon

---

[3] For a recent attempt to unravel these issues, see F. Winward, 'The lives of St Wenefred', *Analecta Bollandiana* 117 (1999), 89–132. See also R. Bartlett, 'Rewriting saints' lives: the case of Gerald of Wales', *Speculum* 58 (1983), 598–613; J. M. N. Smith, 'Oral and written: saints, miracles and relics in Britanny, c. 850–1250', *Speculum* 65 (1990), 309–43, esp. p. 341; and more generally R. R. Davies, *Conquest, Coexistence and Change: Wales 1063–1415* (Oxford, 1987), ch. 7. For the early *vitae* and associated documents concerning the history of the shrine, see C. de Smedt (ed.), 'De Sancta Wenefreda', *Acta Sanctorum*, I (Paris, 1887), pp. 691–759. Late medieval manuscript copies of her life include Bodleian Library, MS Laud. Misc. 114, fols. 140r–(160) (s. xii); BL, Cotton MS Claudius A. V, fols. 136r–145v (s. xiv); BL, Lansdowne MS 436, fols. 107r–109r (s. xiv); BL, Add. MS 35,298 ('Legenda Sanctorum in Englysshe'), fol. 53r (s. xv). She was also incorporated in John Mirk's *Festial* of c. 1401: *A Collection of Homilies*, ed. Theodore Erbe, Early English Text Society, extra series, 96 (London, 1905), pp. 177–82. Additional material on the cult of St Winefride can be found in S. Baring-Gould and J. Fisher, *The Lives of the British Saints*, 4 vols. (London, 1907–13), IV, pp. 185–96. For the confraternity, see *Calendar of Patent Rolls, Henry VII* (London, 1914), p. 158. For Welsh poetry on the saint, see E. R. Henken, *Traditions of the Welsh Saints* (Cambridge, 1987), pp. 141–51 and G. Williams, 'Poets and pilgrims in fifteenth- and sixteenth-century Wales', *Transactions of the Honourable Society of Cymmorodorion* (1991), pp. 69–98.

[4] *Calendar of Papal Registers: Papal Letters*, VII: *1417–31*, ed. J. A. Twemlow (London, 1906), p. 504.

Plate 11.1  Exterior of the chapel over St Winefride's Well. (Crown copyright: Royal Commission on the Ancient and Historical Monuments of Wales).

(plates 11.1, 11.2, 11.3).[5] Holywell's popularity as a site of pilgrimage on the eve of the Reformation epitomised the vitality and resilience of traditional piety at all levels of Welsh society. Its wonder-working waters linked it with a wider penumbra of sanctified springs whose unlicensed cults were looked upon by the Church with greater ambivalence, sites which remind us of the more spontaneous and unruly features of what William Christian has called 'local religion'.[6]

The Henrician Reformation seriously undermined the foundations of the late medieval system of the sacred. The polemical attacks which

[5] See D. Webb, *Pilgrimage in Medieval England* (London and New York, 2000), p. 198; D. J. Hall, *English Mediaeval Pilgrimage* (London, 1965), pp. 32–4 (and see ch. 2 *passim*). Henry V's visit was recorded in *The Chronicle of Adam Usk 1377–1421*, ed. C. Given-Wilson (Oxford, 1997), p. 263. For Caxton's printed text of Robert of Shrewsbury's *vita*, see *The Lyf of the Holy [and] Blesid Vyrgyn Saynt Wenefryde* (Westminster, 1485), discussed in M. J. C. Lowry, 'Caxton, St Winifred and the Lady Margaret Beaufort', *The Library*, 6th series, 2 (1983), 101–17.
[6] See Webb, *Pilgrimage*, ch. 7; W. Christian, *Local Religion in Sixteenth-Century Spain* (Princeton, 1981).

Plate 11.2  Bathing pool of St Winefride's Well. (Crown copyright: Royal Commission on the Ancient and Historical Monuments of Wales.)

Plate 11.3  Interior of the chapel over St Winefride's Well. (Crown copyright: Royal Commission on the Ancient and Historical Monuments of Wales.)

Protestant theologians launched upon the cult of miracles and saints coincided with a concerted campaign to destroy the physical and institutional structures which had given these beliefs their social meaning. By stripping the altars and dissolving monasteries the authorities were seeking to erase concrete artistic and architectural reminders of a false ideology. In attacking relics and icons they set out to demonstrate that mere material objects lacked the magical power which laypeople erroneously attributed to them, to show that hitherto venerated artefacts were inert, impotent and useless. Even the outreaches of Wales could not evade this iconoclastic crusade. In a letter to Thomas Cromwell in 1538, Hugh Latimer linked the famous image of the Blessed Virgin Mary at Penrhys with a similar statue ('our great Sibyll') at Worcester, condemning both as 'the devil's instrument[s] to bring many . . . to eternal fire' and suggesting sarcastically that both would make 'a jolly muster in Smithfield'. Shortly thereafter, it was secretly dismantled and removed to

London for incineration.[7] The miraculous taper of Our Lady at Cardigan was likewise dismissed as a 'develish delusyon' and taken away, while the wooden statue of the great Celtic warrior saint Derfel Gadarn in Merionethshire symbolically fuelled the pyre upon which the Observant Friar John Forrest was burnt for denying the Royal Supremacy in 1538. The determination of the crown's agents to abolish all 'antique gargels of ydolatry' and eradicate all 'memoryall monymentes' of romish 'popetry' resulted in the desecration of St Winefride's shrine in Shrewsbury, but this does not seem to have extended to Holywell, which escaped almost unscathed. The statues of the Virgin Mary and St Winefride inside the well chapel appeared to have been spared the general onslaught and as late as 1612 a picture and stained-glass window depicting the life and death of the martyr remained. This is all the more intriguing in the light of the activities of Henry's commissioners at Buxton, where they defaced even the 'tabernaculle' occupied by the image of St Anne, 'lokkyd upp and sealyd the bathys and welles', and confiscated the 'cruchys, schertes, and schetes' left behind by grateful pilgrims.[8]

There are probably several reasons why Holywell survived the holocaust. Its recent refurbishment as a Tudor shrine undoubtedly supplied it with a certain immunity, but so too did the prospect of diverting the income of the well, estimated at £10 per annum in the *Valor Ecclesiasticus* of 1535, into the Henrician treasury. The right to collect the revenue was leased to a certain William Holcroft, who complained to the Court of Augmentations that several men pretending to be churchwardens of Holywell had sought to reclaim the offerings by telling visitors that the money they placed in the box before St Winefride would 'never be remedy for your souls' but merely help to fill the king's coffers, and then inviting them to put their oblations in two alternative caskets.[9] These ingenious swindlers were all members of the staunchly Catholic Pennant family, whose influence in the area, combined with that of the conservative Mostyns, the new owners of Basingwerk Abbey, must have inhibited more far-reaching reform of the site.[10] This may help to explain

[7] H. Latimer, *Sermons and Remains*, ed. G. E. Corrie, Parker Society (Cambridge, 1845), p. 395. For an overview of the early implementation of Protestantism in Wales, see G. Williams, *Wales and the Reformation* (Cardiff, 1997).

[8] T. Wright, *Three Chapters of Letters Relating to the Suppression of the Monasteries*, Camden Society, 1st series, 26 (London, 1843), pp. 183–7, 189–91, 208–9, and p. 143 respectively. The survival of the mural and windows is attested by John Speed in *The Theatre of the Empire of Great Britaine* (London, 1611–12), book 2, fol. 121.

[9] J. Hunter and J. Caley (eds.), *Valor Ecclesiasticus*, 6 vols. (London, 1810), IV, p. 438; E. A. Lewis and J. C. Davies (eds.), *Records of the Court of Augmentations Relating to Wales and Monmouthshire* (Cardiff, 1954), pp. 96–7.

[10] D. R. Thomas, *A History of the Diocese of St Asaph*, 2 vols. (London, 1870–4), p. 467.

why the Privy Council failed to implement a proposal to remove the Gothic edifice in 1579 and also why Holywell eluded the fate suffered by Capel Meugan in Pembrokeshire. The latter was 'utterlie defaced' in 1592 by order of local magistrates, with the workmen being instructed not to leave a single stone still standing.[11] Nevertheless, over time the sacred charisma associated with the well chapel was diminished by its reappropriation for secular and political purposes. In the seventeenth and eighteenth centuries it seems to have been used as the venue for the assize and quarter sessions.[12] The annexation of this hallowed space as an arena for enacting the formal ceremonies of criminal justice and civil administration may be seen as a deliberate attempt to deconsecrate it and reintegrate it into the sprawling machinery of the monarchy and state.

Even so, throughout the early modern period Holywell remained a magnet for pilgrims. The Council of the Marches made repeated attempts to prevent 'superstitious flocking' to the shrine and Elizabethan and early Stuart commentators repeatedly lamented the stubborn persistence of older opinions and rituals linked with the site. David Powell deplored continuing resort to the spring (*'fons divae Venefredae sacer'*) in a Latin tract of 1585. Thirty years later John Speed likewise disparaged the 'zealous, but blind devotion' of those who immersed themselves in the fountain firmly convinced of the sacred virtue of the waters and supposing that the red spots on the stones deposited at the bottom were 'drops of the Ladies bloud'. He was no less scornful about the belief 'carried for truth by tradition of time' that the violet-smelling moss growing on the side of the well was Winefride's hair.[13] When the lawyer Justinian Paget visited the town in 1630 he too found that 'ridiculous fables' about the saint were still alive and well in Flintshire folklore, including the miracle that 'her head was cutt of and sett on againe and she lived 15 yeares after'.[14]

Such remarks reflect a wider strand of contemporary anxiety about the remnants of popery and idolatry which lingered on in post-Reformation Wales. This was a constant refrain of the bishops of the region. In 1567, for instance, Nicholas Robinson of Bangor wrote to William Cecil that 'ignorance contineweth many in the dregges of superstition', complaining of the continuation of pilgrimages, as well as of vigils for the dead, relic

[11] BL, Cotton MS Vitellius. C. I, fols. 81v–82r; Jones, *Holy Wells*, pp. 59–60.
[12] See Thomas Pennant, *The History of the Parishes of Whiteford, and Holywell* (London, 1796), pp. 222–3. It was also used as a parochial school.
[13] Giraldus Cambrensis, *Itinerarium Cambriae . . . Cum Annotationibus Davidis Powell*, part 2 of *Pontici Virunnii Viri Doctissimi Britannicae Historiae Libri Sex* (London, 1585), book 1, ch. 2, p. 85; Speed, *Theatre*, book 2, fol. 121.
[14] BL Harleian MS 1026, fol. 31v.

worship, and the lighting of candles in honour of the saints.[15] A decade later Richard Davies of St Davids was equally scandalised by the persistence of expeditions to 'Welles and blinde Chappelles' in his diocese, along with other residues of 'the kingdome of Antichrist', and in 1587 the MP Edward Downlee told the House of Commons of the 'supersticion' he had seen people 'us[e] to a springe . . . in castinge it over ther sholders and head' in a speech designed to underline the consequences of the 'lacke of learned and honest ministers' in rural Welsh parishes.[16] Two years later Ellis Price wrote to the government about the intolerable and 'abhominable Idolatrye' practised by some inhabitants of the parish of Clynnog, where he himself had witnessed the sacrifice of bullocks to Beuno, who was also the patron saint of an adjacent well.[17] Sometimes such practices were closely intertwined with nascent Welsh nationalism. A memorandum sent to Lord Burghley around the same time reported that the people 'doe still in heapes goe one pilgrimage to the wonted welles and places of supersticion' on ancient feast days, summoned by 'theire Pencars or heade minstrells'. On these and other occasions 'theire harpers and Crowthers' recounted the lives of the Celtic saints and sang songs celebrating the victories of their ancestors in wars against 'the English nacion'.[18] While man-made structures might be mutilated or removed, it was impossible to denude the landscape of natural topographical features which operated as a mnemonic to time-honoured rituals and orally transmitted traditions and legends. As long as they remained unerased, the hagiographical and historical myths associated with them stubbornly refused to fade from the collective memory and imagination.[19]

Historians have been inclined to regard these practices as evidence of the existence of a seam of pre-Christian belief in the Celtic fringes of Britain, as well as of the inability of the Protestant Church to effect anything more than the nominal conversion and outward compliance of

[15] PRO, S(tate) P(apers) 12/44/27, printed in D. Mathew (ed.), 'Some Elizabethan documents', *Bulletin of the Board of Celtic Studies* 6 (1933), 77–8.

[16] R. Davies, *A Funerall Sermon Preached the xxvi Day of November . . . in the Parishe Church of Caermerthyn* (London, 1577), sig. D2r–v; T. E. Hartley (ed.), *Proceedings in the Parliaments of Elizabeth I*, ii: *1584–9* (Leicester, 1995), pp. 390–1.

[17] PRO, SP 12/224/74 ('Information given by Mr Price of certain idolatries and superstitions practised by the people in North Wales', May 1589).

[18] BL Lansdowne MS 111, fol. 10r–v. It may also be noted that the life of St Winefride continued to circulate in the late sixteenth century in Welsh: e.g., *Bucchedd Gwenfrewy*, edited as an appendix in Baring-Gould and Fisher, *Lives of the British Saints*, iv, pp. 397–423.

[19] Cf. the comments of A. Fox, *Oral and Literate Culture in Early Modern England* (Oxford, 2000), pp. 234, 253–5. M. Aston, 'English ruins and English history: the Dissolution and the sense of the past', *Journal of the Warburg and Courtauld Institute* 36 (1973), 231–55, explores the nostalgia inspired by ruined monasteries and its role in stimulating antiquarian activity.

the Welsh populace. The tenacity of such rituals in this 'dark corner of the land' has also often been cited in support of the contention that the Counter-Reformation in Wales was itself, to quote Glanmor Williams, 'a resounding failure'. Representing 'the carry-over by an unchanging peasantry of a fixed round of custom and habit', the relationship of these vestiges to the doctrinally self-conscious and morally rigorous piety which the seminary priests and Jesuits brought with them from the continent is said to have been very tenuous indeed.[20] According to Michael Mullett, this brand of diffuse survivalism acted as a positive 'barrier to Tridentine observance'.[21] Together with a panoply of lesser sacred sites, Holywell is seen as a paradigm of the resilience of indigenous religion to an exercise in coercive acculturation which closely paralleled that being pursued on the other side of the confessional divide – a drive to internalise dogma, prune away dubious magical accretions, and inculcate a sober culture of discipline.

In the light of recent work, however, these analyses may be in need of reassessment. One of the keynotes of research on European Catholic renewal in the last decade has been an emphasis on the way in which its agents sought to harness and revitalise the late medieval geography of the sacred. As Philip Soergel, Trevor Johnson and Marc Forster have shown, the revival of medieval shrines and the sanctification of new holy places was a hallmark of the Counter-Reformation in Bavaria and other parts of the Holy Roman Empire. Relics were imported to resacralise cities like Munich scarred by successive waves of Protestant vandalism and rulers and clerical Reformers collaborated in attempts to transform Marian pilgrimage sites such as Altötting into focal points of dynastic loyalty and anti-Protestant fervour. This went hand in hand with an effort to 'create and inhabit a mythical past', to mobilise such locations as living links with the holy history of these territories.[22] Jesuit and other missionaries in Brittany and elsewhere in France likewise centred their

---

[20] G. Williams, 'Wales and the Reformation', in G. Williams, *Welsh Reformation Essays* (Cardiff, 1967), pp. 25, 21 and pp. 11–33 *passim*; G. Williams, *Renewal and Reformation: Wales c.1415–1642* (Oxford, 1993 edn), p. 313 and ch. 13 *passim*. See also J. G. Jones, *Wales and the Tudor State: Government, Religious Change and the Social Order 1534–1603* (Cardiff, 1989), pp. 102, 106–7; and B. Bradshaw, 'The English Reformation and identity formation in Wales and Ireland', in B. Bradshaw and P. Roberts (eds.), *British Consciousness and Identity: The Making of Britain, 1533–1707* (Cambridge, 1998), pp. 43–110, for a complex and contentious argument contrasting the success of the Counter-Reformation in Ireland with its ineffectiveness in Wales.

[21] M. A. Mullett, *Catholics in Britain and Ireland, 1558–1829* (Basingstoke, 1998), p. 29 and see p. 97 for the suggestion that Welsh Catholicism was 'far removed from the crusading passions of the Counter-Reformation'.

[22] P. M. Soergel, *Wondrous in his Saints: Counter-Reformation Propaganda in Bavaria* (Berkeley, 1993), esp. chs 4, 6, quotation at p. 229; T. Johnson, 'The recatholicisation of the Upper Palatinate (1621–c.1700)', unpublished PhD thesis (Cambridge, 1991);

evangelical activities on existing loci of sanctity. Tailoring their initiatives to the local environment and seeking to tap into the distinctive traditions of the region, they preached and catechised at wells, megaliths, and wayside crosses and subtly refashioned and sanitised the rituals surrounding them.[23] Similar tactics were used by their counterparts in the Low Countries and Ireland: here too, as Raymond Gillespie and others have revealed, the cults of native saints were rejuvenated and 'a Tridentine veneer' applied to the customs associated with ancient venerated places within the rural landscape.[24] These processes of accommodation and compromise resulted in the gentle evolution of a reformed Catholicism in these contexts.

There is much to suggest that the Welsh and English priests trained in continental seminaries and sent back to reclaim their compatriots to the Church of Rome employed similar strategies, suitably modified to obviate the considerable problems posed by persecution and proscription. Expelled from ecclesiastical buildings commandeered for Protestant services, they collaborated with the laity not merely in reconsecrating private houses and chambers as new arenas for worship but also in sanctifying hitherto neutral locations in the natural world – gardens, orchards, woods and fields – as spaces in which Catholics could meditate, pray and commune with their Maker.[25] In Wales, the missionaries skilfully exploited the rhythms of the country's Celtic heritage and made use of gateways to the sacred which had evaded total obliteration by Tudor iconoclasts. It is no coincidence, for instance, that Morgan Clynnog seems to have chosen an old chapel associated with the dissolved Cistercian monastery at Margam in Glamorganshire as the location for christening a Catholic infant in August 1591.[26] Even in a state of neglect and decay such structures provided a powerful link with a sacred and numinous past. The case of the Skirrid near Abergavenny, a mountain supposedly

T. Johnson, 'Holy fabrications: the catacomb saints and the Counter-Reformation in Bavaria', *JEH* 47 (1996), 274–97; M. R. Forster, *Catholic Revival in the Age of the Baroque: Religious Identity in Southwest-Germany 1550–1750* (Cambridge, 2001), ch. 2.

[23] L. Chatellier, *The Religion of the Poor: Rural Missions in Europe and the Formation of Modern Catholicism, c. 1500–c. 1800* (Cambridge and Paris, 1993), pp. 102–16, 182; and see Elizabeth Tingle's chapter, below.

[24] W. Frijhoff, 'La fonction du miracle dans une minorité catholique: Les Provinces-Unies au xviie siècle', *Revue d'histoire de la spiritualité* 48 (1972), 151–78, esp. 170–1. R. Gillespie, *Devoted People: Belief and Religion in Early Modern Ireland* (Manchester, 1997), pp. 8, 159–60, and ch. 2. For a stimulating but flawed discussion by a sociologist, see M. P. Carroll, *Irish Pilgrimage: Holy Wells and Popular Catholic Devotion* (Baltimore and London, 1999), chs. 3–4.

[25] See L. McLain, 'Without church, cathedral or shrine: the search for religious space among Catholics in England, 1559–1625', *SCJ* 33 (2002), 381–99, esp. 385.

[26] BL Harleian MS 6998, fol. 3r–v.

cleft by an earthquake at the time of the Crucifixion, is even more compelling. An ancient destination of pilgrims, the ruined chapel erected at its summit became a centre for Counter-Reformation activity in the late sixteenth century, a venue for sermons and administration of the Sacraments. In 1676, Clement X granted complete remission of their sins to all those who visited it on the feast of St Michael the Archangel and there prayed for 'the extirpation of heresies and the exaltation of Holy Mother Church'.[27] Far from a haven of unthinking traditionalism, this was a site which the missionaries actively remodelled as a beacon of militant Tridentine Catholicism.

But the centrepiece of this programme to reshape sacred space was undoubtedly Holywell. From the late 1570s, priests made it the headquarters of their long and arduous circuits on foot in the remote villages of Denbighshire and Flintshire. The efforts of John Bennett, Hugh Owen and Humphrey Evans in the area bore fruit in a record of committed recusancy unmatched elsewhere in Wales. By the 1620s, the Jesuits were running a recusant school nearby at Greenfield Abbey, the home of the Mostyns, in flagrant defiance of the Protestant authorities, a situation which their secular rivals feared would 'drawe a persecution upon . . . that holy place of pilgrimadge and the whole cuntrey there aboute'.[28] In due course, however, both the seculars and Jesuits set up permanent residence in two inns in Holywell, the Cross Keys and Star respectively, and it is not surprising that when the Society of Jesus formalised its missionary structures in 1670 it placed its operations in this region under the patronage of St Winifred.[29] Pilgrimage to the well was actively promoted by the Tridentine priesthood and hierarchy. A stray reference in an account of a

[27] J. H. Canning (ed.), 'Catholic registers of Abergavenny, Mon. 1740–1838', in *Catholic Record Society Miscellanea* 27 (1927), pp. 102, 108–9; M. R. Lewis, 'The pilgrimage to St Michael's Mount: Catholic continuity in Wales', *The Journal of Welsh Ecclesiastical History* 8 (1991), 51–4.

[28] See J. M. Cleary, 'Recusant schools in North Wales, 1626–1627', *Worcestershire Recusant* 32 (1978), 13–23, at 14. Space does not permit an exploration of the conflicts which arose between the seculars and Jesuits over control of the site: see C. M. Seguin, 'Cures and controversy in early modern Wales: the struggle to control St Winifred's Well', *North American Journal of Welsh Studies* 3 (2003), 1–17, esp. 10–17. I am grateful to my colleague Andrew Thorpe for drawing this article to my attention.

[29] See H. Foley, *Records of the English Province of the Society of Jesus*, 7 vols. in 8 (London, 1877–84), IV, pp. 491–537; V, pp. 932–46, VII (1), p. 560; P. Hook (ed.), 'Catholic registers of Holywell, Flintshire, 1698–1829', in *Catholic Record Society Miscellanea* III (London, 1906), pp. 105–8; D. Aneurin Thomas (ed.), *The Welsh Elizabethan Catholic Martyrs* (Cardiff, 1971), ch. 3, and pp. 317–21; E. G. Jones, 'Catholic recusancy in the counties of Denbigh, Flint and Montgomery, 1581–1625', *Transactions of the Honourable Society of Cymmrodorion* (1945), 114–33; T. M. McCoog, 'The Society of Jesus in Wales: the Welsh in the society of Jesus: 1561–1625', *Journal of Welsh Religious History* 5 (1997), 1–27.

miraculous cure of 1657 reveals that a plenary indulgence had lately been bestowed on this 'holy place', restoring the pardon which lapsed at the time of the Reformation, before being briefly restored through the efforts of Bishop Thomas Goldwell, close associate of Cardinal Pole, during the reign of Mary I.[30] A note surviving in the archives of the Archdiocese of Westminster shows that by 1664 Catholic clergy in the town had assembled a sizeable library of devotional, liturgical and controversial books in Latin, English and Welsh, including, it seems, fifty-four copies of the life of the seventh-century virgin bound in leather and another forty-seven in vellum. It is tempting to infer that these might have been lent out to visitors. Another item in the same catalogue entitled 'Rules of the Sodality' may suggest that, as at major shrines on the continent, a confraternity had become connected with the site.[31] These societies were the nurseries in which the Counter-Reformation clergy nurtured and refined the piety of the intensely devout. Holywell was thus by no means untouched by the invigorating winds of the early modern movement for Catholic reform.

Another important manifestation of this process was the publication in 1635 of a new printed edition of the life and martyrdom of St Winefride (plate 11.4). Prepared by the Jesuit John Falconer, this pocket-sized book was a modernised version of Robert of Shrewsbury's twelfth-century *vita*. In his dedicatory epistle and preface to the reader, the translator celebrated the Flintshire maiden as 'the patroness of Wales', 'a bright morning-star' which had not ceased to shine in this time of 'darkenes', even when other saints had 'quite vanished out of living mens sights'. He mentioned that many recent miracles attested to the continuing sanctity of the waters of her well but, in keeping with the priorities of the humanist hagiography emerging in Europe, forbore to recount them 'because they have not ben by depositions of persons sworne, and publique Instruments authentically approved'. He also strenuously deflected the objections of Protestants who might reject passages in the tract as 'fabulous legends' and dissociated himself from some of the more improbable traditions surrounding the shrine, notably those concerning the sweet-scented

---

[30] C. de Smedt (ed.), 'Documenta de S. Wenefreda', *Analecta Bollandiana*, 6 (1887), 340. For the renewal of the indulgence under Thomas Goldwell, see de Smedt, 'De Sancta Wenefreda', p. 736. The precocious character of the Marian Counter Reformation in Wales is notable: see G. Williams, 'Wales and the reign of Mary I', *Welsh History Review* 10 (1981), 334–58.

[31] Archives of the Archdiocese of Westminster, xxxii/99, fol. 477r. I am greatly indebted to Thomas McCoog for this reference. The book may have been a copy of the *Rules of the English Sodalitie, of the Immaculate Conception of the most Glorious Virgin Mary* (Mechelen, 1618).

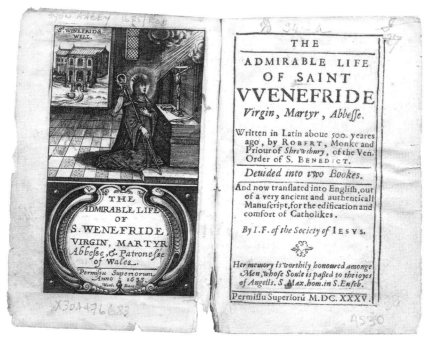

Plate 11.4 Robert, abbot of Shrewsbury, *The Admirable Life of Saint Wenefride Virgin, Martyr, Abbesse*, trans. J[ohn] F[alconer] ([St Omer], 1635), title-page and frontispiece.

moss and blood-coloured stones, which he dismissed as akin to 'Ovids Metamorphosing Fables'.[32]

The Tridentine revival of the medieval cult of Holywell must be seen as part of a wider attempt to recolonise the British past. The relatively smooth progress of the Reformation in Wales owed much to the success of its apologists in depicting it not as a new-fangled foreign implant but rather as the restoration of the apostolic faith once proudly practised by its Celtic inhabitants. Historians like Bale and Foxe presented Protestantism

---

[32] *The Admirable Life of Saint Wenefride Virgin, Martyr, Abbesse*, trans. J[ohn] F[alconer] ([St Omer], 1635), quotations at sigs. *3v–*4r, **1r–v. Abbreviated versions of her life also appeared in the *Roman Martyrologe* authorised by Gregory XIII (St Omer, 2nd edn, 1667), p. 317 and in John Wilson's *English Martyrologe* ([St Omer], 3rd edn, 1672), pp. 249–50. Elizabethan and early Stuart Catholics continued to copy her life in manuscript. She is included in the preceding calendar and almost certainly featured in the lost portion of the text of Nicholas Roscarrock's 'Alphebitt of Saintes': Cambridge University Library, Add. MS 3041, fol. 11r. See also C. Horstmann (ed.), *The Lives of Women Saintes of our Contrie of England . . . (c. 1610–1615)*, Early English Text Society, old series, 86 (1886), pp. 88–91.

as the true heir of the pure religion professed by the ancient Britons prior to the Saxon and Norman invasions and its corruption by agents of the Antichristian papacy.[33] St Winefride was one of the heroines of a rival Catholic narrative of the Christianisation of Britain which revolved around the nation's three conversions by Rome – the first linked with St Peter and the Apostles, the second associated with Pope Eleutherius and King Lucius, and the third launched by Gregory the Great and Augustine of Canterbury. She was repeatedly marshalled as part of a pantheon of saints who bore witness to the unbroken continuity of Roman Catholicism in these islands since the earliest times. She featured in the series of murals painted around the walls of the chapel of the English College at Rome which gave visual expression to this potent myth, in the book of engravings of these paintings published in 1584, generally known as the *Trophaea* (plate 11.5), and in the succession of ecclesiastical histories which culminated with Richard Challoner's *Britannia Sancta* in 1745.[34] St Winefride and her spring provided a tangible point of contact with the hallowed space inhabited by a glorious but contested Catholic past, preserved, defended and perpetuated in polemical images and texts.

A further aspect of Counter-Reformation efforts to transform this pilgrimage site into an icon of resurgent Catholicism was the collection and circulation of carefully attested miracles wrought by the virgin at Holywell. By the seventeenth century the missionary priesthood seem to have been making systematic efforts to record cures experienced at the site in a central register. A manuscript apparently compiled sometime around 1675 contains nearly fifty examples of persons restored to health by its waters, the first dating from 1556 but most clustering after 1600. Others were noted in the Annual Letters of the English Province of the Society of Jesus. These accounts emphasise the efficacy of St Winefride's

---

[33] See G. Williams, 'Some Protestant views of early British Church history', in his *Welsh Reformation Essays*, pp. 207–19; P. Roberts, 'Tudor Wales, national identity and the British inheritance' and B. Bradshaw, 'Identity formation in Wales and Ireland', both in Bradshaw and Roberts (eds.), *British Consciousness and Identity*, pp. 8–42, 43–110. A classic statement of this Protestant version of British history was the vernacular 'Address to the Welsh people' in Bishop Richard Davies' preface to the Welsh New Testament of 1567, trans. in A. O. Evans, *A Memorandum on the Legality of the Welsh Bible and the Welsh Version of the Book of Common Prayer* (Cardiff, 1925), appendix III, pp. 83–124.

[34] The fullest exposition of this rival narrative is Robert Persons' *Treatise of Three Conversions*, 3 vols. (1603–4). Giovanni Battista de Cavalleriis, *Ecclesiae Anglicanae Trophaea* (Rome [1584]), on which see A. Dillon, *The Construction of Martyrdom in the English Catholic Community, 1535–1603* (Aldershot, 2002), ch. 4 and *passim*. Michael Alford, *Fides Regia Britannica sive Annales Ecclesiae Britannicae*, 4 vols. (1663), II, §xx–xxxvii; Serenus Cressy, *The Church History of Brittany, from the Beginning of Christianity to the Norman Conquest* ([Rouen], 1668), book 16, ch. 8; Richard Challoner, *Britannia Sancta* (London, 1745), pp. 244–8.

A. S. Wenefredæ Virgini ob uirginitatem à Cradoco Alani regis filio
in NortWallia caput amputatur, eius capite in Vallem deuoluto
fons erupit adhuc miraculis clarus.

B. Cradocus a Dæmone rapitur.

C. Eiusdem Virginis capite à S. Benone corpori adiuncto ipsa ad
quindecim annos superuixit.

Plate 11.5 The martyrdom of St Winefride, in Giovanni Battista de
Cavalleriis, *Ecclesiae Anglicanae Trophaea* (Rome [1584]).

spring for an extraordinary range of diseases and complaints, from deafness to demonic possession and from leprosy to fevers and epileptic fits, and they typically stress that doctors had relinquished all hope of assisting these patients and the failure of other forms of alternative medicine. Some of the stories, such as the tale of a pedlar saved from drowning by bending a threepenny piece to the saint, are decidedly old fashioned in character, but others are imbued with a distinctly confessional flavour. There are stories of scoffing Protestants providentially punished after polluting the fountain with their dirty boots and of cures that bring about the conversion of hardened enemies of the Catholic faith, including a rigid Quaker. Other miracles follow earnest prayers that relief be granted sooner rather than later, 'least heretiques should laugh at them for having taken so long a journey to no effect', and a number indicate the ways in which the clergy sought to redirect popular devotion into orthodox Tridentine channels. Thus the ailing Mrs Anne Fortescue received the holy sacraments before immersing herself in the waters, while a Staffordshire youth injured while playing football 'first cleansed his soule by general confession and also refreshed it with the most sacred Eucharist'.[35] Indirectly these narratives reveal how the missionaries remoulded pilgrimage piety and publicised the site as a symbol of the ongoing ability of the Church of Rome to work thaumaturgic wonders.

They also provide evidence that it was not merely the 'meaner sort of people' who made journeys to seek the aid of St Winefride at Holywell. Wealthy members of the Catholic gentry and nobility from all over England and Wales also numbered among her grateful clients, along with the Jesuit Edward Oldcorne, cured of cancer of the mouth by sucking one of the distinctive red stones which were deposited at the bottom of the well.[36] Nor was it a case of secretive visits by scattered individuals, like the three daughters and maidservant of a Jacobean man fined £10 for suffering them to go to the spring 'in superstitious manner' under cover of night.[37] In the second decade of the seventeenth century the shrine seems to have become the focus of increasingly overt and audacious assemblies of recusants, often *en masse*. The Council in the Marches

---

[35] De Smedt (ed.), 'Documenta de S. Wenefreda', pp. 305–52, citations at pp. 329–30, 311, 345–6, 336, 339–40, 343 respectively. For examples noted in the Annual Letters, see Foley, *Records*, IV, pp. 536–7. The story of the Protestant paralysed after leaping into the spring with his boots on was also recorded by the Jesuit John Gerard in his memoir: see *The Autobiography of an Elizabethan*, trans. and ed. P. Caraman (London, 1951), p. 47. For further discussion, see Seguin, 'Cures and controversy', p. 3–8.

[36] For Oldcorne, see de Smedt (ed.), 'Documenta de S. Wenefreda', pp. 312–15 and Gerard, *Autobiography*, pp. 45–8. He commended his soul to the saint in his final speech on the scaffold, Foley, *Records*, IV, p. 242.

[37] G. D. Owen, *Wales in the Reign of James I* (Woodbridge, 1988), p. 10.

had only short-term success in stopping 'the great concourse of people thither' for daily service and for sermons on Sundays and feast days in 1617, when it adopted the tactic of administering the oaths of supremacy and allegiance to all strangers who refused to come to the Church of England.[38] In November 1620, when Bishop Lewis Bayley of Bangor went to Holywell in person to arrest the priests and other papists congregated there, it was said that the countryside rose up against him, 'handled him roughly and then threw him into a ditch'.[39] According to John Gee, writing four years later, the midsummer festival of St Winefride was the occasion for an annual gathering of pilgrims from Lancashire, Staffordshire and other counties and a yearly 'Synod or Convention' of the missionary clergy. Not long after Charles I's accession Sir John Bridgeman was charged by the Privy Council with stemming the flow of 'ill affected' visitors to the well.[40] This had only a very temporary effect. In 1629 it was reported that gentlemen and women 'to the number of fourteen and fifteen hundreth' had been present there, together with more than 150 priests. The assembly included Lord William Howard of Naworth and the prominent convert, Elizabeth Cary, Viscountess Falkland, accompanied by her chaplain Mr Everard. Seven years later the same lady and her company came thither on foot, dissembling 'neither their quality nor their errand'.[41] Still struggling to make much impact, Bridgeman talked of 'muringe up the head of the springe'.[42] He did not carry through this threat, but at the Flint Assizes of 1637 orders were issued to the local churchwardens to remove the iron bars surrounding the fountain, to close all except two hostelries in the town, and to disfigure the medieval image of the saint. A statue of Our Lady was another casualty of this iconoclastic outburst, which coincided with growing puritan fury about the Laudian programme to restore and preserve the 'beauty of holiness'. The recusant community retorted by circulating stories of the divine judgements which had befallen the perpetrators of these acts of sacrilege.[43] Pilgrimages continued unabated and in 1640 the local Catholic nobleman George Petre began to erect a building in Holywell, apparently to provide more spacious accommodation for devout visitors. The government stepped in to

[38] BL Royal MS 18B, VII, fol. 1r–v.
[39] A. J. Loomie (ed.), *Spain and the Jacobean Catholics*, II: *1613–1624* (Catholic Record Society, 68, 1978), p. 140.
[40] John Gee, *The Foot Out of the Snare* (London, 1624), pp. 33–4; PRO, SP 16/38/73.
[41] PRO, SP 16/151/13; J. P. Kenyon (ed.), *The Stuart Constitution: Documents and Commentary* (Cambridge, 2nd edn, 1986), p. 146 (Laud's return to the king's Instructions for 1636).
[42] PRO, SP 16/346/25. Further detail about the episode is provided by Seguin, 'Cures and controversy', pp. 13–15.
[43] De Smedt, 'De Sancta Wenefreda', p. 738. The removal of the image of the Virgin Mary is dated to 1635 by Thomas Pennant, *A Tour in Wales*, 2 vols. (1778–83), I, p. 31.

investigate, following rumours that it was intended to house a College of Jesuits.[44] During the Civil War the site seems to have suffered more damage at the hands of parliamentary soldiers and other godly vandals.[45] To zealous Protestants who saw themselves engaged in an apocalyptic struggle with the papal Antichrist, far from a mere hangover from an age of superstitious ignorance and darkness, Holywell was a provocative symbol of a reformed Catholicism which was making disturbing military conquests on the continent and which might yet seek to re-extend its empire into the British Isles.

Indeed, from the mid-Elizabethan period onwards, the Protestant authorities seem to have feared that the spring was becoming a rallying point for recusant militancy and conspiratorial activity. In 1586 the mayor of Chester took the precaution of arresting two gentleman from Essex who travelled to St Winefride's well allegedly 'to seek for ease of some infirmitye', apparently under the impression that this was a cloak to hide more sinister motives.[46] Journeys to resorts like Bath in Somerset and Spa in Germany were arousing similar suspicions.[47] Nothing did more to reinforce this conviction than events which took place in the late summer of 1605, when the Jesuit Henry Garnet led a remarkable pilgrimage to Holywell involving several priests and lay-people closely implicated in the Gunpowder Plot, Fathers Tesimond and Gerard and Ambrose Rookwood among them. On its way through the Midlands the party paused at the houses of Sir Everard Digby, John Grant and Robert Winter. Rumours circulated that 'the company went in such hostile manner for the Catholic cause'. By the time the group reached the shrine, it numbered thirty, not including servants, and the last stages were completed by the ladies of the party on barefoot. Government officials retrospectively interpreted this extraordinary expedition as a journey to pray for the success of the conspiracy and invoked it as telling evidence of Garnet's treasonous complicity, a claim denied by the priest but repeated by Protestant propagandists and by many later historians.[48] The whole

[44] PRO, SP 16/459/49, 16/466/3, 16/467/41; Foley, *Records*, IV, pp. 535–6.
[45] See D. Thomas, 'St Winifred's well and chapel, Holywell', *Journal of the Historical Society of the Church in Wales* 8 (1958), 28. John Taylor noted that the chapel was 'now much defaced by the injury of these late Wars', in *A Short Relation of a Long Journey . . . Encompassing the Principalitie of Wales* (London, 1653), p. 11.
[46] PRO, SP 12/193/14.
[47] See P. Hembrey, *The English Spa 1560–1815: A Social History* (London, 1990), ch. 1.
[48] See J. Morris, *The Condition of Catholics under James I: Father Gerard's Narrative of the Gunpowder Plot* (London, 1872), pp. 78, 240, 258; *CSP Domestic 1603–1610*, pp. 270, 299; PRO, SP 14/216, II, 121 and 153, transcribed in M. Hodgetts, 'Shropshire priests in 1605', *Worcestershire Recusant*, 47 (1986), 24–36, quotation at p. 31; and P. Caraman, *Henry Garnet 1555–1606 and the Gunpowder Plot* (London, 1964), pp. 324–5. For later reiterations of government claims, see D. Jardine, *Criminal Trials*, II: *The Gunpowder Plot* (London, 1835), pp. 200–1; Hall, *English Mediaeval Pilgrimage*, pp. 37–8.

issue is so encrusted in myth that the truth may now be irrecoverable, but we should not rule out the possibility that some of the pilgrims did hope to invoke the support of St Winefride for this desperate crusade. After all, medieval kings had often prayed at major shrines for victory in war and in 1620 Maximilian of Bavaria, patron and devotee of the miraculous Marian image at Altötting, made the Blessed Virgin *Generalissima* of his armies at the decisive Battle of the White Mountain.[49] The parallels are at the very least suggestive.

One other cluster of episodes at Holywell deserves our attention. On 29 August 1687, James II travelled to the well to pay his respects to St Winefride and to ask her to intercede to assist his wife to conceive and bear a son. He presented the shrine with a lock of his hair plaited beneath a crystal and a sacred Stuart relic, the very shift in which his great-grandmother Mary Queen of Scots had been beheaded. Only a few months before Mary of Modena had handed the chapel over to the Jesuits, having persuaded the king to bestow it upon her as a personal gift, in blatant disregard of the legal rights of the Mostyn family, who had long been its proprietors. At the same time she expressed her intention of repairing the chapel and putting it once again to a pious use. The birth of Prince James Francis Edward the following June was attributed to the king's prayers at the well and the queen paid for a priest to say mass at the site in thanksgiving for a child whose arrival would have ensured the Catholic succession to the throne.[50] In a curious way, the miracle wrought by St Winefride may be said to have helped precipitate the Glorious Revolution. Yet what these momentous events have arguably masked is a deliberate attempt to revive Holywell as a royal shrine. It is worth engaging in a little counterfactual speculation: had the Stuart dynasty survived might the site have become the baroque centrepiece of a British Counter-Reformation, a shining exemplar of eighteenth-century Catholic confessionalisation? The politicisation of sacred and historically evocative landscapes was one of the characteristic features of this process on the European mainland. In this context it is hardly surprising that the chapel became the target of renewed Protestant outrages in 1688.

Nevertheless St Winefride's well continued to attract Catholic visitors in significant numbers. When she visited the town in 1689, Celia Fiennes saw an 'abundance of devout papists' kneeling round the spring and the Blundells of Little Crosby in Lancashire made several pilgrimages

---

[49] See R. Bireley, *The Refashioning of Catholicism, 1450–1700* (Basingstoke, 1999), p. 109.

[50] See Pennant, *History*, p. 230; M. Ashley, *James II* (London, 1977), pp. 208, 218; Lord Mostyn and T. A. Glenn, *History of the Family of Mostyn of Mostyn* (London, 1925), pp. 148–9.

to Holywell between 1702 and 1728.[51] According to Philip Metcalf, the Jesuit chaplain of Powis Castle, who published a new edition of St Winefride's life in 1712, during the 'Travelling Season' the town was 'crowded with zealous Pilgrims, from all Parts of Britain'. The well was attended from sunrise until late at night and littered with barrows and crutches left behind as ex-votos, despite repeated efforts to clear them 'by those who envy the Glory of our Saint'.[52] Protestant raids on the site persisted intermittently: a detachment of dragoons was sent in to disperse the pilgrims and arrest the resident priest in 1716.[53] The following year Bishop William Fleetwood launched a scathing attack on the virgin martyr at the centre of the cult, designed to arrest the 'great concourse' to her shrine and undeceive credulous papists who continued to swallow the 'senseless legends' about her decollation and resurrection recently revived by Father Metcalf. Marshalling all his skills as a historian, he set out to demonstrate that St Winefride was 'an Imaginary Saint' and that her medieval *vita* was a post-Conquest fabrication. He gave scholarly substance to the claim that these fables were, in the words of the Kentish rector James Brome, nothing more than 'the Chymical Extracts of some Enthusiastick hot-brained Monks'.[54]

By the late 1770s the resort of pilgrims to the spring had apparently decreased considerably, but no more than a generation later, Bishop John Milner's publicisation of the miraculous cure of the Wolverhampton servant girl Winefrid White, initiated the shrine's nineteenth-century renaissance.[55] Holywell's reincarnation in the late-Victorian period as the Lourdes of the British Isles has served to efface its early modern transformation into an emblem of vibrant Tridentine Catholicism. It has eclipsed the extent to which the missionary priests successfully harnessed this medieval site, along with other sacred landmarks, as a powerful weapon in their campaign to combat and convert heretics, rouse lapsed Catholics

---

[51] C. Morris (ed.), *The Journeys of Celia Fiennes* (London, 1947), pp. 180–1; Margaret Blundell (ed.), *Blundell's Diary and Letter Book 1702–1728* (Liverpool, 1952), pp. 19, 62, 105, 146, 183.

[52] P. Metcalf, *The Life of Saint Winefride. Reprinted from the Edition of 1712*, ed. Herbert Thurston (London, 1917), pp. 83–4.

[53] *The Political State of Great Britain*, xvi (London, 1718), p. 69.

[54] W. Fleetwood, *The Life and Miracles of St Wenefrede, Together with her Litanies, with some Historical Observations Made Thereon* (London, 1713), prefaces 'To the Reader' and 'the Devout Pilgrims', quotations at pp. 7, 22; J. Brome, *Travels over England, Scotland and Wales* (London, 1707 edn), pp. 237–8. In the separately paginated section of *The History of the Worthies of England* (London, 1662) on the principality of Wales (p. 32), Thomas Fuller likewise lashed out against 'this damnable lye' and these 'improbable truths'.

[55] Pennant, *Tour*, i, p. 37 noted the decrease 'of pilgrims of late years to these *Fontanalia*'. J[ohn] M[ilner], *Authentic Documents Relative to the Miraculous Cure of Winefrid White of the Town of Wolverhampton, at Holywell* (London, 1805).

out of their spiritual lethargy, and wean the populace away from superstition and idolatry. Like pilgrimage shrines on the continent it functioned as a focal point of anti-Protestantism and as a nexus with an heroic if spurious past. Bearing the wounds of repeated spasms of evangelical zeal, it was a visible testimony to the defiance and courage of an embattled community and to the resurgent Church of Rome to which it proudly owed its allegiance.

## II

Counter-Reformation renewal is, however, only one facet of the post-Reformation history of Holywell. It would be wrong to suppose that the site was frequented only by Catholics in the sixteenth, seventeenth and eighteenth centuries. Many individuals who considered themselves upright Protestants undertook excursions to this and other springs. By way of an epilogue it may be valuable to consider the character and significance of visits to these formerly sanctified places. What they reveal is that pilgrimage survived as an important cultural phenomenon long after the reformers abolished the theology that underpinned it. When John Chamberlain spoke of Sir Dudley Carleton's two sisters going 'forward for a pilgrimage to St Wenefrides well' in September 1608 he was indicating a gradual migration in the meaning of the word itself, from a journey performed in a spirit of reverence or penitence to one carried out for pleasure, interest or adventure.[56] Some such 'pilgrims', like Samuel Johnson and his companion Mrs Thrale, who passed through Holywell in 1774, were merely curious tourists, intrigued by the sheer power of a fountain which delivered twenty-one tons of water per minute and never froze, and which in time became known as one of the natural 'wonders of Wales'.[57]

Others may have been drawn there by the picturesque architecture of the Gothic chapel: by the 1790s booksellers were selling engraved prints of the elegant structure.[58] This strand of nostalgic fascination with the site was fostered by pastoral verse in the mode of Michael Drayton's *Poly-Olbion* (1622) and embodied in the writings of antiquarians and topographers.[59] In the late seventeenth century the practices connected with holy wells in general were the subject of systematic study by Edward

[56] PRO, SP 14/36/40. See C. Morris, 'Introduction', in C. Morris and P. Roberts (eds.), *Pilgrimage: The English Experience from Becket to Bunyan* (Cambridge, 2002), p. 10.
[57] A. M. Broadley, *Doctor Johnson and Mrs Thrale* (London, 1910), pp. 187, 232.
[58] As noted by Pennant, *History*, p. 219.
[59] M. Drayton, *Works*, ed. J. W. Hebel, 5 vols. (Oxford, 1931–41), IV, pp. 74, 204–5, 483. See Aston, 'English ruins and English history', pp. 231–55.

Lhuyd, Keeper of the Ashmolean Museum, who, with a band of assistants, travelled the Celtic nations of Britain to record surviving remnants of their ancient culture.[60] Forerunners of the nineteenth-century folklorists, Lhuyd and his colleagues regarded these 'druidical' customs as evidence that the populace had never completely abandoned popery and paganism. However, their comments probably tell us more about the developing quest to recover a romantic Welsh past than they do about the degree to which rural society had embraced or evaded the Reformation.[61] The polemical commonplace that these rituals were relics of heathenism obscures the extent to which such sites had been successfully absorbed first into a Christian, and then into a Protestant, universe.

In this regard particular attention should be paid to the recreational nature of many early modern journeys to Holywell. Thus in the summer of 1617 one Lowry Davies of Caernarvon travelled there 'with diverse others of her nighbours, rather out of pastime than devotion', the same year in which the Cheshire authorities disciplined the organisers of a festive expedition to the well, involving nearly two hundred inhabitants of the villages of Shotwick, Rabie, Puddington and Little Neston. Led by a hired piper, these merry-makers spent an entire September Sunday 'in fidlinge and dauncinge to and fro', to the irritation, not to say indignation, of sabbatarian justices.[62] Much later in the eighteenth century Thomas Pennant complained that the first Sunday after St James' day was kept at the spring in 'every species of frolick and excess', but he cleared the local Roman Catholic congregation of 'any part in the orgies, which are, I fear, celebrated by persons of our own religion only'.[63] These practices may reflect the manner in which, in the wake of the liturgical upheavals of the Reformation, traditional religious rituals were slowly displaced out of their original ecclesiastical framework into the domestic and secular sphere and translated from solemn ceremonies into forms of

---

[60] These were intended to be published in a work entitled *Archaeologia Britannica*, only the first volume of which ('Glossography') appeared (London, 1707). The answers to the 'Parochial queries' he issued to his assistants and correspondents, which contain many references to practices at wells, are edited in *Parochialia*, 3 vols., supplement to *Archaeologia Cambrensis* (1909–11). See also the complaints of Erasmus Saunders, *A View of the State of Religion in the Diocese of St David's* (London, 1721), pp. 36–7.

[61] P. Morgan, 'From a death to a view: the hunt for the Welsh past in the Romantic period', in E. Hobsbawm and T. Ranger (eds.), *The Invention of Tradition* (Cambridge, 1983), pp. 43–100.

[62] De Smedt (ed.), 'Documenta de S. Wenefreda', p. 319; PRO CHES. 24/114/2 ('Information of Richard Holland of Little Neston, miller, c. September 1617'); PRO CHES. 21/3, fols. 9v, 12, 19, 22v (Presentments to the Grand Jury). I owe both these references to Steve Hindle.

[63] Pennant, *History*, p. 227. He too thought these customs could be traced to 'primaeval ceremonies'.

entertainment and leisure. In turn the open spaces associated with them seem to have been reconsecrated to play. To adapt a thesis advanced by Ronald Hutton, such developments may offer insight into the ways in which British society made the protracted and difficult passage from Catholicism to Protestantism.[64]

It is also possible to detect signs of an emerging culture of cleanliness and health. In 1610 it was reported that Dame Dorothy Townshend and other gentlewomen of her company did 'so sweat' from the 'good cheer' of their host Sir John Wynn and 'their ill-throwing at dice, that they must needs wash and purify themselves in the Holywell'.[65] And while Celia Fiennes had no time for tales of its supernatural properties, she could appreciate the refreshing taste of a 'good spring water', especially when mixed with wine, sugar, and lemons.[66] Nor was it only Catholics who travelled to the spring in search of relief from debilitating illnesses. In a context of medical eclecticism, many Protestant invalids seem to have pinned their hopes upon its unparalleled reputation for healing. Some even went there on the advice of Catholic physicians and by the mid-1630s smocks were apparently available for hire to visiting bathers. The number of recorded post-cure conversions is one measure of the cross-confessional character of the well's clientele;[67] the callipers and hand-carts they left behind them as grateful testimonies also undermine any suggestion that it was a recusant ghetto. Such visits should not necessarily be seen as a sign of imperfect Protestantism, as evidence of popular resistance to the Reformation precept that miracles had ceased. Protestants did not deny that the well had remarkable sanative qualities: they simply rejected the notion that it derived its virtues from the influence and intercession of St Winefride. Instead they believed that these had been implanted there by Providence. Some attributed the cures experienced at the site to the mineral content of its waters; others stressed the salutary effects of their bracing temperature, seeing them as nothing more than 'the experience'd Effects of a Cold Bath'.[68] Reflecting a theological ambiguity on the issue which historians have often overlooked,

---

[64] R. Hutton, 'The English Reformation and the evidence of folklore', *P&P* 148 (1995), 89–116.

[65] J. Ballinger (ed.), *Calendar of Wyn (of Gwydir) Papers 1515–1690 in the National Library of Wales and Elsewhere* (Aberystwyth, 1926), p. 87.

[66] Morris (ed.), *Journeys*, p. 181.

[67] As reflected in the miracles recorded in de Smedt (ed.), 'Documenta de S. Wenefreda', esp. pp. 311, 316–17, 345–6, 350–1. For reference to the hire of smocks, see R. James, *Iter Lancastrense; A Poem, Written A. D. 1636*, ed. T. Corser, Camden Society, old series, 7 (1845), p. 8.

[68] The quotation is from Metcalf, *Life*, p. 68. See also Pennant, *Tour*, pp. 38–9; [Daniel Defoe], *A Tour Thro' the Whole Island of Great Britain*, 3 vols. (London, 1724–7 edn), p. 99.

William Fleetwood even admitted the hypothetical possibility that they might just be truly miraculous occurrences, though he too concluded that in most cases God chose to work through the medium and within the limits of nature.[69] Protestant providentialism thus retained a place for the belief that interpositions of divine power at particular locations could heal human beings of conditions and diseases which the contemporary medical establishment deemed untreatable and fatal.

The rhetoric that developed around the many therapeutic springs which emerged and flourished in the course of the sixteenth and seventeenth centuries and became fashionable resorts after 1700, notably Bath, Buxton, Harrogate, Tunbridge Wells and Epsom, was no less firmly embedded within a framework of pious assumptions. Some of these were newly discovered; others were sites with a pre-existing reputation for healing which had been resurrected and purged of their 'popish' and ostensibly pagan overtones. Either way the physicians who publicised their medicinal properties celebrated them as 'precious gifts' from God to the British nation – special dispensations from heaven to assist the sick and suffering.[70] And there is at least the possibility that Holywell might have joined the ranks of these famous spas. In 1579 the Privy Council ordered its deputies in the Marches of Wales to test whether the waters of the fountain were 'medicinable' and if so to facilitate the admission of 'dyseased parsons' in an orderly manner to the same. If the result of the trial was negative they were to take steps to dismantle the chapel and to suppress the 'vayne and superstitious use' of the well.[71] As we have seen, although the edifice was not defaced as instructed, it was the latter course of action which shaped the shrine's subsequent fate.

It is necessary, then, to resist the temptation to speak of secularisation. In the guise of healing springs Protestantism preserved, even if it redefined, the concept of a sacralised landscape. The notion that the material world could still be a channel and conduit of divine power survived the Reformation, albeit in a less potent form. This was not merely a consequence of pastors and theologians having to condone what they could not banish and eradicate; it must be seen as evidence that the Protestant religion did not entirely relinquish the idea that the created world might be a vessel for supernatural grace. Holywell, therefore, not only highlights the

---

[69] Fleetwood, *Life*, pp. 11–12, 39–40, 63, 95. On Protestant attitudes towards miracles, see my 'Miracles in post-Reformation England', in J. Gregory and K. Cooper (eds.), *Signs, Wonders and Miracles: Representations of Divine Power in the Life of the Church*, SCH 41 (forthcoming).

[70] For further discussion, see my 'Reforming the Waters: holy wells and healing springs in Protestant England', in D. Wood (ed.), *Life and Thought in the Northern Church, c. 1100–1700*, SCH, Subsidia, 12 (Woodbridge, 1999), pp. 246–55.

[71] BL Cotton MS Vitellius. C. I, fols. 81v–82r.

Counter-Reformation effort to reassert control over this ancient sacred space and to use it as a weapon in its campaign to reclaim Britain for Rome. It also has much to tell us about the 'complex mental and cultural modifications', the dynamic processes of accommodation, exchange and negotiation which accompanied what the late Bob Scribner described as the shift 'from sacramental world to moralised universe'.[72]

---

[72] R. W. Scribner, 'The impact of the Reformation on daily life', in *Mensch und Objekt im Mittelalter und in der Frühen Neuzeit: Leben-Alltag-Kultur* (Vienna, 1990), pp. 316–43, esp. 326, 340–3; R. W. Scribner, 'Reformation and Desacralisation: from Sacramental World to Moralised Universe', in R. Po-Chia Hsia and R. W. Scribner (eds.), *Problems in the Historical Anthropology of Early Modern Europe*, Wolfenbütteler Forschungen 78 (Wiesbaden, 1997), pp. 75–92, at p. 78.

## 12 The sacred space of Julien Maunoir: the re-Christianising of the landscape in seventeenth-century Brittany

*Elizabeth Tingle*

'The faith of [the people of] Brittany has always been so constant and so pure that the heresy of the last century, so widespread in all the provinces of the kingdom, was not able to penetrate this one, and four of her bishoprics never suffered from its shadow.'[1]

Antoine Boschet's preface to his 'Life' of the Jesuit missionary Julien Maunoir echoed the pride of seventeenth-century Bretons that they were among Europe's oldest rural Christians. In the fifth and sixth centuries, missionaries had come from Ireland, Wales and Cornwall to evangelise post-Roman Armorica. Corentin came from Cornwall and founded the diocese of Quimper-Cornouaille, Paul Aurélien founded Léon, and both Brieuc and Malo worked in sees that were to bear their names. In the fifteenth century, religion was revitalised by the preaching of the Dominican Vincent Ferrer, who died in Vannes. The Bretons of the west were little affected by the Calvinist church that appeared in France after 1555, and later in the century fought against the Protestant king Henri IV for longer than any other French province. By the early seventeenth century, an important part of Breton identity and culture, among both elite and popular groups, was a millennium-old Catholicism 'pur et dur'.

But there was a paradox in Breton Christianity by the seventeenth century. Despite strong attachments to Catholicism the religion of the people failed to measure up to the expectations of reformers who emerged in the province after 1600. In 1607, when Michel Le Nobletz returned to the Léon after his studies, he found the religious life of the region to be in a miserable state. The majority of priests lived in ignorance, unable to read fluently in either French or Latin, and the humble folk 'stagnated in extreme blindness, without catechism. In the majority of parishes there were perhaps only 6 people who understood the mysteries

---

[1] A. Boschet, *Le parfait missionnaire ou la vie du Révérend Père Julien Maunoir* (Paris, 1697), p. iv.

of the Holy Trinity and the Incarnation and who knew even the Ten Commandments. The majority confessed and took communion only at Easter. Drunkenness, superstition and other sins . . . were everywhere widespread.'[2] Ignorance and corruption of morals had almost banished faith.[3]

Contemporary criticisms of the limitations of rural Catholicism were taken up by later historians. Jean Delumeau, writing in the 1970s, argued that at the end of the Middle Ages, peasants throughout Europe were only superficially Catholic, with limited knowledge of doctrine, and that religion exercised few moral and behavioural constraints.[4] Historians of Brittany drew similar conclusions. Alain Croix and Ellen Badone have both argued that before the seventeenth century 'laxity on the part of the laity and the clergy, including . . . drunkenness and promiscuity of clerics . . . was largely tolerated . . . Levels of church attendance were low and comportment differed little from that in secular settings such as the tavern.'[5] This behaviour changed only in the seventeenth century with conscientious bishops, better-educated parish priests and missionary religious orders working in the countryside, seeking to implement the rulings of the Council of Trent and the values of Catholic reform. Reformers promoted doctrinal correctness, greater emphasis on the sacraments, especially the eucharist, a penitential piety of contemplation, meditation and devotion, and an altered interior relationship with God.[6] There was a massive attempt at Christianisation through the catechising of common people, 'superstitions' were attacked and there was a drive to reform manners through increasing self-discipline and moral control.[7]

Yet the traditional view of a 'top down' Counter-Reformation does not fit neatly the Breton experience. This was a province in which elites and popular groups were proud of their Catholic past, and where history played an essential role in the affirmation of cultural identity. 'Divided linguistically, sometimes separated politically, Bretons have always had a consciousness of a common historical patrimony. The memory of the Breton migration and the pilgrimages of the early saints . . . provided

---

[2] J. Maunoir, *La vie du vénérable Dom Michel Le Nobletz*, ed. H. Pérennès (Saint-Brieuc, 1934), p. 91.

[3] Boschet, *Le parfait missionnaire*, p. iv.

[4] J. Delumeau, *Catholicism Between Luther and Voltaire: A New View of the Counter-Reformation* (London, 1977).

[5] E. Badone, *The Appointed Hour* (Berkeley, 1989), pp. 174–5.

[6] P. T. Hoffman, *Church and Community in the Diocese of Lyon 1500–1789* (New Haven, 1984), p. 84; Delumeau summarised in R. Po-Chia Hsia, *The World of Catholic Renewal* (Cambridge, 1998), p. 5.

[7] P. Burke, *Popular Culture in Early Modern Europe* (London, 1978), pp. 234–5.

anchorage for this tradition'.[8] From the ninth and tenth centuries, Breton monasteries had produced a rich corpus of *vitae* of early saints. Their stories and themes were well known among all sections of the population: there was a lively oral, popular culture of saints' lives and deeds, as well as printed texts by 1600.[9] What is striking about these *vitae*, according to Bernard Merdrignac, is their promotion of Celtic Brittany as a special zone of evangelism, with a pure and distinctive early Church. Here, the missionary saints had received their mandates to preach directly from Christ himself, not from other apostles or authorities.[10] The Bretons were thus a chosen people of God. After union with France in 1532, there remained a special relationship between the Breton Church and the papacy, and a distinctive arrangement with the Crown. Brittany was exempt from the Concordat of Bologna of 1516 while the Act of Union stated that only natives were to be appointed to Breton dioceses. In the late sixteenth and early seventeenth centuries, there was a resurgence of cultural particularism expressed most clearly in the high-profile publication of historical works sponsored by the provincial Estates. In 1582, Bertrand d'Argentré's 'History' illustrated the particularity of Brittany's politics and identity over time. In 1636 the *Vies, gestes, mort et miracles des saints de la Bretagne Armorique* was published by the Morlaix Dominican Albert Le Grand, and from the middle of the seventeenth century, the Maurist congregation in Brittany undertook a massive work of historical synthesis and publication of primary documents. This work resulted in a number of publications in the eighteenth century including the *Vies des Saints de Bretagne* of Gui-Alexis Lobineau in 1725 and the *Histoire de la Bretaigne* of Dom Morice. All of these works emphasised the role of the early missionaries in creating a special Breton religious culture, which underpinned the Breton duchy and state. Further, historical identity was rooted strongly in place. The landscape of mountain, *landes* and sea was an old one, filled with sites associated with the deeds of saints and heroes. The ancient origins of Armorica, described by Caesar, were given reality by large numbers of surviving prehistoric standing stones and tombs, relics of the Gaulish past. In each parish there were holy wells and fountains, chapels, and literally hundreds of wayside and field crosses of all periods. The Breton countryside was a sacred place, in space and time.

---

[8] N.-Y. Tonnerre, 'Introduction. Douze siècles d'historiographie bretonne', in N.-Y. Tonnerre (ed.), *Chroniqueurs et historiens de la Bretagne du Moyen Age au milieu du xxe siècle* (Rennes, 2001), p. 10.

[9] B. Merdrignac, 'L'apport des sources hagiographiques à l'histoire de la Bretagne médiévale', in Tonnerre (ed.), *Chroniqueurs*, pp. 32–3.

[10] *Ibid.*, p. 22.

However, after 1600 it was no longer enough to be proud of a long Catholic history and tradition, following the rites of the Church. Salvation necessitated a more active engagement with God. The Church militant did not want a faith based only on gestures or rites, but a system of values; *dévôts* and reformers promoted personal responsibility for sin before God, minute examination of conscience, interiorisation of faith and regular use of confession and sacraments. This religion had to be learnt, by the young at school, through catechism, and by adults through preaching and reading, so that people could draw conclusions from the articles of faith in everyday life.[11] To this end Brittany was the subject of a massive campaign of rural evangelism after 1600. The first missionary to work in the west was the priest and mystic Michel Le Nobletz, born into the rural nobility of the parish of Plougerneau in Léon in 1577. After training for the priesthood in Bordeaux, Agen and Paris and a year spent as a hermit on the north Breton coast, in 1608 he began to evangelise in the countryside, preaching and catechising in rural parishes and small fishing ports in the Trégor, Léon and Cornouaille. His method was that of the wandering preacher of the Middle Ages, working alone or assisted by his friend the Dominican Père Quintin, mixing evangelism with a strongly mystical brand of piety of prayers and severe penances, denunciations of lay habits and sins. While his missions had limited success, Le Nobletz was to be influential through the methods he developed, pioneering the use of painted tableaux for teaching and canticles in Breton, and through the friends he made among the newly founded Jesuit college at Quimper. Indeed it was because of inspiration by Le Nobletz that the Jesuit Julien Maunoir began work in Brittany. Born on the borders of upper Brittany in 1606, he became a Jesuit novice and hoped to work among the Huron of Canada but found instead a field for his apostolate while teaching in the college of Quimper in 1630–3. For ten years Maunoir worked much as Le Nobletz had, preaching in the countryside with an assistant, Père Bernard; from 1650 however he sponsored collective missionary effort, organising teams of parish priests to assist him, who served in their benefices while not engaged on missionary work.[12] Between 1640 and his death in 1683, Maunoir conducted 375 missions, mostly in Cornouaille but also Léon, Tréguier and the western part of the diocese of Vannes. Other groups also contributed to missionary work. Le Nobletz inspired several pious women, who adopted secular religious lives, praying, teaching and performing charitable activities from their own homes, such as his sisters Marguerite

---

[11] A. Croix, *L'âge d'or de la Bretagne 1532–1675* (Rennes, 1993), p. 477; L. Châtellier, *The Religion of the Poor. Rural Missions in Europe and the Formation of Modern Catholicism c. 1500 – c. 1800* (Cambridge, 1997), p. 13.
[12] G. Devailly (ed.), *Histoire religieuse de la Bretagne* (Chambray, 1980), p. 183.

and Anne, and Françoise Quisidic of Morlaix.[13] The Jesuit college in Vannes was a centre of mysticism, associated with Vincent Huby, while his contemporary Jean Rigoleuc led missions in the Vannetais. Jean Eudes worked around Saint-Malo in the 1630s and 1640s, and later in the decade Lazarists also began to evangelise in eastern Brittany.

Reformers had to tread carefully. Nobles and urban elites agreed upon the need to improve rural ignorance but they still held that Brittany had a particularly strong and special Catholic culture. In the countryside also, as Châtellier has argued, missionaries did not find a people without God, rather they were shocked by the ease with which he was appealed to: they had the difficult task of substituting workaday familiarity with God and the saints with a sense of divine transcendence while also demonstrating God's omnipresence in the whole universe and every person's life.[14] Increasing numbers of regional studies have shown that Catholic reform was not simply imposed from above but was a result of negotiation and compromise between Tridentine aspirations and local values. It is argued here that the methods of the missionaries of western Brittany were also distinctive, to accommodate her distinctive cultural values. Brittany was culturally and legally distinct from the rest of the kingdom of France, especially the four Breton-speaking dioceses of Tréguier, Léon, Quimper and Vannes of the west, with their Celtic language related to Cornish and Welsh. Two particular features of Catholic reform activity are at the heart of this chapter. Firstly an emphasis upon ritual and the use of physical space, and secondly a conscious reference to the perceived ancient sanctity of the province. The Catholic reform movement in western Brittany had a strong gestural component and was strongly rooted in time and place. Reformers sought to reorder relations with the divine through a re-sanctification of the historical landscape and a refashioning of existing sacred sites. There was above all a conscious attempt to reconstruct the mental and physical world of the early Breton saints and Church, albeit under Roman Catholic control. Vincent Huby called this process 'the second conversion' of the province.[15]

## I    The sacred space of the parish: the reordering of ecclesiastical monuments in the sixteenth and seventeenth centuries

Reforming bishops in late-medieval Brittany had eagerly sought to improve the morality and religious comportment of the laity. From the early fifteenth century there had been a growing concern over appropriate

[13] Maunoir, *La vie du vénérable Dom Michel Le Nobletz*, pp. 117–18, 145–6, 156.
[14] Châtellier, *Religion of the Poor*, p. 107.    [15] Croix, *L'âge d'or*, p. 477.

marital unions, sexual morality and illegitimacy. Episcopal injunctions ordered the public registration of baptisms to enhance morality by preventing marriages between spiritual kin and to shame women who lived in concubinage or who produced illegitimate children. Parish registers in Brittany are the earliest in Europe; the first injunction to keep records occurred in the Nantes diocese in 1406 and by 1500, parishes in all Breton dioceses were keeping registers. Comportment was also subject to sporadic regulation. For example in 1462 an episcopal injunction from Tréguier ruled against the playing of games, mummeries and dancing in churches and cemeteries, and there were orders for annual examination by rectors of all their parishioners on the Credo, Pater Noster and Ave, while children were to be instructed on Sundays.

A new campaign took place after *c.* 1630 when bishops of the four western dioceses began to reform their sees. A concern with sacred space, both intellectual and physical place, was central to the general Catholic reform movement, and to the work of the Breton episcopacy. Bishops were increasingly resident, as a result of royal policy which installed them as agents of internal politics and as brokers at the provincial estates; the smaller, remote and unfashionable bishoprics of the west were filled with men who served for long periods of time, living in their dioceses. They sought to reform the religious life of the laity through modification of behaviour, at home and in church. Despite the emphasis of contemporary written texts on interior spirituality and intellectualisation of faith, outward behaviour was still the central object of episcopal regulation. Catholicism continued to be a religion of actions and gestures for both elites and popular groups, especially in a province so recently involved in a confessional war.

As gesture could represent interior thought, so reform of outward behaviour could modify internal piety. Firstly, there was a particular effort to define behaviour during religious services and on holy days.[16] In the diocese of Léon, there were rulings in the late 1620s against frequenting taverns and dances, particularly on Sundays and feast days.[17] Reformers 'sought to rivet the worshipper's attention on the divine, to the exclusion of secular distraction'.[18] Secondly, there was a renewed campaign to eliminate profane activities from sacred ground, within churches and cemeteries, and to separate religious sites physically from the everyday world. Boschet complained in his 'Life' of Maunoir that the peasantry 'regarded the church less as a holy place where God wished to be honoured than as a meeting place where they made up their parties for

---

[16] *Ibid.*, p. 500.     [17] *Ibid.*, pp. 367–8.
[18] Hoffman, *Church and Community*, pp. 130–2.

debauchery and vengeance such that after high mass, everyone went to satisfy their passions'.[19] Thus, in the Léon there were injunctions against holding seigneurial courts in churches (1624) and against drying grain in porches (1630).[20] Ceremonies were to be orderly, disciplined and subject to clerical control. Festivities were to be banished from the sacraments, such as after baptisms; there was to be orderly and quiet behaviour during mass. The church was not to be a place for socialising but 'for holiness and prayer, where mingling and gossip were inappropriate. Silence and contemplation were to be enforced.'[21] The aim was to impose a distance and a respect with regard to the values, places, usages and persons of the church hitherto treated with familiarity by the laity.

The refashioning of interior, personal space went hand in hand with the reordering of the physical site of ritual and worship. The interest in religious comportment received its clearest outward manifestation in western Brittany with the great rebuilding of parish churches, a movement that began as early as c.1530 and which grew more intense after 1630. During these years, western Breton parishes and confraternities undertook the physical reordering of their religious monuments on a grand scale. In the organisation, execution and use of the new buildings, we see a twin concern with the need to refashion ritual to achieve greater spiritual merit, and to bring religious life much closer to the centre of the parish. Local interests and Tridentine concerns fused; the exteriorisation of faith in stone and mortar was both an indicator and a motor of the reordering of spiritual practices.

Throughout Europe, the Catholic reform movement had an important impact upon the design of church buildings and fittings. By the 1530s, reformers were emphasising the liturgy and Sacraments in worship, especially eucharistic devotion, trends which led to changes in the church design. Chancels were enlarged and rood screens taken down, to increase lay participation in the communion service. The high altar became a central focus in the church although side altars continued to be erected for the celebration of obit masses and special prayers. Simultaneously, there was an increase in preaching and a growing popularity of sermons. Naves were built or modified to increase the space available for crowds to hear sermons, lessons and catechisms, with flat or wooden roofs for better acoustics. Large pulpits were erected to propagate the word of God and more windows inserted for light. The most famous example of this baroque architecture was the church of the Gesù in Rome. Images and statues were also used to glorify God and to teach principles of the

---

[19] Boschet, *Le parfait missionnaire*, p. 187.
[20] Croix, *L'âge d'or*, pp. 367–8.    [21] Hoffman, *Church and Community*, p. 85.

faith. Session xxv of the Council of Trent in 1563 proscribed images that would inspire false doctrine and instructed artists to avoid impurities. It exhorted the artist 'to delight, teach and move the faithful to piety through a simple, straightforward and accurate representation of Christian doctrine and church history', a message internalised by many artists and their patrons.[22]

Particularly distinctive in the west was the construction of a suite of religious monuments known as parish closes. Between 1500 and 1700, most parishes in the western dioceses undertook some or all of the following: reconstruction or embellishment of the parish church, its tower and south porch; construction of high walls around the cemetery, pierced by a monumental gateway arch; a calvary, and a monumental ossuary or charnel house, added either to the south side of the church or built as a free-standing chapel in the cemetery. For example, at Argol (diocese of Quimper), the parish church was rebuilt in the mid-sixteenth century, a monumental gateway and walls enclosed the cemetery precinct in 1569, a calvary was erected in 1617, and an ossuary added in 1665. At Saint-Thégonnec (Léon), the parish church was rebuilt after 1563 and the tower after 1589. High cemetery walls and an archway were built in the 1580s, a calvary followed in 1610 and an ossuary after 1676. There was a clear definition, elevation and separation of the sacred domain at the heart of parish life. Catholic reform emphasised the drawing of religious life closer to the parish church so it could be better supervised by the priest. In the Trégor after 1600 for example, there was a proliferation of foundations of rosary and holy Sacrament confraternities based in the parish church, to encourage the faithful to stay close to home.[23]

If we take the example of the parish close of Saint-Thégonnec, we can see clear evidence for new ideas being set literally into stone.[24] The high altar continued to be placed against the east wall of the apse, but three modifications to the chancel made it highly visible to the body of the church. Wide steps were constructed up to the altar, which was built on a platform so that it was in an elevated and visible position. Alterations to the nave after the mid-sixteenth century saw the demolition of the rood screen. A great retable was built behind the altar, covering

---

[22] M. D. W. Jones, *The Counter-Reformation. Religion and Society in Early Modern Europe* (Cambridge, 1995), p. 103. See also Hsia, *The World of Catholic Renewal*, pp. 155ff.

[23] A. Croix (ed.), *Les Bretons et Dieu. Atlas d'histoire religieuse 1300–1800* (Rennes, 1985), sect. 26.

[24] E. C. Tingle, 'The Catholic Reformation and the parish: the church of Saint-Thégonnec, Finistère, France, 1550–1700', in D. Gaimster and R. Gilchrist (eds.), *Archaeology of Reformation, 1480–1580* (Leeds, 2003), pp. 44–57. The discussions of Saint-Thégonnec church draw heavily upon this essay. For details on architecture and furnishings see Y. Pelletier, *Saint-Thégonnec* (Luçon, 1992); P. Thomas and de L. Cargouët, *Saint-Thégonnec – le calvaire* (Montreuil-Bellay, 1999).

the apse walls, to concentrate the eye down on the central focus of the church. Similar refashioning took place all over western Brittany. Croix has interpreted the enclosure of parish church precincts and the greater ritualisation of the use of sacred space as a product of the impact of Counter-Reformation.[25] It appears from the chronology of building however that Catholic reformism, enhanced by the confessionalisation of the wars of religion, began to influence new fashions in building well before 1600.

The parishioners of Saint-Thégonnec were not just concerned with the church but with the provision of a range of buildings and spaces in which the sacred would prevail. The high walls erected around the churchyard accessed through a triumphal arch, provided a monumental entry to the separate domain of the sacred and the dead. There was a clear demarcation of the holy, its separation from the profane, to delimit physically the sacred zone at the heart of parish life, keeping it safe from animals and people, and even from everyday vision. Within the precinct there was a large calvary, decorated with scenes from Christ's passion, and from 1676 an ossuary chapel. This chapel had several functions. It was a depository for remains displaced from their original resting place by subsequent inhumations. Wills and parish register evidence show that in the Léon, the most common form of interment for the laity was in the nave of the parish church in this period.[26] Competition for space was fierce and corpses were regularly lifted and placed in the ossuary. Second, there was great concern for the souls of the departed. Inside the ossuary there was an altar for requiem masses and prayers for the dead. Thirdly, the ossuary contributed to a total pedagogical experience. Entry into the church through the arch and the yard became a religious procession from the secular into the sacred world, past tombs, the ossuary (on the left) and the calvary (on the right) before entering into the south porch of the church – a symbolic journey from sin, through death to redemption symbolised by the scene of Christ's passion, on into Mother Church. The living were thus invited to reflect on the means by which they might avoid damnation and gain grace and salvation. For those who could read French and Latin, a small minority of this parish, an inscription on the ossuary was instructive: 'It is a good and holy thought to pray for the faithful departed – o sinners repent while you are living because for we dead there is no longer time – pray for us the departed because one day you will be as we are – go in peace.'[27]

[25] A. Croix, *La Bretagne aux xvie et xviie siècles: la vie, la mort, la foi* (Paris, 1981), ii, see ch. 18.

[26] R. Leprohon, *Vie et mort en Bretagne sous Louis XIV* (Brasparts, 1984), pp. 142–4.

[27] Croix, *La Bretagne aux xvie et xviie siècles*, ii, pp. 1102–4; Badone, *The Appointed Hour*, pp. 173–82.

The close relationship between action and interior thought in Brittany is shown by the intellectual underpinnings of these building projects. Tridentine-inspired piety was important in the parish close movement, but the origins and context lie in the traditional theology of good works and charitable giving important long before 1600. Salvation came through grace bestowed as a gift from God which men and women came to deserve through their actions, works of mercy, charity and the sacraments.[28] Gifts for church construction, repair and embellishment were one outlet for this pious behaviour. This theology was given greater stress by Tridentine reformers, who promoted activism as the duty of Christian men and women. But the parish closes did more than allow for the remission of the sins of those who gave money for these good works. They enshrined in their stones and enforced upon their users through their plan and their layout, a new perception of the sacred, modifying ritual behaviour and action. A new form of sacred space was created, which in turn was designed to promote new interior actions through re-ordered physical gestures. The spiritual and the material cannot be separated in these rural communities. There is a second indicator that physical gesture and ritual participation could offer a route to inward knowledge. We see in the Catholic reform years the growth of new types of confraternity, whose aim was modification of personal behaviour through ritual action. As early as 1530, in Saint-Martin-de-Morlaix, the rector created a confraternity for the Holy Name of Jesus, to eliminate swearing.[29] Between 1620 and 1660, the Confraternity of the Rosary spread to 40 per cent of parishes in the diocese of Vannes and to 85 out of 101 parishes of Tréguier.[30] The reformation of interior, moral space and the reordering of the physical site of ritual and worship were interdependent.

## II     Missionaries, landscapes and history

The rebuilding and embellishment of churches, and the new use of sacred religious space, did not always impress the reformers of the early seventeenth century. For Michel Le Nobletz, outward manifestations of piety were but a substitute for an inward spiritual zeal; people sheltered behind public devotions while ignoring the interior life. The people of lower Brittany 'contented themselves with pilgrimages . . . and visits to churches where indulgences could be obtained, without striving to learn the fundamental truths, without frequenting the Sacraments and without ordering their morals. Much was spent on pious foundations, sacred ornaments

---

28 Châtellier, *Religion of the Poor*, p. 13.
29 Croix *L'âge d'or*, p. 380.     30 Croix, *Les Bretons et Dieu*, sects. 25 and 26.

and presents to churches, yet people neglected to acquit their debts or to pay their servants and labourers'; care was taken to pray to God for the dead but charity for the living was cold.[31] The central concerns of Le Nobletz, Maunoir and other reformers, were knowledge and prayer. Rural people needed education in the articles of the faith and appropriate moral teaching: 'if people were taught their prayers and how to examine their consciences, individuals would suddenly become spiritually empowered and society as a whole, having internalized the teachings of catechism, would be regenerated'.[32] As in missions throughout Europe, primary emphasis in Brittany was on teaching, through preaching, catechism, the sacraments and the adoption of new devotions. However, much of this still took place within an older devotional repertoire. For example, preaching themes remained those of the 'Loys des trespassez' first published in 1485: that thoughts of death must direct actions in life, and with a central preoccupation of sin, correction, justification and redemption.[33] Croix comments that the missions were new in terms of their intensity, form and style but they also worked within a solid tradition of ecclesiastical discourse and their methods and form were inspired largely by a powerful medieval emotion.[34]

Further, despite rhetorical emphasis on instruction, it is clear that missionary activity in the west also had a strong ritual and gestural component. Trevor Johnson has noted for the Upper Palatinate that missionaries not only stressed formal acquisition of knowledge through religious instruction, but also performance and ritual; they were prepared to persuade through vivid symbols as well as indoctrination.[35] Gestures and actions remained important means of expressing and engendering piety. Missionaries in Brittany adopted and adapted a number of traditional practices. A distinctive feature of the Breton countryside was the large number of wayside and field crosses. Yves Castel has estimated that there were at least 1,500 in the small diocese of Léon alone at the beginning of the seventeenth century and some of these sites were reused in missionary activity.[36] Le Nobletz and Père Quintin frequently preached and gave catechism lessons in fields and at roadsides, next to wayside crosses.[37] At the end of missions, many communities erected new crosses as tangible

---

[31] Devailly (ed.), *Histoire religieuse*, p. 166.
[32] Quotation from Juan de Ávila in S. T. Nalle, *God in La Mancha. Religious Reform and the People of Cuenca 1500–1650* (Baltimore, 1992), p. 105.
[33] Croix, *L'age d'or*, pp. 362–3.    [34] *Ibid.*, p. 509.
[35] T. Johnson, 'Blood, tears and Xavier-water' in R. Scribner and T. Johnson (eds.), *Popular Religion in Germany and Central Europe 1400–1800* (Basingstoke, 1997), p. 193.
[36] Croix, *L'âge d'or*, p. 347.
[37] G.-A. Lobineau, *Les vies des saints de Bretagne*, edited by Abbé Tresvaux, 6 vols. (Paris, 1836–39), IV, p. 163.

symbols of renewal. Crosses old and new became the objects of veneration, decorated with flowers, rosaries, tiny images of saints and votive offerings.[38] Secondly, there was a tradition of pardons, feast days held at chapels and sacred wells, for which indulgences had been granted by past bishops. Although holy in their institution, Boschet deplored that they had become trading fairs and meeting places for dances and debauchery. Maunoir encouraged the return of pardons to their sacred purpose. At the pardon of the chapel of St Tugdual, he preached against dancing and debauchery; at Notre Dame de Gueaudetz, a healing shrine, he encouraged the pilgrims to say every day a short rosary, which he designed and had sold on the site.[39]

Rituals were necessary to legitimise and validate the work of the new religious groups working in the Breton countryside. Despite a long tradition of anchorites and mystics, wandering preachers and religious enthusiasts, evangelists faced hostility. Parish priests resented outside clerics interfering in their benefices; Le Nobletz irritated nobles with his harsh criticism of their avarice and vice, while villagers could turn nasty: Maunoir was driven from the village of Saint-Gildas in 1649, accused of being a werewolf.[40] But God and His saints could show divine sanction for missionary work. Louis Châtellier has shown that Counter-Reformation missionaries promoted themselves as the envoys of God, whose mandate was proved, as in the days of Christ and the early church, by miracles.[41] Julien Maunoir cured many ailments with blessed rosary beads. Jesuit-authored saints' lives and reports of missions are full of miracles and signs of wonder. Reformers depended upon a widespread belief in the 'constant and direct intervention of the divinity and his saints in the life of everyday' to promote their cause.[42]

The most distinctive characteristic of the missions of Le Nobletz and Maunoir was their invocation of the protection of the early saints of Brittany and their attempts to recreate the mental and physical world of their holy predecessors. Imitation of the deeds of the heroes of Breton history gave cultural validity to their actions. The model and hero of Le Nobletz was the founder of the diocese of Léon, Paul Aurélian, who had evangelised in north western Brittany in the sixth century. Following in Aurélian's footsteps, Le Nobletz began work outside of his native parish with a mission to the remote islands of Ouessant and Molène. Next, he went to the island of Batz, off the north Breton coast, where Aurélian

[38] See Châtellier, *Religion of the Poor*, pp. 115–16.
[39] Boschet, *Le parfait missionnaire*, pp. 220–2.
[40] Devailly (ed.), *Histoire religieuse*, p. 180; G. H. Doble, *A John Wesley of Armorican Cornwall (Father Julien Maunoir)* (Truro, 1926), p. 7.
[41] Châtellier, *Religion of the Poor*, pp. 102–3.    [42] Devailly, *Histoire religieuse*, p. 199.

had founded a monastery and had died.[43] Le Nobletz also evangelised in the remote promontory of Saint-Mathieu, then in 1613 on the island of Sein. Sein held particular terrors for land folk. It was a site of old paganism, famous for its history as a cult centre and oracle during the Gallo-Roman period.[44] Its people lived harsh, primitive lives: there was no resident priest on the island and the population lived on seaweed and fish, leavened by cargoes salvaged from wrecked ships. It was a wild and terrible place. Maunoir, too, began his missionary career with journeys to Ouessant, Molène, and then to Sein, which were hailed as great successes. The population was warm and receptive to his message while a sailor from Sein was persuaded to train as a priest, to provide the islanders with a permanent dispenser of the Sacraments. Both Le Nobletz and Maunoir can be seen here consciously recreating the desert retreats, wilderness walks and sacred journeys of St Paul Aurélien, putting their work under his protection and recreating themselves in his image.

Likewise, the cult of St Corentin was revived by Jesuits working in Quimper. Although relics of the saint were housed in the cathedral and he remained the patron of the city, his cult had declined in popularity. During missions in the diocese, Le Nobletz put himself under the protection of its founder.[45] The Jesuits of Quimper were also eager to establish their credentials in the city through an association with its first bishop. In 1638, during an outbreak of plague, an angel appeared to Père Bernard, ordering him to pray to St Corentin. Bernard organised a public procession with the saint's relics and used the occasion to restore Corentin's fountain, placing a new statue under its vaulted roof.[46] Maunoir's ministry was likewise put under the protection of Corentin. After their missions to the western isles of Brittany, Maunoir and Bernard went on pilgrimage to the abbey of Landévennec, to say mass on the tomb of St Gwénolé, companion to the saint.[47]

Maunoir in particular encouraged the revival of early saints' cults in the countryside. An example of this occurred at Mûr, where the rector built a new chapel to house the tomb of the holy anchorite Elouan, to whom he believed he owed recovery from illness. Maunoir was invited to preach at the laying of the first stone of the new chapel, where he spoke of the ancient devotion to St Elouan and the long-time neglect of the veneration of his tomb.[48] Croix has argued that cults became more localised in the

---

[43] Maunoir, *La vie du vénérable Dom Michel Le Nobletz*, pp. 165–7.
[44] A. de Saint-André dit Père Verjus, *La vie de Monsieur Le Nobletz, prestre et missionnaire* (Paris, 1666), p. 193.
[45] Lobineau, *Les vies des saints*, IV, pp. 176–7.
[46] Boschet, *Le parfait missionnaire*, pp. 66–8; Lobineau, *Les vies des saints*, IV, p. 268.
[47] *Ibid.*, p. 137.    [48] *Ibid.*, p. 201; Lobineau, *Les vies des saints*, V, p. 81.

seventeenth century. The strong attachment of local people to their religious places was reinforced by a Church which encouraged a parish-based religion and short, collective journeys in place of the long, individual pilgrimages favoured in the later Middle Ages.[49] But Breton cults were not only insular; a wide range of new devotions were adopted in this period. The parish church was the site where international cults achieved a local, physical reality. To turn again to the example of Saint-Thégonnec, the principal dedication of the church was to St Thégonnec or Conog, a monk who came to Armorica from Wales with St Paul Aurélien; both saints were represented by their statues as was St Jaoua, their companion. Saints rooted in the tradition and culture of the locality, were certainly important. But most saints venerated here were shared with the wider Christian world. In the south porch and the choir were statues of evangelists and apostles. Altars in the north aisle were devoted to Mary, Anne and Joseph, and in the south, to St Jean the Baptist, with statues of Christopher, Sebastian and Roch, traditional protectors from the plague. There is also evidence for new devotions in the guise of two confraternities, the Rosary and the Holy Sacrament, both favoured by Catholic reformers. The Rosary had an altar and retable in the north transept, with a mixture of old and new imagery. On the first stage of the retable, the central image is of the Virgin giving rosaries to St Dominic and St Catherine of Siena, Dominicans whose mission was the defence of true doctrine. On the second stage of the retable, above, was a depiction of souls in purgatory, flanked by statues of St Louis, promoted by the Jesuits, and of the angel Raphael with Tobias. Several of the saints in the church were newly favoured in the early modern period, for example, Joseph, the Counter-Reformation exemplar of the loving father and the patron of the good death.[50] The 'residents' who occupied the sacred space at the heart of the parish, evolved over time.

Direct association of the Breton missionaries and the early Celtic apostles was further perpetrated by the writings of their Jesuit colleagues. In the mid and late seventeenth century a series of saints' lives appeared, written by members of the Society of Jesus, recording the deeds and miracles wrought by the missionaries. Verjus and Maunoir both wrote 'Lives' of Le Nobletz; Boschet wrote a 'Life' of Maunoir and in the early eighteenth century the Benedictine Lobineau gathered 'Lives' of all the missionaries and lay *dévôts* of Brittany. The 'Lives' were consciously modelled on those of the early medieval saints. The miracles of Le Nobletz in particular recalled those of earlier figures: he extinguished fire using prayers, beads and relics, cured illness and raised the dead. The missionaries themselves and their hagiographers tapped into an enduring

---

[49] Croix, *L'âge d'or*, pp. 379–80.     [50] See also Hoffman, *Church and Community*, p. 119.

contemporary belief in the miraculous intervention into the natural world by supernatural beings, and a Breton pride in their own particular saints. Further, this world view had strongly physical dimensions. There were sacred objects and above all sacred places where the divine presence was especially strong.[51] Le Nobletz and Maunoir benefited from the opinion that, 'Armorican Brittany has always been honoured, more than any other country, with particular signs of the total power of God'.[52]

A second distinctive feature of the Catholic reform movement in western Brittany was the rediscovery and re-sanctification of ancient Christian sites. The countryside of the west was extremely rich in the cult centres of saints, many of which were of local origin. These sites were associated with chapels and particularly fountains or wells, their main function being curative. Mamert's shrine specialised in curing stomach problems, Livertin's, headaches and Houarniaule was efficacious against fear. Biblical saints were also associated with local sites, particularly Our Lady and her mother, St Anne. Brittany was an old, sacred landscape where a special place for contacting the divine was always close to hand. During the seventeenth century, all over Catholic Europe, old shrines were reinstated, new ones built and reformers from the religious orders revived cults and pilgrimages, 'tapping into a vast popular appetite for the holy and channel[ing] the magical towards ecclesiastically sanctioned practices'.[53] Brittany, too, participated in this trend. Validation by reference to the sacred past was vital in the legitimation and acceptance of these new cult centres.

The most famous 'rediscovery' of an ancient, sacred landscape occurred near to Auray in 1624. On 25 July, her feast day, St Anne revealed herself to a farmer, Yves Nicolazic. She told him that on Christmas Day 900, a chapel had been built in her honour in the field which he worked called Bocennu, in the hamlet of Keranna, parish of Plunéret. The field was well known locally as the site of an ancient building; masonry was frequently cleared from its surface and Nicolazic's father had built a granary with some of the stone, including pieces that resembled window tracery. The visions of St Anne continued; one night, Nicolazic and some friends uncovered an ancient statute of the saint from Bocennu, revealed to him in a vision, and in 1625, twelve gold coins miraculously appeared on his kitchen table, for the rebuilding of the site. The Capuchins of Auray took up the cause: they assisted in the collection of alms and promoted the site as a pilgrimage centre.[54] A

[51] Jones, *The Counter-Reformation*, p. 119.
[52] Verjus, *La vie de Monsieur Le Nobletz*, preface.
[53] R. Po-Chia Hsia, *Social Discipline in the Reformation. Central Europe 1550–1750* (London, 1989), p. 154.
[54] Lobineau, *Les vies des saints*, III, pp. 358–63.

similar 're-discovery' took place in northern Brittany, twenty years later. In Corseul in 1644, a spring became the focus of miraculous cures. In October of that year, a statue of Our Lady was discovered in the waters of the fountain of Plancoët, the day after the feast of the rosary. A merchant was healed of dropsy and within days pilgrims flocked to the shrine for cures. Again, strong references to an early Christian past can be seen, for Corseul was a former Roman town; sculpture and masonry occurred here and a Gallo-Roman temple still survives. Roman towns were often associated with sites of early martyrs and miracles; Corseul retained a tradition of its early Christian past. Encouraged by the local religious orders, both Auray and Corseul gave good evidence to contemporaries of the special and ancient nature of Breton Christianity, of the importance of the past in contemporary renewal and the immanence of the divine presence in the countryside.

A third and final distinctive feature of the 'second conversion' of the Breton countryside, and of the relationship between reformed Catholicism and popular spirituality, was the re-Christianisation of 'dark' places in the physical landscape, where evil spirits and paganism lingered. The Counter-Reform campaign against superstitions and abuses throughout western Europe is well documented and there were plenty such practices in Brittany. Le Nobletz found that in maritime Cornouaille, women would sweep their local chapels, gather up the dust and throw it into the wind, to have favourable winds for the return of their husbands and sons.[55] When a person died, all the water containers of the household were emptied, so that the soul of the deceased would not drown, and on St John's Eve, when bonfires were lit, each family would put a stone close to their fire, so that the souls of their ancestors could sit and warm themselves.[56]

There were also many physical indicators of the pagan past of the 'Gauls', who inhabited Armorica before the Roman invasion of Julius Caesar. Principal among these were megalithic monuments, dolmens (chambered tombs), menhirs (standing stones) and cromlechs (stone circles).[57] There were also ancient springs, lakes and forests. These places, both natural and man-made, were frequently marginal to the human communities of the early modern period, on common land and on the boundaries and edges of cultivation and settlement. Richard Bradley argues that it was not until the seventeenth century at the earliest that scholars learnt to distinguish between artificial constructions and geological features of the landscape but the difference did not matter to

---

[55] Maunoir, *La vie du vénérable Dom Michel Le Nobletz*, p. 215.

[56] *Ibid.*, p. 216.

[57] A. Millon, *Pauvres Pierres! Les mégalithes bretons devant la science* (Saint-Brieuc, s.d.), p. 7.

Plate 12.1 Fountain of St Philibert, commune of Trégunc, Finistère, France.

contemporaries.[58] What was important about these sites was that they were places in the landscape imbued with supernatural properties. They were locations for communications and encounters between different worlds.[59]

Sites associated with water featured strongly in the sacred landscape of Brittany. Springs and wells where water came directly out of the ground were particularly important throughout the pre-modern centuries, as places where the outer world could communicate with the depths, special locations where the sacred world could be revealed.[60] Many of these sites were overtly Christian long before 1600; each parish had at least one well or fountain associated with a saint and healing, their functions explained in terms of the intercession of saints as with other holy relics, and the water used as an unofficial sacramental.[61] But the use of these sites was ambiguous. Pagan and superstitious practices rubbed shoulders with

[58] R. Bradley, *An Archaeology of Natural Places* (London, 2000), p. 103.
[59] *Ibid.*, p. 11; R. Bradley, *Altering the Earth. The Origins of Monuments in Britain and Continental Europe* (Edinburgh: Society of Antiquaries of Scotland Monograph Series, 8, 1993), pp. 4, 34.
[60] Bradley, *An Archaeology of Natural Places*, p. 27.
[61] W. Christian Jnr, *Local Religion in Sixteenth-Century Spain* (Princeton, 1981), p. 176.

quasi-orthodox behaviour. In Cornouaille fountains were used for divination. On the first day of the New Year, people threw presents of buttered bread into the local fountain, and others threw in pieces to represent family members, to see if there would be any deaths in the coming year.[62] The waters of St Gobrien's fountain in the parish of Mesquer cured colic; when they failed to work, the saint's statue was plunged into the spring until the ailment disappeared.[63] Springs and water courses were also liminal locations, gateways between the supernatural and natural worlds. Olive Blandin heard voices around the fountain of Ruellan, where the cult of Notre Dame de Plancoët came to be developed. She thought at first that it was her recently deceased daughter, asking for masses to be said for her soul, until she came to realise that it was Our Lady who was addressing her.[64] The mystic and visionary servant girl known as 'La Bonne Armelle' had several religious revelations while next to water. One day, while bathing in a river with her mistress, Armelle wept because she was reminded by this water of the torrent of Cedron, and the sufferings of the Son of God.[65] Missionaries encouraged rather than frowned upon the use of water shrines, but greater emphasis was put upon prayer and healing rather than divination. Le Nobletz and Maunoir both cured using water from fountains. At these sites, official cults merged with popular religion 'to create a powerful locus of sanctity'.[66]

As for prehistoric monuments, we have no record of how these were explained in the seventeenth century, but by the first half of the eighteenth, they were linked with pagan religion. They were seen as sacred sites for worship, oracles, altars for ancient sacrifices and burial places, associated with the ancient Gauls and their druids, described by classical authors. Since the Middle Ages, there had been a campaign to re-Christianise or to neutralise these ancient sites and any lingering pagan spirits with which they were associated. In a survey of 1910, G. Guénin found that 111 communes in Brittany had prehistoric monuments associated with Christian sites. Fifty-seven per cent of these comprised a church or chapel built within or very close to a prehistoric site; 26 per cent had crosses sculpted or engraved on them; 13 per cent had been moved into a cemetery or church and an unknown number had simply been destroyed.[67] While it is not possible to date closely the Christianisation of these sites, the iconography found on menhirs and dolmens shows that many were Christianised or re-Christianised in the sixteenth and

---

[62] Maunoir, *La vie du vénérable Dom Michel Le Nobletz*, p. 216.
[63] Croix, *L'âge d'or*, pp. 377–8.     [64] *Ibid.*, pp. 389.
[65] Lobineau, *Les vies des saints*, IV, p. 383.     [66] Hsia, *Social Discipline*, p. 155.
[67] G. Guénin, 'Les rochers et les mégalithes de Bretagne (légendes, traditions et superstitions)', *Bulletin de la Société Académique de Brest*, 2nd series, 35 (1910–11), 191–280.

Plate 12.2 Menhir at Men-Marz, commune of Brigognan, Finistère, France.

seventeenth centuries. At Loctudy, a menhir was incorporated into the early modern cemetery wall; at Saint-Duzec in the parish of Pleumeur-Bodou, a menhir was sculpted in 1674 with a crucifixion and signs of the apostles.[68] At Men-Marz in Brigognan and at Trégunc for example, large menhirs had their tops re-sculpted as crucifixes, in the style of the stone crosses of the region. Christian rituals and symbols purified pagan sites, closing off realms from where malign spirits might appear. The use of special signs changed the ways in which the sacred spaces of the past were perceived.

The notion that 'God's grace was more common at certain places' may have disturbed some elite churchmen and *dévôts*, but it was a belief shared by lay elites and popular groups in Brittany, including the missionaries themselves. There was not cynical accommodation of rural beliefs to effect religious and moral reformation, but a shared experience of spirituality. As Johnson has pointed out, 'far from attempting to eradicate the magical aspects of popular religion . . . the Jesuits actively supported them. Not only did they decline to wage war on superstition they also imported their own magical goods.'[69] Missionaries did not seek to destroy local traditions, because they themselves accepted many of them. Rather, they sought to increase clerical authority over them.[70] Through prayers and rituals they tried to 'sanitize local religious custom and ensure that it was under clerical control', for 'they claimed alone to know the difference between true religion and false superstitions'.[71]

## III    Conclusions

The parishioners of Plévin knew full well the importance of saints of the church and their association with physical places. When Julien Maunoir died in the parish in 1685, the bishop and chapter of Quimper came to remove his body for burial in the cathedral. The people of Plévin took up arms and refused to let Maunoir's body be taken from their church, where they interred him; his bones and dust remain part of the spiritual patrimony of the parish.[72]

How successful was the work of Catholic reformers in the countryside of western Brittany? It is clear that reform was dogged with practical difficulty and some opposition at all social levels. Bretons were not an ignorant, superstitious group of insular peasants but communities

---

[68] B. Bender, *The Archaeology of Brittany, Normandy and the Channel Islands* (London, 1986), p. 74.
[69] Johnson, 'Blood, tears and Xavier-water', p. 201.
[70] Christian, *Local Religion*, p. 161.    [71] *Ibid.*, p. 162; Hsia, *Social Discipline*, p. 183.
[72] Boschet, *Le parfait missionnaire*, p. 411.

with great pride in their distinctive political and social histories, their Catholic religious culture and they were actively engaged in rebuilding their religious patrimony to meet changing spiritual needs. There could be resentment of criticism of old values and practices shown in hostility to missionaries but there was also an on-going interest in new forms of spirituality and sympathy with pious men, so the missions had some successes. In Brittany as elsewhere in Europe, by 1700 there had been 'improvements'; the rituals and sacraments of the church were more Romanised and standardised than in the past, when every diocese had its own breviary; Christian dogma was better known; piety became more personal for many and new devotions such as the rosary and the holy sacrament were widely adopted.[73] Religious activity had become more solemn and reverential and there was a new emphasis on charitable works and the needs of the poor.[74]

The successes of the Catholic reformers, and their enduring popularity in Breton folklore, came from their adaptation to the culture and interests of their flocks. Reform activity, especially missions, had a distinctly Breton flavour. The history and landscape of Brittany provided a specific context for the methods and the legitimation of missionary work. This was a province in which history was an important badge of identity and the historical landscape was an essential source of pious experience, and there persisted in Brittany a strong notion that saints could have especially favoured relations with particular communities. Missionaries used the history and landscape of memory particularly that of the early saints, to reinforce their message of reform and salvation. This brief study of Brittany confirms results of other studies that throughout Europe, the Catholic reforms 'affirmed the local side of religion and merely tried to correct what it saw as its excesses. Religion remained tied into the landscape, with specially sacred places; healing and spiritual grace was obtained from physical objects, relics, water and even the dust of sacred sites.'[75]

Secondly, this study has shown that the gestural and ritual nature of seventeenth-century reformism was as important as doctrinal education and the stress on interior faith. There was a strongly ritualised and physical, site-centred element to old and new Catholic belief and practice. At special places in the landscape, divine intervention and even miracles could occur at any moment. Parish churches were 'reformed' to allow for

---

[73] M. R. Forster, *Counter Reformation in the Villages: Religion and Reform in the Bishopric of Speyer 1560–1720* (Ithaca, 1992), pp. 101, 106–7; Châtellier, *The Religion of the Poor*, p. 13.
[74] R. Briggs, *Communities of Belief* (Oxford, 1989), p. 403.
[75] Christian, *Local Religion*, p. 179.

more dignified worship and sacramental rituals. Sites of past Christian achievements were revived. Benign landscape features, such as wells and springs, often associated with former saints, were re-used and were resurrected to give legitimacy and inspiration to present actions. Malign reminders of superstition and a pagan past were neutralised with a range of symbols and rituals. The reformers sought to bring a more orthodox practice and understanding to all of these sites and to bring new perceptions of the sacred. Robin Briggs argues that the result of Catholic reform was not a separation of the intellectual and physical world, but often 'the intensification of ostentatious devotional practices which at least bordered on the superstitious, in the hope of redeeming weaknesses of the flesh'.[76] The Catholic reform movement was not a monolithic effort, with centralised aims and agendas. What is becoming clear in local studies is that, as with medieval Catholic practice everywhere, devotions varied and evangelism was tailored to suit local interests and needs. The Catholic reform movement in Brittany 'was a question of evolutions more than results'.[77]

[76] Briggs, *Communities of Belief*, p. 371.    [77] Croix, *L'âge d'or*, p. 513.

# 13 Sacralising space: reclaiming civic culture in early modern France

*Amanda Eurich*

In recent years, some of the richest analysis of confessional violence in early modern France has focused on the deeply embedded ideologies of pollution and corruption that articulated the physical as well as the spiritual dangers posed by the religious Other. As Natalie Davis, Barbara Diefendorf, Denis Crouzet and others have argued, Catholic polemicists nurtured the belief that the presence of heretics, living or dead, endangered the body politic and social. While Calvinist theologians rejected medieval body politics as superstition, they nonetheless defined spiritual purity in terms of separation. Thus, state-sponsored peace initiatives, such as the Edict of Nantes, often turned on the careful articulation of space which proclaimed the neutrality of civic culture, while allowing the two religions to maintain a separate and distinct place in the community. The right to construct houses of worship, to conduct religious processions, to bury the dead, and to carry out the contours of devotional life without interference were all considered fundamental safeguards of confessional coexistence. The delineation of sacred spaces which acknowledged the legitimacy of each confession offered irrefutable, visible proof of the incorporation of both Catholics and Protestants into the larger civic community.

Spatial cohabitation, however, was a fragile achievement, subject to frequent renegotiation as the demographic and political boundaries of religious communities shifted and transformed urban geographies. In Huguenot strongholds throughout southern France, Reformed communities interpreted the establishment of bipartisan regimes as a punitive, rather than protective measure. In towns where Protestants had excised visible manifestations of Catholic devotion, the reintroduction of Catholicism – the clergy, churches, rituals and symbols – almost inevitably produced bitter legislative contests over the contours of sacred and civic space. The principality of Orange, a Dutch protectorate situated within the larger embattled landscape of southern France, provides an excellent opportunity to explore how Calvinists and Catholics contested the parameters of religious coexistence set in place by state and local authorities, and in the process, redefined the boundaries of the sacred, especially in the capital city of Orange itself. Through the use and abuse of sacred and profane space, Orangeois of both confessions manipulated and reordered the urban topographies around them to articulate distinctive visions of faith and community and assert their authority over the dangerous, heretical Other.

For much of the sixteenth century, the Dutch protectorate of Orange was the site of bloody religious wars, which repeatedly challenged efforts by the house of Nassau to impose regimes of parity and pacification in absentia on its subjects. In 1607, however, Phillip-William of Nassau promulgated the Edict of Toleration, which like the Edict of Nantes, established the framework for confessional coexistence in the principality for most of the seventeenth century. While Catholics and Protestants in Orange lived side by side, often in relative harmony, the two faiths continuously tested the boundaries of sacred space. The high holy days of the Christian calendar almost inevitably increased tensions between the two communities, but even more routine expressions of religious devotion, such as viaticum processions, could transform civic space into a deeply entrenched battlefield of competing confessional visions. From 1650 onward, the internecine struggles within the house of Nassau during the minority of William III, intensified sectarian tensions in the principality and provided the pretext for the French invasion and occupation of the principality from 1660 to 1665. Two successive periods of French rule from 1672 to 1678, and again from 1685 to 1697, introduced the increasingly restrictive religious policies of the Bourbon state which challenged and eventually undermined the local construction and practice of religious coexistence and its spatial configurations.

A mere twenty miles from the papal enclave of Avignon, the nerve centre of Catholic renewal and Tridentine reform in southern France, the principality of Orange often was defined in relation to its more important and powerful neighbour. Shared economic interests, commercial ties and social networks complicated the religious antagonism that developed between the two principalities after a radical Huguenot party seized control of the local government in Orange in the early 1560s. While the steady exchange of men, matériel and capital encouraged a relatively porous confessional frontier, contemporary chroniclers still cast the Dutch principality and its eponymous capital city as '*une petite Genève*', situated in the shadow of a puissant French Rome. As early as the 1560s, Orange became a critical *étape de passage* as religious refugees sought temporary asylum in the principality while en route to more stable bastions of

Protestantism beyond the borders of France, such as Geneva.[1] The principality was also a final destination for a number of relatively prosperous, well-educated Huguenots, whose presence reinforced the nascent Reformed community and encouraged the shifting balance of power in favour of an increasingly vocal Protestant party.[2] A century later, as the Bourbon government tightened its religious policies in the 1670s and 1680s, Orange became a key *pays de refuge* for thousands of Protestants from the surrounding regions of Languedoc and Dauphiné.[3] While contemporary estimates which placed the number of refugees at 10,000 to 12,000 are probably gross exaggerations, more recent calculations suggest that the population of Orange, which reached 6,000 to 7,000 in the late seventeenth century, may have almost doubled – albeit temporarily – between 1682 and 1685. In the months preceding the promulgation of the Revocation of the Edict of Nantes, the local Protestant minister, Jacques Pineton de Chambrun recorded that the city's two temples were so crowded with communicants during Easter and Pentecost that makeshift communion tables had to be set up to accommodate the faithful.[4]

Over the course of the sixteenth century, Orange also became home to two cultural institutions – the academy and *collège* – which assured the principality would play a major role in the sustenance of Calvinist communities beyond its territorial borders.[5] By virtue of letters patent granted by Louis of Nassau in 1573, the university of Orange, which had been established in 1365, was transformed into a Huguenot academy for the training of Protestant ministers throughout the Midi. For much of the late sixteenth and early seventeenth centuries, local Protestant ministers dominated the faculty of theology at the academy and monopolised teaching positions in the *collège*, thus assuring that both institutions would serve as important educational alternatives to the well-established

[1] W. F. Leemans, *La principauté d'Orange: une société en mutation*, 2 vols. (Hilversum, 1986), I, pp. 455–7. When French governor La Molle ordered a census of the Huguenot community during the French occupation of 1568, rosters indicate about 39 per cent of resident population could be loosely identified as Huguenot. Approximately half of those were considered 'foreigners'.

[2] *Ibid.*, pp. 440–2, 448–52.

[3] See *Catalogue exposition: La Révocation de l'Edit de Nantes: Orange, terre d'accueil et d'exil* (Orange, 1985), p. 19.

[4] J. Pineton de Chambrun, *Les larmes de Jacques Pineton de Chambrun* ([1688] Paris, 1888), pp. 86–90.

[5] K. Maag, 'The Huguenot academies: preparing for an uncertain future', in R. A. Mentzer and A. Spicer (eds.), *Society and Culture in the Huguenot World, 1559–1685* (Cambridge, 2002), pp. 144–5; D. Bourchenin, *Etude sur les académies protestantes en France au XVIe et XVIIe siècles* (Geneva, 1969), pp. 111–12.

network of Catholic *collèges* and universities in Avignon and surrounding territories.[6] In the 1670s and 1680s, the Academy of Orange, which drew only a small international circle of Protestant students throughout much of the seventeenth century, saw its foreign enrolments soar with the forced relocation or closure of more renowned academies of Montauban, Nîmes, Sedan and Die.[7]

The letters patent of 1573 also made provision for the establishment of another important locus of Protestant influence in the city of Orange: the printing house. A year later, after some vigorous lobbying on the part of *collège* officials, the Protestant printer, Simon de Colombier opened up operations in Orange in a shop near the college. Over the course of the next two decades, he was succeeded by a number of printers, each engaging in a self-consciously, Protestant printing programme.[8] Thus by the mid-1570s, the institutional and religious landscape of the city of Orange had changed to reflect the critical mass of Protestants worshipping within its borders. In addition to their own house of worship (which will be discussed later), Protestants could see around them the physical evidence of their cultural and political power.

Seventeenth-century engravings of Orange show a cityscape dominated by an imposing fortress situated above the city on Mont St Eutrope.[9] From the late sixteenth century onwards, the chateau-fort became one of the most potent symbols of Protestant militancy and resistance. Home to Orange's military governor, the citadel also housed a large garrison of soldiers, the majority of them foreign mercenaries. In the late 1590s, the Huguenot minister, Vincent Serres, spearheaded efforts to strengthen the fortifications, appealing to the Reformed churches of Languedoc and Dauphiné for financial aid to fund the project. By the late 1620s, anxious to protect the principality from the renewal of religious hostilities between Catholics and Protestants in the French Midi, Maurice of Nassau transformed the city into one of the most powerful strongholds in Europe. Military plans drawn up by Nassau's chief architect, Servole, expanded the lines of fortifications around the existing citadel and town below with eleven massive towers for defence. Servole's fortifications firmly established Orange's reputation as an impenetrable *place de sûreté* within the broader network of garrisoned cities created as a consequence of the military concessions granted to Huguenot communities by the

---

[6] Maag, 'Huguenot academies', p. 145.     [7] *Catalogue terre d'accueil et d'éxil*, pp. 17–19.
[8] Leemans, *Principauté d'Orange*, I, pp. 444–5.
[9] See, for example, the illustrations that appeared in the classic history of Orange by Joseph de La Pise, *Tableau de l'histoire des princes et principauté d'Orange* (The Hague, 1639). Reproduced in *Cité des princes à l'aube du grand siècle: évocation de la ville d'Orange à travers le cadastres de 1616* (Orange, 1990).

Edict of Nantes. After the Peace of Alès in 1629 effectively terminated these promises of military protection, Orange became an even more critical bastion in the increasingly contested confessional landscape of the Midi.

## I          Reconfiguring the sacred landscape of the city

As elsewhere in Europe, the earliest Protestant services in Orange were clandestine meetings held within the protective embrace of private dwellings.[10] While the secrecy of early Protestant communities sometimes provoked violent attacks on the places where Catholics suspected Protestants of defiling the landscape by their profane, heretical worship, Catholic–Protestant confrontations over the uses and abuses of sacred space only reached fever pitch once Protestants began to press for more legitimate public expressions of their faith within the community.[11] The first militant expression of Protestantism in Orange manifested itself in a series of violent, iconoclastic attacks, triggered by the festivities surrounding All Saints' Day in 1561.[12] Brandishing muskets and pistols, bands of roving Protestants invaded churches and chapels, cleansing them of their statues, relics and other cultic devices. As Bob Scribner and others have argued, iconoclastic action must be understood as a highly ritualised form of de-sacralisation, keenly attuned to the power of sacred space. To reveal the purely material nature of man-made images required physically removing the offending objects from their sacred context to profane locales, where their authenticity could be tested, taunted and exposed.[13] In Orange, the Catholic notary, Jean Perrat, recorded how the perpetrators of the All Saints' Day riot tore down crosses and saints' statues and then dragged them through the muddy streets of the city, kicking and hurling insults at them.[14] The methodical purification of the city's Catholic spaces culminated two months later with a vicious assault on the sacred centre of the Catholic community, the Cathedral of Notre Dame de Nazareth.[15] Celebrating each victory by gathering for worship in these newly cleansed spaces, the Protestants of Orange were not only battling

---

[10] See Leemans, *Principauté d'Orange*, I, pp. 438–9.

[11] See, for example, B. Diefendorf, *Beneath the Cross: Catholics and Huguenots in Sixteenth-Century Paris* (Oxford, 1991), pp. 50–4, 83–8.

[12] M. Venard, *Réforme protestante, réforme catholique dans la province d'Avignon au XVIe siècle* (Paris, 1993), pp. 465–8.

[13] For a chronicle of the events, see J. Perrat, *Chronique d'un notaire d'Orange*, ed. L. Duhamel (Paris, 1881).

[14] R. W. Scribner, *Popular Culture and Popular Movements in Reformation Germany* (London, 1987), esp. ch. 5.

[15] Comte de Pontbriant, *Histoire de la principauté d'Orange* (Avignon, 1881), pp. 76–7.

for a legitimate place within the sacred landscape of the city, they were threatening to overtake it completely.

The Huguenots' campaign to reconfigure the sacred landscape of Orange and adapt it to suit their own theological imperatives and devotional aesthetic was short-lived. In 1563 Prince William of Nassau proclaimed the first of many edicts of pacification, which reaffirmed the basic spatial contours of medieval Catholicism by ordering the restitution of Catholic ecclesiastical properties. In turn, William accorded the city's Protestants the right to worship in the former chapel of the Jacobins for six months while the Parlement of Orange determined a more permanent solution to the problems posed by cohabitation.[16] Three years later, Orangeois Protestants were still meeting in the chapel, when city consuls petitioned William to cede the building formally to the Reformed Church, arguing that 'the Roman Catholics have for the exercise of their religion the three most spacious temples in the city'.[17] Something of the frustration and resentment that Protestants must have felt being relegated to this makeshift accommodation, while the city's Catholic minority monopolised key spaces within the city, permeates the municipal records. Seven months later, however, the Reformed community scored a singular victory when the governor of Orange accorded them the right to construct their own place of worship within the city walls in the eastern sector of the city near St Martin's Gate (see figure 13.1); within a year, the Temple of St Martin welcomed its new congregation.[18]

Elsewhere in France, the location of Huguenot places of worship was often hotly contested, and many were sited in insalubrious and incommodious properties in the suburbs beyond city walls. Royal commissioners may have been motivated by a sincere desire to keep the peace by avoiding the clashes that inevitably occurred when the two communities worshipped in close proximity to each other, but contemporaries on both sides of the religious divide interpreted the decisions as punitive and exclusionary, especially in urban areas where walls and gates were potent markers of *communitas*.[19] The haste with which Orangeois Protestants built a place of worship uniquely their own testifies to their eagerness to insinuate themselves permanently into the urban tissue of the city. For the next sixty years the *petit temple*, as it came to be called, was the most potent symbol of the inclusion of Protestants within the body politic. Perhaps even more importantly, the erection of the Temple of St Martin

---

[16] *Ibid.*, p. 79.    [17] Archives Communales (hereafter AC) Orange, BB16, fol. 40.
[18] AC Orange, BB16, fol. 67; CC7.
[19] P. Roberts, 'The most crucial battle of the wars of religion? The conflict over sites for reformed worship in sixteenth-century France', *Archiv für Reformationsgeschichte* 89 (1998), 246–9.

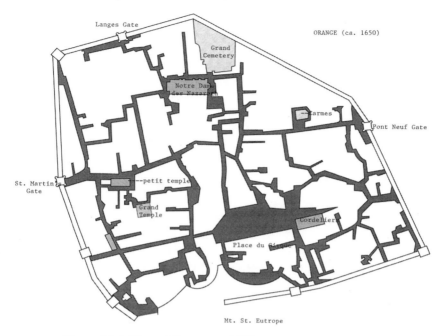

Figure 13.1 Map of Orange, *c.* 1650.

established a competing centre of sacred power in Orange which challenged the Cathedral of Notre Dame as the central locus of religious authority in the principality.

Orangeois Calvinists were keenly aware of the hierarchies of religious space within the city. Their energetic efforts to demystify the sacred 'hot spots' of the local Catholic community resurfaced with each new wave of sectarian violence. During the 1560s and 1570s the Cathedral of Notre Dame and the chapel of St Eutrope were subjected to repeated iconoclastic attacks. The intensity and frequency of these hostilities certainly owes more to mere opportunity and can be clearly linked to the central importance of these churches within the sacred geography of local Catholicism. In 1563, for example, local Protestants climbed up the bell tower of the Cathedral and managed to detach its massive bells, sending them crashing through the roof of the nave.[20] In so doing, they silenced the carillon that marked the boundaries of Catholic community and laid claim to the acoustic landscape. The mythic traditions surrounding the chapel of St Eutrope rendered it an even more problematic

---

[20] Pontbriant, *Histoire*, p. 77.

space for Protestants in Orange. Widely believed to be the site of the first Christian church, established by the city's patron saint, the twelfth-century church enjoyed enormous popularity among local pilgrims, who came to venerate the relics of the bishop-saint and worship at the most ancient locus of Christianity in the city. Pillaged in the iconoclastic frenzy of 1562, the chapel was attacked again in 1563, and then completely destroyed on the orders of the Protestant warlord, Montmorency, in 1578.[21]

Across the Midi, the confessional conflicts of the 1560s and 1570s inspired the ritual appropriation and inversion of worship sites which Wolfgang Kaiser has described as a kind of 'typography of violence'.[22] In Aix-en-Provence, for example, Catholics transformed the garden near the city walls where Protestants had gathered for worship into an execution site, hanging Protestant rebels from the pine trees growing there.[23] In Orange, after Catholics briefly regained control of the city after the so-called Notre Dame massacre of 130 Protestants in February 1571, they appropriated the Temple of St Martin for their own services, claiming that the Cathedral had been rendered unfit for worship by Protestant degradations. In practical terms, this was a curious action, given the modest size of the Protestant temple and the availability of more spacious places – even sacred spaces – in the city. Nonetheless, this 'tit-for-tat' appropriation of rival sacred space demonstrates just how critical the battle over Reformed sites of worship was in the minds of contemporaries.

The conflicts generated over sites of worship extended to cemeteries as well. While some members of the Huguenot community in Orange in the early days of the Reform movement sought burial beyond the boundaries of the city walls and the meddlesome authority of Catholic clerics, many Protestants and Catholics apparently also continued to bury their dead side by side in the large urban cemetery located behind Notre Dame de Nazareth.[24] In fact, among Catholics outdoor burials actually increased during the 1570s since the desecration and destruction of local churches had deprived the community of the opportunity to bury its dead

---

[21] AC Orange, BB19, fol. 143; C. Feuillas, *Orange: métamorphoses* (Marguerittes, 1992), p. 37.

[22] W. Kaiser, *Marseille au temps des troubles, 1559–1596* (Paris, 1992), p. 102 as cited in Roberts, 'The most crucial battle', 251.

[23] *Ibid.*

[24] In 1561, for example, a funeral procession of some 100 men and women gathered in the cemetery of St Pierre, outside the city walls without priests, bells, or crucifixes to bury Antoine Farineaux 'in the Genevan manner' in what was probably the first public Protestant burial in the city. City and church officials took note, since even the spare, clandestine burial rites of early Huguenot communities were still public affirmations of faith. See Leemans, *Principauté d'Orange*, I, p. 438.

in the uncompromised, consecrated spaces of church interiors.[25] At the same time, Protestants vigorously resisted efforts to create separate burial grounds, which given the tight spatial confines of early modern Orange, almost inevitably meant the relocation of their dead to the suburbs.[26] They appealed to family honour and *amitié ancienne*, touching on the values of friendship, status and lineage shared by members of both communities, and argued that both communities should continue to bury their dead in family grave sites or tombs irrespective of confession.[27] By the late sixteenth and early seventeenth centuries, however, it appears that the indiscriminate sharing of burial space gradually gave way to the partitioning of the cemetery into distinct Protestant and Catholic sections, perhaps in part to hinder the occasional vandalism that heightened tension between the two communities.[28]

From 1572 to 1598 with the support of resident Calvinist governors, Protestants enjoyed a virtual monopoly over municipal and parlementary offices, forcing Catholics, including the bishop of Orange, to seek refuge in the rural hinterland or in papal territories of the Comtat Venaissan. This de-centring of Catholic authority together with the desecration and destruction of key sacred spaces altered the urban grid and encouraged Protestants to transform the civic landscape even further by establishing 'points of stability', that is, the creation of sites or monuments which recalled and transfixed local events and their meanings in civic memory.[29] In the 1570s, for example, members of the Protestant community lobbied civic and military authorities for the right to construct a monument to commemorate the infamous Notre Dame Massacre of 1571, when Catholic vigilantes, inspired by the inflammatory preaching and festivities surrounding the Feast of the Purification of the Virgin, had killed local Protestants in the streets of the city.[30] For the Reformed community, the massacre was a defining moment, giving the community its first

---

[25] Based on a random sampling of 250 wills registered with Orangeois notaries and housed in the Archives Départementales (hereafter AD) Vaucluse, series E.

[26] See K. Luria, 'Separated by death? Burial, cemeteries and confessional boundaries in seventeenth-century France', *French Historical Studies* 242 (2002), 182–222.

[27] For a discussion of the rhetoric employed by Protestants, see C. Desplat, 'Sépulture et frontière confessionnelle: protestants et catholiques de Béarn (XVI–XVIIe siècles)', *Centre d'études du protestantisme béarnais* 9 (1996), 67–75.

[28] In the 1580s, for example, city accounts record a bill of fifteen livres to exhume a donkey buried in the cemetery, an act of vandalism that seem clearly rooted in confessional tensions, although it is unclear from the records which side perpetrated it. AD Vaucluse, cc535.

[29] D. C. D. Pocock, 'Place and the novelist', in K. Foote (ed.), *Re-Reading Cultural Geography* (Austin, 1994), p. 369. See also G. Justitz, 'Reforming space, reordering reality: Naumburg's Herren Gasse in the 1540', *SCJ* 33 (2002), 625–48.

[30] For an evocative description of the massacre, its perpetrators and victims, see Leemans, *Principauté d'Orange*, I, pp. 450–1.

martyrs and establishing the real dangers of the Catholic Other. With civic resources as well as privately collected funds, a column of martyrs was constructed in the Place du Cirque, the Roman amphitheatre where popular tradition held that early Christian martyrs had suffered a similar fate at the hands of the Romans. The location of the monument thus conjoined two examples of Christian persecution in time and space, creating a singular point of stability in an evolving and contested cityscape.

The promulgation of the Edict of Nantes also signalled the end of Protestant hegemony in the principality of Orange. On 2 May 1598, Henri IV confirmed Phillip-William of Nassau, son of William the Silent, as sovereign of Orange. A devout Catholic, Phillip-William lost no time in ordering the re-establishment of Catholic worship in Orange and the creation of a bipartisan Parlement and consulate, a programme which put the Dutch absentee prince at odds with his resident Calvinist governor, Alexandre Blacons. Over the next decade, Huguenot ministers in Orange backed Blacons in his vehement refusal to implement the full measure of Phillip-William's decrees. They vociferously opposed the restoration of Catholicism and lobbied to retain their control over the sacred geography of the city, urging authorities to restrict the practice of Catholicism to liminal places in the city for the preservation of peace and order in the principality. In 1599 before the assembly of the Estates of Orange, the Huguenot minister Julian Sebastian requested that the exercise of the Roman religion be confined to one neighbourhood in the city of Orange, charging that the mendicant orders, 'the authors and instigators of the last massacre perpetuated in the present city of Orange', should not be readmitted to the principality.[31]

On 23 August 1607, Phillip-William's ten-year struggle to assert his sovereignty over Orange culminated in the proclamation of a new edict of toleration, which established the general guidelines for religious coexistence in Orange for most of the seventeenth century. For both practical and symbolic reasons, Phillip-William staged the public proclamation of the Edict of Toleration in the Place du Cirque.[32] Within the densely settled urban centre of Orange, the Place du Cirque was the only public space large enough to assemble the community as a whole that could not be fully claimed by one confession or the other. Both the *petit temple* and the Cathedral of Notre Dame, for example, had often been used for official gatherings too large to assemble in the town hall, but both were obviously unsuited for a ritual intended to underscore the common identities and allegiances of Orangeois of both confessions. While Protestants

---

[31] Bibliothèque Municipale (hereafter BM) Avignon, MSS 5264, fols. 50–2.
[32] Pontbriant, *Histoire*, p. 107.

had attempted to appropriate the meanings attached to the amphitheatre by placing the column of martyrs there, the Cirque still remained an open and polyvalent space. Phillip-William himself cannot have been immune to the potent symbolism of the antique site, which allowed him to conflate his own contested claims of sovereignty with Roman imperialism. Thus, with the magnificent façade of the Augustan theatre as a backdrop, Phillip-William appeared before his subjects, performing the twin role of beneficent prince who bestowed the blessing of peace upon his subjects and of conquering Caesar who demanded a visible sign of loyalty from his subjects. Local chroniclers described how Phillip-William stretched his sword over the gathered assembly while his subjects repeated their vows of loyalty and acquiesced to his designs. From this point on, the Roman amphitheatre, which had been identified as a place of martyrdom, became the one official site in Orange which symbolised the inclusion of both confessions in the body politic.

Closely modelled on the principles and language of the Edict of Nantes, the edict of 1607 was guided by the spirit of *oubliance*, or forgetfulness, which enjoined both confessions to set aside their past differences by embracing the civic and national identities they shared in common.[33] A number of the edict's articles reinforced this policy by mandating the complete obliteration of any references to the religious conflicts of the sixteenth century from civic memory and space. Private and public discourse which revived the spectre of religious violence was banned. Monuments which commemorated 'les temps des troubles' were razed. One of the first casualties of this policy was the column of martyrs in the Place du Cirque. The edict of 1607 thus redefined the physical topography of the city, dividing Orange into three distinctive zones of influence: Catholic, Protestant, and those neutral spaces – the streets, markets, and public squares, including the Place du Cirque – shared by members of both communities.

The triumphant return of Jean Tulles II, bishop of Orange, in August 1609, and the celebration of Catholic rites in the cathedral for the first time in thirty years, marked the beginning of a bitter struggle to re-sacralise the civic landscape. Tulles initiated a vigorous campaign to reclaim and restore sites that had fallen into ruin, or even worse, had been profaned by even more mundane uses during the Protestant ascendancy. Over the next decade, Huguenot ministers protested each public advance of Catholicism in Orange from the establishment of a Capuchin

---

[33] For a discussion of *oubliance* in the Edict of Nantes, see D. Margolf, 'Adjudicating memory: law and religious difference in seventeenth-century France', *SCJ* 17 (1996), 399–418.

monastery in the ruins of the church of St Florent at the northern edges of town to the annual assemblies of Catholic clergy.[34] The restoration and re-consecration of Catholic religious sites made it possible to transform churches, monasteries and convents once again into sacred space for both the living and the dead. Over the course of the seventeenth century, the confessional delineation of burial space increased as Catholic elites began to demand burial both inside the chapels of the various monastic orders that had returned to the city as well as in the cemeteries attached to them.[35] The shifting balance of demographic power between the two confessions also may have helped fuel anxieties about the resurgence of Catholicism in Orange. By the early seventeenth century, baptismal rates in the Catholic community began to rise dramatically. By the 1620s Catholic baptisms had outstripped those in the Protestant community by a ratio of 3 to 2.[36]

Under the governorship of Christophe Dohna (1630–7) and the regency government of his widow, Ursule de Solms (1637–49), however, the Huguenot community flourished and even more boldly inscribed itself on the civic landscape.[37] A Calvinist from the Palatinate, Dohna encouraged the construction of two institutions critical to the perpetuation of the Reformed community: the new *collège* and the *grand temple*.[38] In 1633, he presided over the ground-breaking ceremonies for the new Protestant temple, which became one of the most potent symbols of the political and cultural power of the Huguenot community in Orange until Louis XIV ordered its destruction in 1685.[39] The construction of the *grand temple* in Orange coincided with the dramatic expansion in the number of Protestant temples throughout the kingdom of France, prompted in large

---

[34] BM Avignon, MSS 5238, fol. 742; MSS 5286, fol. 251. The language of the notarial record which recognised the right of the Capuchins to build on the ruins of the church of St Florent is an unequivocal statement of the evangelical mission of the order and conveys something of the sense of crisis that gripped the Huguenot elite. It reads: 'oct 1611 . . . Monseigneur Rvd Jean de Tulles évesque d'Orange depuis son advenant . . . désire de édiffier en ceste ville d'Orange ung couvant de pères capuchins pour l'augmentation de la foy catholique et que despuis il heust faire entandre son dessaing à son excellence en France le quel agréant l'intention dudict Monseigneur évesque par ses lettres patentes données à Paris 3 sept 1610 . . .' AD Vaucluse 3E51/91, fols. 255–6.

[35] Between 1640 and 1679, for example, over 60 per cent of all testators in Orange specifically requested burial in churches, monasteries or convent chapels. These calculations are based on a sample of 1,100 wills housed in the AD Vaucluse.

[36] AC Orange, GG1–GG7 (Catholic registers); GG38–GG40 (Protestant registers).

[37] Pontbriant, *Histoire*, pp. 197–202.

[38] On the importance of Huguenot temples to the construction of Calvinist community and identity, see A. Spicer, '"Qui est de Dieu oit la parole de Dieu": Huguenots and their temples', in Mentzer and Spicer (eds.), *Society and Culture in the Huguenot World*, pp. 175–92.

[39] Pontbriant, *Histoire*, p. 198.

part by growing congregations and overcrowding. Affluent Protestant communities, such as those at Charenton, La Rochelle and Montauban, spared no expense, hiring renowned architects to design temples in the latest style and finest materials.[40] No records, unfortunately, survive detailing the design or cost of the great temple in Orange, but its physical location adjacent to the grounds of the *palais de justice* signalled the dynamic nexus of confessional politics and religion. Touring southern France in the 1670s, John Locke proclaimed it 'a very pretty sort of building, one long stone arch like a bridge, running the whole length of the building', suggesting that it conformed to the longitudinal plan of a number of temples in the Midi.[41]

The interior of the *grand temple* underscored the deep bonds of political patronage which sustained the Huguenot community in Orange and guaranteed its legitimacy. The coat of arms of the house of Nassau hung strategically on the wall near the pews reserved for the Protestant members of Parlement, a conscious visual layering of the emblems of civic authority within this sacred space.[42] In 1637, the Reformed community in Orange established an even more potent physical marker of its connection to the principality's political elites by constructing a funerary monument for the ashes of the recently deceased Christophe Dohna.[43] The tomb, which honoured the governor who had been the impetus behind the construction of the temple and had worshipped among their ranks, was a source of intense pride.

The construction of temples often provoked Catholic hostilities, especially in towns where Protestants accounted for a sizeable percentage of the population but in Orange, the even-handed policies of local authorities and resident military officers tempered Catholic opposition, and efforts to protect the sacred sites of both communities from confessional vandalism mitigated tensions between the communities.[44] The city council, for example, allowed Protestants to rebuild the 'column of martyrs', provided they enclosed it behind a gate to discourage potential vandals 'from molesting the spot by dumping garbage there'.[45] Military authorities were vigilant when reports surfaced that soldiers had 'pissed in the

---

[40] Spicer, 'Qui est de Dieu oit la parole de Dieu', pp. 175–92; R. A. Mentzer, 'The Reformed churches of France and the visual arts', in P. Corby Finney (ed.), *Seeing Beyond the Word* (Grand Rapids, 1999), pp. 205–11; M. Prestwich, 'Patronage and the Protestants in France, 1598–1661: architects and painters', in R. Mousnier (ed.), *L'âge d'or du mécénat (1598–1661)* (Paris, 1985), pp. 77–88.

[41] As quoted in H. Guicharnaud, 'An introduction to the architecture of Protestant temples', in Corby Finney (ed.), *Seeing Beyond the Word*, pp. 141, 149.

[42] Chambrun, *Les larmes*, p. 110. See also Guicharnaud, 'An introduction to the architecture of Protestant temples', p. 139.

[43] Chambrun, *Les larmes*, p. 110.

[44] Spicer, 'Qui est de Dieu oit la parole de Dieu', p. 179.     [45] AC Orange, BB26.

holy water' in the Cathedral.[46] Rumours that a local roustabout had uttered grievous blasphemies while playing boules in an alleyway near the Protestant burial grounds were the cause for an extensive military inquest.[47] This kind of judicial arbitration was critical in a dense urban landscape where the boundaries between the sacred and profane, as well as between confessions, were tightly configured.

## II    Eucharistic devotions and the reordering of public space

While official policy in effect proclaimed the neutrality of public space, the devotional activities of both confessions tested the notion that the streets and squares of the city belonged to members of both communities. By virtue of the edict of 1607, Protestants were obliged to manifest at least nominal respect for the Catholic festal calendar by closing their shops and refraining from business of any kind during religious holidays. In theory, Catholics were also obliged to render a kind of reciprocal deference to Huguenot festivities, but in practice the law favoured Catholics for whom the processional aspect of religious devotion was much more highly developed.[48] Over the course of the seventeenth century, the resurgence of confraternities and Marian sodalities, whose devotional axes centred on the contested rituals and icons of Catholicism, tapped collective religious sensibilities and linked rich and poor together in the sacred effort to resanctify the body politic. Through ritual devotions and processions, Catholic lay men and women as well as clergy in Orange reasserted their authority through the reordering of civic space and time. Nowhere is this clearer than in the numerous conflicts generated by Corpus Christi festivities in Orange.

The central element of Corpus Christi was the procession of the Host, housed in an ornate monstrance carried by the clergy, who marched underneath a highly decorated canopy through the town. In biconfessional communities, such as Orange, local traditions developed to minimise the possibility of confessional conflict. Catholic processions generally followed a carefully prescribed route – one that mapped out the sacred topography of the Catholic community while circumventing Protestant temples and cemeteries. Nonetheless, Eucharistic processions effectively sacralised both time and space within the city. Protestants were not only

---

[46] AD Vaucluse, Parlement d'Orange B1087.    [47] *Ibid.*

[48] With perhaps the exception of the funeral corteges, liturgical processions were not an integral part of the Reformed culture. See Luria, 'Separated by death? Burial, cemeteries and confessional boundaries', 185–222; B. Roussel, '"Ensevelir honnestement les corps": funeral corteges and Huguenot culture', in Mentzer and Spicer (eds.), *Society and Culture in the Huguenot World*, pp. 193–208.

obliged to close their shops but also to vacate the streets, unless they wanted to suffer the humiliation of genuflecting before the passing Host. Catholic faithful hung tapestries from their windows to honour the passing Host, and priests proclaimed the verities of Eucharistic devotion in the squares and streets of the city as well as at the high altar. During Corpus Christi, the fixed, holy sites of the Catholic community expanded into the neutral spaces of the city, transforming the streets, squares and structures around them into 'virtual' churches, visible manifestations of the Church triumphant.[49] The spectacular processions of the Eucharist, prayer vigils around the Host (the so-called Forty Hours Devotion), and the week-long cycle of public sermons which punctuated the octave of Corpus Christi were powerful, tangible affirmations of the *corpus mysticum*, the sacred Christian community, to which heretical Protestants, conspicuous by their absence or by their marginalised presence at the edges of the crowd, did not belong.[50] Moreover, by the 1660s participation in Corpus Christi processions became the most visible symbol of outward conformity to the Bourbon state and its religious agenda. Accordingly, for the first time since the Reformation had taken a foothold in Orange, French military commanders joined civic leaders, Catholic sodalities and clergy in Corpus Christi processions, ordering volleys of cannon fire to mark the occasion.[51]

The persistent refusal of Huguenots to venerate the Eucharist threw into even greater relief the dangers that religious heterodoxy posed to the body politic. Offenders invariably were subjected to punitive ritual processions that manipulated the potent intentions attached to Catholic processions. In 1661, for example, magistrates charged a nine-year-old Protestant boy, Louis Villeneuve, with blasphemy for urinating in a communion chalice in a local Dominican chapel. Imprisoned for a week in the town, Louis was condemned to make amends for his crime the following Sunday in a public procession during which he was repeatedly forced to acknowledge the dominion of the Catholic sacred world around him and the inviolable purity of its rituals and sacred spaces. In its essential elements, the procession reproduced a kind of *auto da fé*, an essentially

[49] M. Rubin, *Corpus Christi: The Eucharist in Late Medieval Culture* (Cambridge, 1991), pp. 243–71.

[50] On the structure and meaning of eucharistic devotions in France, see K. Luria, 'Rituals of conversion: Catholics and Protestants in seventeenth-century Poitou', *Culture and Identity in Early Modern Europe (1500–1800)* (Ann Arbor, 1993), pp. 69–72; B. Dompnier, 'Un aspect de la dévotion eucharistique dans la France du xviie siècle: Les prières des Quarante-Heures', *Revue d'histoire de l'Eglise de France* 67 (1981), 5–31.

[51] For comparison see P. Soergel, *Wondrous in his Saints: Counter-Reformation Propaganda in Bavaria* (Cambridge, 1993), pp. 87–9.

medieval ritual which had been designed to separate, punish and then integrate repentant heretics back into the Christian fold.[52]

Two different accounts of the event by Protestant witnesses exist, both of which suggest the growing sensitivity of the Reformed leadership to temporal dimensions of long-standing traditions concerning the uses and abuses of public places. In a series of clandestine letters, Jean Sauzin, a former parlementary secretary, kept the authorities in Holland appraised of events in the principality after the first French occupation in 1660. A draft of the letter he penned detailing the Villeneuve affair as it unfolded in July 1661 still exists among his family papers.[53] Sauzin's carefully crafted description of the procession (replete with revisions which only serve to heighten the sense of injustice and outrage that provoked the letter in the first place) is a revealing document both in term of its rich ritual details as well as its emotional resonance. Sauzin described how the young Villeneuve, stripped to the waist, with ropes hung round his neck and body, was forced to carry a twelve-pound candle on an expiatory procession throughout Orange. Flanked by a sixteen-man armed guard, drummers, and the municipal executioner, Louis marched solemnly along the processional route that included mandatory stops at each of the city's five Catholic churches, where he begged forgiveness before the municipal executioner administered a few exemplary lashes. The procession, which physically reaffirmed the sanctity of Catholic churches and shrines within the city, culminated at the public square before the Cathedral of Notre Dame de Nazareth, where drummers summoned local citizens to witness the final pitiful display. According to Sauzin, such violent actions 'on such a holy day as Sunday which is normally reserved for serving God' scandalised members of both confessions.

In Jacques Pineton de Chambrun's account of the affair, recorded some twenty years after the fact, the pivotal transgression of traditions is temporal as well.[54] Villeneuve, he writes, was paraded to the public square at ten the Sunday following his arrest, where he was whipped for his crime at precisely the hour that the city's Huguenots were walking to religious services. Outraged by what he perceived as an overzealous miscarriage of justice, Chambrun also protested at the violation of long-standing, local agreements that had recognised the practical necessity of allowing the members of each community to construct separate and inviolable worship rituals. As elsewhere in Europe, Protestants and Catholics not only worshipped at separate churches, they often also worshipped at separate hours to minimise the inevitable conflicts that developed when the

---

[52] E. Muir, *Ritual in Early Modern Europe* (Cambridge, 1997), pp. 207–12.
[53] BM Avignon, MSS 2914, fols. 764–8.    [54] Chambrun, *Les larmes*, p. 12.

two worshipping communities competed for control of both physical and acoustic space. While Orangeois authorities shrewdly observed the letter of the law in staging Villeneuve's procession, Chambrun complained that the affair was yet another example of the progressive disintegration of the temporal and spatial arrangements of cohabitation.

## III    Planting crosses and claiming souls

By the late seventeenth century, the cumulative effect of two periods of French rule encouraged the complete transformation of public life in Orange. The strict application of Bourbon policies provided Orangeois Catholics with numerous opportunities to reclaim and re-sacralise the civic landscape. Their efforts were directed towards a number of sacred points, but focused in particular on one site invested with particular meaning for the Catholic community: Mont St Eutrope. In August 1661, Louis XIV ordered the Orangeois to raze the chateau on St Eutrope and its surrounding fortifications, an action easily identifiable in seventeenth-century political culture with the repression of Protestantism in France.[55] Protestant leaders in Orange were well aware of similar actions taken against the Protestant strongholds of La Rochelle, Loudun, or in the Provençal region at Les Baux. In his memoirs, Chambrun linked the material and symbolic loss of political sovereignty and independence effected by the destruction of the chateau and fortifications to a consequent loss of religious liberty. Catholics invested the action with religious significance and lobbied to reclaim and re-consecrate the site they revered as one of the most ancient Christian places in the city by planting a cross there. Even among members of the broader Catholic community in France, the site was considered significant. In a speech delivered in November 1661, the bishop of Lavaur commended the destruction of the fortress 'as a most glorious deed since one of the bastions was erected on the ruins of a Church where several councils met'.[56] To contemporary polemicists for whom the continuity and antiquity of the Catholic Church was one of the major rhetorical weapons wielded against Protestant apologists, the reclamation of St Eutrope was a singularly effective material example of the enduring vitality of the Roman Catholic Church.

---

[55] The cemetery was one such place, and in 1670 after a vigorous campaign waged by the bishop of Orange, the city consuls ordered that a wall be constructed to separate formally the Catholic and Protestant burial grounds. The destruction of the citadel took over a decade to complete. In 1673, for example, the comte de Grignan, under royal orders, laid siege to Orange on the pretext that its 'fortifications were not yet fully demolished'. See Feuillas, *Orange*, p. 41.

[56] *The History of the Persecutions in the Reformed Churches in France, Orange and the Piedmont from the Year 1655 to This Time* (London, 1699).

For precisely this reason, it remained a highly contested site as the city's Protestants attacked the cross of St Eutrope on at least three separate occasions.

By the mid-seventeenth century, the iconoclastic fury of Huguenot communities across the Midi was directed towards the large outdoor crosses planted by Catholic missionaries as a sign of territorial conquest and conversion. While Calvinist contempt for the medieval veneration of the cross produced a flurry of iconoclastic scandals in the early days of the religious wars, the strategic positioning of crosses at wayside shrines, crossroads, and even on Neolithic dolmen, became an even more militant feature of post-Tridentine Catholic renewal in the seventeenth century.[57] Louis Châtellier has argued that the ceremonial planting of crosses assumed an increasingly important role in Catholic missions and protocol after 1650.[58] Mission campaigns, especially in the deeply contested religious borderlands of southern France and the eastern marches of the Holy Roman Empire, routinely culminated in the erection of a monumental cross in a highly visible space, such as the centre of the village or on a hilltop overlooking it. The various meanings ascribed to this ceremony suggest the expansive, polyvalent nature of Catholic ritual. In more traditional Catholic preserves, such as Brittany, for example, where monumental reconstructions of Christ's crucifixion called *calvaires* were common, processions could assume an almost penitential function, prefiguring the late eighteenth- and early nineteenth-century predilection for the stations of the cross.[59]

In southern France, the penitential aspects of the ceremony were often eclipsed by the symbolism of territorial possession. Here, as along other religious frontiers, the cross became 'a rich political and religious symbol . . . a sign of the triumph of the True Church over heretics and infidels'.[60] The dual symbolism is evident in the missionary activities of the celebrated Capuchin preacher, Father Honoré de Cannes, who organised several large-scale missions in southern France. Cannes crowned his Toulouse mission in 1678 with a ceremonial cross-planting outside the city gates, but refused to head the procession without the participation of the city's Black Penitent confraternity, the nucleus of a militant Catholic party drawn from among the town's parlementary elites, renowned for

---

[57] See, for example, Diefendorf, *Beneath the Cross*, pp. 85–8, 130, 172–9; R. Sauzet, *Contre-réforme et réforme catholique en bas-Languedoc: le diocèse de Nîmes au XVIIe siècle* (Brussels, 1979), pp. 196–9; E. Tingle, 'The sacred space of Julien Maunoir: the re-Christianising of the landscape in seventeenth-century Brittany' in this volume.

[58] L. Châtellier, *The Religion of the Poor: Rural Missions in Europe and the Formation of Modern Catholicism, c. 1500–1800* (Cambridge, 1997), pp. 108–9.

[59] *Ibid.*     [60] *Ibid.*

their legal offensive against the Huguenots of the Midi.[61] In relatively quick order, the Toulousan cross became a sort of pilgrimage site for local Catholics, and Cannes was forced to install a local priest in a hut built nearby to receive offerings and protect the monument from local relic-seekers. He may also have been worried about iconoclastic attacks, especially in a region where Protestants had transformed cross-battering into a kind of clandestine sport.[62]

The increasingly violent clashes between Catholics and Protestants in Orange resulted in at least three attacks on the crosses of St Eutrope between 1675 and 1681. On 13 May 1675, for example, the Parlement of Orange threatened the unknown perpetrators for battering a cross at St Eutrope with a fine of 500 livres, and ordered local priests to reveal any information that they had concerning their own in-house investigation.[63] A few years later, after a violent storm struck down one of the crosses planted on Mont St Eutrope, city inspectors reviewing the damage found a white banner draped over the cross, inscribed with 'blasphemous attacks against the dogma of the Religion'.[64] By far the most infamous iconoclastic attack on outdoor crucifixes, however, was the 1679 assault, which inspired a full-fledged Catholic counter-attack. Under the cover of night in the spring of 1679, the perpetrators of the scandal crept up the hillside and destroyed one of the crosses that had been erected on the ruins of the chateau. The initial attack produced a flurry of letters between the bishop of Orange and officials in Paris and a massive public outcry.[65] In the early days of the scandal, Orangeois Protestants insisted that the action had been perpetrated by Catholic thugs who hoped to provoke attacks on the Reformed community, but suspicions eventually fell on Jean Poudrier, a local artisan and ardent Protestant.[66] Although Poudrier was formally accused of the crime and summarily punished, the bishop of Orange insisted on an expiatory procession that drew hundreds of Catholics from around the principality and the Comtat Venaissin. The entire *corps de la ville*, including Protestant consuls, paraded in full regalia (*en chaperon*) to St Eutrope to dedicate a new cross. Musicians came from

---

[61] Châtellier, *Religion of the Poor*, p. 39. On militant Catholicism elsewhere, see C. Delprat, 'Les magistrats du parlement de Toulouse durant la Ligue', *Annales du Midi* 108 (1996), 39–62; R. A. Mentzer, 'The Edict of Nantes and its institutions', in Mentzer and Spicer (eds.), *Society and Culture in the Huguenot World*, pp. 109–12.

[62] For early eighteenth-century evidence of this activity, see Archives Nationales, TT437, art. 23.

[63] BM Avignon, MSS 5233, fol. 269.

[64] AC Orange, BB33.      [65] BM Avignon, MSS 5275, fol. 231.

[66] L. Duhamel (ed.), *Inventaire-sommaire des Archives municipales antérieures à 1790 de la ville d'Orange*, 2 vols. (Orange, 1917), I, p. 100; AC Orange, BB32, fols. 178–80; Chambrun, *Les larmes*, pp. 50–4; Pontbriant, *Histoire*, pp. 229–34.

Avignon along with several penitential confraternities, who joined their Orangeois *confrères* in the liturgical exercise. A brief memoir left by a priest from the village of Mornas testifies to the importance of this event to the larger Catholic community in the principality. In jubilant tones, Pelhardi described how the bishop of Orange convoked the support of local clergy by sending around a circular that arrived almost too late for him to attend the process.[67] In his description of the procession itself, Pelhardi went to great pains to underscore the humiliation of the city's Huguenots, who were obliged to close their shops and watch from the sidelines as the extended Catholic community filed through the streets to mark their victory.

The scandal of the crosses of St Eutrope inspired Catholics in Orange to expand their sacralisation campaign beyond the historic, sacred sites of the city to the shared public spaces that belonged to both confessions. An especial target of this re-Catholicisation campaign was the Place du Cirque. Throughout the seventeenth century, the Roman amphitheatre had become identified as the site where the Princes of Nassau or their agents reaffirmed the unique liberties and biconfessional privileges of Orange. In 1607, as we have seen, Phillip-William commandeered the space to proclaim the Edict of Toleration. In 1665, the Place du Cirque again became the obvious site for the numerous celebrations that commemorated the restoration of Dutch sovereignty.[68] In late March 1665, Catholics and Protestants marked the departure of the French garrison with two distinct religious ceremonies: the traditional *Te Deum* mass of thanksgiving scheduled an hour before Protestants gathered for their prayer service. At the conclusion of each service, salvos of cannon fire rang out from the chateau-fort, marking the beginning of the civic celebrations that culminated with a huge public procession to the Place du Cirque. When the new Dutch governor, Zulychem arrived in April, the Place du Cirque again functioned as the site of communal pacification and reconciliation. Welcomed into Orange with a triumphal entry that recalled the city's Roman past and impressive antiquities, Zulychem concluded the lengthy, formal process of pacification with the public proclamation of amnesty in the Place du Cirque. In a ceremony reminiscent of Phillip-William's proclamation of the Edict of Toleration almost sixty years earlier, Zulychem appeared on a raised dais before the assembled community, the Prince's empty throne on a scaffolding overhead, while the attorney general pronounced the amnesty decree. To mark the occasion even more permanently in civic memory, city officials planted a tree

---

[67] AC Mornas, GG6.
[68] J. Pineton de Chambrun, *Relation de ce qui s'est passé au rétablissement d'Orange* (Orange, 1666), n.p.

in the amphitheatre as a monument to the shared liberties and allegiances of both confessions.[69]

Thus in 1679, when ecclesiastical officials demanded the right to plant a second cross at the Place du Cirque in a final expiatory procession for the attacks on the crosses of St Eutrope, local Protestants considered it a particularly worrisome assault on the purported neutrality of civic space.[70] Moreover, the action also represented a shrewd riposte to the Protestants' construction of their own historic identity, since it was here that the earliest Huguenot community had erected a shrine to its martyrs in 1572.

In 1685, the French invaded Orange for a third time. With the help of local Catholics, French dragoons eagerly applied the full measure of the Revocation of the Edict of Nantes, reconfiguring and re-Catholicising the central urban grid by destroying a number of institutions – sacred and secular – which had served as symbols of Protestant identity and inclusion. The pattern of destruction varied in some particulars, but subscribed to the general pattern followed in other recalcitrant Huguenot strongholds across France, where bit by bit the physical symbols of Huguenot hegemony and independence – walls, temples, cemeteries, academies – were dismantled and integrated into a new political reality.[71] Even in spite of protests from a local priest, the Temple of St Martin was summarily razed to the ground. The *grand temple* followed quickly thereafter, although Chambrun noted with pride in his memoirs that local labourers struggled for fourteen days to destroy the edifice until they finally employed explosives.[72] Several days later, the portal of the *grand temple*, one of the few material remains that survived the explosion, was sold to the rectors of the hospital general for eighty-six livres. A few weeks later, workmen transported it to the hospital where it became the new entry to the hospital's chapel, an action which symbolised the physical integration of the city's Huguenot community into the very heart of the Roman Catholic Church.[73]

The timely intervention of William of Orange prevented the total reconstruction of the urban and institutional grid under French rule. Under his patronage, the university which was closed briefly in 1682, reopened again a year later, surviving until the early eighteenth century.[74] After the Treaty of Ryswick in 1697 restored Dutch sovereignty, the great temple was rebuilt with William's help. Local officials wrested control of the hospital general from the bishop and restored governance to a bipartisan

[69] *Ibid.*    [70] Chambrun, *Les larmes*, pp. 110–14.
[71] See K. Robbins, *City on the Ocean Sea: La Rochelle, 1530–1650* (London, 1997), ch. 5.
[72] *Ibid.*    [73] AC Orange, GG164/2.
[74] Leemans, *Principauté d'Orange*, I, pp. 455–6.

administration, doing the same for the college which had been turned over to the Catholic Church in 1685 as well. However, this last efflorescence of Protestantism in Orange was a pale reflection of the vibrant community that had helped govern the principality for over a century, and within two decades, the provisions of the treaty of Utrecht sent most members of the community into exile again.

Early modern theories of religious coexistence were predicated upon the separation of urban space into distinct spheres: those sacred spaces (principally churches, cemeteries, but also shrines and monuments) monopolised by the members of each confessional community, and those public spaces shared by everyone. The processional features of early modern devotion, however, challenged legal and political efforts to delineate the boundaries and contours of confessional communities. While local authorities relentlessly hammered out the details of cohabitation, determining which public spaces could be appropriated for worship and burial, they were continuously confounded by the fact that sacred space was both *fixed* and *fluid*. Sacred communities defined themselves as much by their rituals as by their sacred buildings and sites. Processions were by their very nature transgressive, the means by which the sacred community permeated and purified the profane. In medieval Europe, this fusion of sacred and civic worlds was a powerful metaphor of the unity of Christendom – one that the Tridentine Church was quick to reclaim through the use of the physical cult of the cross and Eucharistic devotion. In the mixed communities of early modern France, however, both became instead a confessional threat, symbolising the marginalisation and eventual exclusion of Huguenots from the urban landscape completely.

The goal of Catholic renewal implicitly challenged the legal acknowledgement of neutral civic space, aiming instead to resanctify the body social and politic through the appropriation of this shared public space. As Elizabeth Tingle has argued, seventeenth-century missionaries paid particular attention to the reordering of the physical world, particularly to those places used as nodal points for contacting the divine.[75] The re-consecration of local shrines, Marian sanctuaries, and pilgrimage sites gave Catholics access to particularly powerful centres of sanctity, where the supernatural and natural conjoined through the intercession of Catholic saints, living and dead. In the isolated landscapes of Brittany, missionaries like Julien de Maunoir reclaimed the pagan sites of ancient Celtic worship for the Church. In the densely populated communities

---

[75] Tingle, 'The sacred space of Julien Maunoir'.

of the Huguenot crescent, state and church officials often worked hand-in-hand to recast and reorder the urban landscape, claiming not only the most ancient sites of early Christian worship but also contemporary public spaces and institutions in a final, comprehensive victory over heresy. In the process, they posited an integral relationship between physical space and the communities that inhabited it.

# 14 Breaking images and building bridges: the making of sacred space in early modern Bohemia

*Howard Louthan*

From the revolutionary Hussite wars of the early fifteenth century to the decisive defeat of the Bohemian estates at White Mountain in 1620, religion was the most divisive issue between the Czechs and their central European neighbours. The followers of Jan Hus, the Utraquists, eventually succeeded in creating a semi-autonomous Church in the fifteenth century. Though they reached a compromise with the Holy Roman Emperor, a new spirit of religious discontent in the sixteenth century fuelled in part by the Lutheran Reformation further complicated an already uneasy relationship between Vienna and the Bohemian kingdom. By the mid-sixteenth century the Czech lands had a well established reputation as a homeland of heresy. A proverb that widely circulated during this time may have captured popular sentiment best as it proudly proclaimed that Germany was admirably self-sufficient. Swabia provided her prostitutes, Franconia her thieves, Frisia her perjurers, Saxony her drunkards and Bohemia her heretics.[1] The situation changed dramatically after 1620, for following their victory on the battlefield, the Habsburgs launched an aggressive campaign of re-Catholicisation. A century later Bohemia's religious crisis was definitively resolved. A spirit of dissent that had so characterised this region from the time of Hus had been virtually extinguished and replaced by a new expression of Catholicism. The nature and scope of this confessional transformation is complex. This chapter will analyse two aspects of the complicated process by which Catholic elites sought to 'sanctify space' in a kingdom that had been defiled by heresy for over two centuries.

There are few regions north of the Alps that can match the rich landscape of the Bohemian baroque. Leading an artistic and architectural makeover of unprecedented proportions, a host of painters, sculptors and craftsmen transformed the Czech kingdom in the seventeenth and early eighteenth centuries. Marian columns, wayside chapels, pilgrimage

---

[1] Cited in G. Strauss, *Sixteenth-Century Germany: Its Topography and Topographers* (Madison, 1959), p. 11.

complexes along with new or restored churches, convents and monasteries sprung up across the region. These monuments, the most visible signs of Bohemia's new confessional identity, have been the subject of considerable study. From the statuary of Matthias Braun to the architectural production of the Dientzenhofer family, art historians have produced a formidable body of research on this period. In much of this literature, however, there has been a tendency to discuss aesthetic developments in isolation from the historical circumstances in which they are grounded. Though scholars of the Bohemian baroque would certainly acknowledge that the artistic activity of their period was a product of the new religious climate, they have often failed to integrate their work into a broader historical narrative. Bohemia's baroque art and architecture were not simply a by-product of the Habsburg victory of 1620, but a jubilant expression of triumphant Catholicism. The role and function of religious art was a matter of long debate and considerable controversy in Czech society and in the end became a fundamental issue in the military confrontation between King Frederick and Emperor Ferdinand that culminated at White Mountain. The matter of sacred space, its desecration, preservation or re-creation, became pivotal in this clash between international Calvinism and resurgent Catholicism.

Though Jan Hus had once commented, 'It is as great a shame to destroy a valuable picture as a valuable book', the revolution that followed his death developed in an entirely different fashion.[2] It is difficult to underestimate the destruction that accompanied the Hussite wars. They unleashed an iconoclastic frenzy that could not be matched even by the zeal of the Reformation's most ardent image breakers. There were few churches or monasteries that were left untouched by the great unrest. It is important to note that this first wave of iconoclasm was essentially over by the time Emperor Sigismund reached an agreement with the Hussites at Jihlava in 1436. The Hussite legacy, however, would never completely disappear. It lived on in splinter groups that drew their inspiration from the more radical Hussite wing. Occasionally there would be an incident such as the one in 1504 when a Prague tailor pulled down a statue of Christ and began whipping it with his colleague.[3] But in general Bohemia's religious culture from the middle decades of the fifteenth century onwards was relatively conservative in nature. Images, processions and even a moderate Marian cult, what Eamon Duffy has described in the English context as traditional religion, remained important elements

---

[2] Cited in K. Stejskal, 'Ikonoklasmus českého středověku a jeho limity', *Umění* 48 (2000), 206.

[3] J. Macek, 'Bohemia', in R. Porter and M. Teich (eds.), *The Renaissance in National Context* (Cambridge, 1992), p. 211.

of Czech ecclesiastical culture after the initial dislocations of the Hussite revolution had passed.[4] It was only when more extreme ideas of the Protestant Reformation reached Prague in the second decade of the seventeenth century that iconoclasm once more became a significant issue.

The relationship of the Reformation to the visual arts is of course a complicated matter. Lutherans were generally conservative while Calvinists often assumed a more aggressive stance. In the *Institutes* Calvin concluded that religious images were contrary to Scripture. He did not, however, advocate iconoclasm. According to Calvin it was the role of the magistrate to remove such objects from former Catholic churches in an orderly fashion. The problem arose when local authorities were resistant to these views. In regions such as France and the Low Countries Calvinist adherents found no support from secular rulers and thus took it upon themselves to execute this commission. As a result, there would be waves of violence when mobs ransacked churches and destroyed sacred art. The situation in Bohemia, however, was very different. With the election of Frederick of the Palatinate, the so-called Winter King, the Czech estates installed a regime that vigorously promoted an iconoclastic agenda. The *éminence grise* behind this programme was the king's court preacher and advisor, Abraham Scultetus. Initially educated at Wittenberg, Scultetus was part of the university's crypto-Calvinist faction. He eventually found a more congenial home at Heidelberg. Scultetus would accompany his patron to his new kingdom where a significant challenge lay before him.

Changes began in Prague on 15 October, 1619 when St Vitus cathedral was officially handed over to Frederick's entourage with plans to transform it into the new king's court church. The dean and the canons were promptly evicted and given three days to quit the premises while the cathedral itself was sealed and guarded by Frederick's men. Though the Palatine elector would be crowned in the church a few weeks later, more substantial alterations would need to be executed before St Vitus was suitable for Calvinist worship. In the days surrounding the Christmas holiday Scultetus launched a thorough 'cleaning' of the cathedral. To appreciate the bold and aggressive steps taken by Scultetus it is necessary to put these events of late December in a broader context. Those princes implementing a 'second Reformation' in Lutheran territories during this period frequently met significant resistance from the populace when they attempted to remove religious images from the churches. In the Upper Palatinate these actions were often stealthily undertaken at night while

---

[4] See A. Molnar, 'The catholicity of the Utraquist church of Bohemia', *Anglican Theological Review* 41 (1959), 260–70. We have an account, for example, of an Utraquist celebration of the Corpus Christi festival in 1574. See C. Straka, 'Jak slavilo se Boží tělo v Praze v XVI. a XVII. století', *Časopis katolického duchovenstva* 57 (1916), 162.

in Berlin the decorating changes in the cathedral precipitated a riot in 1615 where Prince Johann Georg of Brandenburg-Jägerndorf was physically attacked.[5] Scultetus, in contrast, was not inclined to work furtively nor afraid of popular opposition. One of the German workers engaged to take down the images reported that Scultetus turned to the crew during their work and loudly exclaimed, 'O you Lutherans, come to me and I will open your eyes, for you most assuredly stink of Rome.'[6] At the centre of this protracted operation at the cathedral was a celebrated sermon Scultetus delivered on 22 December.[7]

Structuring his homily around Exodus 20: 4–6, Scultetus made three simple and direct points. God clearly forbids the portrayal of his likeness. Moreover, he does not permit the worship of images. It is thus incumbent upon the prince to ensure that proper worship is restored by removing all items that would be offensive to God. Scultetus' subsequent remarks, however, indicate how sweeping his vision for this action actually was. In the Low Countries in those instances where the magistrates did support Calvinist reforms, religious art was often disassembled in an orderly fashion or returned to their original donors, and as we have noted earlier, Calvin himself did not support iconoclastic activity. Frederick's court preacher was of another mind altogether. He would cite a series of examples from the Old Testament where the Israelites threw down and completely destroyed the idols and altars of their heathen neighbours.[8] In his autobiography he would elaborate further on this theme. In recalling these events, he turned once more to Scripture. God has called us to remove all idols from our heart, and as a sign of this inner conversion, outward action is necessary. The Lord enjoins all true believers to 'take pictures away; that is, *to break them or consign them to the flames*'.[9]

This is exactly what occurred during the last two weeks of December. Scultetus' offensive actually began the day before he preached his sermon exhorting the faithful to action. An eyewitness to the events, Šimon Kapihorský, reports that on 21 December Frederick began his war against the images and saints. The Winter King's followers started their work by taking down the large crucifix opposite the high altar before

---

[5] W. Troßbach, 'Volkskultur und Gewissensnot: Zum Bilderstreit in der "zweiten Reformation"', *Zeitschrift für Historische Forschung* 23 (1996), 477.

[6] V. Kramář, *Zpustošení Chrámu svatého Víta v roce 1619* (Prague, 1998), p. 118.

[7] I have been using the Czech version *Krátká, avšak na mocném gruntu a základu Svatých Písem založená zpráva o modlářských obrazích* (Prague, 1620). The text was most widely distributed, however, in a German version.

[8] *Krátká, avšak na mocném gruntu a základu Svatých Písem založená zpráva o modlářských obrazích*, D, iii.

[9] *Die Selbstbiographie des Heidelberger Theologen und Hofpredigers Abraham Scultetus*, ed. G. A. Benrath (Karlsruhe, 1966), p. 81. Here he refers to I Samuel 7: 3. The italics are my own.

moving on to the tomb of John Nepomuk, which they quickly dismantled. Finally, they proceeded to the high altar itself. Apart from the images
and the statues they also gathered together the chairs of the archbishop
and canons and then burned them all in a heap. They returned the next
day, and as Kapihorský relates, the heads and bones of the saints were
thrown away, trampled upon and burned. The iconoclasts continued their
campaign two days after Christmas. We learn from another account that
they focused their attention on the cathedral's stone altars, which they
systematically reduced to rubble. Among the casualties that day was
an altar painting of Lucas Cranach that had been commissioned by
Ferdinand I.[10]

Unlike more typical incidents of Reformation iconoclasm in France,
Switzerland and the Low Countries, the 'cleaning' of St Vitus Cathedral was not a movement with a broad base of support. Even some of
the men who had been hired to do the work had serious qualms about
the business. A certain Jakob Hübel reported that when he complained
that many of the valuable objects were being mistreated, one of Frederick's advisors responded with a laugh, 'We would like to do this to
Rome as well.'[11] The Catholics, of course, were the most vociferous in
their opposition to Scultetus' programme. The cathedral was the only
parish church in Prague that had remained faithful to Rome, and its
dean and canons saw it as one of the last Catholic redoubts in the city.
For their part the canons of the chapter wrote an impassioned letter
of lament to Archbishop Lohelius who was in exile in Vienna. They
described the destruction of the cathedral furnishings and saw this as a
token of the end of Catholicism altogether in Bohemia.[12] The resistance
to Frederick's policies, however, extended far beyond the small Catholic
community. The Utraquists, too, were concerned with his ecclesiastical
innovations and desecration of the kingdom's holy sites. Cooperating with
the Catholics, they were able to preserve the St Wenceslas chapel, far and
away the cathedral's most important shrine.[13]

After the St Vitus incident Frederick turned his attention to another
of Prague's famous landmarks. A cross had stood on the third pier of
the Charles Bridge since 1361. Though it was pulled down during the

---

[10] Kapihorský's account is reprinted in T. Pešina, *Phosphorus septicornis, stella alias matutina*
(Prague, 1673), pp. 350–5. Also see *Grewel der Verwüstung*, Prague, 1620 (National
Museum, 42 D 17)

[11] Kramář, *Zpustošení Chrámu svatého Víta*, p. 117.

[12] 14 January 1620. Letter is reprinted in Pešina, *Phosphorus septicornis*, pp. 356–7. Helpful
here is the archival material of the Prague Castle. See Archiv metropolitní kapituly u Sv.
Víta, Codex VI 9, fols. 156v–171v.

[13] Pešina, *Phosphorus septicornis*, pp. 642–3; C. A. Pescheck, *The Reformation and Anti-
Reformation in Bohemia*, 2 vols. (London, 1845), I, 365.

early years of the Hussite wars, it had been re-erected in the middle of the fifteenth century and joined by two flanking statues. When Frederick arrived, it was his wife, Elisabeth Stuart, who seems to have been most offended by what she referred to as the bridge's 'naked bath attendant'. Shortly after Christmas 1619, Frederick conferred with his council concerning the fate of this object. In no uncertain terms, they warned the king against removing the cross, as they feared a great public outcry were it to disappear. Though no official steps were taken, some time later it mysteriously disappeared at night.[14] As we see both at St Vitus and with the cross, Frederick was clearly operating on a very different level than that of his subjects. For the Palatine prince his actions were based on well-defined theological principles. Religious objects, however, can possess a multiplicity of meanings, and what was merely a doctrinal issue for the Calvinist court was perceived as an attack on traditional Bohemian culture by the general populace.[15]

The backlash against Frederick and Scultetus was substantial. The St Vitus incident became a *cause célèbre* initiating a significant flurry of pamphlets. Both Catholic and Lutheran theologians jumped into the fray as strong denunciations of the action were quickly issued from Ingolstadt, Mainz, Tübingen, Wittenberg and Leipzig.[16] One of the most interesting of the publications was an illustrated broadsheet that depicted Frederick flying high above Prague and accompanied by the devil who has led the prince through a series of three temptations. As indicated by the crucifix prominently displayed on Charles Bridge, one of these trials concerned the treatment of Prague's sacred images and statues. Failing to detect the devil's clever stratagem, Frederick fully embraced Scultetus' iconoclastic programme. This decision, as the commentator informs us, contributed to the Winter King's final downfall.[17] Pamphlets were also produced in

---

[14] Pešina, *Phosphorus septicornis*, p. 353. Also note the scandalous reports of Elisabeth's impiety and its consequences, 655–6. Though the Czech exile and historian Pavel Skála would downplay public reaction to the disappearance of the cross, a legend would later circulate that those who attempted to remove the cross would be punished directly by God as in the case of Elisabeth who was forced to flee the city in 1620. See J. Svátek, *Pražské pověsti a legendy* (Prague, 1997), pp. 107–8.

[15] For a comparative example see Joel Budd, 'Rethinking iconoclasm in Early Modern England: the case of the Cheapside Cross', *Journal of Early Modern History* 4 (2000), 402.

[16] Specific publication details can be found in Benrath's edition of Scultetus' *Selbstbiographie*, 80–1.

[17] For this illustration see *Deutsche illustrierte Flugblätter des 16. und 17. Jahrhunderts*, ed. W. Harms, 7 vols. (Tübingen, 1980–2004), II, p. 321. For a broader collection of these illustrations depicting the struggle between Frederick and Ferdinand see the valuable collection of the National Museum in Prague (102 A 1–199). Mirjam Bohatcová has compiled a useful catalogue for this collection (*Sborník Národního Muzea v Praze*, Řada C, 27, no. 1 (1982)).

Prague that attacked the policies of the Calvinist court. One fascinating tract recounts a dialogue between an Utraquist, a Catholic and a Lutheran. Distressed by Scultetus' zeal, the Utraquist remarked to his Lutheran colleague, 'It would be better for you and me to follow the Jesuits than the Calvinists, for they have never thrown such a big rock in our garden as the Calvinists have just done.' At his turn the Lutheran passed on the rumour that a thousand English iconoclasts were even now preparing to descend on Bohemia and finish the business that Scultetus had begun.[18] In the end, all three individuals banded together and condemned the religious innovations that threatened the kingdom's spiritual and cultural heritage.

One of the most interesting responses to the desecration of sacred space at St Vitus came from Tomáš Pešina, a future dean of the cathedral who would compile a series of accounts from Frederick's iconoclastic campaign. The workman commissioned to demolish the tomb of St Vitus was knocked senseless and lost the use of his hands for a significant period of time. Much worse, however, was the fate in store for those charged to remove the grill around the grave of St John Nepomuk. A Hussite blacksmith who was initially sent in to do the job knew better and refused the assignment directly. The Saxon Lutheran who replaced him was sent sprawling when he tried to take down the railing. In a state of delirium and great pain, he was consumed by an internal fire that slowly killed him.[19] As Pešina pointed out, these developments were in no way surprising for there had long been a popular saying in Prague that whoever destroys St Vitus would be promptly sent to hell.[20]

The memory of December 1619 would become a permanent feature of the cathedral itself. In the early 1620s the cabinet maker Caspar Bechteler would carve four large and intricate panels that depicted these events for the ambulatory of St Vitus.[21] The first two scenes illustrate the Calvinists at work destroying the furnishings of the church. One worker has climbed a ladder intent on bringing down the crucifix in front of the altar. Others are busy smashing or breaking objects with axes, hammers and mallets. Even the incident at Nepomuk's tomb is recorded. While two men are continuing to dismantle the railing, another two are carting off the Saxon ironworker who has just been knocked senseless (see plate 14.1). It was the intent of the artist and designer to recall the destruction of

---

[18] *Einfältiges Gespräch über den kurtzen aber unschriffttmässigen Bericht von den ungötzen Bildern und die Christliche Gemein zu Prag . . .* (Prague, 1620), pp. 1, 6.

[19] Pešina, *Phosphorus septicornis*, pp. 645–8. For similar accounts of images defending themselves against the outrages of French Huguenots see O. Christin, *Une révolution symbolique: l'iconoclasme huguenot et la reconstruction catholique* (Paris, 1991).

[20] Pešina, *Phosphorus septicornis*, p. 633: 'Kdo Swatého Wita boři, snadno se Pekla dobořj'.

[21] On the issue of dating see Franz Matsche, 'Das Grabmal des hl. Johannes von Nepomuk im Prager Veitsdom', *Wallraf-Richartz-Jahrbuch* 38 (1976), 95–6.

Plate 14.1 Photograph of Caspar Bechteler's carving of the iconoclasts in St Vitus' cathedral, Prague.

Solomon's Temple through these two panels, and the connection with the biblical narrative was strengthened by one of the most prized possessions of the cathedral. According to the chronicle of Dalimil (1314), the Jerusalem Candelabrum which had stood in St Ludmila's chapel, had been taken originally by Titus from Jerusalem before passing on to Bohemia in the twelfth century.[22] The story is completed on the other side of the ambulatory. With an inscription recounting the destruction of Pharaoh's army at the Red Sea, Frederick and his entourage are shown crossing the Moldau in haste, confusion and fear after their unexpected rout at White Mountain.[23]

An ironic testament to the brief reign of the Winter King, the panels, which are themselves a beautiful work of religious art, memorialised the policies of an individual who attempted to remove all such images

[22] A Latin inscription ran across the two scenes, 'Deus venerunt gentes in haereditatem tuam polluerunt templum tuum. Ps LXXVII.' See the special instructions that were given by the cathedral chapter to save the Jerusalem candelabrum from destruction during Scultetus' initial campaign. Archiv metropolitní kapituly u Sv. Víta, Codex VI 9, fol. 164v. Also note the legend of the Jerusalem candlestick. Svátek, *Pražské pověsti*, p. 55.

[23] Here the inscription reads, 'Irruit super eos formido et pavor in magnitudine brachii tui. Exod. XV Anno MDCXX'.

from the cathedral. The carving, however, was more than a clever joke at Frederick's expense, for all those who busied themselves restoring St Vitus were making a broader statement concerning the nature of artistic activity. The Jerusalem Candelabrum, which had been badly damaged, would be carefully repaired and returned to the cathedral with a new shaft topped by the lamb triumphant and surrounded by four of Bohemia's patron saints. Emperor Ferdinand would donate a new triptych to replace the retable that had been destroyed by the Calvinists. Its central scene, now the focal point of the church, was St Luke painting the Virgin. The apostle at work on his portrait would become a common motif in this period. After the desecration of the Calvinists, the images had returned to St Vitus victorious, and now the making of religious art was celebrated in and of itself as an act of orthodoxy.

## I    From commercial thoroughfare to devotional space: the remaking of Charles Bridge

Switching our perspective from the iconoclasts to iconodules, we will now consider how Catholics used religious art to create or re-create sacred space in the post-White Mountain period. Towards that end we will turn to a monument that is arguably Prague's best-known landmark, the Charles Bridge and its celebrated statuary. A close examination of this structure and its subsequent transformation after the Thirty Years War are illustrative of broader dynamics at work in Bohemian society. The bridge would gradually become an informal but important centre of popular piety. A certain Englishman visiting the city in the middle of the eighteenth century would note:

In every part of the town people are seen kneeling before statues, but especially on the big bridge across the Moldau where there is the greatest crowd of passers by. This bridge is richly decorated by statues of saints, so that the walker must pass them on both sides like two rows of musketeers. Travellers, especially those coming straight from Berlin, will marvel at the piety of the people here, specifically at the burning passion they display before the saints of the bridge.[24]

The young and often acerbic Arthur Schopenhauer would later remark that 'the bigoted inhabitants of Prague would consider it the worst sin to cross the bridge without at least doffing their hats'.[25] Such was not the case, however, at the beginning of the seventeenth century, for the bridge had a rather dubious reputation. It is important then to review the

[24] Cited in *Město vidím veliké . . . Cizinci o Praze*, ed. V. Vojtíšek (Prague, 1940), pp. 101–2.
[25] *Ibid.*, p. 162

structure's history, for its entire character was transfigured in the decades after 1648.

The bridge itself, which did not acquire the name of its builder until the nineteenth century, had been constructed by Charles IV to replace an older structure that had been destroyed by floods in 1342. The new bridge quickly became notorious. Even before its completion, local felons, often in the hire of a third party, found it a useful place to do away with their enemies. In the late fourteenth century three important church officials, including a future saint, were hurled from its ramparts.[26] The fate of its first monuments also reflected the turbulent nature of this period. Though the stone bridge remained relatively free of decoration in these early centuries, a crucifix had been erected in 1361 to mark the spot where Martin Cink, a priest of the cathedral, had been flung into the river. The cross, which became an informal centre of devotion, would first be destroyed by the Hussites in 1419. Replaced in the second half of the fifteenth century, it would be tossed in the river by a supporter of Elisabeth Stuart. It would reappear for a third time in 1629 only to be shot down by the Swedes in 1648. The bridge acquired other unsavoury connotations over time. In its early days it had been used as an official place of execution. Across from the crucifix, a headsman had dispatched local felons where a column of Justice had stood.[27] More recently, the impaled heads of prominent Czech rebels who had been executed in 1621 were grimly displayed on the eastern tower of the span, while in 1648 the bridge actually served as the frontline in the Swedes' brief but bitter siege of the city. When the invading army finally withdrew, many must have wondered what new tragedy would next unfold on this structure. For Bohemia's Catholics the Charles Bridge was an apt symbol of a faith that had been under siege for nearly three centuries. Those who worked on the bridge in the late seventeenth and early eighteenth centuries endeavoured to transform a site of death, rebellion and heresy into a space that celebrated the triumph of orthodoxy.

It was the *Ponte degli Angeli* in Rome that originally inspired the decoration of Prague's stone bridge.[28] But this relatively modest set of angels over the Tiber would soon be surpassed by a virtual army of saints that quickly appeared on the span across the Moldau. The first monument to go up was the crucifix that had been shot down by the Swedes. In 1657 the Bohemian court chancellery decided that a more permanent and dignified memorial should stand in the place of the old wooden cross. They sent

---

[26] J. F. Hammerschmied, *Prodromus gloriae Pragenae* (Prague, 1723), p. 591.

[27] J. Schaller, *Beschreibung der königlichen Haupt- und Residenzstadt Prag*, 4 vols. (Prague, 1795), II, p. 364.

[28] K. Neubert, I. Kořan and M. Suchomel, *Charles Bridge* (Prague, 1991) p. 46.

two craftsmen to Dresden where they purchased a large bronze replacement from the workshop of Hans Hillger. The first of the statues, John Nepomuk, was raised in 1683. Though two more would appear in the 1690s, it was not until the first decade of the eighteenth century that the saints began arriving in significant numbers. In a frenetic flurry of activity, twenty-four of the original twenty-eight statues were erected between 1706 and 1714. No single individual, institution or religious order dominated this phase of construction. Of the twenty-eight monuments raised between 1659 and 1714, thirteen were sponsored by individuals, nine by religious orders and six by other institutions.[29] Participation among the orders was particularly wide. The Cistercians, Dominicans, Jesuits, Premonstratensians, Augustinians, Theatines and Servites were all patrons.

The patrons who erected these statues clearly hoped that the bridge would become an important devotional space. The Jesuits, who may have been the most keenly attuned to the issue of audience, noted in 1709 that most passers by stared merely with curiosity at the statues around them. It was only Nepomuk and the crucifix that consistently elicited a pious response from the viewer.[30] The design of specific monuments thus became a matter of considerable importance to the Jesuits and others active on the bridge. Contemporary reports indicate that over time their efforts were successful. The bridge would become an important locus of popular devotion. Hats would be doffed, candles would be lit, prayers would be said, and heads would be bowed. More significantly, many of the models on Charles Bridge would be replicated across the region. Jan Mayer's 1708 statue of the apostle Jude leaning on his cudgel helped initiate this saint's cult in Bohemia and set the pattern for many churches outside Prague. In his dramatic portrayal of the Cistercian nun, St Luitgard, Matthias Braun evidently drew his inspiration from the graphic work of J. K. Liška in the monastery of Plasy in western Bohemia. The same theme would be repeated by Peter Brandl for the Sedlec cloister in the eastern half of the kingdom. The most famous of these examples is the statue of John Nepomuk. Jan Brokoff's saint with hands clasping a crucifix to his chest, head slightly askew and eyes clearly fixed on the hereafter became the prototype for the hundreds of Nepomuks that would appear in nearly every Bohemian village.[31]

The originality or novelty of the bridge's statuary was thus a matter of secondary importance. Patrons and artists were more concerned with

[29] Data on dates and patrons provided by E. Poche and K. Novotný, *Karlův most* (Prague, 1947), pp. 88–112.

[30] Státní Ústřední Archiv, Stará manipulace, J 20/17/11, fols. 1v–2r.

[31] Neubert, Kořan and Suchomel, *Charles Bridge*, pp. 46, 58, 60, 64.

producing effective and compelling models that could be replicated in other settings as aids to devotion. The Jesuits in particular saw the bridge's battery of saints as a type of outdoor theatre. An interesting discussion occurred within the order concerning the design of the Francis Xavier statue. In the creation of this towering memorial with multiple levels and figures, the sources illustrate that the Jesuits utilised their experience with school theatre to help compose a design that from their perspective would prompt the appropriate pious response from the viewer.[32] Older monuments would also be restored and expanded heightening both their dramatic effect and religious significance. The new bronze crucifix from Dresden would be gilded adding a greater sense of dignity and honour to the oldest monument on the bridge. In 1681 Karl Adam of Říčany would provide funds for two lamps to remain constantly lit at either side of the cross. At the beginning of the eighteenth century a small Golgotha, complete with skulls, frogs and lizards, would be added to the base of the crucifix.[33] The originally modest marker, which had been first intended to commemorate the death of Martin Cink, was being transformed into a more prominent and permanent wayside shrine along this commercial thoroughfare.

As work on the statuary drew to a close, the printers took over where the sculptors left off. More than half a dozen books on the new landmark quickly appeared, most of them with a practical religious agenda. Joachim Kamenitzky's *Eigentlicher Entwurff und Vorbildung der vortrefflichen kostbahren und Welt-berühmten Prager Brucken* (Prague, 1716) was a detailed guide to the structure with a decidedly spiritual orientation. Each chapter contained an edifying biography of the specific saint or saints along with a prayer 'so that the physical eye of the viewer when observing the statue would illuminate the inner eye and refresh the spirit'.[34] Joannes Müller's *Triginta devotiones ad Christum et Sanctos eius* (Prague, 1712) was an aid to quiet meditation and worship across the bridge, an informal type of pilgrimage that could be performed during the bustle of everyday life. Augustin Neürautter's magnificent *Statuae Pontis Pragensis* (Prague, 1714) had no text at all though his handsome quarto-size illustrations were certainly intended for devotional purposes. Even in the early nineteenth century this literature retained its pious character.

---

[32] One Jesuit commentator observed that trivial decorations such as crabs were wholly inappropriate for the Xavier monument that was designed for such an important spiritual purpose. Státní Ústřední Archiv, Stará manipulace, J 20/17/11, fols. 1r–1v.

[33] J. Kamenitzky, *Eigentlicher Entwurff und Vorbildung der vortrefflichen kostbahren und Welt-berühmten Prager Brucken* (Prague, 1716), pp. 54–7.

[34] *Ibid.*, A6v.

W. F. Welleba's *Die beruehmte Prager Bruecke und ihre Statuen* (Prague, 1827) helped the passer by decode the often complicated iconography of the statuary.[35]

The iconography of the stone bridge reflected many of the general themes of the Catholic Reformation at high tide. Not unexpectedly, the Virgin was well represented. Apart from three statues of Mary herself, the first two monuments on the Old Town side of the bridge aggressively promoted her cult. In 1709 the Cistercians commissioned Matthias Jäckel to depict Bernard genuflecting before the Virgin. Jäckel cast the scene as a reversal of the Annunciation where a triumphant Mary greets the saint, who assuming the position of Gabriel will announce her status as Queen of Heaven. The previous year the Dominicans had funded a similar work featuring Dominic and Aquinas as her disciples. The adoration of the Host was another theme that was attended to. Vít Seipl, the abbot of Strahov, sponsored a statue of St Norbert defending the Sacrament from the blasphemies of the twelfth-century heretic Tanchelm while immediately opposite, Francis Borgia piously directs the viewer's attention to a monstrance and Host held by an angel. Catholic martyrs were scattered across the span highlighted of course by both the statue of Nepomuk and a plaque that marked the actual spot where he was thrown into the river for his refusal to disclose the secrets of the confessional to a jealous Wenceslas IV (1361–1419). The bridge's decoration also complemented civic and confraternal activities. The imperial counsellor Jan Václav Obytecký charged Ferdinand Brokoff with the creation of a trio of saints – Elizabeth, Margaret and Barbara (see plate 14.2). Barbara, the central figure of the group and the patron saint of the dying, is holding the chalice for the final Sacrament, a scene that would have surely resonated with so many of Prague's confraternities that were concerned with the 'good death'.[36] To her left is Elizabeth giving alms to a poor beggar. This theme of Christian charity, which was reflected in a number of the monuments, is the most obvious example of the performative nature of the bridge. A society organised by Prague's many servants would shortly develop around Ferdinand Brokoff's *Pietà* where individuals would contribute to the maintenance of the widows of their community.[37] Finally, there is the decidedly affective nature of the statuary. This strain of Catholic

---

[35] See for example Welleba's detailed explanation of Ferdinand Brokoff's St Cajetan. W. F. Welleba, *Die beruehmte Prager Bruecke und ihre Statuen* (Prague, 1827), p. 129.

[36] On death and the confraternities, see J. Mikulec, *Barokní náboženská bratrstva v Čechách* (Prague, 2000), pp. 62–4. Obytecký may well have been ill himself as he died the year after the statue was erected. The inscription beneath the statue reads *Orate pro nobis nunc et in hora mortis.*

[37] Schaller, *Beschreibung*, II, pp. 363–4.

Plate 14.2 Ferdinand Brokoff, St Elizabeth, St Margaret and St Barbara, Charles Bridge, Prague.

mysticism, which is clearly evident in the figures of Bernard and Francis, reaches a climax in Matthias Braun's magnificent figure of St Luitgard. Bohemia's answer to Bernini's St Theresa, this blind Cistercian saint lost in ecstasy is gently pulled to drink from the wounded side of the crucified Christ (see plate 14.3).

These general concerns of the Catholic Reformation were balanced with more local themes specific to the Czech context. The sacred space of the bridge effectively merged religious and patriotic interests. On the bridge's eastern tower a plaque was installed that helped set the tone for the entire structure, transforming a casual stroll across the river into a patriotic meditation of the city's recent past. Commemorating the 1648 siege of the city, this panel urged the traveller to wander slowly across the bridge remembering the Old Town citizens who fought with 'fire and sword' against the Swedish invader.[38] This historical moment would become indelibly etched into the public memory of the bridge. Kamenitzky's guide recounts in obsessive detail the events of the fourteen-week siege. During this period the Swedes launched six separate attacks on the bridge, fired 186 shells and spent 12,587 rounds of ammunition in their vain attempts to reach the river's eastern bank.[39] One of the most important features of the siege was the melding of patriotic concerns with religious sentiment. Key to the city's defence was the leadership of Jiří Plachy. On the night of 26 July when the Swedes stole down from Castle Hill, it was supposedly the Jesuit Plachy who rallied a few citizens to man the barricades and hold the bridge until morning and the arrival of reinforcements. The Jesuits assumed critical positions both militarily and spiritually during the siege. When they were not coordinating student militias, they were calling the city to repentance. They instituted fasts, led prayer services and even organised processions of flagellants.[40] They also helped sacralise the events of the war endowing the bridge with a greater sense of sanctity. When a Swedish sharpshooter levelled the crucifix, it was they who took Christ's intact head to the Clementinum where it remained for many years as a treasured relic.[41] There were other reminders of the heroic defence of the bridge. The iconography of the

---

[38] Welleba, *Die beruehmte Prager Bruecke*, pp. 7–8.

[39] Kamenitzky, *Eigentlicher Entwurff*, p. 14.

[40] Significant here is the unpaginated eighteenth-century manuscript history of Johannes Miller, *Historia Provinciae Bohemiae Societatis Jesus ab anno Domini 1555 quo eadem societas primum in Bohemia pedem fixit ad annum usq 1723 quo Provincia Bohemiae primum suum saeculum finivit*. See book 3, number 21, section 9, 'Auxilia spiritualia, & militaria tempore obsidionis Pragensis anno 1648 a nostris pro bono communi praestita'. Strahov Monastic Library, Shelfmark DG III 19.

[41] Svátek, *Pražské pověsti*, p. 108. See the 1891 painting of Karel and Adolf Liebscher that features the 1648 struggle on the bridge with a specific reference to the incident at the cross.

Plate 14.3  Matthias Braun, St Luitgard, Charles Bridge, Prague. Today housed in the Prague Lapidarium.

St Vitus statue is particularly interesting. The kingdom's patron saint stands undaunted before three lions cowering before him, not unlikely to be a reference to both the saint's bravery before the beasts loosed by Diocletian and the valour of the Catholic Czechs before the Protestant lion of the north. The figure was funded by Matěj Vojtěch Macht, dean of the chapter of Vyšehrad. His father had been one of the students on the barricades, and for his service the emperor had granted the family the title *Löwenmacht*.

Art historians have noted that the bridge and its statuary represent an important stylistic fusion of international trends with a more local tradition.[42] What is true in terms of aesthetics is also a significant feature of its content. There are a number of monuments, in fact, that feature some rather strange pairings between a local saint and a figure of more international significance. Ferdinand Brokoff coupled the great missionary Vincent Ferrer with Bohemia's St Procopius, the founder of the monastic community of Sázava. Slightly more jarring is the statue celebrating the Trinitarian order that had been founded in 1198 to redeem Christian captives from the Muslims. Standing next to its founders, John of Matha and Felix of Valois, is the kingdom's most rustic of saints, the hermit Ivan. Though these juxtapositions of figures might strike our eye as odd today, they served an important function when they were erected. The statues of the stone bridge were in many respects an attempt to reintegrate Bohemia's problematic past into a broader ecclesiastical narrative of the church triumphant. It is significant that with both Vincent and the Trinitarians their Bohemian partner was a saint who predated them by nearly three centuries, perhaps a way to remind the kingdom's believers that they too shared an old and distinguished Catholic heritage. The bridge's martyrs mirror the same theme. Nepomuk and Wenceslas are balanced by Jude and the Jesuit martyrs of Nagasaki. By focusing on the victories of an earlier period, the designers of the stone bridge were trying to reach past the relatively recent troubles of Scultetus and Hus and reconnect Bohemia both to its earlier cultural traditions and the wider Catholic world.

If there is a characteristic common to all these monuments, it is victory and celebration. As we observed at the outset, the Charles Bridge had a rather ambiguous past. Its history had been marred by the assassinations of priests, the machinations of Protestant queens and the assaults of Swedish soldiers. But the political and religious climate was changing, and these changes would be made manifest on the bridge. The year 1648 was of course one important turning point for Bohemia. Another moment would come in the early 1680s when a bloody peasant revolt was suppressed, and the Turks were turned back at Vienna. The crisis of the early seventeenth century was passing and giving way to a new period of stability. From the Catholic perspective the Church had been tried and had emerged triumphant. A number of the statues were built specifically to celebrate noteworthy events. Brokoff's Nepomuk commemorated the

---

[42]  T. DaCosta Kaufmann, *Court, Cloister and City* (Chicago, 1995), p. 361.

300th anniversary of the saint's martyrdom. The Trinitarian memorial of 1714 marked John of Matha's death five centuries years earlier. And then there were the statues themselves. Two of the tallest monuments on the bridge, the twin towers of Xavier and Loyola, are perhaps the best examples of this new sense of confidence. A theatrical Ignatius is perched on a laurel wreath that symbolises the victory of the Catholic cause. The wreath itself is resting on a globe, which in turn is supported by allegorical representations of the four continents. Scattered across the structure are emblems and inscriptions that announce the valiant work of the Jesuits in turning back heresy and re-establishing the true faith. The equally massive Xavier has a slightly different orientation. Gesturing to a cross that he holds in his left hand, the tireless missionary is proclaiming the gospel to a savage who is bowing at his feet while an engraving to his right informs us that the saint has baptised 1.2 million new believers.[43]

The theme of conversion introduced here by Xavier is significant as it illustrates to what extent the bridge had become an identity marker for Bohemia's Catholics. Conversion is a process of interaction, a dialogue between two parties. On the one hand, it points to the ultimate triumph of one's own faith. Apart from Ignatius and Xavier the bridge was filled with missionary saints. There was Norbert, bringing the gospel to central Europe, Dominic, combating the Albigensians, Vincent Ferrer, working among the Turks and Jews and even the usually mild Anthony of Padua known in some quarters as the 'hammer of heretics'. All these figures reminded Czech believers on what side they stood. But conversion also points to the faith of the other, and it is this side of the dialogue that is often more important in the formation of identities. Conversion reminds us of whom we are not. It distinguishes our enemies and exposes their weaknesses. This dual dynamic of highlighting one's friends while recognising one's foes may have been the most important social function of the bridge.

Czech Catholics would recognise three sets of confessional opponents scattered across the bridge. The Muslims as Turks and Saracens, or more vaguely described as Moors, were well represented. Kamenitzky identified the four individuals supporting the Xavier monument as Muslims.[44] Thematically, they play a more central role in the statues of the Trinitarians and Vincent Ferrer. The Trinitarian group depicts the liberation of Christians held captive by the Muslims. At the base of this structure is a prison where a seemingly bored Turkish gaoler is guarding a group of believers who are beseeching God for deliverance. Vincent Ferrer, in contrast, is represented as an apostle to the heretics. Below him is a turbaned

---

[43] Kamenitzky, *Eigentlicher Entwurff*, p. 129. Also significant are Kamenitzky's substantial remarks on the iconography of the Ignatius monument, pp. 82–128.
[44] Kamenitzky, *Eigentlicher Entwurff*, p. 129.

Plate 14.4　Luther, Charles Bridge, Old Town Bridge Tower, Prague.

figure of a new Saracen Christian who bears an inscription celebrating the saint's conversion of 8,000 Muslims. More interesting are the multiple references to the only non-Catholic community that existed in late seventeenth-century Prague, the Jews. Next to the Muslim convert on the Ferrer monument is a rabbi who with hand across his chest is admitting the errors of his faith. Evidently, Ferrer had greater success with the Jews, for the engraving below the rabbi informs us that he succeeded in bringing 25,000 to the Catholic faith. There is a more subtle allusion on the statue of the Dominicans. Originally below Dominic was an inscription from I Corinthians, 'We preach Christ crucified, unto the Jews a stumbling block.' This reference takes on special meaning when we consider the monument immediately to its right, the famous crucifix. In the mid-1690s a Jew had crossed the bridge and as a gesture of mock adoration had bowed backwards to the cross. For this blasphemous behaviour, the Jewish community had been compelled to erect at their own expense a gilded inscription proclaiming Christ's sanctity in Hebrew. At the bottom of the cross three plaques were installed that described in Czech, Latin and German the crime of the Jew.[45] The last of these confessional

---

[45] Schaller, *Beschreibung*, II, pp. 349–50.

enemies were the Protestants. How the stone bridge came to include these heretics is an intriguing story that reflects to what extent this structure had become an identity marker for Bohemian Catholics. The supporters of neither Luther nor Calvin were officially represented in the bridge's statuary. By the early eighteenth century, however, there was a popular legend concerning two figures that decorated the corner of Old Town Bridge Tower. A man with a lascivious smile has slipped his hand under the dress of a woman (see plate 14.4). The tale that circulated and was told to foreign travellers identified this indecorous couple as an earthy Luther and a lusty Katherine von Bora.[46]

The contrast with events a century earlier could not have been greater. While Bohemia's Calvinist king had launched a campaign against most forms of religious art, this decidedly Catholic mode of cultural expression had grown and flourished after White Mountain. Marian columns would be erected in virtually every town. Votive images would appear on everything from trees to bedroom walls while statues of St John Nepomuk were so widespread that Rainer Maria Rilke would later compose a poem that playfully satirised their ubiquity.[47] In his study of pilgrimage patterns in Bohemia, Franz Matsche has observed that those who designed these routes and sites of popular piety were attempting to sacralise the landscape.[48] The rapid proliferation of this type of art would help create a *terra sancta* in a kingdom that had been stained by heresy for over two centuries. From the pilgrimage shrine to the wayside chapel, from the statue in the village square to the image in the humble kitchen, Bohemia's devotional art helped create a web of sanctity and sacredness that penetrated everyday life. This dynamic process of seizing the mundane and making it holy was at the heart of the aesthetic revolution that transformed Bohemia in the century after White Mountain. Religious art had expanded far beyond traditional ecclesiastical space and had now become one of the most significant markers of a new Czech identity.

---

[46] See for example the story told to three English travellers in 1734. 'The travels of three English gentlemen, in the year 1734', *The Harleian Miscellany*, v (London, 1810), p. 349; Svátek, *Pražské pověsti*, p. 111.

[47]         Aber diese Nepomucken!
         Von des Torgangs Lucken gucken
         und auf allen Brucken spucken
         lauter, lauter Nepomucken.
Rainer Maria Rilke, *Sämtliche Werke*, 7 vols. (Frankfurt, 1955–97), I, pp. 31–2.

[48] Noted in Jan Royt, *Obraz a kult v. Čechach: 17. a 18. století* (Prague, 1999), pp. 112–13.

# 15    Mapping the boundaries of confession: space and urban religious life in the diocese of Augsburg, 1648–1750

*Duane J. Corpis*

For more than a century after the Reformation, German Protestant and Catholic rulers waged war over the confessional status of the Holy Roman Empire as a whole. However, with the conclusion of the Thirty Years War (1648), political authorities shifted their attention away from inter-confessional rivalries across political borders to an internal programme of social discipline and confessionalisation.[1] Certainly, the confessional Other remained an object of suspicion and hatred. Protestants continued to launch attacks on Catholic superstition and error, just as Catholics bombarded Protestants with accusations of heresy. But after the Peace of Westphalia, the legitimacy of employing military coercion to 'convert' competing confessional polities and communities had evaporated. Of course, the confrontation between Catholics and Protestants across confessional boundaries remained potentially explosive and imminently violent. But in general, religious conflicts between competing confessional polities became absorbed in prolonged legal disputes before the imperial courts rather than on the battlefield.

The one place where confession and coercion still went hand-in-hand was *within* the political community. Here, governments could exercise coercive power to maintain the religious uniformity and conformity of their subjects through the force of judicial punishment. Cities in this region displayed such concern about religious uniformity primarily because the Bishopric of Augsburg was *not* a confessionally uniform landscape. Although the region included Catholic cities like Dillingen (the bishop's primary residence) and Donauwörth, significant urban pockets of Protestantism also existed. Protestantism had swept the imperial

---

[1] For an English-language overview on confessionalisation and social discipline, see R. Po-Chia Hsia, *Social Discipline in the Reformation: Central Europe, 1550–1750* (London, 1989). The vast body of German scholarship starts with W. Reinhard, 'Zwang zur Konfessionalisierung? Prolegomena zu einer Theorie des konfessionellen Zeitalters', *Zeitschrift für Historische Forschung* 10 (1983), 257–77 and H. Schilling, 'Die Konfessionalisierung im Reich. Religiöser und gesellschaftlicher Wandel in Deutschland zwischen 1555 und 1620', *Historische Zeitschrift* 246 (1988), 1–45.

cities of Kempten and Memmingen in the sixteenth century, and even after the brutal repression of the Peasants' Revolt, the citizens of these towns maintained their commitment to Luther's new teachings despite the pressures of neighbouring Catholic regimes.[2]

In addition to cities that were either exclusively Lutheran or Catholic, three cities in the bishopric were 'biconfessional'. For the times, these three cities reflected rare experiments indeed. Kaufbeuren, a predominantly Lutheran city with a large Catholic minority, granted Catholics full political rights as citizens after 1648. However, the distribution of seats on the city council remained fixed at thirty Lutherans and eight Catholics, even when the Catholic population began to grow in the eighteenth century.[3] The Lutheran patricians secured a relatively stable peace with the Catholic minority by extending them equal protection under the law but simultaneously secured their own power by denying Catholics equal representation in city government.

In contrast to Kaufbeuren, Augsburg and Dinkelsbühl were not only biconfessional; they also possessed a policy of strict confessional parity.[4] As delineated in the Treaty of Osnabrück (one of two treaties referred to jointly as the Peace of Westphalia), official parity imposed political and legal equality for Protestant and Catholic citizens in these cities. First, all citizens were to tolerate the religious faith of all other citizens, so long as they were either Catholic or Lutheran. Second, the Peace Treaty rescinded the Restitution Edict of 1629, which the Holy Roman Emperor had issued at the highpoint of Catholic victories during the war. The Restitution Edict aimed to recreate a pre-Reformation confessional map by transferring all Protestant properties and titles back to Catholic hands. The Peace of 1648 restored these losses to their former Protestant communities based on the so-called 'Normal Year' 1624. Thus, the confessional boundaries imposed by the Peace of Westphalia in 1648 used the year 1624 as the standard to determine how the geography of the Holy Roman Empire should be divided between the confessions. If this component of the Treaty looked backward in time to restore a moment in the past, the third requirement instituted something new, for it mandated that all civic offices and institutions be divided equally between Catholics and Lutherans. Thus, unlike the situation in Kaufbeuren, Catholics and Lutherans would have parity in the number

[2] B. Moeller, *Imperial Cities and the Reformation: Three Essays* (Durham, 1982).

[3] F. Junginger, *Geschichte der Reichsstadt Kaufbeuren im 17. und 18. Jahrhundert* (Munich, 1965), p. 156.

[4] P. Warmbrunn, *Zwei Konfessionen in einer Stadt: das Zusammenleben von Katholiken und Protestanten in den paritätischen Reichsstädten Augsburg, Biberach, Ravensburg und Dinkelsbühl von 1548 bis 1648* (Wiesbaden, 1983).

of city council seats. In Augsburg, two *Stadtpfleger* – one Catholic and one Lutheran – simultaneously presided over the city council, which consisted of twenty-three Catholic and twenty-two Lutheran magistrates. Most other civic offices were doubled to allow dual occupation by both confessions, and in a few cases, a single position would alternate between Catholic and Lutheran officeholders.[5]

Authorities in all of these cities – whether Catholic, Protestant, or biconfessional – exerted great effort to discipline a variety of practices that challenged religious orthodoxies. Significantly, many of these efforts to impress confessional conformity upon the urban landscape attempted to shape the uses of physical space. Disciplining religious life entailed disciplining the space in which religious life unfolded by imposing order upon the disorder of the churchyards, the cemeteries, the streets. In the process, urban authorities fashioned a confessionalised urban landscape in which citizens lived their everyday lives: where they bought and bartered, worked and played, raised their children, and (of course) where they worshipped. Secular officials joined forces with clergymen to regulate a variety of practices that challenged how urban authorities mapped the contours of the city's sacred and profane spaces. Most importantly, these authorities fashioned their mental map of the confessional landscape by imposing clear spatial boundaries surrounding and separating Catholics and Protestants and by regulating those urban spaces where the two faiths inevitably encountered one another. Each of these urban communities recognised the necessity of creating a confessionally stable landscape, whether based on absolute confessional uniformity or a highly regulated form of biconfessional tolerance.

I use terms such as confessional boundaries, geography, and landscape in part as metaphors for the intersection between religious and political communities, but in fact, contemporaries literally recognised the significant role that space played in forging a post-Peace regime. For example, as early as August 1649, shortly after the city council of Augsburg had instituted the Peace of Westphalia's standard of religious parity, tensions concerning the reorganisation of the city's confessional landscape emerged when a Catholic day labourer named Hans Zeberle appeared before the city court after several quarrels with two Lutheran ministers.[6] The minister Leonhard Fustennegger reported that Zeberle had appeared before him requesting to be instructed in the faith of the Augsburg confession. Fustennegger naturally thought that Zeberle

[5] E. François, *Die unsichtbare Grenze: Protestanten und Katholiken in Augsburg 1648–1806* (Sigmaringen, 1991).
[6] Stadtarchiv Augsburg (hereafter StAAug), Strafamt, Urgichten, 1648–1650, Nr. 330.

wanted to convert. Fustennegger soon realized that Zeberle actually intended to interrogate the tenets of Lutheranism and defend the Catholic faith. For example, Zeberle questioned whether a sin imagined was itself a sin, and the minister argued the Lutheran position that it in fact was. The Catholic day labourer attempted to demonstrate the absurdity of this position by asking whether the unfulfilled intent to kill a person made one as culpable as an actual murderer. This line of discussion remained unresolved as they turned to an even more troubling topic. Zeberle claimed that the Peace of 1648 – the very settlement that had divided Augsburg by granting Lutherans and Catholics legal equality and by distributing church properties according to the principle of the Normal Year – was an 'accursed, godless Peace that dishonoured God, trampled the Queen of Heaven under its feet, scorned the saints, and destroyed the papacy'.[7] Having turned away from a disagreement over dogma, the conversation ended with a direct attack on the political regime of the city.

The subversive implications of Zeberle's criticisms were even more explicit in a later conversation he had with the minister Hans Mair. In the presence of Mair, Zeberle criticised the Peace because 'there's nothing about the Mother of God in it'. Mair responded, 'The virgin Mary has nothing to do with this Peace.' Zeberle then claimed that the church where Mair preached rightfully belonged to the Catholics. It was, after all, called the *Barfüsser Kirche*, a reminder that the church had once been in the possession of the Franciscans, the oft-nicknamed 'barefoot' order of monks. 'My answer was', Mair wrote, 'that it doesn't matter what [the church] is called; we are not bound to the external church built of stone and wood. It could just as well be called the Barfüsser Church or St George. Rather, we are speaking about the living community and church.' Zeberle, however, stubbornly maintained that the church belonged to the Catholics and called all Lutheran preachers 'heretics, soul murderers, and thieves who spread a devilish, damnable teaching'. As his temper flared, he warned Mair that the Lutherans would soon be required to return the churches to their rightful owners.

The political authorities of Augsburg had hoped to prevent precisely such inflamed confessional passions by granting legal equality to Catholics and Lutherans. If both confessions had equal political privileges and equal access to the city's resources, perhaps the everyday antagonisms between the two faiths would subside. But the city council also knew how deeply confessional antagonism ran. Thus, in their attempt to prevent confessional disorder, Protestant and Catholic city councillors agreed to outlaw all religious libel and calumnious speech. However,

[7] *Ibid.*

Zeberle laid bare the limits of the city's attempt to suppress religious antagonisms. Even when he was brought before the court for interrogation, his tone was confrontational, confident and self-righteous. The city officials who presided over the interrogation asked Zeberle whether he knew of the city's 'serious and exemplary punishments [against] disparaging speech, libel, blasphemy, calumny, and threats'. The court scribe recorded Zeberle's answer: 'The defendant is astonished that much is forbidden but little is punished, and he will speak the truth, even if it should cost him his life ten times.' When asked why he attacked the legitimacy of the Peace, he responded, 'Because no one can be saved outside of the Catholic faith and since so many Catholic churches have been surrendered due to the Peace, anyone can imagine for themselves that . . . no one will be able to find the straight and narrow way to heaven.'[8]

For Zeberle, the boundary between Catholicism and Lutheranism was a theological line between true religion and heresy, between salvation and damnation. But it was also a boundary etched into the physical space of the city. He recognised that the division of the city into Catholic and Protestant spaces was a political act of the state and hence artificial, arbitrary and contestable. Eventually, he believed, Catholicism would triumph over Lutheranism, and the Lutherans would be forced out of their churches and, we can assume, out of the city as well. Here, his understanding of the city's sacred landscape differed from official attitudes. While the city councillors saw the official boundaries between denominations as necessary for the maintenance of peace and order, he saw them as a dangerous compromise with heresy. According to Zeberle, this compromise had de-legitimised the city governments, justifying his defiance of the Lutheran clergy and the city's laws. In general, the attempt to maintain religious order in Augsburg by fashioning a divided but balanced confessional landscape succeeded. But occasionally Catholics and Lutherans alike contested this landscape by laying claim to the city, in part or as a whole, in ways challenging the official spatial boundaries that split the city in two.

In the seventeenth and eighteenth centuries, popular dissatisfaction with the official confessional landscape regularly resurfaced in other biconfessional cities as well. For example, in 1730, a Lutheran farmer was arrested for disrupting Sunday mass in a Catholic church in Dinkelsbühl. He had entered the church in a drunken rage shouting anti-Catholic curses. The Lutheran was beaten by several Catholic parishioners, arrested, and charged with disturbing the peace. In the official proceedings against the farmer, Catholic witnesses recollected an incident

[8] *Ibid.*

that had occurred decades earlier in 1690. In that year, two Lutheran trespassers had entered the church during mass, stormed the altar, and ridiculed the Catholic priest. One even urinated on the altar.[9] Such an act of desecration seems to conform to a script that Lutherans performed generations earlier during the early phases of the Reformation, when Protestant iconoclasts smeared spit or faeces on Catholic holy objects in what Robert Scribner called 'antiritual' or 'counterliturgical' acts intended to negate the power of Catholic sacred spaces.[10] It appears that Lutheran collective memory still re-enacted the basic script of ritual desecration decades after the Reformation. In turn, the confessional antipathy generated by the specific circumstances of 1690 had remained lodged in the collective memories of Catholics in Dinkelsbühl, ready to resurface as evidence of Lutheran misconduct in a court trial forty years later.

Such symbolic acts of desecration took place not only in biconfessional cities within the diocese. Even in officially Lutheran cities such as Memmingen and Kempten, where small numbers of Catholic artisans or day labourers lived on the margins of urban society, confrontations between members of the official and the minority religious communities occasionally erupted into open hostility. Confessional antagonisms could become especially acute in Memmingen, where, in addition to Catholic labourers, Catholic clergy lived in the cloister of the Holy Ghost, the only Catholic place of worship that the Lutheran city council tolerated within the city.[11] In 1684 several inebriated Protestant journeymen began throwing snowballs at one such Catholic priest. The priest rushed back to the cloister to evade his three antagonists. One of the journeymen chased the priest into the cloister church where his misbehaviour intensified. There, he tried to kiss the church attendant's maid, who succeeded in escaping his clutches. Then, as if he were in a tavern, he asked several people standing nearby whether they had any tobacco. One person responded by asking him if he was trying to make a pigsty out of the

---

[9] Archiv des Bistums Augsburg, BO 1573, letter from Jerg Bernhard Walch in Dinkelsbühl, dated 29 May 1690 and letter from Catholic mayor and city council of Dinkelsbühl, dated 11 May 1730.

[10] R. W. Scribner, 'Ritual and Reformation', in R. Po-Chia Hsia (ed.), *The German People and the Reformation* (Ithaca, 1988), pp. 122–44. See also N. Z. Davis, 'The rites of violence', in *Society and Culture in Early Modern France* (Stanford, 1975), pp. 152–87.

[11] Before the Reformation, the monks who operated the cloister were independent of the city's jurisdiction. Though the cloister successfully fought to maintain its presence in the city, its autonomy was eroded during the Reformation, visually demonstrated by the Lutheran city council seal emblazoned on the cloister's external wall. The seal symbolically announced that the already marginal Catholic presence in the city was tolerated only by the political grace of the Lutheran magistrates. See Kiessling, 'Konfession als alltägliche Grenze – oder: Wie evangelisch waren die Reichsstädte?', in W. Jahn (ed.), *Geld und Glaube. Leben in evangelischen Reichsstädten* (Augsburg, 1998), p. 53.

church, at which point the Lutheran youth began meowing like a cat and whistling. Finally, at least according to the priest's accusations, he tried to knock over the baptismal basin.[12] In addition to striking out against the body of the Catholic priest, the Lutheran primarily responsible for the incident directed his abusive mockery against the space of the church itself. The onlookers certainly understood the meaning of his strange behaviour – he was trying to desecrate the sole existing sacred space for Catholics in Memmingen with his carnivalesque sexuality and animalistic excesses. One of the other young Lutherans later reported that his personal antagonism towards the Catholic priest resulted from the cleric's anti-Protestant sermons. 'I have worked in many Catholic places', he explained, 'but nowhere have I heard the Lutherans so blasphemed as here.'[13] At stake was the integrity and honour of the local Protestant community in a city that was officially Lutheran. For these journeymen, the presence of Catholics in the city marred the purity of the confessional landscape, no matter how narrowly the city council had circumscribed that presence to a single place.

The city authorities of even a staunchly Protestant city like Memmingen could not excuse such an attack on the Catholic Church as playful revelry. The magistrates wished to eliminate all excess and disorder from the city streets. Thus, proper behaviour in the name of the official Lutheran faith could not include such disorderly conduct. Although we do not know whether and how the men involved were punished, we do know that they were brought before the magistrates for questioning, during which the men admitted to at least some of the indiscretions reported by Catholic witnesses to the city council. The concern shown by the magistrates in this case – they even demanded that all citizens with knowledge of the case bear witness against the culprits in accordance with their oaths of citizenship – again reflects the differing attitudes towards the religious landscape held by authorities and commoners. Both the Lutheran magistrate and the common resident found the presence of Catholicism within the city threatening, but the magistrates found equally disruptive the expression of public religious conflict between Lutherans and Catholics. In this instance, the city council's goal of creating a stable and ordered urban landscape with contours defined by orthodox Lutheranism came into conflict with a more general urge to produce a confessionally pure landscape that questioned the presence of Catholicism within the city.

In some sense, I have started backwards by highlighting evidence demonstrating how urban residents challenged or questioned the official confessional landscapes that the city councils wished to fashion and

---

[12] Stadtarchiv Memmingen (hereafter StAMem), 378/2.     [13] *Ibid.*

preserve. I have done so in order to emphasise the degree to which the 'confessional landscape' is not merely an analytically useful metaphor, but actually clarifies one of the central ways that people understood the expression of religious piety and confessional hostility. As the evidence above suggests, the contours of religious life and the boundaries between religious communities were, in an important sense, physical and spatial. The question we must now answer is, how did secular and ecclesiastical authorities actually map the official contours and boundaries of the urban confessional community?

For most Catholic cities in the diocese of Augsburg, the primary directives for organising and disciplining religious life (and space) came from the bishops. In a series of mandates reissued continuously over the seventeenth and eighteenth centuries, the bishops used what coercive authority they possessed to impose order on the urban spaces of the Catholic communities under their jurisdiction. Because their jurisdiction extended over a large territory that was difficult to coordinate and control, they could never completely root out gambling, dancing and merry-making. Nevertheless, the bishops criminalised such unofficial festive practices, especially when they occurred on hallowed ground. Any appropriation of the churchyard for worldly purposes received the critical attention of Catholic authorities. Furthermore, the bishops ordered restaurants, inns and public markets to remain closed during church services. Catholic citizens found at home or on the street at this time could be punished, usually with a hefty fine.[14] The home, the street, the tavern – indeed, all secular spaces that competed with the church – became off-limits during high mass, thus granting the church a monopoly on urban space, at least on Sundays.

City councils throughout the diocese independently implemented similar legislation. In 1750, the Protestant and Catholic magistrates of Kaufbeuren prohibited residents from walking in the streets, sitting in their gardens, or loitering in front of their stores during church services. Whenever people should have been in church, city magistrates tried to empty the secular public spaces that competed with the sacred space of the parish church. The Kaufbeuren city council authorised two city officials to patrol the city streets and visit private homes during services to ensure that residents were in church.[15] The city council of Memmingen issued a decree in 1713 to respond to the divine wrath that God had apparently let loose upon the world to punish human wickedness, manifested in the

---

[14] Staatsarchiv Augsburg (hereafter SAA), Hochstift Augsburg MüB Lit. Nr. 154, mandates dated 1643 and 1750.
[15] Junginger, *Geschichte der Reichsstadt Kaufbeuren*, pp. 150–1.

recent bloody wars and the material hardships of inflation. In the eyes of the magistrates, the festive culture of everyday urban life posed a threat to the spiritual health of the entire commune, a situation that the magistrates could alter by encouraging residents to lead a 'righteous, Christian and godly life'. In the early modern religious worldview, moral decadence and spiritual lassitude not only affected one in the hereafter, but had consequences in the material, mundane world as well. Thus, the magistrates desperately desired to rid the urban landscape of ungodly practices that threatened to bring God's punishment upon the town. Specifically, the decree forbade dancing and musicians at weddings and festive gatherings as well as entertainments involving games and other miscellaneous excesses (*vielfältigem außschweiffen*) in the taverns. In addition, the magistrates ordered residents to attend Sunday church services and the weekly days of penance to pray for God's forgiveness.[16] Thus, the ordinance positioned the city's Lutheran parish church as the moral and spiritual centre of Memmingen's confessional landscape by transforming it into a space for shared communal penance. The worldly crises confronting the city of Memmingen generated an almost eschatological materialism that linked human sinfulness to the worldly suffering experienced by the urban commune and connected the moral reform of physical space with the restoration of communal grace.

Likewise, Kempten's city council issued a decree banning dancing and gambling on Sundays and requiring stores to remain closed on major holidays and during regular Sunday services.[17] City residents were banned from hanging their laundry in the churchyard on Sundays and warned that any cattle or chickens found wandering around the churchyard would be impounded. The Kempten magistrates seemed peculiarly concerned with the presence of animals in the church grounds that disturbed the peace and sanctity of the service. In 1730, to prepare for a church jubilee, the city council ordered several city officials to stand guard by the church doors with whips in order to keep stray dogs from entering the building. Even once the congregation had assembled and the doors to the church were closed, the mayor told the church attendant 'that he should constantly carry a whip with him to hunt dogs out of the church'.[18] This concern for ordering church space seems to have occupied the proceedings of the Kempten city council frequently, whether to control the chaotic rush of parishioners wishing to make confession simultaneously (the solution was to permit no more than two families to approach the confessional at one

---

[16] StAMem, A BD. 18, Ratsdekrete (1713–33), 21 May 1713.

[17] On Sundays that were not holidays, stores could open once the church service was over. SAA, Reichsstädte Akten, Kempten, Nr. 16.

[18] Stadtarchiv Kempten (hereafter StAKem), Ratsprotokolle, 23 June 1730.

time), to discipline children who played in the churchyard, or to ensure that parishioners wore the appropriate clothes in church.[19]

The threat of apostasy posed a particularly acute problem for maintaining the stability of confessionalised space in such cities. For example, on 8 April 1729, the city council minutes of Kempten proposed that 'if, in the future, someone moves over to the papists through rashness or malice, that person should be held as an outsider (*einen abtrünnigen Menschen*)'. The city council adopted the proposal, which essentially required not only the social expulsion of converts from the community, but also their physical exile from the city. The new policy also stipulated how a person who reconverted to Lutheranism might once again join the community: '[The convert] will be accepted into the community and recognised as a member of our church again when he does public penance in the church.'[20] The public, ritual act of penance conducted in the church cleansed the impurity and pollution that resulted from a person's apostasy. At this moment of ritual transformation, the church physically embodied a threshold that marked the reconvert's entrance back into the confessional and political community.

Nonetheless, such reintegration could potentially remain an incomplete process. In 1772, an elderly man and his wife fled Kempten to the cloister at Ottobeuren where they wanted to convert. Due to the husband's frailty, they never reached their destination. They returned to Kempten, where they asked to regain their status as Lutherans and citizens. Before they were readmitted into the community, they had to endure the public humiliation of sitting in front of the church altar in direct view of the congregation while the minister delivered a sermon about the evils of their deeds. They were then confined to the city's workhouse for the remainder of their lives.[21] This example highlights not only the social stigma attached to apostasy; it also shows how the actions taken by city officials simultaneously to punish and reconcile the couple made use of the symbolism of space. The couple's shaming in the public forum of the church and their confinement within the workhouse were powerful methods available to the secular and ecclesiastical authorities in Kempten to purify and contain the contamination that had tainted the community as a consequence of the couple's religious transgression. It also served as a strong warning to all other citizens that conversion brought with it severe political consequences and social stigmatisation. There was no place for

---

[19] See respectively StAKem, Ratsprotokolle, 13 Nov. 1699, 9 April 1731 and 4 June 1731.
[20] StAKem, Ratsprotokolle, 8 April 1729.
[21] StAKem, B129u. *Cronik von der Heil. Römisch. Freÿen Reichs Stadt Kempten, vom Jahr 1600 bis 1795, zusamengetragen von Peter Gebhart, des Gerichts und Handelsman Ao. 1799. den 31 Decbr.*

the convert within the city walls, and even a person who reconverted might remain permanently on the social and spatial margins of the community.

The policies issued by Catholic bishops or Lutheran city councils suggest how urban authorities tried to impose a rigid confessional order upon the space of the cities they controlled. But how was the fragmented landscape of the biconfessional city organised, given the fact that Catholics and Lutherans constantly competed with one another in such cities to define the sacred centres of the city? Perhaps the clearest example of this competition was the church complex of St Ulrich and St Afra, a volatile hotbed of controversy in biconfessional Augsburg. The building complex consisted of two churches and a monastery, architecturally joined together. According to the religious settlement of 1648, the monastery and main basilica belonged to the Catholic Church. The chapel built on the side of the basilica, however, was given to the Lutheran community. One final compromise permitted the Catholic clergy to use the St Jacob's chapel inside the Lutheran church for occasional baptisms. A wall with a locked door separated the basilica and the chapel.

Towards the end of the seventeenth century, the Lutheran clergy began complaining that Catholic clergy and laymen were sneaking into the Protestant chapel through the door and desecrating it. The complaints intensified in the early eighteenth century. Catholics had allegedly thrown broken glass through the door.[22] They sneaked in and cut holes in the altar cloths. They were even accused of damaging the painted decorative name plates that adorned the pews and indicated who sat where. This was a significant affront, since the plates that were damaged or stolen came from the first several rows of pews – the name plates belonging to the parishioners with the highest social status.[23] Starting in 1709, the Protestants began renovating the chapel. In order to rebuild the façade, they wanted to tear down the old exterior wall, which was decorated with a fresco of the Virgin Mary. The Protestant architects also planned to remove the cornerstone which had the date 1458 emblazoned on it, the year when St Ulrich's church was originally added to the monastery.[24] Catholics protested, for these were important reminders to their community of the time before Luther, when all sacred spaces in the city belonged

[22] StAAug, Evangelisches Wesensarchiv (hereafter EWA) 941 T.II, letter dated 1681.

[23] StAAug, EWA 941 T.I, 'Verschidene Turbationes, so die Ulricaner Mönch und Papistin unter währendem Gottesdienst der Evangelischen, und sonsten ausserhalb dem selben in der Pfarr Kirch zu St Ulrich verübet.'

[24] The architectural addition of St Ulrich's Church to the basilica began in 1457 and was completed in 1458. E. von Knorre, 'Material zur Geschichte der evangelischen Ulrichskirche in Augsburg', *Zeitschrift des Historischen Vereins für Schwaben* 69 (1975), 47.

to the Catholic Church. This controversy raged on for decades and was even brought to the attention of the imperial court system.[25]

Many similar controversies emerged after the Peace of Westphalia over the need for Catholics and Lutherans to share the city's spaces, serving as a constant reminder to the magistrates that Augsburg's urban spaces were in fact riddled with religious tensions. How then could Catholic and Lutheran magistrates fashion a coherent confessional landscape out of the inherent religious diversity of the biconfessional city? One way that Catholic and Lutheran magistrates tried to consolidate their confessional communities involved the careful organisation of religious rituals that coordinated fragmented confessional spaces into an imagined whole. Augsburg's Lutherans began to feel the need for consolidating their community urgently in the first half of the eighteenth century, when the relative proportion of Lutherans to Catholics in the city began to decline, largely due to the influx of Catholic day labourers from the countryside.[26] While Augsburg's Lutherans recognised that they could not alter unfavourable demographic trends, they did believe that they could strengthen their community from within through a strong, defensive posture that secured its perimeters.

These perimeters were etched repeatedly onto the civic landscape during particular holidays through the spatial and temporal coordination of events in each parish church throughout the city. Thus, in 1730, the secular and ecclesiastical authorities published an *Intimation or Proclamation of the Herein Discussed Evangelical Jubilee and Thanksgiving Festival this Year 1730: How such [Proclamation] should be read on . . . June 18th before the Morning Sermon and after the Reading from all Pulpits in the 6 Evangelical Parish Churches of the Free Imperial City Augsburg.*[27] The title of the document says it all – the six churches served as the spatial nodes in a temporally coordinated event linking each different parish into a single, shared, imagined community that transcended the confessionally fragmented landscape of the city. Each separate parish became united in an official effort to propagate the exact same message, fixed through the use of printed text, to the city's entire Lutheran community.

In addition to the medium of the message, the content of the announcement fed into the logic of imagining the geographic consolidation and even expansion of the boundaries of Lutheranism. The *Intimation and*

---

[25] StAAug, Katholisches Wesensarchiv (hereafter KWA) B2[22].

[26] On demographic shifts in Augsburg, see François, *Die unsichtbare Grenze*, pp. 33–72.

[27] StAAug, EWA Nr. 534 T. I, *Intimation oder Verkündigung des innstehenden Evangelischen Jubel- und Danck-Festes dieses 1730. Jahrs; Wie solche Dom. II. Post Trinit. D. 18. Junii vor denen Morgen Predigten / nach dem Vorlesen / Von allen Cantzeln / in den 6. Evangelischen Pfarr-Kirchen der Freyen Reichs-Stadt Augspurg solle abgelesen werden* (Augsburg, 1730).

*Proclamation* asked parishioners to 'pray not only for you and your dear hometown, but for the evangelical churches throughout the entire circumference of the world, that the Gospel remain steadfast until the end of days and that it be preached unhindered with much blessing'. The announcement even exhorted parishioners to provide donations to support Lutheran missionaries in India for the 'further propagation of the Gospel among the pagans'.[28] The message also served as a warning to members of the Lutheran community to maintain their moral discipline on this particular day of remembrance and celebration: 'Abstain from all carnal lusts, which assail the soul . . . Do not waste time with excess in eating and drinking; by visiting the taverns, cafés, or pubs; [or] by associating with sinful company engaged in all kinds of idle gossip, untimely religious disputes, playing, dancing, shooting, suspicious walking and strolling, and other such things.'[29] Here again we see how civic officials attempted to impose order on the confessional landscape by patrolling various urban spaces within the community that became off-limits during the holiday, as well as monitoring particular activities that might take place in those spaces.

In 1771 the evangelical mayor and city council issued a decree to the ministers of the six Lutheran churches in Augsburg with goals similar to those expressed in the announcement published in 1730. This decree carefully organised one of the evangelical community's most important holidays, the Day of Penance and Prayer. Though not as significant as Good Friday and Easter, the Day of Penance and Prayer was important for Augsburg's Lutherans because it was an invented holiday. It did not conform to the traditional liturgical cycle. In fact, every year the date for the Day of Penance and Prayer changed – the Lutheran authorities arbitrarily established its date according to the particular needs of the community. In years of famine or other hardships, the Lutheran community might even celebrate more than one Penance and Prayer Day. The central significance of this invented holiday lay in the fact that it was *not* celebrated by Catholics. As a special Lutheran holiday, it contributed to the creation of a separate and distinct Lutheran communal identity. This holiday forged a Lutheran sacred *time* – a liturgical calendar of holy days different from those celebrated by Catholics. In addition, this day of devotion offered yet another opportunity for the six separate Lutheran parishes in Augsburg to unite into a single collective whole.

This is especially clear in the 1771 decree. The ministers of all six parishes were to deliver sermons drawn from the same biblical text and ensure that the same songs would be sung in each church. They would

[28] *Ibid.*    [29] *Ibid.*

also compose a 'special prayer' for recitation to their respective parishioners requiring the approval of the city council. There was to be no deviation in the service from one Lutheran church to the next. In order to guarantee the uniformity of the songs and prayers, these were to be published and circulated before the holiday. The various Lutheran parish ministers normally organised their own services. However, on this particular holiday, every Lutheran in Augsburg would enter his or her church, hear roughly the same sermon, sing the same songs, and take communion at about the same time. The bells of all six churches would ring throughout the city, marking the beginning and end of the service.[30] The city council's meticulous coordination of events shaped both time and space, organising the fragmented landscape into a homogenous whole. Distinct evangelical communities that typically defined themselves normally on the level of the parish would simultaneously act through collective rituals as a single community, thus overcoming the physical distance that separated the various Lutheran churches, while symbolically marginalising the Catholic presence in the city.[31]

A comparable attempt on the part of Augsburg Catholics to organise the religiously fragmented landscape of the biconfessional city is reflected in a mandate issued jointly by the Catholic and Lutheran magistrates in 1754.[32] The mandate ordered that artisans of both faiths momentarily cease working whenever a Catholic priest passed by their workshops in order to transport the consecrated Host to the home of a sick person. In such instances, the priest carrying the Host signalled his passage through the streets by ringing a hand-held bell. A recent incident had prompted the issuance of this new decree: a Catholic priest carrying a consecrated Host to the home of a patient passed the workshop of two Lutheran artisans. The artisans did not hear (or did not pay attention to) the signal of the bell, and they continued to work as normal. Apparently one of them threw a stone out of the window, just missing the head of the priest. Although no one was hurt, the magistrates were nonetheless concerned that, in addition to the 'danger [to] body and life', a similar incident could in the future 'lead to great difficulties, which might disturb the general peace'. Thus, the mandate instructed that the priest and his assistants 'let themselves be heard frequently and continuously with the signal of the bell whenever visiting a patient with the venerable Host, as in other places such as Vienna, Munich, etc., so that all disorder can be prevented, and

---

[30] Bells organised communal time and space long before this period. G. Dohrn-van Rossum, *The History of the Hour: Clocks and Modern Temporal Orders* (Chicago, 1996), pp. 197–215.

[31] StAAug, EWA 326.     [32] StAAug, EWA 631.

so that a person from either religious confession may behave appropriately, either by the observance of devotion or by the suspension of work and noise'. Although the city's public spaces were shared by both confessions, the magistrates agreed that the consecrated Host and its Catholic carrier deserved special treatment as they passed through the streets. By forcing even Lutherans to respect the passage of the Catholic Host through the city, the mandate authorised the ritualised fashioning of a Catholic space that cut its way through confessionally mixed neighbourhoods. It attempted to forge a confessionally ordered space out of the confessional fragments and everyday disorder that characterised social life within Augsburg.[33]

This example fits comfortably within a broader strategy of consolidating the Catholic landscape in Augsburg by integrating public spaces normally shared by people of both faiths into a sacred Catholic landscape through ritualised acts of processions and pilgrimages. The most important religious processions were held on holy days like Corpus Christi or during Holy Week preceding Easter Sunday. Participants journeyed from one church to another or to a pilgrimage shrine outside of the city altogether, often while singing liturgical songs and carrying banners, candles, relics and saints' images.[34] The Corpus Christi procession involved the entire Catholic community in a visually impressive parade through the city that included brotherhoods and city councillors in full regalia carrying flags and candles to accompany the elaborate monstrance transporting the consecrated Host. Even the Catholic members of the city guard participated in the procession, which necessitated that the city lock its gates during the event.[35] While the locking of the gates was a practical solution to the temporary understaffing of the city fortifications, it also represented a moment in which the Catholic Church and secular magistrates could expand the circumference of the Catholic community to the spatial boundaries of the city. The elaborate liturgical calendar of the Catholic Church afforded parishioners countless opportunities on official holy days and saints' days to take to the streets in processions

---

[33] In a similar ordinance, the Bishop of Augsburg decreed that whenever a priest carried the Holy Sacrament to the houses of sick parishioners, Catholics in the street should 'show all due reverence [to the Host] with curtsies and veneration' (SAA, Hochstift Augsburg MüB Lit. 154, dated 5 March 1672).

[34] On pilgrimage and sacred landscape, see W. Christian, *Local Religion in Sixteenth-Century Spain* (Princeton, 1981); P. Soergel *Wondrous in His Saints: Counter-Reformation Propaganda in Bavaria* (Berkeley, 1993); R. Habermas, *Wallfahrt und Aufruhr: zur Geschichte des Wunderglaubens in der frühen Neuzeit* (Frankfurt am Main, 1991); W. Freitag, *Volks- und Elitenfrömmigkeit in der frühen Neuzeit. Marienwallfahrten im Fürstbistum Münster* (Paderborn, 1991).

[35] F. Herre, *Das Augsburger Bürgertum im Zeitalter der Aufklärung* (Augsburg and Basel, 1951), p. 26.

and pilgrimages.[36] In addition, the Augsburg Catholic clergy organised processions on other special occasions. For example, according to the report of one Lutheran cleric, the Catholic Church held a 'very pompous procession' in 1698 to parade the relics of five saints, newly delivered from Rome, through the city.[37] Much like the carefully coordinated rituals used by Protestants on the Days of Penance and Prayer, the processions linked the spatially fragmented Catholic community into an imagined whole.

Those processions which began in the city but ended in Andechs or some other nearby shrine further connected the urban community to an even larger Catholic sacred geography, one that encircled the city and seemed to drown the city's Lutheran community in a sea of Catholicism. The cathedral preacher Franz Xavier Pfyffer explained specifically how the members of the Trinity Brotherhood organised their annual pilgrimage to Andechs in order to 'combat the errors of Luther and his followers' by 'publicly confessing to the ancient Catholic faith and bringing forth before the world the bright light of day against the darkness of the Lutheran pseudo-religion'. This pilgrimage site (*Gnaden-Ort*, or literally 'place of grace') was a useful weapon in the war against Lutherans because it housed three miraculous hosts, a venerable image of the Virgin Mary and numerous relics of other saints, which had been 'confirmed and protected against the false teachings of Lutheranism through so many clear miraculous signs'.[38]

Catholic communities in other biconfessional cities also utilised processions to strengthen the faith of the local Catholic community by inscribing a sacred landscape within and throughout the city. In 1669, the Jesuits in Kaufbeuren explained that the procession they organised to Ottobeuren would help Kaufbeuren 'remain still somewhat Catholic and not completely eaten up by the damnable heresy of Lutheranism'.[39] Ottobeuren, a cloister that housed several pilgrimage shrines and relics, was a particularly efficacious site of supernatural power for Catholics. The link between Kaufbeuren and the broader sacred geography beyond its walls was ritually constituted through the repeated script of bodies moving through space. Such processions bolstered the faith of Kaufbeuren's Catholics

---

[36] P. Rummel, 'Fürstbischöflicher Hof und katholisches kirchliches Leben', in Gunther Gottlieb *et al.* (eds.), *Geschichte der Stadt Augsburg von der Römerzeit bis zur Gegenwart* (Stuttgart, 1984), p. 539.

[37] Marcus Mattsperger the Younger, *Kirchen Calender* (undated), Archiv bei St Anna, Seniorats Archiv, Nr. 8.

[38] F. Pfyffer, *Die Schätz den Göttlichen Gnaden gesucht und gefunden auf dem Heiligen Berg Andechs / als Die hochlöbliche Bruderschafft der Allerheiligsten Dreyfaltigkeit zu Augsburg* (Augsburg, 1743), pp. 18–19.

[39] SAA, Klosterakten, Kloster Ottobeuren, Nr. 104, letter dated 30 July 1669.

by allowing them to participate in an elaborate spectacle of faith that included music, costumes and banners. The pilgrimage represented the ritual sanctification and reconfiguration of Kaufbeuren as a Catholic space. Kaufbeuren's Catholic minority could claim the city and flaunt themselves at the Lutheran majority during religious processions, if not during political elections. Processions and pilgrimages in biconfessional cities thus provided Catholics an opportunity to confront their Lutheran cohabitants by occupying public urban spaces with the symbols and rituals of the Catholic faith. Even in officially Lutheran cities, Catholic residents might claim space through public processions, although the city governments carefully circumscribed the scope of such events. So, for instance, Kempten authorities complained in 1702 that one annual procession 'moves further and further into the city every year' and insisted that the Catholics revert to their more limited traditional observances.[40] Although the Lutheran magistrates had reached a compromise with the Catholic minority, they were unwilling to sacrifice their ultimate control over the city's space.

In addition to the church and the street, the school became a key place where the boundaries of the local confessional community were laid down. Urban officials saw the religious and political aims of education as part of a single mission: to create citizens obedient to God and to the city council. An eighteenth-century proposal for the reform of evangelical schools in Augsburg, for example, highlights the perceived connections drawn between well-catechised parishioners and obedient citizens: 'Such a large portion of the local Lutheran parents unfortunately show so little concern for the education of their children, especially regarding what is necessary and indispensable for a happy life and a Godly death.' The lack of parental concern led many 'patriotic' citizens (*Patrioten*) to wonder 'what kind of citizens such children will grow up as. There is nothing more base than to find children in the German primary school who, after attending school for three to four years . . . are as unknowledgeable about our most holy religion, as if they had never received any instruction at all.'[41] Those parents who neglect their children's education produce 'male and female citizens in whom we can find no true fear of God, no respect for superior government authority, no love for one's neighbour, no ability to discipline their children, and instead in whom we find only imprudence and a rude, intractable character'.

In 1748, shortly after this anxiety-ridden demand for educational reform reached the attention of the city council, the Lutheran magistrates

---

[40] SAA, Fürststift Kempten, Acta Civitatica, Nr. 114, letter dated 23 May 1702.
[41] StAAug, EWA 1130.

published a revised ordinance for the evangelical schools of the city. The ordinance clearly defined the school as a site for inculcating students with a moral discipline that they would bring with them outside of the school house: 'Whenever school is held, it should open and close with prayers, and when the children are allowed to return home, they should be diligently reminded to be well-behaved on the streets.'[42] To accompany the school ordinance, the city council also printed the METHODUS *and Means of Teaching* to instruct schoolmasters how to fulfil their duties more effectively. This text reinforced the concern to order urban space that the school ordinance had voiced, for the schoolmaster should teach students that 'discipline and good morals should [be maintained] above all in the church, the school, at home, and in the streets'.[43] Together these two documents demonstrate how the general anxiety about religious conformity and political obedience expressed in the initial proposal for school reform, which were not conceived of at first in spatial terms, became inextricably linked to the city council's other mandates trying to impose confessional order on the urban landscape. Both the school ordinance and the METHODUS transformed the school from a space in which catechism took place to a locus within a larger network of spatial regulation encompassing the church, the home and the streets.

The school might also become a contested space, one seen by the city officials as harbouring the potential for disorder. Such was the case when the Jesuits refounded their gymnasium in the biconfessional city of Kaufbeuren in 1715, more than sixty years after the predominately Lutheran city council closed the original Jesuit school in 1649. In a gesture of fairness, the Lutheran authorities had permitted the Catholic minority community to maintain a Latin school funded from civic revenues to complement the Protestant school. But when Catholics began raising private money to re-found the Jesuit school in the early eighteenth century, the Lutheran city officials responded with hostility. In a ruling on the lawsuit brought by the Lutheran city councillors against the Jesuits, the imperial court in Regensburg decided that the Jesuits could organise an educational institution in the city. But even the imperial court could not deny that only the Kaufbeuren city council could approve the building of a completely new schoolhouse. So, the predominately Lutheran city

---

[42] *Ibid.*

[43] The city council of Kempten also expected teachers to discipline students' behaviour in spaces outside of the school. After hearing that several girls had thrown berry seeds at each other during the midday sermon, the city council ordered the two schoolmasters who ran the girls' school 'to pay greater attention to the maidens in the church and to make sure that they enter and leave the church in pairs' (StAKem, Ratsprotokolle, 31 Aug. 1705).

council strategically denied the Catholic community the authorisation to construct a new building, forcing the Jesuits to convert already existing Catholic spaces into temporary classrooms.

The arguments mustered by the Lutheran councillors embodied a conservative anxiety that any change in the confessional landscape would destabilise the existing balance between the confessions and threaten the Lutheran community politically and religiously. Since the existing Latin schools in Kaufbeuren, both Catholic and Lutheran, required parents to pay for their children's education, the free schooling received at a well-endowed Jesuit gymnasium might entice Lutheran parents to send their children to a Catholic school. Furthermore, the Jesuit school would attract a large number of boys from outside the city, which would heighten the potential for disorder due to the presence of many rowdy, young students, especially since the Jesuits were liable to teach them that 'they [are not] subjects of any worldly authority'.[44] It is thus not surprising that the Lutheran councillors tried desperately to thwart the Catholic community's plans. At the very least, they could minimise the Catholic community's institutional growth by containing its architectural expansion. This strategy worked until the Jesuits began building their school on the grounds of the bishop's residence, a particular space in the city that was both incontestably Catholic and beyond the jurisdictional reach of the city council, since it technically (much like a modern-day embassy) belonged to a foreign power.[45]

The fears of the Lutheran authorities were not totally unfounded. Kaufbeuren's Lutherans understood that Jesuits would use the city as a base of operations as they mobilised and manoeuvred around the city's surrounding territories. The newly imported Jesuit teachers also served as missionaries within the city and beyond to energise Tridentine Catholicism in the countryside and to push back the boundaries of Protestantism.[46] The Jesuits' promotion of public-student theatre as a forum to attack heresy was also well known, and their students began performing plays almost immediately. Until the Jesuits had the funds to build a theatre in the school, the plays were often performed openly in city squares before a confessionally mixed public, and even after the theatre stood complete, the audiences contained many curious Lutherans.[47] The

---

[44] H. P. Schmauch, 'Das Jesuitengymnasium in Kaufbeuren. Ein Beitrag zur Kaufbeurer Schulgeschichte, 2. Teil', *Kaufbeuren Geschichtsblätter* 12 (December 1991), 370.
[45] *Ibid.*, 370–1.    [46] *Ibid.*, 371.
[47] H. P. Schmauch, 'Das Jesuitengymnasium in Kaufbeuren. Ein Beitrag zur Kaufbeurer Schulgeschichte, 3. und letzter Teil', *Kaufbeuren Geschichtsblätter* 12 (March 1992), 417–18.

Jesuits in Kaufbeuren were keen to organise religious processions within the city and pilgrimages to nearby Cloister Irsee in which their students participated.[48] Both plays and processions increased the possibility of interconfessional interactions, whether hostile or sympathetic. Communal fears of apostasy emerged strongly when individual Lutheran parents began sending their sons to the gymnasium for a free, high-quality education, for these Lutheran boys were strongly encouraged to attend mass every day at 7.00 a.m. with their Catholic classmates and were otherwise exposed to a heavy dose of Catholic catechism.

Throughout their lives, Lutherans and Catholics found themselves in a variety of spaces and places that exerted tremendous influence on their religious identities, from the very first time they entered a church to become baptised or a school to learn their alphabet and catechism. Even after death, the body entered a final space charged with religious significance – the cemetery. In Augsburg, the cemeteries served as critical sites for defining membership in the divided confessional communities of the city. After 1648, the Lutherans laid claim to one communal cemetery inside the city walls located next to St Stephan (*Unterer Gottesacker*) and one that had been built just outside of the city in front of the Red Gate (*Oberer Gottesacker*). Augsburg Lutherans had control over the city's main intramural cemetery by St Stephan decades before the Thirty Years War, though both confessions made use of it. In 1600 the Jesuits insisted that the city permit the construction of an exclusively Catholic cemetery, but due to the lack of space inside the city, this cemetery had to be built outside of the city walls. Thus, after 1600 most Catholics buried their dead in a plot of land just outside of the Gögginer Gate (*Katholischer Gottesacker*), although many elite Catholic families continued to inter their kin in the cemetery next to the cathedral in the part of the city belonging to the bishop.[49]

This topographical arrangement differs from the recent findings of historian Craig Koslofsky, who identifies the increasingly common practice of extramural burial as a Lutheran development during the period of the early Reformation. Although some medieval medical experts had suggested moving urban cemeteries outside of the city walls for health reasons even before the Reformation, many Catholics resisted this change since the separation of the dead from the living challenged both official theology and popular practices. Catholics identified cemeteries as

---

[48] *Ibid.*, 415.
[49] See the entry 'Friedhöfe' in G. Grünsteudel, G. Hägele and R. Frankenberger (eds.), *Augsburger Stadtlexicon* (Augsburg, 1998), p. 414.

sacred spaces, since they were typically located on or near the sacralised ground of churches or chapels. Especially for Catholic patricians, burial in consecrated land at the sacred centre of the community – the parish church – helped constitute their elite social status. In medieval Germany, only the dishonoured and those who died during epidemic plagues were buried outside of the city. In contrast to Catholic thinking, Luther denied the sacrality of the cemetery altogether, just as he had argued that the physical structure of churches themselves held no special sacred power. As Koslofsky notes, Luther advocated extramural burial in part because he acknowledged the arguments concerning health concerns and in part because he saw the cemetery as a profane space with no inherent sacred worth.[50]

In Augsburg, however, the association of extramural burial with Lutheranism does not hold true, for Lutherans clung to their intramural cemetery. To abandon the cemetery by St Stephan after the Peace of Westphalia would have meant abandoning one of the properties granted to them by the Normal Year of 1624. Thus, the Lutherans in Augsburg eagerly claimed the intramural cemetery, not because it was inherently sacred, but because it had strategic worth in the confessional competition over civic space. But while this topographical configuration seems to contradict Koslofsky's findings, in one important sense it does not. The cemeteries became places that marked and reinforced the spatial distance between the Catholic and Lutheran communities. In this sense, the creation of distinct places of burial was intended to impose order on the confessional landscape by creating boundaries to separate Catholics and Lutherans, both living and dead.

Like the two cemeteries, other institutional spaces in Augsburg were spatially divided into Catholic and Lutheran sites. Even apparently secular institutions such as the city orphanages and poorhouses were doubled, one each for Lutherans and Catholics.[51] While this institutional doubling was typical, a few spaces were shared by both confessions, including Augsburg's sanitarium and hospital. However, shared space could produce confessional trouble. For example, Lutherans complained that Catholics recited the Ave Maria too loudly and too often in the sanitarium, while Catholics in the hospital grumbled about the Protestant

[50] C. M. Koslofsky, *The Reformation of the Dead: Death and Ritual in Early Modern Germany, 1450–1700* (London and New York, 2000).
[51] On Augsburg's civic institutions, see François' *Die unsichtbare Grenze*. On Augsburg's orphanages, see Thomas Max Safley, *Charity and Economy in the Orphanages of Early Modern Augsburg* (Atlantic Highlands, 1997).

hymns sung by Lutheran patients.[52] Such conflicts highlight the utility of doubling most urban institutional spaces. By spatially distancing Catholics and Lutherans, the magistrates hoped to preserve order both within and between the two religious communities.

But even the decision to separate certain Catholic and Lutheran institutional spaces did not always succeed in preventing people on the ground from troubling the confessional map imposed from above. Such was the case with Apolonia Frischhauptin, an unmarried Protestant woman originally from Ulm who had been confined in Augsburg's Lutheran *Zuchthaus* (literally, a disciplinary house), probably for begging. In 1720, Frischhauptin fled her confinement and appeared before the Catholic mayor to ask for his protection, for she wanted to convert to Catholicism.[53] Not yet knowing where she had fled, the Lutheran mayor issued a warrant for her arrest in order to return her to the *Zuchthaus*. By the eighteenth century, many cities had created similar institutions, which fused the spatial segregation and physical confinement of delinquents with a daily regimen of moral discipline based on religious observances and forced labour. The *Zuchthaus* rid the streets of beggars and other morally suspect people in an attempt to empty the city of unwanted social pollution.[54] Although the archival documents do not narrate the conclusion of Frischhauptin's story in full, the evidence suggests that her conversion had secured her the formal political protection of the Catholic mayor and her release from Lutheran custody. Shortly after these events, Jacobina Osweldin, also confined in the Lutheran *Zuchthaus*, converted. The Lutheran mayor suspected that the example of that 'brazen woman Apolonia Frischhaubtin' had influenced Osweldin's decision. Although he agreed to turn Osweldin over to the legal jurisdiction of the Catholic political community, this time he insisted that the convert be transferred to the Catholic *Zuchthaus*, where she would still complete the term of confinement originally imposed upon her by the Lutheran authorities.[55]

In Augsburg, where parity demanded the creation of separate but equal institutions for the two faiths, the founding of both a Catholic and a Lutheran *Zuchthaus* (along with separate civic charities, hospitals and orphanages) reaffirmed the institutional autonomy of the two competing communities. It also limited the sites where confessional contact – and hence conflict – might occur. By building two separate *Zuchthäuser*, the

---

[52] StAAug, KWA E14[3], letters dated 27 July 1651, 2 September 1651.
[53] StAAug, Reichsstadt Akten 841, 1720, letter dated 11 March 1720.
[54] See R. Jütte's *Poverty and Deviance in Early Modern Europe* (Cambridge, 1994), pp. 174–5.
[55] StAAug, Reichsstadt Akten 841, various letters dated 11 March 1720.

magistrates reinforced a set of practices existing since 1648; they were forging an urban landscape in which the space was confessionally fragmented but carefully ordered, divided but nonetheless highly organised. Yet in the two cases discussed above, the act of conversion disrupted the biconfessional organisation of the urban landscape and challenged official attempts to create a spatial order that would preserve religious order both within and between the two confessional communities. Crossing the boundary of belief through conversion involved crossing spatial boundaries, but while in other cities that usually meant some sort of exile from one's home town, for Apolonia Frischhauptin and Jacobina Osweldin, it potentially promised freedom from confinement in a Lutheran disciplinary space.[56] Conversion for these two women represented a useful strategy that took advantage of the instability of the official biconfessional landscape. Individuals could relocate themselves within new confessional boundaries through the act of changing faiths, but only by leaving the spaces belonging to their prior community of belief. In an age when city magistrates vigorously imposed religious conformity through the organisation of the urban landscape in order to protect social and political order, conversion represented an act of *non-conformity* that transgressed the social, cultural, and physical boundaries between Catholics and Lutherans.

The creation of Catholic and Lutheran confessional communities required imposing boundaries to separate one faith from another. In part, these boundaries consisted of intangible cultural and social distinctions between Catholics and Lutherans. But urban authorities also inscribed abstract religious distinctions into the tangible, physical landscape. Catholic and Lutheran interactions on the street, the marketplace, or the churchyard represented a potential threat to civic order, either because such interactions might lead to violent confrontation or to corrupting influences resulting in conversion. From the perspective of secular and ecclesiastical authorities, the best way to avoid these possibilities was to vigorously monitor the confessional landscape internally and along its borders. Secular magistrates therefore assisted the ecclesiastical authorities in the project of imposing religious conformity within the boundaries of the confessional community well into the eighteenth century. They also attempted to minimise the moments when either their citizens or outsiders crossed over those boundaries. But such moments nevertheless happened. The conversion of Apolonia Frischhauptin in

---

[56] For an overview of conversion and migration, see D. Corpis, 'The geography of religious conversion: crossing the boundaries of belief in southern Germany, 1648–1800', unpublished PhD thesis (New York University, 2001).

the Augsburg *Zuchthaus* is but one example of how transgressing the boundary of belief challenged the city government's attempts both to organise urban space into a uniform confessional landscape and to use space as a means to discipline the behaviour of city dwellers. In everyday practice, space was much more dynamic, contested and negotiated than the rigid maps that competing confessional authorities used to imagine their urban landscapes.

# Index

*A choice drop of seraphic love* (1734) 117
abbeys 4, 22, 249
abbots 23, 32, 151
Aberdeen 84, 99, 100
Aberdeenshire 99
Abergavenny 221
Abraham 41
academies 279
Accession day 107
accidental death 136
acoustics 243, 265
Act of Union (Brittany) (1532) 239
*Acts and Monuments of These Latter and Perilous Days* (1563) 37
Acts of Parliament 88
Adam 164, 194
Adam, Karl 293
adoration of images 47, 55, 56, 213
*Against the Heavenly Prophets in the Matter of Images and Sacraments* (1525) 41, 46, 48
age and the elderly 9–10, 34, 58, 108, 133, 143, 311
Agen 240
Agincourt, battle of (1415) 213
Águeda 199
aisles 128–9, 130, 133, 134, 135, 141, 250
Aix-en-Provence 266
Alba, Duke of 207
Albigensians 299
Alcalá 198
Alcántara, Pedro de 196
Aldersey, Hugh 134
Aldersey, William 134
Aled, Tudur 213
Alehouses, *see* taverns
ales and beers 18, 22, 28, 31
Alès, Peace of (1629) 263
Alexandru cel Bun 149, 155
Alexandru Lăpuşneanu 153, 154, 155
Al-Hajari 119
Alkmaar 119

All Saints' Day 263
Alldridge, N. 132
Alps 282
altar cloths 312
altars and altarpieces 5, 9, 39, 40, 41, 43, 45, 46, 47, 48, 50, 54, 55, 56, 57, 58, 59, 68, 72, 75, 83–4, 85, 88, 104, 114, 119, 124, 127, 130, 133, 134, 144, 147, 150, 151–6, 177, 216, 243, 244–5, 250, 254, 273, 285–6, 288, 307, 311
Altdorf 57
Altötting 31, 220, 228, 230
America and the Americas 1, 193, 207
amphitheatres 268, 269, 278–9
Amsterdam 137
Anastasia Bubuog 159
Anastasis 164
Anabaptists and Anabaptism 27, 31, 33, 42
*Anatomie de la messe et du messel* 65
ancestors, *see* kin
anchorites 4, 163, 193, 195, 196, 248, 249
Ancient of Days 160
Andechs, Holy Mountain of 34, 317
Andrews, Lancelot 98, 102
Angelic Salutation 50, 53
angels 65, 86, 94, 159, 206, 209, 210, 249, 250, 291, 294
Angelsey 137
Anglo-Saxons 225
animals 245
*Annales Ecclesiastici* (1588–1607) 171, 175, 176
Annunciation 294
*Answer to Valetin Campar* (1525) 46
Anthony of Padua 299
Antichrist 94, 219, 229
anti-popery 42, 72, 100, 218, 228, 230, 233, 235
antiquarians 232
Antwerp 190

Ap Rees, Evan 137
apostles 84, 97, 161, 164, 192, 225, 239, 250, 256, 299
apprentices 36
apse 78, 146, 160, 178, 244
Arbore 159, 160
Arbore, Ana 159
Arbore, Iuliana 159
Arbore, Luca 159
Arbore, Nichita 159
Arbore, Toader 159
archaeology 3, 16, 144, 147, 149, 150, 152
arches 244, 245, 271
Archilleus 124
architects and architecture 3, 9, 45, 84, 145, 166, 206, 213, 216, 232, 262, 271, 282, 283, 312
arcosolium 159
Argol 244
Aringhi, Paolo 189, 190
Aristotle 16, 191
Ark of the Covenant 94–5
arms, see heraldry
Arnage 34
Arnheim 189
art, artists and artistic heritage 3, 14, 35, 41, 46, 48, 53, 213, 216, 244, 282, 292
articles 122
artisans 21, 23, 26, 277, 307, 315
ascetics and asceticism 159, 163, 195, 199, 205, 206, 209
ashes 271
Ashmolean Museum, Oxford 232
Askew, John 137
aspergillum 44
assizes, see courts and court records
Assumption of the Virgin 50
Aston, M. 12, 46, 132
atmosphere 45
Augsburg 23, 25, 299, 303, 304–6, 312, 318, 321–4
  Barfüsser Kirche 305
  Bishopric of 302
  Cathedral 321
  Gögginer Gate 321
  mayors of 304, 323
  Red Gate 321
  Sanitarium 322
  St Jacob's Chapel 312
  St Stephan 321, 322
  St Ulrich and St Afra 312–13
  The Three Moors 23
  Zuchthaus 323–4, 325
Augustinians 292

aural experiences, see sounds and soundscapes
Auray, Brittany 251, 252
Ave Maria 242, 322
Avignon 260, 261, 262, 266, 277
awe and reverence 43, 112, 116, 117, 122, 232

Baal 111, 199
Babylon 196
Bačkovo 160
Badone, E. 238
Baia, Battle of (1467) 155
Bale, John 224
Balkans 149
ballads 36, 105
Baltic 40, 46
Bamberg 58
Bancroft, Richard, Archbishop of Canterbury 111
banners, see flags
baptism 36, 43, 67, 73, 92, 98, 99, 100, 102, 136, 137–8, 221, 242, 243, 270, 299, 312
baptismal registers, see parish registers
bards 213
barefoot (Carmelites) 195, 210, 229, 305
Barfoot 123
Barnes, Anne 135
Barnes, Rowland 135, 141
barns 45, 95
Baronio, Cesare 167, 170–8, 179, 190
baroque 6, 11, 14, 51, 195, 210, 230, 243, 282, 283
barricades 296
bars 92, 228
Barstow, Mr 123
basilicas 144, 148–9, 164, 170, 172, 184, 211, 312
Basingwerk Abbey 217
Basingwerk, Flintshire 213
basins 92, 308
Baslow, Derbyshire 113
bastardy, see illegitimacy
Bath, Somerset 229, 235
battle sites 162
Batz 248
Bavaria 19, 21, 22, 23, 25, 26, 27, 31, 32, 33, 33, 34, 36, 220
bawdy houses 23, 24
Bayerbach, Bavaria 27
Bayley, Lewis, Bishop of Bangor 228
beads 250
beadsmen 115
bears 114

Beaufort, Lady Margaret 213
Bechteler, Caspar 288
Bede 173
beds and bedrooms 95, 199
beer, see ales
beggars, see the poor
belfries 71–2
Bellenden, Adam 93, 98, 99, 102
bells 14, 43, 71, 105, 108, 117, 118, 120,
    129, 264, 265, 266, 315
bema, see sanctuary 144
benches, see seating
Benedictines 21, 212, 250
benedictions, see blessings
Benfeld, Alsace 33
Benham brothers 35
Bennett, John 222
Bentham, Thomas, Bishop of Coventry
    and Litchfield 116
Berlin 285, 290
Bern 19, 22, 23, 26, 27, 28, 29, 31, 32,
    33, 34, 67
Bernard, Père 240, 249
Bernini, Gian Lorenzo 296
Bethlehem 195
Betzenstein 57
Bèze, Théodore de 76
Bible 14, 26, 33, 73, 90, 95, 172, 284,
    285, 314, see also Old Testament and
    Word of God
Bickley, Thomas, Bishop of Chichester
    107
Birnie, William 90, 91, 93
Birr, Bernese Aargau 31
bishop's transcripts 126
bishops 19, 23, 34, 42, 83, 84–6, 93, 98,
    99, 100, 107, 114, 115, 119, 151, 161,
    218, 238, 241, 242, 248, 249, 256,
    266, 275, 302, 309, 312, 320, 321
Bistrita 144, 149, 155
blacksmiths 288
Blacon, Cheshire 125, 140
Blacons, Alexandre 268
Blair, Robert 96
blasphemy 26, 31, 57, 272, 273, 277, 294,
    300, 306
blessings 43, 47, 48, 59, 102, 200
blood 92, 94, 184, 218, 224
Blundell family 230
Blythburgh, Suffolk 117, 118
Bocennu, Brittany 251
bodies 38, 64, 94, 178, 184, 193, 209,
    210, 211, 245, 256
Bogdan 146, 147, 150
Bogdan III 156, 162
Bohemia 6, 45, 282–301

Bolarque 198, 202, 205
Boller, John 114
bones, see relics
bonfires 252
Book of Canons (1636) 82, 85–6
Book of Common Order (Scottish) (1556)
    81–2
Book of Common Prayer (English) (1559)
    81
Book of Martyrs, see Acts and Monuments of
    These Latter and Perilous Days 37
books 101, 223, 225, 283, 293
Bordeaux 240
borders, of Scotland 93
Borgia, Francis 294
Borromeo, Carlo 184
Boschet, Antoine 237, 242, 248
Bosio, Antonio 164, 166, 167, 172, 178,
    190
Bosio, Giacomo 169, 170
bosses 213
Bottari, Giovanni 189
boundaries and borders 9, 23, 28, 47, 55,
    124, 134, 135, 194, 196, 199, 252, 259,
    260, 262, 265, 266, 280, 302, see also
    liminality
Bourbon dynasty 260, 273, 275
bowing, see prostration
boyars 145, 153–4
Boydle, Robert 134
Boyleyn, George, Dean of Lichfield 120
boys 28
Boyton, Cornwall 113
Bradley, R. 252
Brandenburg 36, 43, 48
Brandl, Peter 292
Braun, Matthias 283, 292, 296
bread 118, 254
Brechin 84
breviaries 172, 213
breweries 22
Bridgeman, Sir John 228
bridges 20, 28, 29, 31, 271
Briggs, R. 258
Brigognan, Brittany 256
Britain 2, 98, 212, 219, 224, 229, 233
Britannia Sancta (1745) 225
Brittany 220, 237–58, 276, 280
Brokoff, Ferdinand 294, 298, 310
Brome, John 231
Bromfield, Mrs 134
Brookes, John 136
Browne, Ellen 137
Bruce, Robert 94, 97
Bruck, Bavaria 33
Bruyn, John 134

Bucer, Martin 109
bull baiting 117
Bullinger, Heinrich 65, 87, 89
bullocks, *see* cattle
Buñuel, Luis 209
burial 10, 72, 88, 89, 93, 98, 124–43,
    144–66, 179, 180, 245, 254, 256,
    266–7, 270, 280, 321–2
Bury St Edmunds 111
busts, *see* statues
butchers 31, 114
Buxaco 199, 205
Buxton, Derbyshire 217, 235
Byzantine Empire 145, 149–50, 151–2,
    156, 162, 200

Caernarvon 233
Caesar 269
Caius, John 114
cakes 48
Calderwood, David 94
calendar 13, 51, 167, 172–3, 260, 272,
    314, 316
Calne, Wiltshire 115
calvaries, *see* crosses
Calvin, Jean 4, 46, 62, 63–5, 68, 71, 73, 74,
    76, 86–7, 97, 109, 203, 284, 285, 301
Calvinism i, 2, 6, 17, 237, 259–81, 284–7,
    301
Camaldolesi 195
Cambridge 197
    Peterhouse 102
Cambridgeshire 118
Canada 240
canals, *see* waterways
candles 14, 43, 55, 57, 58, 59, 73, 179,
    183, 211, 219, 274, 292, 316
Canisius, Peter 204
cannon 108, 273, 278
canopies 51, 70, 76, 272
Canterbury, Cathedral 122
Canterbury, Province of 213
canticles 240
Capel Meugan, Pembrokeshire 218
Cappadocia 144, 163
captives 299
Capuchins 251, 269, 276
Caradoc, prince and decapitator 211
Cardigan 217
cardinals 177
Careless, John 111
carillons 265
Carleton, Sir Dudley 232
Carmelites 11, 210, *see also* barefoot
Carnival 172, 308
carpet 83

Cartaro, Mario 170
Carthusians 195
cartography 14, 170
Casentino 195
Castanizqa, Juan de 195
Castel, Y. 247
Castille 195, 197, 200
catacombs 171–2, 178, 179, 183, 190
*Catechism of the Church of Geneva* (1542)
    61–4
catechisms and catechising 221, 237, 238,
    240, 243, 247, 321
catechumens 151
*Cathedra Petri* 175
cathedrals 4, 9, 14, 82, 83, 84–5, 87, 88,
    102, 115, 122, 212, 249, 256, 285, 317
Cathelan, Antoine 72, 76
Catherine of Aragon 213
Catholic Reformation 3, 6–7, 11, 12, 16,
    167–92, 193–210, 211–36, 237–58,
    259–81, 282–301
Catholics and Catholicism i, 2, 4, 5, 6, 7,
    9, 16, 17, 19, 26, 28, 32, 33, 34, 39, 41,
    42, 43, 44, 47, 51–2, 54, 58, 59, 72, 81,
    83, 86, 92, 100, 108, 144–66, 167–92,
    211–36, 259–81, 283–301, 302, *see also*
    recusancy
cats 115, 308
cattle 57, 120, 219, 310
caves 4, 95, 164, 202, 206
Caxton, William 213
Cay, Elizabeth, Viscountess Falkland 228
Cecil, William, Lord Burghley 218, 219
Cedars of Lebanon 199
Cedron 254
cells 196, 199, 206, 209, 210
cemeteries, *see* churchyards and cemeteries
censers and censing 42
ceremonial, *see* rituals, rites and
    ceremonials
chalices 31, 273, 294
Challoner, Richard 225
Chamberlain, John 232
chancellors
chancels and the east end of churches
    39–59, 83, 85, 116, 118–19, 120, 127,
    129, 130, 133, 134, 137, 243, 244
chantries 5, 87–8, 128, 132
chapels i, 4, 9, 12, 13, 14, 18, 19, 20, 23,
    24, 41, 45, 49, 70, 75, 82, 85, 87, 88,
    99, 102, 121, 124, 150, 160, 199, 213,
    216, 217, 219, 221, 222, 230, 232,
    235, 239, 244, 245, 248, 251, 252,
    254, 263, 264, 273, 279, 282, 301, 312
Chapels Royal 82, 84
Charenton 271

charity 240, 246, 247, 257, 294
Charlemagne 46
Charles I of Scotland and England 81–2, 95, 129, 228
Charles IV, Holy Roman Emperor 50, 291
Charles V, Holy Roman Emperor 195
charnel houses 244, 245
chastity 201–3
Châtellier, L. 241, 248, 276
Cheddar, Somerset 113
cherubim, see angels
Cheshire:
    county of 137, 233
    Sheriffs of 131, 134
    Cathedral 126, 134
    Holy Trinity 124–43
    mayor of 229
    Palatinate of 126
    Roodeye 125
    St John 132, 134
    St Oswald 134
    St Peter 135
    St Werburgh 134
    Watergate 125
Chichester 107
    diocese of 118–19
chickens 310
childbirth 135
children 44, 77, 78, 99, 100, 112, 115–16, 119, 121, 123, 130–1, 134, 136, 137–9, 150, 157, 158, 221, 242, 252, 273, 299, 304, 311, 318–21
Chilterns 20
choir (as group) 107, 111
choir (as zone) 31, 45, 48, 51, 68, 69, 70, 75, 78, 84, 85, 130, 151, 250
choir screens see screens
Chora (Kariye Djami) 150
chrism 42
Christendom 280
Christian, W. 214
Christinger, R. 16
Christmas 82, 118, 168, 251, 286, 287
Chronicle of Dalimil (1314) 289
church ales 7, 18
church goods 31
Church of England 122, 123, 228
church orders and ordinances 40, 41, 43, 46, 48
churches, parochial i, 4, 5, 6, 9, 10, 11, 13, 17–38, 39–59, 60–80, 81, 84, 87, 88, 93, 96, 98, 99, 103, 104, 124–43, 144–66, 169, 212, 242, 243, 244, 250, 252, 254, 257, 259, 263, 270, 274, 280, 283, 284–7, 305, 311, 312, 313, 314, 315, 319, 322

churching 136, 137
churchwardens 31, 32, 114, 116, 126, 130, 131, 133, 137, 217, 228
churchwardens' accounts 2, 106, 108, 113–14, 128, 130, 131
churchyards and cemeteries 9, 10, 11, 12, 42–3, 44, 46, 57, 93, 98, 104, 124, 130, 134, 135, 136–43, 242, 244, 245, 254, 266, 267, 270, 272, 279, 280, 299, 304, 309, 310, 311, 321–2, 324
Cink, Martin 291, 293
Cistercians 213, 221, 292, 294, 296
cities see urban centres
city walls see walls
civic culture 12, 302
civic offices and officers 298, 303, 310, 314
Clark, P. 17
class consciousness 166
Clement I, Pope 176
Clement X, Pope 222
clergy 4, 9, 20, 22–3, 23, 27–9, 31, 33–4, 36, 45, 45, 57, 58, 62, 68, 71, 74, 75, 76, 77, 78, 82, 86, 89, 90, 93, 94, 96–7, 98, 104, 105–6, 116, 117–18, 134, 145, 151, 163, 168, 203, 213, 220, 221, 222, 228, 229, 231, 235, 237, 238, 240, 241, 242, 243, 244, 246, 248, 249, 259, 261–2, 266, 268, 269–70, 272, 273, 277, 278, 279, 284, 286, 291, 298, 299, 304–6, 307, 311, 312, 314, 315–16, 317, see also preachers and preaching
clocks 129
Clodock 113
cloisters 199, 317
clothing 74, 90, 178, 195, 210, 230, 234, 311, 318, see also vestments
cloths 83, 92, 99
Clynnog Fawr, Caernarvon 113, 219
Clynnog, Morgan 221
Clyve, Richard 130, 133
coast 240, 248
coffins, see sarcophagi
collection boxes 217, see also poor boxes
colleges 76, 87, 229, 240, 241, 262
Cologne 189
columns 282, 291, 301
commandments 42, 55, 61, 73, 76, 123, 238
commissioners 264
communion tables 5, 31, 45, 66, 68, 76, 83, 85, 118–19, 130, 261
communion, see Eucharist
communities and communality 7, 11, 12, 23, 24, 25, 28, 31, 33, 34, 35, 37–8, 41, 42, 59, 72, 77, 79, 117, 124–43,

190, 259, 260, 263, 264, 266, 272, 273, 294, 317–25
compounds (monastic) 206
Comtat Venaissin 267, 277
Concordat of Bologna (1516) 239
concubinage 242
confession 227, 238, 240
Confession of Augsburg (1530) 55, 304
confessional conflict 56, 59, 259, 265
confessionalisation 17, 245
confirmation 82
confraternities 75, 213, 223, 243, 244, 246, 250, 272, 276, 278, 294, 316
congregations 4, 45, 56, 75, 78, 79, 82, 85, 86, 87–8, 89, 90, 93, 94, 95, 96, 97, 105, 106–23, 271, 311
consecration 39, 41, 42, 43, 46, 48, 59, 65, 84, 86–7, 89, 90, 91, 97–103, 104, 125, 127, 142, 143
consistories 26, 28, 31, 32, 78
Constantine, Emperor 174
Constantinople 150
Constantinople, Patriarchate of 148
conventicles 96, 98
convents 270, 283, see also nuns and nunneries
copes 83
Corcelles 23
Corinthians 300
Cornouaille 240, 252, 254
Cornwall and Cornish 237, 241
coronation of the Virgin 50
coronations 82
coroners 136
corpses, see bodies
Corpus Christi 54, 55–6, 272–3, 316
corridors 178
Corseul, Brittany 252
cosmology 16, 47, 206
Cotgrave, John 135
Council of the Marches 218, 227
Council of Trent 6, 34, 54, 172, 175, 180, 220, 221, 222, 224, 231, 238, 241, 243, 244, 246, 276, 280, 320
councils and corporations, civic 48, 50, 53, 56, 68, 100, 134, 271, 299, 303–4, 305, 307–8, 309, 312, 315, 316, 318, 319
Counter-Reformation, see Catholic Reformation
Court of Augmentations 217
courtiers 145
courts and court records 2, 4–6, 7, 26, 28, 31, 32, 92, 117, 218, 228, 243, 306, 307, 313
courtyards 41

covers and coverings 50, 54, 57, 69
Cox, J. Charles 120–1
Crachley, Richard 138
craftsmen 125, 282, 292
Cranach workshop 40, 46
Cranach, Lucas 286
Creed (Apostles') 62
Creed 242
Cressy, D. 127
Crier, Widow 138
crime and criminal behaviour 24, 56
Cristoforo, Roncalli 177
Croix, A. 238, 245, 247, 249
Cromwell, Thomas, Earl of Essex 216
crosses 4, 41, 46, 48, 51, 53, 57, 71–2, 79, 88, 97, 192, 196, 199, 200, 207, 221, 239, 244, 245, 248, 254, 264, 266, 275–8, 285–7, 288, 291, 296
crossroads 139, 276
Crouzet, D. 259
Crown, policy of, in Scotland 81, 84, 94, 100–2
Crown of Thorns 207
crowns 162, 184
Crucifixion 222, 256, 276
crusades 230
crypts 146
crystal 230
Cuhea 147
Culford, Suffolk 121
cult of the Saints, see saints
cultivation 172
Culworth, Lancashire 113–22
cupboards 71
customs houses 28
cyberspace 15
cycles, see time
Czech 300

D'Argentré, Bertrand 239
Dairsie, Fife 85, 102
Dällenbach, Christian 31
Dalmeny 100
dances and dancing i, 7, 26, 28, 33, 35, 111, 233, 242, 248, 309, 310, 314
Daniell, C. 135
Daniil 164
Danzig 44
  Marienkirche 44
Dauling, Robert 100
Dauphiné 261, 262
Davies, Lowry 233
Davies, Richard, Bishop of St Davids 219
Davis, N. Z. 1, 60, 259
Day of Penance and Prayer 314–15, 317
De Bus, César 26

*De Canibus Britannicis* (1570) 114
De Cannes, Honoré 276–7
De Chambrun, Jacques Pineton 261, 274–8, 279
De Colombier, Simon 262
De Jesús María Doria, Nicholás 197–8
De Jesús María, Alonso 198
De Jesús María, Diego 201, 205
De Jesús, Diego 199
De Jesús, Fray Tomás 197–8, 199, 200, 201, 203, 204, 208
De Jesús, Juan 198
De La Cerda, Doña Bernarda Ferreira 205
De la Flor, F. 193, 199, 209
De la Madre de Dois, Beatriz 202
De la Miseria, Juan 196
De la Miseria, Mariano 196
De Manuel, Tomás Gonzálex 208
*De martyrologio romano* (1586) 176
De Nacimiento, Cecilia 208
*De ritu sepeliendi mortuos apud veteres christianos et eorundem coemeteriis liber* (1568) 179
De Santa María, Francisco 198, 202, 203, 204
De Santa Teresa, José 202
De Solms Ursule 270
De Vega, Lope 207
De Witte, Emanuel 119
dean and chapter, or dean and canons 115, 256, 284, 286, 288, 297
death and the dead 4, 10–11, 43, 93, 124, 180, 184, 218, 244–7, 250, 254, 259, 266, 270, 280, 291, 294, 318, 321, 322, *see also* burial; tombs and mausoleums *and* accidental death
debauchery, *see* immorality
decoration and ornament 68, 73, 74, 84
dedication of churches 4, 35, 41, 43, 95, 162, 250
Dee, River 125, 136
*Deesis* 159, 160–1
defecation 121, 307
Delumeau, J. 238
demons and the demonic 194, 207, 227
Denbigh 113
Denbighshire 222
Derfel Gadarn 217
desacralisation 6, 263
desecration 31, 40, 42, 44, 46, 92–3, 117, 118, 217, 228, 266, 283, 290, 307–8, 312
deserts, *see* wilderness
desks 120, 131
Despotus, Jacobus Heraklides 152

Devil 18, 25, 31, 42, 161, 168, 203, 207, 216–17, 287
Devonport 139
Dickson, David 96, 97–8
Die, academy of 262
*Die Beruehmte Prager-Bruecke und ihre Statuen* (1827) 294
Diefendorf, B. 259
Dientzenhofer family 283
diet 199
Diet, Imperial 56
Dietrich, Veit 56
Digby, Sir Everard 229
Dillingen 302
Dinkelsbühl 303, 306–7
Diocletian, emperor 176, 297
Discaled, *see* barefoot
disease 26, 36, 56, 115, 140–2, 143, 227, 249, 250, 322
Dissolution of the Monasteries 216
divination 254
divinity and the divine 146, 158, 209, 242, 251, 280
Dixon, S. 57
Dobrovăţ 153, 155, 160, 161
Dod, Anne 135
Dod, Hugh 135
dogs 44, 92, 105, 113, 310
dogwhippers 113, 310
Dohna, Christopher, governor of Orange 267, 270, 271
Dolan, F. 7
Dolheştii Mari 160
Dominicans 237, 240, 250, 273, 292, 294, 300
Domitian, Emperor 174
donations 55
Donauwörth 302
donkeys 25, 267, 270
Donne, John 112
doom paintings 14
doors 47, 92, 100, 116, 120, 129, 130, 131, 133, 137, 310–17
Downlee, Edward 219
Dowsing, William 15
drama and dramatists 207
Drayton, Michael 232
Dresden 292, 293
dress, *see* clothing
Drinkwater, Thomas 134, 138
druids 233, 254
drunkenness 25, 238, 282, 306, 307
Dublin, Synod of (1634) 98
Duffy, E. 56, 283
Dundas, George 100

Duperac, Etienne 170
Durham Cathedral 85
Durkheim, E. 11, 13, 17
Duruelo 196
dust 257
Dutch 268, 278, 279, *see also* Holland *and* Netherlands
dynasties 100, 146, 162, 166, 214, 220

earth 208
earthquakes 107, 109–13, 221
East Anglia 15
East Dereham, Norfolk 113
east end of church, *see* chancels and the east end of churches
Easter 27, 31, 82, 95, 172, 238, 261, 314
Easter Sunday 316
Eden 194, 205, 208, 210
Edict of Toleration (1607) 260, 268, 269, 278
edicts of pacification 264
Edinburgh 93, 95–6, 100
Edinburgh, Provost of 95
Edinburgh, St Giles 82, 85
Edinburgh, Tron Church 93
education 318–21
Edward IV of England 213
Edward VI of England 129
Eggiwil 34
Egypt 170
*Eigentlicher Entwurff und Vorbildung der votrefflichen kostbahren und Welt-berühmten Prager Brucken* (1716) 293
El Burgo 199
El Greco 195
Elbe, River 42
elders 78
election 62
Eleutherius 225
Elgin 87
Eliade, M. 1
Elijah 198, 199, 200–1, 203, 204
Elisabeta of Moldavia 156
Elishah 200
Elizabeth I of England 129
Elouan 249
Eltersdorf 57, 58
Emmental 31, 34
Emperors, Byzantine 150
England and the English 11, 17, 19, 20, 26, 27, 36, 39, 46, 56, 81, 83, 84, 92, 98–9, 102, 104–23, 124–43, 288, 290
English Civil Wars 15, 229

engraving and engravings 40, 40, 225, 232, 262
Enlightenment 23, 25, 208
epitaphs 158
Epsom, Surrey 235
Erfurt 32
eschatology 146, 160, 161, 194, 310
Escorial 195
Essenes 200
Essex 229
estates (provincial) 239, 242, 268
estates of Bohemia 284
Eucharist 14, 23, 34, 39, 44, 44, 45, 46, 51, 54, 57, 61, 62, 66–7, 68, 73, 75, 76, 79, 82, 83–4, 85, 87, 94, 95, 96–7, 98, 100, 101, 118, 121, 178, 180, 227, 230, 238, 243, 249, 254, 272, 273–4, 280, 306, 307, 309, 310, 315, 321
Eudes, Jean 241
Evangelists 84, 250
Evans, Humphrey 222
Evans, Mary 135
Evans, Thomas 135
Eve 164
Everard, Mr 228
evil 161
excommunication 61, 100–2, 136
executions 136, 155, 159–60, 230, 266, 291, 294
Exodus 285
explosives 279

façades 70, 269, 312
fairs 35, 248
Falconer, John 223
family 36, 75, 131, 133, 134–5, 138, 139, 141, 143, 147, 150, 151, 152, 153–6, 159, 190, 204, 252, 254, 267, 317
famine 314
Farel, Guillaume 67, 68, 73
Farineaux, Antoine 266, 268
farmers 251, 306
fasting 31, 197, 202, 296
Fathers of the Church 168, 196, 200, 204, 209
fauna 194, 209
feast days and festivities 35, 50, 51, 54, 55, 58, 162, 164, 172, 174, 202, 211, 213, 219, 222, 228, 242, 248, 251, 252, 263, 267, 316, *see also* holidays and holy days
Feast of the Assumption 175
Feast of the Circumcision 200
feasting 33
Featley, Daniel 112

Ferdinand I, Holy Roman Emperor 286
Ferdinand II, Holy Roman Emperor 283
Fernbalm, Bern 33
Ferrer, Vincent 237, 298, 299
festivals, *see* feast days and festivities
Fethiye Camii 150
fields 97, 221, 247, 251
Fiennes, Celia 230, 234
*Fifty Godly and Learned Sermons Divided
    Into Five Decades* (1549–51)
fighting 31, 44, 115, 118, 121, *see also*
    violence
fire and incineration 83, 110, 217, 250,
    285, 286
firearms 263
*First Book of Discipline* (1561) 87, 89, 98
fish 44
Five Articles of Perth (1625) 82, 85, 91,
    94
Flacius Illyricus, Matthias 203
flags 277, 316, 318
Flanders 197
Fleetwood, William, Bishop of Ely 231,
    235
Fletcher, Thomas 141
Flint 228
Flintshire 222
floods 291
floors and flooring 70, 85
flora 194, 206, 209, 248
folklore and folklorists 24, 120, 218, 233,
    257
fonts 5, 15, 43, 45, 129, 133
food and drink 17–38, 314, *see also* feasting
football 227
Forbes, Patrick, Bishop of Aberdeen 84
forests, *see* woods and forests
*Form of Prayer and Ecclesiastical Songs*
    (1542) 61–4
fornication, *see* sex, sexuality and sexual
    offences
Forrest, John 217
Forster, M. 51
Fortescue, Mrs Anne 227
fortifications 262–3, 275, 316, *see also*
    walls
Foster, M. 220
Foucault, M. 15
founders (of churches) 145, 151–2, 153,
    161
fountains 41, 199, 205, 211–36, 239, 249,
    251, 252, 254
Foxe, John 37, 110, 121, 224
Foxe, Simon 110
Foxley, George 109–10

France 4, 8, 18, 26, 34, 119–20, 121, 220,
    237–58, 259–81, 284, 286
Franciscans 305–6
Franconia 47, 51, 282
Frederick V, of the Palatinate 283, 284–90
Free-willers 111
Freising 21, 25
French (language) 237, 245
French Wars of Religion 242, 245
frescos 177, 178, 312
Freudenstadt, Schwarzwald 45
Fribourg 28, 29
Frischhauptin, Apolonia 323–4, 325
Frisia 282
Froment 67
frontiers 9, 12, 276, *see also* borders, of
    Scotland *and* liminality
funerals, *see* burial
funerary rooms 144–66
furniture and furnishings 45, 50, 66, 68,
    69, 83, 89, 102
Fustennegger, Leonhard 304–5

Galata 155
galleries 45, 50, 57, 129
Gallicus, Nicholas 206
gambling 33, 234, 309, 310
games and gaming 28, 31, 35, 92, 115,
    242, 272, 304, 310, 314
gardens 66, 204, 205, 208, 221, 266, 309
Garnet, John 229
gates 21, 130, 244, 254, 264, 266, 276,
    316
Gaukönigshofen 33
Gee, Henry, mayor of Chester 130
Gee, John 228
gender 9–10, 132–3, 143, 157, 272
genealogy 156, 157
General Assembly of the Church of
    Scotland 82, 98
Genesis 41
Geneva 6, 26, 27, 60–80, 260–1
    Cathedral (Saint-Pierre) 68–70, 71, 75,
    78
    psalm books 106
    Saint-Gervais 69, 70, 78
    Temple of the Madeleine 68, 69, 70
gentiles 86, 202
gentlemen 110, 111, 125, 130, 133, 134,
    135, 228, 229
genuflecting 47, 57, 58, 118, 273, 294
Gerard, John, Father 229
German and Germany 4, 17, 19, 19, 22,
    23, 25, 33, 36, 39–59, 189, 220, 229,
    276, 282, 285, 300, 302

German Peasants' War 303
Gibson, Robert 100–1
gilding 53
Gillespie, R. 221
Gipkyn, John 119–20
girls 28
Giuleşti 148, 149, 150
Glasgow Assembly (1638) 83–4, 93, 97, 99, 100
Glasgow Cathedral 92
glass 312
globe 298, 299
Glorious Revolution 230
gluttony 27
God, as father, as Trinity and as creator 25, 28, 36, 39, 41, 42, 46, 48, 55, 61, 62, 65, 66, 73, 75, 77, 78–9, 85, 86, 89, 90–2, 94, 96, 97, 99, 102, 106, 108, 109–10, 111, 115, 117, 147, 192, 196, 202, 206, 208, 209, 210, 221, 235, 238, 240, 241, 242, 243, 244, 246, 247, 248, 251, 256, 274, 285, 299, 305, 309, 310, 318
godparents 138, 242
gold 41, 51, 74
Goldwell, Thomas, Bishop of St Asaph 223
Golgotha 293
good 161
Good Friday 314
Gordon, John 100
Gospel, see Word of God
gossip 243, 314
Gothic architecture 144, 218, 232
Gothic Revival 39
Gräbern 57
grace 65
Gräfenburg 57
Graff, P. 44, 47
grain 243
Grant, John 229
gravestones 70
graveyards, see churchyards and cemeteries
Great Abington, Cambridgeshire 33
Greece 1
Greenfield Abbey 222
Gregory I (the Great), Pope 177, 178, 225
Gregory XIII, Pope 197
Griffeth, Widow 137
Griffiths, P. 132
grills 51, 288–9
groaning, see sighs and groans
Guadalajara 198
Guarinonius, Hippolytus 18

Guazzelli, Guiseppe 173
Guénin, G. 254
guildhalls 127
Gunpowder Plot 229
Gwytherin 212
Gyttones, Mrs 133

Haarlem 119
habits, see vestments
Habsburg dynasty 282–3
Hacket, William 111
hagiography 179, 183, 212, 213, 223, 231, 239, 248, 250
hair 230
hair shirts 195
halls, village and town 32, 37
Hampshire 135
Hand, Alice 140
Hand, James 140
Harding, V. 126, 127
Harfleur 213
harlots, see prostitutes
Harp, John 137
Harrab, Thomas 108
Harrison, William 107
Harrogate, Yorkshire 235
Harsnett, Samuel, Bishop of Chichester 116, 117
Härtl, Hans 31
hats 123, 204, 290, 292
hawks 114, 117
healing, see sickness and the sick
heathens 285
heaven 16, 28, 61, 99, 202, 209, 210, 235, 294
heavens, see cosmology
Hebrew 300
Hebron 204
Heidelberg 284
hell 16, 164, 209, 288
Helvetic Confessions 65, 73–4, 89
Henderson, Alexander 98
Henrician Reformation 214
Henry IV of France 237, 269
Henry V of England 213
Henry VII of England 213
heraldry 15, 68, 72, 213, 271
herbs 43
heretics and heresy 6, 203, 204, 222, 227, 231, 237–58, 259, 260, 263, 273–4, 276, 280, 281, 282, 291, 294, 298, 299, 301, 302, 305, 306, 317
hermits and hermitages 4, 163, 164, 194–6, 198, 199–200, 206, 208, 209, 210, 240, 298

Hersche, P. 34
Hertfordshire 120
Herz, A. 177
*Hetoimasia* 161
Hicks, Clement 130
Hicks, Ellen 130
hierarchy, *see* status
Hieronymites 195
Higham, Sir John 110
highways 20, 29
Highworth, Wiltshire 114
Hill, Robert 100
Hillger, Hans 292
hills 276
Hinchman, Mr 123
*Histoire de la Bretaigne* (1750–6) 239
*Historia general profetica de la Orden de
    Nuestra Señora del Carmen* (1630) 203
historical writing 239
historiography 155
Holcroft, William 217
Holgate, Robert, Archbishop of York 115
holidays and holy days 26, 28, 32, 82, 260,
    272, 310, 314–15, 316, *see also* feast
    days and festivities
holiness and sanctity as a concept 61–3
Holland 274
holy ground 20, 86
Holy Kindred 50
holy objects 4, 9, 31, 43, 284, 307
Holy Roman Emperor 53, 282, 298, 303
Holy Roman Empire, *see* German and
    Germany
holy sites and places 34, 39
Holy Spirit 61, 64, 65, 109–11
Holy Trinity 61, 160, 238
holy water 42, 44, 48, 272, 273
Holy Week 172, 316
Holy Word, *see* Word of God
Holyrood Abbey 82
Holyrood, Chapel Royal 82, 84
Holywell, Cross Keys 222
Holywell, Flintshire 211
Holywell, the Star 222
Home, Randle 126
homes and houses 13, 27, 28, 46, 65, 66,
    67, 77, 83, 95, 96, 97, 98, 133, 137,
    199, 204, 221, 240, 242, 259, 309,
    319
homilies 106, 178, 285
Hopkins, John 108
Hopwood, Mr 129
Hosios Loukas 160
hospices 211
hospitals 323

Host 175, 272, 273, 294, 315–16,
    317
House of Commons 219
house signs 51
How, Samuel 23
Howard, Lord William of Naworth 228
Howes, Sara 135
Howle, Christopher 138
Hübel, Jakob 286
Huby, Vincent 241
Hughes, Piers 138
Huguenots 8, 119, 259–81
Hüll 57, 58
humanism 168, 169, 170, 179, 223
humility 74
Humor 155, 157, 159, 160, 161
*Hundepeitscher* 44
Hungary 146–7
Huron 240
Hürsch, Johann Jacob 27, 28
Hus, Jan 282, 283, 298, 299
husbandmen 133, 142
husbands 28, 135, 252
Hussite wars 282, 283, 287
Hussites 283, 288, 291
Hutchens, Alice 141
Hutchens, Jane, elder 142
Hutchens, Jane, younger 141
Hutchens, John 141, 142
Hutton, R. 234
hymnals 14

iconoclasm 5, 15, 39, 40, 45, 46, 53, 68,
    216, 221, 228, 263–4, 265, 266, 276,
    277, 283–7, 307, *see also* desecration
*iconostasis, see* templon
icons and iconography 146, 150, 151, 163,
    180, 214, 225, 254, 294–6, 297
idolatry 40, 46, 50, 56, 57, 58, 72, 83, 87,
    88, 89, 94, 127, 217, 218, 232, 272,
    285
Ieremia Movilă 153, 154, 155, 156–60
*Ignea sagitta* (1270) 206
Ilam, Staffordshire 120
Iliaş Rareş 152
illegitimacy 139, 143, 154, 242
imagery 36, 39, 87, 104, 250
images 9, 39, 45, 46, 47, 48, 50, 52–4, 55,
    56, 57, 58, 59, 68, 69, 72, 73, 74, 104,
    129, 155–62, 213, 216, 225, 228, 230,
    243–4, 248, 250, 263, 283, 284, 285,
    290, 301, 316, 317, *see also* adoration of
    images; statues; roadside images and
    crosses
immorality 26, 248

immunity 9
Imperial court 319
Incarnation 238
Ince, Priscilla 137
Ince, Randle 138
Ince, William 137
incense 14
indulgences 211, 213, 223, 246, 248
Ingolstadt 287
injunctions 106, 115–16, 118, 242
innkeepers, see publicans
inns 19–38, 228, 304, 309
inscriptions 162, 174, 245
*Institutes of Christian Religion* (1536) 86,
    284
intercession and intercessors 56, 62, 150,
    158, 159, 160, 161, 162, 163, 166
*Intimation or Proclamation of the Herein
    Discussed Evangelical Jubilee and
    Thanksgiving Festival this Year 1730*
    313–14
Ioanichie (Ion Movilă) 159–60
Ion Rareş 158–9
Iona 85
Ireland 121, 137, 138, 220, 221, 237
Irvine 96
Isabella, Countess of Warwick 213
islands 87, 240–8, 249
Israelites 285
Italy 9, 197
Ivan the Hermit 298
ivory 74

Jäckel, Matthias 294
Jackson, Thomas 111
James Francis Edward, Prince of England
    and Scotland (the 'Old Pretender')
    230
James VI of Scotland and I of England
    81–2
James VII of Scotland and II of England
    230
Jegenstorf 23
Jenner, M. 115
Jermyn, Sir Robert 110
Jerusalem 91, 168, 195, 289
Jerusalem Candelabrum 289–90
Jesuits, see Society of Jesus
Jesus Christ 31, 41, 45, 46, 48, 51, 55, 61,
    62, 63, 73, 75, 77, 78, 83, 89, 94,
    110, 156, 158, 160, 161, 162, 164,
    165, 168, 172, 177, 192, 199, 201,
    202, 204, 239, 245, 246, 248, 276,
    283, 296, 300, 317, 319–21
Jewel, John, Bishop of Salisbury 108

Jews 7, 86, 91–2, 191, 299, 300, see also
    Israelites
Jihlava, Battle of (1436) 283
Joachimstal, Bohemia 45
Johann Georg, Prince of
    Brandenburg-Jägerndorf 285
John XXII, Pope 197
Johnson, Samuel 232
Johnson, T. 220, 247, 256
Jones, N. 8
Joseph 199, 250
journeymen 307–8
Jubilees of the Church 310
Julius Caesar 239, 252
Juncker, Bentz 27
jurisdictions 58
Jussy 71, 73
Justice of the Peace, see magistrates and
    officials
justification by faith 42

Kaiser, Wolfgang 266
Kamenitzky, Joachim 293, 299
Kapihorský, Šimon 285–6
Karant-Nunn, S. 74
Kastoria 164
Kaufbeuren 303, 309, 317–18, 319–21
    Gymnasium 319–21
Kempten 303, 307, 310–12, 318
Kenndek, Jane 137
Kennyough, William 136
Kent 231
Keranna, Brittany 251
kermis 28, 35
Kevelaer 20
keys 100–1
Kickes, Clement 135
kin and kinship 10, 36, 134–5, 139, 162,
    252, 267, 321, see also godparents
kings 151, 202, 213
Kirk of Scotland 81–103
Kirk Sessions 87–8, 92, 95
Kirkwall, Orkney 84
kitchens 200, 301
kneeling, see prostration
Knights, Mary 117, 118
Knox, John 97
Kobelt-Groch, M. 27
Koloritissa 164
Koriša 160
Koslofsky, C. 42, 321–2
Kraft, Adam 51, 54
Krauchthal 23
Krauss, Ulrich 59
Krautheimer, R. 174, 177

La Baux, Provence 275
La Bonne Armelle 254
La Rochelle 271, 275
labourers 26, 125, 136, 142, 247, 279, 304, 307–8, 313
Ladder of Jacob 209, 210
laity 113, 146, 147, 190, 197, 216, 221, 229, 238, 241, 242, 243, 245, 312
Lake, Arthur 111
lakes 252
Lamb of God 290
lamps and lights 54, 55, 56, 293
Lancashire 228
Landévennec 249
landholding and landholders 142, 147, 154
landscape 51, 237–58, 263, 301, 304
Landshut 31
language 241
Languedoc 261, 262
Las Batuecas 198, 200, 201, 206, 207, 208
Las Hurdes 209
*Las Hurdes, Land without Bread* (1932) 209
Las Nieves 198, 199
Last Judgement 43, 160, 161
Last Supper 45
Lațcu of Moldavia 147
Latimer, Hugh, Bishop of Worcester 216
Latin 237, 245, 300, 319, 320
Laud, William, Archbishop of Canterbury 15, 118, 122–3, 129, 140, 228
laudi 172
Laudianism 83–6, 92, 102, 118–19
laundry 310
Lauperswil 31
Lavaur 275
law 25, 26, 91, 94, 145
lawyers 218
laystalls 130, 139
Lazarists 241
Le Bras, G. 18
Le Grand, Albert 239
Le Nobletz, Anne 240
Le Nobletz, Marguerite 240
Le Nobletz, Michel 237, 240–1, 246, 247, 248–9, 250, 252, 254
Lee, John, prebend of Calne 122, 123
Lefebvre, Henri 3, 15
left, *see* right–left polarity
Leipzig 47, 61, 287
Lent 169
Leo III 177
Léon 237, 238, 240, 241, 243, 244, 245, 248
Léon, Plougerneau 240

Leverton, Lincolnshire 113
Lhuyd, Edward 232–3
libraries 199, 223
licences 23
light and illumination 40, 48, 55, 73, 206, 243
lightning 120
lights, *see* lamps and lights *and* candles
liminality 8–10, 17, 133, 194, 199, 208, 260, 268
Lindsay, David, Bishop of Edinburgh 83–4, 86, 90–2, 93, 95, 98, 100–2
lineage, *see* kinship
lions 297
Lippe 19
Lips 150
Liška, J. K. 292
litany 123
literacy and illiteracy 107, 240
Little Crosby, Lancashire 230
Little Neston, Cheshire 233
liturgy and liturgical uses 3, 15, 39, 40, 42, 43, 45, 53, 55, 59, 66, 67, 68, 74–5, 76, 77, 79, 81, 93, 98, 102, 104, 145, 151, 170, 172, 179, 198, 213, 233, 243, 314, 316
Liverpool 130
Liverpool, Katherine 136
Liverpool, William 136
Livingstone, John 96, 97
Llanynys, Denbigh 113
Lobineau, Gui-Alexis 239, 250
local elites and dignitaries 125, 130, 131, 134, 141, 143, 238, 240, 241, 242, 256, 264, 270, 273, 276
Locke, John 271
locks 312, 316
Loctudy, Brittany 256
Lohelius, Jan, Archbishop of Prague 286
London 19, 20, 23, 84, 105–6, 108, 115, 126, 217
    Nag's Head 23
    St Botolph Aldersgate 105
    St Katherine Cree 15
    St Margaret Pattens
    St Mary Woolnoth 106
    St Paul's Cathedral 122
    St Paul's Cross 108, 112, 120
    St Stephen Waldbrook 106
'long reformation' 3
'long sixteenth century' 3
Longe, John 136
Loudun 275
Louis of Nassau 261
Louis XIV of France 270, 275

Lourdes 211, 231
Loys des trespassez (1485) 247
Lübeck 6
Lucius, King 225
Lüder, Wolfgang 48
Ludlow, Shropshire 113–22
Luther, Martin 4, 25, 36, 41–3, 44, 45,
	46, 50, 203, 301, 303, 317, 322
Lutherans and Lutheranism i, 2, 6, 25,
	28, 36, 39–59, 282, 284–5, 287, 288,
	303
Lyon 1, 119

Macht, Matěj Vojtěch 297
Madgeburg Centuriators 203
magic 5, 57, 216, 251, 254, 256
magisterial Reformation 3
magistrates and officials 26, 27, 28, 31,
	34, 68, 69, 70, 134, 141, 218, 233,
	272, 273, 284, 285, 304, 308, 309,
	313, 315, 316, 318, 323, 324
maids, see servants
Mainardo, Agostino 65
Mainz 287
Mair, Hans 305
Maisach 31
Málaga 198
mankind 208
mannerism 178
manors 36
Manresa 195
Mans 34
map galleries 170
maps and mapping 133, 169, 303, 304,
	309, 325
Maramureş 146, 147, 150
Marches of Wales 235, see also Council of
	the Marches
Margam, Glamorganshire 221
Margaret of Moldavia 147
Marghita, Princess 152
Maria, Princess 156
Marian exiles 108, 109–13
markets and market places 12, 47, 49,
	269, 309, 324
Märki, Heinrich 31
Marprelate tracts 119
marriage 242
marriage registers, see parish registers
Marsh, C. 127, 133
Martin V, Pope 213
Martin, Gregory 168, 169, 189–90
Martyr, Peter 108
Martyrologium romanum (1598) 174–6,
	177

martyrs and martyrologies 4, 111, 161,
	163, 167, 173, 178, 189, 192, 217,
	252, 267, 269, 294, 298, 299, 311
Mary I of England 128, 129, 223
Mary of Modena 230
Mary, Queen of Scots 230
masonary, see stones
mass, see Eucharist
Massy, William 130, 141
masters 77
Matha, John of 298, 299, 312
Matsche, F. 301
Maunoir, Julien 237, 280, 281
Maurice of Nassau 262
Maximilian, Duke of Bavaria 26, 230
Maxwell, John, Bishop of Ross 83
Mayer, Felix 36
Mayer, Jan 292
mayors, see local elites and dignitaries
Mayrhofer, Joseph 27
McClain, L. 7
Mean, John 96
meat 40, 44, 199
meeting houses 5, 14
Megara 165
Memmingen 36, 303, 307–8, 310
Memmingen, cloister of the Holy Ghost
	307–8
Memorie sacre delle sette chiese di Roma
	(1630) 179
men 77, 112, 114, 116, 156, 157, 246
mendicant orders 45, 152, 268
Men-Marx, Brittany 252, 256
Menologion 161, 166
mercenaries 262
merchants 96, 134, 137, 141, 252
Merdrignac, B. 239
Merionethshire 217
Mesnerpflichtbuch 54
Mesquer, Brittany 254
Metcalf, Philip 231
METHODUS and Means of Teaching (1748)
	319
Méziéres 36
Michael VIII Palaiologos 150
Michalski, S. 40, 46
Midi 261, 262, 263, 266, 271, 276,
	277
Mildenhall, Suffolk 110
military leadership 146
millenarianism 229
Milner, John, Bishop and Vicar Apostolic
	231
minds 38
ministers, see clergy

miracles 218, 223, 225, 230, 234, 248, 250, 252, 257
missions and missionaries 27, 148, 204, 207, 220, 221, 222, 228, 237–58, 276–7, 280, 298, 299
*Mistführer* 44
Mitchell, Thomas 99
Mitchell, W. J. T. 191
moderation 53
modesty 74
Moldau, River 289, 290
Moldavia i, 2, 144–66
    Princes of 145, 146, 150, 151, 152, 153–7, 162, 164
Moldoviţa 160, 161
Molène 248, 249
monasteries and monasticism 4, 5, 9, 10, 12, 21–2, 87, 148, 150, 151, 153, 159, 160, 163, 164, 193–210, 212, 221, 231, 239, 249, 250, 269–70, 283, 292, 298, 312
money 88
monstrance 272
monks, *see* monasteries and monsasticism
Montague, Richard, Bishop of Norwich 118
Montaigne, Michel de 170
Montmorency 266
monumental brasses 130
monuments 51, 87, 130, 168, 242, 243, 252, 254, 267, 269, 271, 276, 280, 293, 294, *see also* tombs and mausoleums; shrines *and* statues
moors 299
Morlaix 239, 241
Morocco and Moroccans 119
Morrens 23, 24
Moryson, Fynes 20
Moses 42, 161
Mostyn family 217, 222, 230
Mount Carmel 111, 193, 194, 196, 198, 200–1, 202
mountains 20, 91, 94, 204, 208, 209, 221, 239
Mountauban 262, 271
Muir, E. 9
Müller, Joannes 293
Mullet, M. 220
Munich 20, 315
Münsingen 23
Münster 17, 26
Mûr, Brittany 249
murder 25, 305
music 26, 106–8, 318
musicians 28, 219, 233, 274, 277, 310

Muslims 152, 298, 299
mysticism 241, 248, 254, 294

Nagasaki 298
name plates 312
names and naming 137
Nantes, diocese of 242
Nantes, Edict of (1598) 259, 260, 261, 263, 268, 269, 279
*naos* 144, 151, 164
*narthex, see* nave
Nassau, house of 260, 278
National Covenant (1639) 81
nationalism 219
nature 11, 193–210, 219, 232, 251, 252, 256
nave 45, 68, 75, 84, 121–2, 144–5, 148, 151, 159, 160, 163, 164, 170, 177, 243, 244, 245, 265
Naxos 165
Neamţ 144, 149, 155
necropolis 150, 152, 153–4, 161, 166
neighbours and good neighbourliness, *see* communities and communality
Nereus 178
Neri, Phillip 171–2
Nero 168
Netherlands 119, 137, 221, 259, 284, 285, 286
Neuenegg 23, 27, 28–9, 31, 32
Neumair, Veith 33
Neürautter, Augustin 293
New World, *see* America and the Americas
New Year's Day 254
Newton 100
Nicolazic, Yves 251
Nieremberg, Juan Eusebio 208, 209, 210
Nimes, academy of 262
nobles and the nobility 67, 78, 97, 114, 146, 213, 228, 240, 241, 248
noise, *see* sounds and soundscapes
Normal Year (1624) 303, 305, 322
Normans 225
Nortorf 23
Norwich 37
    St Peter Mancroft 113
nostalgia 167, 170, 194, 195, 232
Notre Dame de Gueaudetz 248
Notre Dame massacre (1571) 266
Nova Scotia 99–100
Noyes, John 115
nuns and nunneries 4, 10, 196, 202, 208, 211, 292, *see also* convents
Nuremberg 6, 40–59
    Frauenkirche 39, 49, 59

Heilig-Geist-Spital 49
Lorenzkirche 48, 51, 54, 55
Sebalduskirche 48, 51
St Egidien 48
Nussdorfer, L. 190, 191

oaths 88, 116, 228, 308
obelisks 170
Obermenzing, Bavaria 20, 34
Observant Friar 217
Obystecký, Jan Václav 294
Odochia 164
offerings 57, 162, 180, 217, 248
oil 87, 178
Old Testament 41, 203, 285
Oldcorne, Edward 227
*On procuring the salvation of all peoples,*
    *schismatics, heretics, Jews, Saracens and*
    *other infidels* (1613) 204
open air 41, 96, 103
oracles 249, 254
Orange 259–81
  academy 261–2
  Bishop of 277, 278
  cathedral of Notre Dame de Nazareth
    263, 265–6, 269, 272, 274
  chapel of St Eutrope 265
  chapel of the Jacobins 264
  Chateau-Fort 262–3, 275–6, 277
  collège 261–2, 270, 280
  Column of Martyrs 268, 269, 271
  Corps de la Ville 277
  governor of 262, 264, 267, 271, 278
  Grand Temple 270–1, 279
  Hospital General 279
  Mont St Eutrope 262, 275, 277
  Palais de Justice 271
  parlement of 264, 271, 276, 277
  Place du Cirque 268, 269, 278–9
  St Florent 270
  St Martin's Gate 264
  St Pierre 266
  Temple of St Martin (petit temple) 264,
    266, 268, 279
  town hall 268
  University 261, 279
Oratorians 170–2, 177, 179, 190
oratory 210
orchards 221
ordination 102
organs 84, 105, 107, 111
orgies 233
Ormesbye, John 37
ornament, *see* decoration and ornament
orphanages 322, 323

Orthodox Christianity i, 2, 11, 144–66
Osiander, Andreas 43, 48, 50, 53, 55, 56
Osnabrück, Treaty of (1648), *see*
    Westphalia, Peace of
ossuary, *see* charnel houses
Osweldin, Jacobina 323–4
Otto, R. 14
Ottobeuren 311, 317
Ottomans, *see* Turks
Ouessant 248, 249
Oundle, Northamptonshire 23
Our Lady of Carmel 199, 204
Ovid 224
Owen, Ellen 137
Owen, Hugh 222

Paccioti, Francesco 170
Pacomius, Anthony 204
paganism 168, 194, 207, 233, 235, 249,
    252, 253, 254, 258, 314
Paget, Justinian 218
paint 72, *see also* whitewashing
painters, *see* art, artists and artistic
    heritage
paintings 39, 41, 46, 54, 225, 240, 286
Palatinate (Lower) 270
Palatinate (Upper) 58, 247, 284
palms 43, 184, 195
pamphlets 83, 287
panels 39
Pannvinio, Onofrio 179
Pantoktrator (Zepek Camii) 150
Panvinio, Onofrio 179
Papists, *see* anti-popery
*Paradis of 1564* 119
paradise 194, 202, 208
pardons 248
Paris 189, 240, 277
parish clerks 105–6, 126, 133
parish closes 244
parish registers 2, 71, 125–6, 128, 242,
    245
parishes 19, 34, 313, 314
parishioners 10
parliament 93, 94
Pasquale I 184
Passion 164, 172, 245
pastors, *see* clergy
Pater Noster 242
paths 199
Patristic writings 172, 179, *see also* Fathers
    of the Church
patrons and patronage 6, 32, 58, 152, 153,
    198, 202
Paul V, Pope 178

Peartree 99
peasants 31, 36, 53, 220, 238, 256, 298, 304
pedlars 227
Pelhardi 278
penance and penitents 78, 79, 151, 194, 197, 199, 205, 232, 238, 240, 298, 311
Pennant family 217
Pennant, Thomas 233
Pennines 20
Penrhys 216
Pentecost 261
periphery 190
perpendicular 213
Perrat, Jean 263
*Perth Assembly* (1619) 94
Pešina, Tomáš 288
Peter the Hermit 160
Peterson, Katherine 139
Petre, George 228
Petru II of Moldavia 147
Petru Rareş 154, 155, 156, 158
Petru Şchiopul 155
pews, *see* seating
Pezzl, Johann 23, 25
Pfyffer, Franz Xavier 317–25
Pharaoh 289
Philip II of Spain 195
Phillip-William of Nassau 260, 268–9, 278
physicians 227, 234, 235
Pictet, Bénédict 66
pictures 73, 283, 285
piety 36, 109, 110, 147, 220, 223, 227, 235, 238, 240, 244, 246, 257, 290, 298, 301, 309
pigs 25, 44, 57
pigsties 308
pilgrims and pilgrimage i, 4, 5, 9, 19–20, 34, 47, 51, 55, 58, 87, 88, 104, 167, 169, 170, 198, 211–36, 238, 246, 248, 249–50, 251, 266, 277, 282, 293, 301, 316, 317, 321
pillars 69, 70, 77, 137
*pisania* 163
Pius VI, Pope 33
Plachy, Jiří 296
plague cabins 141
plague, *see* disease
Plancoët, Brittany 252, 254
planets, *see* cosmology
Plasy 292
platforms 244
play, *see* games and gaming
Pleumeur-Bodou 256
Plévin, Brittany 256

Plunéret, Brittany 251
poetry, *see* verse
Poland 146, 147
Pole, Reginald, Cardinal 223
pollution 64, 227, 259, 311
*Poly-Olbion* (1622) 232
*pomelnic* 164
Pont, Robert 90, 91
Poole, Robert 117
poor boxes 130
poor houses 322
poor, the 77, 115, 117, 130, 137, 139, 143, 257, 272, 294, 323
Pope and the papacy 4, 19, 42, 43, 56, 184, 192, 201, 203, 211, 225, 267, 305
population 20, 126, 141, 143, 144, 261, 271, 313
porches 243, 244, 245, 250
portals 144
portraits 158–60, 162
ports 95, 126, 130, 136, 240
Portugal 196, 205
possessions 41
Postles, D. 12
postmodernism 15
post-revisionism 3, 16
Poudrier, Jean 277–8
Poundsgate, Devon 23, 25
Powell, David 218
Powis Castle 231
Prague 284
    Archbishop of 286
    Castle Hill 296
    Charles Bridge 286–7
    Clementinum 296
    Old Town 294, 296, 301
    St Ludmila's chapel 289
    St Vitus cathedral 284, 291
    St Wenceslas chapel 286
prayer and praying 23, 25, 26, 41, 42, 43, 44, 54, 57, 64, 65, 72, 77, 78–9, 86, 88, 90, 91, 93, 96, 99, 100, 104, 106, 108, 109–13, 158, 159, 160, 163, 189, 195, 197, 200, 221, 229, 240, 243, 245, 247, 249, 250, 254, 256, 273, 278, 292, 293, 296, 315, 319
Prayer Book, Scottish (1637) 81, 82–4, 85, 86
prayer books 14, 109
preachers and preaching 23, 25, 33, 41–2, 44, 48, 50, 56, 65, 66, 67, 70, 73, 74, 76, 82, 86, 87, 88, 89, 96, 97, 98, 99, 104, 111, 112, 115–16, 119, 122, 123, 221, 237, 239, 240, 241, 243, 247, 248, 267, 276, 284, 285, 305, 317, *see also* sermons

preaching halls 50
preambulation 102
precincts 245
precious stones 74
Premonstratensians 292
Presbyterians and Presbyterianism 82, 83, 103
presbyteries 88, 92, 100, 177
Price, Ellis 219
pride 74
priests, see clergy 264, 266
princes 78–9, 114, 211, 269, 284
printing 262, 293, 313
priories 4, 12
prisons and prisoners 111, 299
private and public space 12, 24, 66, 98, 108, 190, 263, 272, 316, 318
private worship 94, 95, 96, 98, 109, 111–12
Privy Council of England 218, 228, 235
Probota 144, 149, 155, 158, 159, 160, 161
processions 23, 34, 43, 47, 54, 55, 57, 59, 174, 245, 249, 259, 272, 273–5, 276, 278, 280, 283, 316–18, 321
profanation, see desecration
profane 39, 41, 245, 263, 269, 322
property 41, 46, 53
prophets and prophesy 161, 200, 202, 203
Proskynesis 162
prostitutes 168, 282
prostration 82, 83–4, 85, 88, 94, 95, 111, 120, 123, 159, 162, 290
Protestants and Protestantism 5, 6, 10, 13, 16, 40, 46, 48, 50, 51, 104–23, 152, 168, 212, 227, 233, 234, 259–81, 301, 302, see also heretics and heresy
prothesis 164–5
Provence 275
proverbs 282
providence 234–5
provosts 55
Prucker, Paul 27–8
Prudentius 171
Prussia 45
psalm books 105
psalms 26, 36, 101, 104–8
psalters 105–6
Ptolemy 16, 193
public worship 42, 95
publicans 18, 27–8, 31, 34, 36–7
Puddington, Cheshire 233
pulpits 23, 24, 28, 41, 43, 45, 46, 48, 50, 68, 69–71, 76, 77, 78, 86, 92, 97, 102, 120, 129, 131, 243
punishment 274
Purgatory 4, 10, 250

Purification of the Virgin 267
Puritans and Puritanism 17, 110, 121, 228
Putna 144, 149, 155

Quakers, see Society of Friends
Quarter Sessions, see courts and court records
Quimper 240, 241, 244, 249, 256
Quimper-Cornouaille 237
Quintin, Père 240, 247
Quisidic, Françoise 241

rabbis 300
Rabie, Cheshire 233
Rădăuţi 148, 149, 155
Radical Reformation 3, 27, 36, 40, 46, 47, see also Anabaptists and Anabaptism
rails and railing 118–19, see also grills
railways 211
Râşca 159–60
Rasch 57, 58, 59
Războieni (Valea Albă) 162
Reading, St Laurence 113
recusancy 5, 7, 136, 222, 228
Red Sea 289
refectories 199
Reformation i, 4–6, 7, 10, 12, 13, 15, 16, 36, 38, 40, 43, 51, 52, 55, 56, 57, 60, 66, 75, 82, 84–5, 86, 87, 127, 134, 136, 138, 203, 233, 235, 282, 284, 307
Reformed Protestantism 40, 45, 60–80, 81–103, see also Calvinism and Zwinglians and Zwinglism
refugees 261
refuse 271
Regensburg 32, 319
registers of miracles 225
relics 5, 39, 54, 55, 104, 174–89, 212, 218, 220, 230, 245, 249, 250, 253, 256, 257, 263, 266, 277, 286, 288, 296, 310–17
reliquaries 51, 54, 72, 178
remains, see ruins
repairs 89
requiem masses 245
Restitution, Edict of (1629) 303
Reuseni 162
revenues 22, 32, 217
reverence, see awe and reverence
Revisionism 2
Reynolds, Dr 135
Rhine, River 20
Ribadeneira, Pedro 190
Říčany 293
rich, the 77
Rig, William 96

right–left polarity 157, 158
Rigoleuc, Jean 241
Rilke, Rainer Maria 301
rites of passage 8, 36, 166
rituals, rites and ceremonials 4, 8, 10, 26,
    39, 41, 42, 44, 48, 51, 58, 59, 72, 73,
    81, 82–4, 102, 151, 221, 233, 243,
    245, 246, 247, 257, 258, 259, 269,
    270, 272, 273, 311, 318
rivers 208
roadside images and crosses 51, 247, 276
Roberts, P. 8
Robinson, Nicholas, Bishop of Bangor 218
Rochet 83–4
rocks 206
Rodrigo de Ávila 196
rogation 47, 55
Rogerson, Mr 138
Rohan, Duc de 72
*Roma sotterranea* (1635) 167, 180–9
Roman Empire 168, 252, 269, 278
*Roman Martyrology* (1584) 173
Romanesque 144
Romanticism 211
Rome 6, 167–92, 260, 285, 286, 317
    Caelian Hill 172
    Capitoline Hill 169, 174
    Caracalla baths 173, 174
    catacombs of S. Priscilla 171
    catacombs of S. Sebastiano 171
    Collegio Romano 191
    English College 225
    Forum 174
    Gesù 170, 174, 243
    Gianiculum 169
    Old St Peter's 177
    Palatine Hill 174
    Ponte degli Angeli 291
    St Adriano ai Fori 174
    St Callisto 180
    St Giovanni 170
    St Ignazio 191
    St Maria in Vallicella 170
    St Maria Maggiore 170
    St Prassede 184
    Senate House 174
    St Nereo and St Achilleo 177, 189, 190
    St Peter's Basilica 6, 169, 191
    Vatican palace 170
    Via Appia 171, 180, 183
    Via Salaria 183
    Villa Mattei 172
roods, lofts and screens 5, 39, 41, 48, 68,
    69, 75, 104, 121, 129, 131, 139, 243,
    244, *see also* screens

roofs 243, 249, 265
Rookwood, Ambrose 229
rooms 42, 67
rosaries 50, 244, 246, 248, 250, 252, 257
Roşca, Grigore 159
Rosenwein, B. 9, 12
Roth, E. 58
Rothkrug, L. 4
Roussel, B. 72
Royal Supremacy 217
ruins 87–8, 168, 180, 222, 269, 275, 277
Rule of St Albert 197, 201
*Rules of the Sodality* 223
Rummer, Stefan 58
rural communities and regions 11–13, 17,
    18, 19, 23, 26, 32, 56, 69, 70, 71, 76,
    124, 193, 207, 222, 233, 237–58,
    276, 278, 292, 313, 320
Russia 152
Rysto, George 120
Ryswick, Treaty of (1697) 279

Sabbath and sabbatarianism 13, 17, 26,
    27, 31, 34, 91, 96, 117, 228, 233,
    242, 273, 274, 306, 309, 310
Sabbatine Bull 197
Sacrament houses 50, 51, 54, 59
Sacraments and sacramental theology 5,
    25, 54, 61, 62, 65, 67, 73, 74, 79, 81,
    82–4, 86, 87, 88, 89, 94, 95, 97, 98, 99,
    100, 101, 104, 118, 179, 222, 227, 238,
    240, 243, 244, 246, 247, 249, 250, 257,
    294, *see also* baptism; confession;
    Eucharist; penance and penitents; *and*
    marriage
Sacred Congregation for the Propagation
    of the Faith 197
Sacred Congregation of Rites and
    Ceremonies 173, 190
Sacred Congregation of the Holy Office
    173
Sacred Congregation of the Index 173
sacrifices 42, 254
sacrilege, *see* desecration
sacristies 58, 147
Saenredam, Pieter 119
sailors 125, 135, 138, 249
Saint Anthony (Cornwall) 120
Saint Gall 32
Saint-Duzec, Brittany 256
Saint-Gildas, Brittany 248
Saint-Martin-de-Morlaix 246
Saint-Mathieu, Brittany 249
saints 5, 10, 13, 36, 39, 41, 46, 48, 50, 51,
    52, 54, 55, 56, 57, 62, 87, 104, 134,

161, 162, 166, 172, 174–7, 192, 195,
199, 219, 221, 228, 238–9, 241, 248,
249, 250, 251, 253, 256, 257, 258,
266, 280, 285, 290, 291, 293, 298,
305, 316, 317
Achilleo 174
Agatho 175
Andrew 199
Anne 199, 217, 250, 251
Augustine of Canterbury 225
Barbara 294
Basil 209, 210
Bernard 294
Beuno 211, 219
Brieuc 237
Catherine 88
Catherine of Siena 250
Christopher 250
Corentin 237, 249
Deocarus 55, 56
Dominic 250, 294, 299, 300
Elizabeth 294
Flavia Domitilla 174, 175
Francis Xavier 293, 296, 298, 299,
312
Gabriel 294
Gobrien 254
Gwénolé 249
Houarniaule 251
Ignatius Loyola 195, 299, 316
James 233
Jaoua 250
Jerome 171, 195, 204
John Chrysostom 204
John Nepomuk 286, 288, 292, 294,
298, 301
John of the Cross 134, 195, 196, 199,
252
John the Baptist 160, 161, 162, 166,
195, 199, 200, 202–3, 204, 250
John the Evangelist 129, 194, 196, 199,
204
Jude 292, 298
Lawrence 192
Livertin 251
Louis 250
Luitgard 292, 296
Luke 290
Malo 237, 241
Mamert 251
Margaret 294
Martin 57
Mary Magdalene 195, 199–200
Mary the Egyptian 195, 196
Michael 161, 222

Nereo 174
Nicholas 158–9, 160, 161, 199
Norbert 294, 299
Patrick 128–9, 132, 133, 134, 135
Paul Aurélien 237, 248–9, 250
Paul the Hermit 195
Peter 25, 35, 38, 168, 177, 192, 225
Priscilla 173
Procopius 298
Pudenziana 173, 174
Raphael 250
Roch 250
Romulado 195
Sebald 51, 55
Sebastian 250
Simon Stock 197
Stephen of Hungary 147
Teresa of Ávila 195–6, 199, 202, 209,
210, 296
Thariscus 175
Thomas Aquinas 294
Tobias 250
Tugdual 248
Vitus 288, 297
Wenceslas 298
Winefride 217
saints' days, see feast days and festivities
saints' lives, see hagiography
Saint-Saëns, A. 195
Saint-Thégonnec 244, 245, 250
Salamanca 198, 207
Salisbury Cathedral 122
salt 48
San José del Monte 207
sanctification 39
sanctuary 86, 93, 144, 150, 151, 280
Saracens 299
sarcophagi 146, 189
Sarica Kilise 160
Sauzin, Jean 274
Savage, Eleanor 135
Saxons and Saxony 40, 46, 282, 288
Sázava 298
scaffolding 278
Schangnau 21
Schleswig Holstein 23
Schloß Hartenfels, Torgau 41, 45
Schmalkaldic Articles 43
schoolmasters 319
schools 32, 76, 87, 222, 240, 293, 318–21
Schopenhauer, Arthur 290
Schwabhausen 33
Schwarzwald 45
Scotland 81–103
Scott, G. G. 39

Scott, J. C. 18
screens 45, *see also* roods, lofts and screens
scribes 306
Scribner, R. W. 5, 8, 47, 51, 55, 57, 236, 263, 307
Scripture, *see* Bible
sculpture and sculptures 50, 252, 282
Scultetus, Abraham 284–7, 298, 299
sea 239
seating 9, 10, 14, 45, 50, 67, 68, 69, 70, 71, 75, 76, 77, 82, 84, 86, 92, 94, 105, 120, 123, 130, 131–3, 134, 141, 149, 178, 271, 286, 312
Sebastian, Julian 268
Second Margrave's War (1552–5) 57
Second World War 39
Secret Council 95
sectarian conflict, *see* confessional conflict
Sedan, academy of 262
Sedkec cloister 292
Seemanshausen 22
Sein 249
Seipl, Vít 294
seminaries 221
Şendrea 160
Sense, River 27, 28
Sensebrücke 28–9, 35, 56
senses 74
Septimus Severus 174
Serbia 146, 152, 157, 166
*Sermon Upon the Sacraments* (1591) 97
sermons 23, 24, 25, 27, 41, 42, 43, 44, 44, 45, 56, 69, 73, 76, 79, 90, 99, 100, 107, 111, 112–13, 119, 137, 178, 222, 243, 273, 284, 285, 308, 311, 314
*Sermons on Genesis* 45
Serres, Vincent 262
servants 9, 77, 89, 227, 229, 231, 247, 254, 294, 307
services 26, 27, 33, 34, 44, 57, 62, 69, 74, 86, 90, 91, 96, 97, 104–18, 122, 123, 242, 263, 274, 296, 304, 309–10, 315
servile 262
Servites 292
Settle, Thomas 110
Severano, Giovanni 179, 190
Seville 202
sex, sexuality and sexual offences 31, 44, 92, 238, 242, 308
sexes 108
sextons 57, 115
Shaw, John 133
sheep 120, 172
shooting 314

shops 278, 309, 310
Shotts 96–7
Shotwick, Cheshire 233
Shrewsbury 213, 217
Shrewsbury, Abbey of St Peter and St Paul 212
Shrewsbury: Robert, abbot of 211, 212, 223
shrines 4, 5, 9, 10, 12, 13, 41, 46, 48, 49, 50, 51, 55, 56, 59, 88, 104, 124, 198, 211, 212, 213, 216, 217, 223, 229, 248, 254, 274, 280, 286, 293, 301, 316, 317, *see also* tombs and mausoleums; *and* saints
sickness and the sick 55, 94, 95, 109, 180, 211, 212, 234, 235, 248, 249, 250, 251, 252, 253–4, 257, 315
sieges 296–8
Sierra de Francia 207
sighs and groans 105, 107, 109–13
Sigismund, Holy Roman Emperor 283
silence 76, 195, 197, 200, 243
Silsbury, Diocese of 114
Silvan 159
silver 41, 54, 55
Simion Movilă 155
sin 25, 26, 62, 73, 78, 138, 209, 210, 238, 240, 245, 246, 247, 290, 305, *see also* gluttony; murder; pride; theft and thieves; *and* sex, sexuality and sexual offences
Siret 152
Sixtus IV 177
Sixtus V 168
Skirrid, the 221
skulls 196
Slatina 155
smells 14, 205, 218, 224, 285
Smithfield 216
social control 27
social order or structure 9, 114
Society of Friends 227
Society of Jesus 31, 170, 195, 208, 220, 222, 223, 227, 229, 230, 231, 237, 288, 292, 293, 296, 298, 299, 317
sodalities 272, 273
Soergel, P. 220
soldiers 136, 229, 231, 262, 279, 298, 299
Sollern 32
Solomon 99
Solomon's Temple 289
song books 105–6
songs and singing 14, 26, 36, 43, 101, 172, 219, 314–15, 316, 322, *see also* psalms

souls 25, 79, 110, 112, 161, 163, 196, 209, 210, 217, 245, 250, 252, 254, 305, 314
sounds and soundscapes 13, 44, 45, 104–23, 316
South Queensferry 100–2
Southampton 99
Spa 229
Spain 11, 193–210
Spalding, John 100
speech 306
Speed, John 218
Speyside 88
spirits 252, 254, 256
*Spiritual Instruction for those Professing the Eremitical Life* (1629) 201
spiritual kin, *see* godparents
spirituality 11, 16
spitting 307
Spottiswoode, John, Archbishop of St Andrews 85
springs 4, 211–36, 252, 253, 258
sprinkling, *see* holy water
squares 169, 272, 273, 274, 301
squires 120
St Albans, George Inn 23
St Albans, Hertfordshire 22, 23
St Andrews, Scotland 88
St Jean de Luz 119
St Mark's Gospel 90
Staffordshire 227, 228
stained glass 15, 68, 70, 72, 104, 217, *see also* windows
stalls, *see* seating
standing stones 221, 252, 256, 276
Stanford, Berkshire 113
Stapleford, Cheshire 134
Staplegove, Somerset 113
Star Chamber 115
*Statuae Pontis Pragensis* (1714) 293
statues 41, 46, 50, 51, 54, 55, 57, 59, 72, 84, 150, 165, 216, 217, 228, 243, 244, 249, 250, 251, 252, 254, 258, 263, 283, 287, 290, 294, 298, 310
status 9, 45, 114, 133, 135, 142, 143, 157, 222–3, 263, 267, 283, 312
*Steckenknecht* 44
steeples 136
Ştefan cel Mare 153, 155, 162
Ştefan II of Moldavia 154
Ştefan the Young 159
steps 244
Sternhold, Thomas 108
Stevenson, Elizabeth 141
Stevenson, William 141

Stocksbury, Kent 120
stone circles, *see* standing stones
stones 39, 41, 95, 130, 212, 218, 223, 239, 243, 246, 247, 249, 251, 252, 271, 286, 305, 312, 315
stores, *see* shops
Stoß's, Veit 50, 53
Stow, K. 191
Strahov 294
strangers 136, 228, 230
streets 24, 54–5, 169, 170, 263, 267, 269, 272, 273, 304, 308, 309, 319, 323, 324
Stuart Dynasty 81–3, 230
Stuart, Elisabeth 287, 291
Stubbes, Katherine 115
studies 199
sub-culture 18
subterranean space 178
suburbs 264, 267
Sucevița 155, 156, 159, 160, 161
Suffolk 110
suicides 136
supernatural, *see* magic
superstition 43, 47, 57, 68, 88, 98, 218–19, 227, 232, 235, 238, 252, 253, 256, 258, 259, 302
Swarbia 282
swearing 246
Sweden and the Swedish 291, 296, 298
Switzerland 19, 28, 32, 36, 286
swords 269
swornmen 131
symbols and symbolism 129, 168, 194, 196, 256, 258, 259, 276, 311, 318
Symons, Garrat 137
synagogues 91–2
Syria 141

tabernacles 39, 41, 46, 48, 209, 210, 217
tables 73, 82–4, 130
tailors 283
Tanchelm 294
tapestries 273
taverns 13, 17–38, 238, 242, 307, 309, 310, 314
taxation 32, 120
Te Deum 278
Tedlow 118
teenagers, *see* youth, youths and the young
Temperley, N. 108
Tempesta, Antonio 169–70
temples 4, 64–80, 86, 91–2, 93, 94, 119, 252, 261, 264, 266, 270–2, 279
templon 151

Ten Commandments, *see* commandments
Tennenlohe 57, 58
Tesimond, Oswald, Father 229
*The Groanes of the Spirit or the Triall of the Truth of Prayer* (1639) 109
Theatines 292
theatre 293, 320–1
theft and thieves 282
Theodora 150
theology and theologians 26, 41, 44, 48, 57, 65, 66, 82, 89, 102–3, 161, 216, 232, 235, 259, 261, 262, 266, 287, *see also* sacraments and sacramental theology
*Theotokion* 161
Thirty Years War 43, 290, 302, 321
Thomas, K. 114
Thomas, William 168
Thrale, Mrs Hester 232
Throckmorton, Job 111
thrones 158, 159, 160, 162, 178
thunder 25, 108
Tiber, River 169, 291
Tillyfour 99–100, 102
time and set times 13, 23, 24, 37, 42, 44, 54, 55, 63, 87, 88, 106, 164, 239, 272, 274–5, 314, 315, *see also* feast days and festivities
Tingle, E. 6, 280
Titus, Emperor 174, 289
Toader Bubuog 159
tobacco 307
Toggenburg 32
toleration 13, 50, 304
tombs and mausoleums 8, 12, 72, 72, 130, 141, 143, 144–66, 177, 178, 184, 189, 239, 245, 249, 252, 267, 271, 286, 288
tombstones 155, 161
tongs 113
Torgau 41, 42, 43, 45
Totty, Elizabeth 138
Totty, Henry 138
Totty, John 126
Toulouse 276–7
Tower of David 209, 210
towers 46, 205, 244, 262, 265, 291, 296, 299, 301, 312
towns, *see* urban centres
Townshend, Dame Dorothy 234
tracts 24, 94
traders, trades and tradesmen 21, 23, 125, 133, 134, 137, 138, 141
transepts 69, 250
Trautmannshofen 58
*Travel Journal* 170

travellers 29, 36, 51, 114, 290
treason 159
*Treasury of Natural Wonders* (1629) 208
trees 196, 206, 208, 212, 266, 278, 301
trefoil plans 144, 148
Trégor 240, 244
Tréguier, diocese of 240, 241, 242, 246
Trégunc, Brittany 256
Tridentine and post-Tridentine, *see* Council of Trent
*Triginta devotions ad Christum et Sanctos eius* (1712) 293
Trinitarians 298, 299, 311
Trinity Brotherhood 317
triptychs 39, 290
triumphal arches 174
*Trophaea, the* (1584) 225
Tübingen 287
Tudor dynasty 213, 217
Tudosie 164
Tulles, Jean II, bishop of Orange 269
Tunbridge Wells, Kent 235
Tuntenhausen 33
Turks 25, 162, 298, 299, 309
Turner, Dr William 119
Turner, H. 15–16
Twann 32
Tyndale, William 109
Tyrol 18

Ulm 323
United States of America 113, *see also* America and the Americas
universities 262
Unterdolling 32
urban centres 6, 8, 9, 11–13, 14, 17, 20–1, 25, 26, 32, 39, 40–59, 100–2, 108, 110, 124–43, 167–92, 220, 241, 252, 259–81, 302
urination 92, 118, 121, 271, 273, 307
Ursenbach 23
utensils 68
Utraquists 282, 286, 288
Utrecht 119
Utrecht, Treaty of (1713) 280

valleys 21, 32, 34, 207–8, 209
Valois, Felix of 298
*Valor Ecclesiasticus* 217
Van Gennep, A. 8
Van Vliet, Hendrik 119
Vannes 237, 240, 241, 246
Vannetais 241
vassalage 157
Vaud 72

vaulting 213
veils 175
vergers 115, 123
Verjus, Père 250, 256
vernacular 108
verse 53, 108, 196, 208, 232, 301
Vespers 44, 54
vessels 42
vestments 68, 158, 159
vice, *see* sin
Vienna 282, 286, 298, 315
*Vies des Saints de Bretagne* (1725) 239
*Vies, gestes, mort et miracles des saints de la Bretagne Armorique* (1636) 239
vigils 202, 218, 272, 273
villages, *see* rural communities and regions
Villanuevva de la Jara 210
Villeneuve, Louis 273–5
violence 93, 266, 269, 284, 302, 324, *see also* fighting
Viret, Pierre 67, 79
Virgin Mary 50, 51, 52, 57, 58, 128–9, 132, 150, 157, 159, 160, 161, 162, 166, 175, 198, 202, 216, 217, 220, 228, 230, 250, 251, 252, 254, 272, 280, 282, 290, 294, 296, 305, 312, 317
Virgin of Mercy 50
virgins and virginity 192, 201, 211
virtues 74, *see also* charity
Vischer, Peter the Elder 51
visitations and visitation articles 32, 56, 59, 115, 129
visual experiences 45
*Vita Beati Patris Ignatii Loyolae* (1609) 190
*vitae, see* hagiography
Vodă, Ion 153
voices 254
Voievod 146–7
Volovăţ 149
vomiting 31
Von Bora, Katherine 301
Vorniceni 149
Voroneţ 153, 164
vows 269
Vyšehrad 297

Wales and the Welsh 113, 137, 211–36, 237, 241, 250
walking 213, 222, 249, 314
wall hangings, *see* cloths
walls 36, 43, 66, 67, 70, 74, 85, 92, 104, 124, 130, 151–2, 159, 169, 170, 178, 184, 199, 244, 256, 261, 262, 264, 266, 266, 279, 301, 312, 321–2
Walsham, A. 5, 6, 7

Wandel, L. P. 73
Wardhouse, Lady Elizabeth Leslie of 93, 99–100
Wardhouse, Sir John Leslie of 99
Warmington, Issac 138
Warmington, Rafe 138
wars 26, 260, 310
Warwick, St Nicholas 113
water 184, 252, 253, 254, 257
waterways 20, 20
wax 48
wayside images and crosses, *see* roadside images and crosses
wealth and the wealthy 117
Weber, M. i, 5, 15, 60
weddings 31, 36, 310
Weihenstephen monastery 21
Welleba, W. F. 294
wells i, 4, 5, 88, 89, 211–36, 239, 248, 251, 253, 258
Wells, Cathedral, Somerset 119
Welsh, John 94
Wenceslas IV of Bohemia 294
werewolves 248
Westminster, Archdiocese of 223
Westphalia, Peace of (1648) 302, 303–4, 306, 312, 313, 317, 322
Wever, Thomas 129
Whighton, John 121
white 74
White Mountain, Battle of the (1620) 230, 282, 283, 289, 290, 301
White, Francis, Bishop of Ely 102
White, Winefrid 231
whitewashing 14, 69, 70, 73, 104
Whitgift, John, Archbishop of Canterbury 115–16
Whithorn 85
Whitsun 55
whore of Babylon 168
Widdecombe-in-the-Moor, Devon 23, 25
widows 137, 138, 294
wilderness 11, 172, 193–210, 249
William I of Nassau 264, 268
William III of Nassau 260, 279
William, G. 220
Williams, R. 11
wills 2, 245
wind 252
windows 31, 33, 68, 72, 97, 120, 243, 251, 273, *see also* stained glass
wine 22, 23, 34, 34, 234
Winter, Robert 229
Wirth, Rudolf 65, 74

Wishart, George 97
Wistable, Kent 121
Wittenberg 23, 25, 42, 284, 287
wives 28, 57, 132, 133, 134, 138, 157,
    168, 311
Wolverhampton, Staffordshire 231
women 33, 58, 66, 77, 78, 93, 111,
    112, 114, 136, 151, 157, 175,
    228, 229, 240, 242, 246, 252,
    301, 323
wood 305
woods and forests 24, 42, 95, 221, 252, *see
    also* trees
Worb, Bern 34
Worcester 216
Worcester, Cathedral 115
Word of God 41, 42, 45, 47, 48, 61, 62,
    65, 67, 73, 74, 76, 79, 82, 86, 87, 89,
    90, 96, 99, 104, 129, 158, 243, 298,
    299, 314
workhouses 311
workmen 119, 218, 279, 285, 288
worship, *see* services
Wren, Matthew, Bishop of Norwich 102,
    107, 116–17

Wrightson, K. 123
Wüzburg 33
Wynn, Sir John 234

yeomen 114, 124–43
York, All Saints Pavement 113
York, Minster 115
Yorkshire 118
youth, youths and the young 27, 28, 108,
    123, 132, 138, 150, 227, 240, 308,
    320
Yugoslavia 160
Yuste 195

Zaragoza 200
Zeberle, Hans 304–6
Zeeden, E. 44
Zhupans 152
Zulychem 278–9
Zurich 26, 65
Zurich, Great Minster 46
Zutrinken 25
Zwingli, Huldrych 46
Zwinglians and Zwinglism 19, 23, 26, 27,
    28, 33